THE
HUMAN
TRADITION
IN
LATIN
AMERICA

Latin American Silhouettes
Studies in History and Culture

William H. Beezley and
Judith Ewell
Editors

Scholarly Resources celebrates the Columbus quincentenary of 1992 with a series in Latin American Studies. The publisher and the editors seek outstanding works in the humanities and social sciences that illustrate the interplay between the images of the past and the realities of the present.

Latin America combines and recombines diverse cultures, wealth and poverty, sophistication and innocence, modernity and tradition in a fascinating historical kaleidoscope. Attempting to accommodate valued and vital traditions with a heritage of deference and oppression, many Latin Americans experience a living past that seems more real than the facade of modern life that surrounds them. They and outsiders alike struggle to understand and reconcile the images and realities that have created the historical and contemporary mosaic of Latin America.

The myriad cultural dimensions of Latin America provide the subjects for this series of scholarly monographs, translations, reprinted classics, and general studies. Biographies and case studies that illuminate larger social themes also are included. The human aspect offers the focus for authors who aim both to educate and entertain classroom and general readers. The volumes of **Latin American Silhouettes** stimulate our curiosity about the region and interpret the cultural and historical character of the peoples of Latin America. Exposure to the rich traditions and multifaceted histories of the greater part of the Americas will encourage better understanding among the nations and enrich our domestic culture.

Volumes Published

William H. Beezley and Judith Ewell, eds., *The Human Tradition in Latin America: The Twentieth Century* (1987)
Cloth ISBN 0-8420-2331-3 Paper 0-8420-2332-1

David G. LaFrance, *The Mexican Revolution in Puebla, 1908-1913: The Maderista Movement and the Failure of Liberal Reform* (1989)
ISBN 0-8420-2293-7

THE
HUMAN TRADITION
IN
LATIN AMERICA

THE NINETEENTH CENTURY

EDITED BY
JUDITH EWELL
AND
WILLIAM H. BEEZLEY

A Scholarly Resources Imprint
WILMINGTON, DELAWARE

The paper used in this publication meets the minimum requirements of the American National Standard for permanence of paper for printed library materials, Z39.48, 1984.

Scholarly Resources Inc.
104 Greenhill Avenue
Wilmington, DE 19805-1897

Library of Congress Cataloging-in-Publication Data

The Human tradition in Latin America.

   (Latin American silhouettes)
   Bibliography: p.
   Includes index.
   1. Latin America—Civilization—19th century.
2. Latin America—Biography. I. Ewell, Judith,
1943–   . II. Beezley, William H. III. Series.
F1413.H86 1989   980.03′1   89-10317
ISBN 0-8420-2331-3 (alk. paper)
ISBN 0-8420-2332-1 (pbk. : alk. paper)

I believe in aristocracy, though—if that is the right word, and if a democrat may use it. Not an aristocracy of power, based upon rank and influence, but an aristocracy of the sensitive, the considerate and the plucky. Its members are to be found in all nations and classes, and all through the ages; and there is a secret understanding between them when they meet. They represent the true human tradition, the one permanent victory of our queer race over cruelty and chaos. Thousands of them perish in obscurity, a few are great names. They are sensitive for others as well as for themselves, they are considerate without being fussy, their pluck is not swankiness but the power to endure, and they can take a joke.

—E. M. Forster, *Two Cheers for Democracy*

Introduction

"The past is a foreign country," writes novelist L. P. Hartley; "they do things differently there."[1] Indeed, nineteenth-century Latin America is for us one of the most foreign of "countries," with cities and pampas, mountains and rivers, that must be traversed in our imaginations in order for us to meet a host of exotic people. On these journeys, we are occasionally explorers, sometimes travelers, maybe even tourists. Paul Fussell, author and literary critic, says that "the explorer seeks the undiscovered, the traveller that which has been discovered by the mind working in history, the tourist that which has been discovered by entrepreneurship and prepared for him by the arts of mass publicity."[2] The traveler's mind has more trouble "working in history" if it has never experienced the physical landscape in the present. Can the Rockies prepare us for the Andes, or the Mississippi for the Amazon? When Argentine writer and president (1868–1874) Domingo Faustino Sarmiento explains the difference between the civilized city and the barbaric countryside, do we see in our mind's eye Kansas City and the Nebraska plains? Do we understand "civilization" in the way that he meant it? Contemporary analogies can erect barriers between us and the reality of the past. The word "city" applied to Buenos Aires in 1820 or to Lima in 1870 may conjure up mental snapshots of New York or Miami or Raleigh in the 1980s. For that matter, present-day Guayaquil, Ecuador, bears but slight resemblance to that sleepy little town in the 1830s. The space, the terrain, the language, and the people are foreign to us even as we travel through time to try to penetrate Latin America in the nineteenth century.

Although the people whose stories appear in this book seem far removed from our lives, most have the qualities that E. M. Forster admires as part of the "true human tradition." We may cringe at the suffering that some of them endured—or contributed to—or at the violence that pervaded their lives. Still, we can empathize with the courage and ability that gave most of them the "power to endure" through the "cruelty and chaos" of nineteenth-century Latin America.

In terms of years the lives in this book are not as distant from our own time as they might at first seem. These people lived during what historians often call the long nineteenth century, roughly from the 1780s to 1920. The earliest to be born, Maria Antônia Muniz, gave her first shriek in Mexico in 1762, just twelve years before Thomas Jefferson penned the Declaration of Independence. Soledad Román de Núñez uttered her last sigh in Colombia in 1924 and could have taken tea with the grandmother of a college student of the 1990s. None of these individuals is "typical" of Latin America or even of his or her own country or era. Still, none is atypical either, and as we peer into their lives, walk around in their courtyards, meet their friends and relatives, follow them through the streets of their cities and into the mountains or broad plains of their nations, and hear their voices, we can use them to guide us through their times.

We might reflect, as historian Lucien Febvre does about life during the French Renaissance, on the effect of physical surroundings on people. A late twentieth-century individual—urban, sedentary (or sweaty after jogging), and refined—must exercise great imagination to understand people who were none of those things. "What a large place the word 'comfort' has come to occupy in our language, modern comfort in which we take such pride," Febvre muses. "What implications the word has, of convenience and material ease: a light turned on or off at the flick of a finger, an indoor temperature independent of the seasons, water ready to flow hot or cold, as we wish, anytime, anywhere."[3] We take these things for granted, yet surely they affect the implicit assumptions we make about the past. A traveler in 1820 on the mule trail from steamy La Guaira, Venezuela, up to the cooler heights of Caracas experienced one kind of discomfort, and needed one-half day for the journey. In 1989 one can make the same journey in an air-conditioned taxi, perhaps in thirty minutes without traffic on the *autopista* or, alas, in six hours if all Caraqueños decide to return from the beach at the same time. Is the attitude of the mule rider, at leisure although perhaps drenched by tropical showers, different from that of the passenger encased in steel and glass, impatient to reach a high-rise condominium or a favorite restaurant?

How then to understand people who lived in a less comfortable past? In addition to their different physical and material environments, they inhabited different moral and intellectual environments than our own. What does "freedom" mean to a sneaker-shod California teenager? What did it mean to a bandit in early nineteenth-century Mexico, to an Indian leader in mid-nineteenth-century Argentina, or to an intelligent, ambitious woman in 1840s Bolivia? How would they define "liberalism," "conservatism," "federalism," "progress," "selfishness," and "community"? For that matter, did the abstraction liberalism have any more meaning to the average person in nineteenth-century Latin America than the abstraction existentialism has to most twentieth-century North Americans? Perhaps their operative meanings are similar to what historian Eric Hobsbawm suggests for his social bandits; that is, a bandit can play out a gut-level meaning of freedom or justice without being able to write a treatise on these words. Can we intuit from an individual's behavior what he or she believes, what his or her world view is?

Febvre has an answer. "Renaissance, Humanism, Reformation are not mere abstractions, personifications wandering over the heavens where the Chimera chases Transcendent Ideals. To understand these great changes we must recreate for ourselves the habits of mind of the people who brought them about."[4] Yet reconstructing "habits of mind" is probably more of a challenge than that which confronts the contemporary archaeologist who must reconstruct an eighteenth-century brick, ceramic jug, or building. It is impossible, Febvre concedes, to recreate the people of the Renaissance. But, he insists, we must "evoke them, projecting onto the screen of our imaginations some typical silhouettes."[5] By studying these silhouettes we should be able to comprehend the texture of a society, its ambience, how it differed from our own. The essays in this book constitute a guide for the late twentieth-century traveler to a beginning understanding of the inhabitants of that foreign country of nineteenth-century Latin America.

II

If abstractions such as humanism can lead us astray so, too, can general terms such as "Latin America" or even "nineteenth century." Latin Americans had no common experience during the nineteenth century. Arguably, Antonio López de Santa Anna in Mexico in the 1820s may have had less in common with Emilio Coni in Argentina in the 1890s than he did with his contemporary Andrew Jackson of Tennessee. Other abstractions—

modernization, progress, liberalism, positivism, caudillism, anti-clericalism, federalism, centralism, and Indianism—fill the history books. The biographies in this volume offer an opportunity to consider these concepts from the vantage point of individual lives. In some cases, the lives will confirm and enliven the abstractions. In others, they will prompt a reexamination of the terms.

Traditional histories of nineteenth-century Latin America have divided the period and imposed intellectual and thematic order on disparate people and places. The most common subperiods have been the age of independence (1800–1830), dominated by the arrogant profile of Simón Bolívar, the tragic figure of Father Miguel Hidalgo, and the self-deprecating image of General José de San Martín; the age of the caudillos (1830–1860), in which Juan Manuel de Rosas forever gallops on horseback across the pampas, scourge of *unitarios* (Liberals), foreigners, and indigenous peoples alike; and the age of positivism, or modernization (1860–1900), where we discern railroad cars, barbed wire, European immigrants, and cities replete with Parisian boulevards and gracious parks. Each of these ages itself has become an abstraction, a stereotyped silhouette, if you will, to represent part of the long nineteenth century. Textbooks can leave us with sharp images of the period, but their stereotypes sometimes foster easy generalizations and misunderstanding. They also omit much of the rich historical tapestry of the time.

Some historians reject narrative textbook imagery in favor of more analytical treatment. Speaking of the century as a whole, E. Bradford Burns refers to a "poverty of progress" in which the liberal urban values that measure progress by production slowly overtake the communal traditions of the folk. Stanley and Barbara Stein write of the expansion of capitalism, which gradually has drawn Latin America more securely into the world economic system. Still others see real modernization and advancement in the political, social, and economic institutions of Latin America with the advent of technology, educational opportunities, increased trade, and improved communications and transportation. Each of these intellectual models helps us to understand the century, just as the notion of the age of the caudillos does, and provides a good basis for comparative world history. But the people in these constructs often remain encased, frozen, and nonhuman in the reified categories of class, community, region, and modes of production.

In "real life" people can play many roles, and different historians might describe the same behavior in various ways. Louis A. Pérez, Jr., writes of vagrants and social bandits in Cuba, and he observes that "in 1895 the bandits became patriots."[6] Richard Slatta similarly notes that the mere passage of a law turned gauchos from free men into vagrants, hounded by the police.[7] Rebecca Scott points out that Cuban slaves were actors in their own drama in addition to being extras in plays written by the white elite.[8] Frank Safford warns us that even when we generalize about the upper class, "the use of such categories as landowner, merchant and professional as ways of dividing social interest groups is implausible, because the upper classes in nineteenth-century Spanish America lacked the specificity of function that this description implies."[9] Thus, examination of individual biographies, although inadequate alone as "history," can help to reveal the complexities beneath both historical narrative and analysis.

Both the narratives and the grand constructs tend to leave out the people. The followers of Juan Manuel de Rosas remain as shadowy background figures, bit players in an epic drama. Nor do the folk, the *jornaleros* (dayworkers), or the proletariat stand out any more clearly in most of the analytical studies. There are several reasons for the absence of real people in the historiography. Most obviously, the civil conflicts of the time occupied more attention than did official record keeping. It requires painstaking research to study the lives of obscure individuals in the nineteenth century. Even the more distant colonial period, fed by the Iberian mania for documents, has much richer sources. As important as the lack of sources has been is the way in which historians have viewed the nineteenth century in Latin America. After the drama of the Independence Wars, historians have tended to scurry through the century treating the period as a transition, a necessary but boring link between an Iberian colonial past and contemporary nation-states in an international setting. Thus the people who are the actors on this grand stage are not seen as individuals, at least in part because the whole century is seen as only a parenthesis between two more dramatic epochs. When historians do examine the period more carefully, they tend to look for surviving colonial institutions and traditions or for precursors of future conditions. The nineteenth century becomes part of a purposeful unfolding of history in which "each link in the genealogy, each runner in the race, is only a precursor of the final apotheosis and not a manifold of social and cultural processes at work in their own time and place."[10]

Historians tend to assume a unilinear transition, the hackneyed "seamless web" of history. As Florencia Mallon argues, those who have written about political revolutions and the development of national ideologies in the nineteenth century have a "positivist unilinear view of historical development that by definition assigns no creative role to nonbourgeois classes, pre-Enlightenment politics, or non-Western regions in the genesis of nationalism."[11] It matters not whether the direction of the line rises, hailing modernity and progress, or falls, lamenting the distance from a more generous and humane past; the direction draws our attention rather than the plots on the line along the way.

Some historians recently have begun to examine more carefully the nineteenth century and to question assumptions about this transitional period. Most agree that the late colonial crisis and the wars for independence did indeed provide a shock to the colonial system. Nor do they overlook the dramatic upheavals of the century, sources of valuable information about change and continuity. Yet they urge closer study of the social history of the period to test our assumptions about change, about its direction and its meaning. Steve Stern argues, for example, that examination of political action during abnormal times may lead us to assume that people passed through intermittent waves of passivity and reaction. With regard to peasants or country people, we see them only as victims who react to the changes forced upon them by others or by the dynamism of the capitalist system. Looking at people's daily adaptations and resistance to change can give us a fuller appreciation of how change occurs. People, after all, are "continuously involved in the shaping of their societies."[12] Their responses cover not only political values but also economic and social ones.

III

A transition between two dimly illuminated models or constructs can be difficult to see in and of itself. Yet foreign travelers, who began to visit Latin America in the 1700s, may show us a way to focus more closely on the period. With lively curiosity, they asked many of the questions that we also would like to pose. Their observations must be used with care, for many of them were both travelers in the best sense of the word and tourists in the worst sense.

Most travelers wanted to know what made the people of Latin America tick. In what ways were they like Europeans or U.S. citizens? How were they different? In their exotic surroundings, with coffee and rubber trees, bananas and mangoes, rain forests and the mighty Amazon, maté and *guaraná* (herbal drink), llamas and ostriches, did they think the same thoughts as the travelers? Did indigenous peoples recall the glories of pre-Columbian civilizations or evoke the barbaric beginnings of the human race? Were black slaves more or less eager for freedom than they were in the north? Were women supposed to be, as were their sisters to the north, pious, chaste, domestic, and silent? Did the sight of steamboats on the Magdalena inspire the same excitement as that sight had on the Hudson? Did Latin Americans worship both the Catholic church and the popular cults and saints? Would an immigrant have a good chance to travel that fabled path from rags to riches? How did the political conflicts that swirled about them touch their everyday lives? Just as the nineteenth-century travelers filled their notebooks with conflicting impressions, we too will leave our historical journey, either with many of our questions unanswered or with too many answers.

We might plan three trips through this long nineteenth century. First, we would like to understand what attitudes and realities prevailed from the late eighteenth century until the last Spanish soldier was defeated in the Independence Wars in 1826. Second, we might turn to studying the new republics (and the Brazilian empire) during their most chaotic times, from the late 1820s until the 1870s. The quickening pace of change would draw us to make a third inspection between 1880 and World War I. The people we encounter may seem similar in many ways over our three trips, or they might differ as much as those we would have met had we visited Spain under Francisco Franco in 1948 and then returned forty years later after his death. Fate also will introduce us to different kinds of people on each trip. We might enjoy a chat with the Colombian priest José de Calasanz Vela in 1870 but have little to say to the Mexican mystic Teresa Urrea in the 1890s.

If we had traveled to Latin America around the beginning of the nineteenth century, we would have seen the effects of what some people have called the second conquest of Latin America. As the Bourbon monarchs of Spain (and their counterparts in

Portugal) sought to tighten their authority over their empire (much as King George III had tried in British America), life changed for the colonists. Trade blossomed, still hampered by mercantilist restrictions but freer than previously. People in port cities such as Caracas and Buenos Aires especially enjoyed the new prosperity and also had quicker access to new books and European ideas. The wars that swept Europe and the Americas in the late eighteenth century also contributed to opening Latin America to the outside world, for Spain could not enforce its rule, especially when Napoleon occupied the Iberian Peninsula in 1808.

The quickening pace of life had several effects. Creoles became impatient as their expectations of greater political influence and wealth rose. Although they echoed the egalitarian slogans of the French Revolution, they feared the consequences of full implementation in their multiracial societies. Indigenous peoples, slaves, and *castas* (legally inferior people of color) sometimes chafed at new and harsher economic demands or absorbed the liberating ideas of the French Revolution. Each effort at resistance inspired others. To be sure, there were no telegraphs or satellites, but many indigenous peoples heard of the large-scale revolt of Túpac Amaru II in Peru in the 1770s. Around the Caribbean especially, news of the slave revolt that culminated in the independence of Haiti in 1804 spread like wildfire. Hot-blooded agitators like Francisco Miranda fanned the flames and tried to encourage the Creoles to throw off their Spanish chains. His failed effort, as well as the ultimate successes of Simón Bolívar, José de San Martín, Agustín Iturbide, and Dom Pedro I, gave hope to both individuals and the new nations.

The generation born in the late eighteenth century and living into the independence period formed a unique cohort. They straddled two worlds, one of which crumbled in their lifetime. Their education and experience were formed during the late colonial period. They grew up as part of the Iberian empires and only with difficulty could imagine any other situation, except perhaps the idealized utopia that the grand words of the French Revolution had evoked. Some, like Agustín Marroquín or Atanasio Tzul, became part of the independence struggles with little understanding of their importance. Their inchoate ambitions remained stillborn. Others, either luckier or more prescient, like Antonio López de Santa Anna, benefited from the Independence

Wars and new attitudes. Basil Hall, a Scottish naval captain, referred to people like Santa Anna when he commented, on a visit to Guayaquil in 1821, that "the people have acquired a knowledge of their own consequence and power, and, instead of submitting quietly, as heretofore, to be cheated at every turn, and letting all things pass unregarded, from utter hopelessness of amelioration, they take a deep and active interest in whatever affects their fortunes in the slightest degree."[13] He marveled that changing times had stimulated even the local women to discuss politics.

The Prussian traveler Alexander von Humboldt reinforced the general spirit of optimism in his extensive catalog of the resources of and economic possibilities for Latin America. He wrote that "the shores of Venezuela from the beauty of their ports, the tranquility of the sea by which they are washed, and the fine ship timber that covers them, possess great advantages over the shores of the United States. In no part of the world is there found firmer anchorage, or fitter positions for the establishment of military posts."[14] Humboldt cautiously predicted that after its recovery from the destruction of the Independence Wars, Latin America would develop into prosperous republics no less civilized than, although probably different from, the European nations from which they had sprung. On his visit to Mexico in 1803–04, he also had been impressed with the colony's great prosperity, but, he added, "Enormous sums are accumulated in the hands of a few individuals, but the indigence of the people cannot help striking those Europeans who travel through the country."[15] He concluded that the Spanish Crown (and the Creoles) needed to recognize "that the prosperity of the whites is intimately connected with that of the copper-colored race, and that there can be no durable prosperity for the two Americas till this unfortunate race, humiliated but not degraded by long oppression, shall participate in all the advantages resulting from the progress of civilization and the improvement of social order!"[16]

Unfortunately, most Latin American rulers during the next generation (and subsequently, for that matter) neither understood nor heeded Humboldt's warning. Like Bolívar, many believed that the independence generation had "plowed the sea." Seeing ruin all about them, they usually reacted pessimistically and defensively to the challenges of nationhood. The economy that had blossomed during the late eighteenth century had wilted.

War had destroyed plantations, cattle herds, and mines. European goods flowed into the open economies, competing with the products of local craftsmen. Spanish and Portuguese merchants and settlers frequently left in disgust, taking with them valuable capital and skills. Cities stagnated, with little more to offer than the ravished countryside. Flight of capital, lack of transportation, and sometimes scarcity of labor limited efforts to reawaken the economy. Individuals and governments both experienced a chronic shortage of funds. Without money, political leaders could neither hire civilians nor pay the army—two sure sources of dissatisfaction. Even the church shrank in importance, as the Vatican refused to name bishops to the new countries and as Latin Americans turned away from the priesthood as a career. Many of the elite continued to vacillate between fear of the colored majority and scorn for them. Weak and vulnerable but still possessing legendary mineral wealth and geopolitical importance, the young nations suffered under numerous foreign threats and from invasions, both formal and informal. The contrast between the sonorous phrases of the first constitutions and the dreary reality of weakness, isolation, and poverty was too great to allow hope to survive.

Foreign travelers who ventured to Latin America during the first fifty years of the new republics shared much of the pessimism expressed by the ruling elite. Nature remained as bountiful as Humboldt had painted it, but human capriciousness and weakness doomed the region to constant civil conflict and enduring misery. Visitors measured the new nations against their own and pronounced the new states wanting.

Charles Blachford Mansfield, a British vegetarian, utopian, and chemist, turned his observant eye on Latin America in 1852–53. Ignorant of Portugese or Spanish, he discussed and confirmed his impressions almost exclusively with his English-speaking compatriots. Things in Latin America were better or worse, larger or smaller versions of what he knew back home. He characterized a Brazilian sugar plantation house as comparable "in point of elegance to a third-rate farm-house in England,"[17] and the Parahyba River was "about as broad as the Thames at Hammersmith, much more picturesque, but not quite so useful."[18] Despising the cool, sunless damp of England, Mansfield basked in Brazil's sunshine; expressed wonder at the tropical flora and fauna; and complained of the dirt, inconveniences of travel, and sometimes foul, although not uniquely so, smells that he encountered. "Pernambuco . . . is a dreadfully dirty place; there is not a drain of any sort, and all imaginable filth lies in the streets: yet it does not smell bad: to Lisbon it is sweet, and to Cologne it is a rose in comparison."[19] Buenos Aires, with its abandoned cattle carcasses in the streets, offended his sense of smell much more, perhaps for the hypocrisy of its calling itself the city of "good airs." The contrast between natural abundance and human incompetence led him frequently to exclaim, as many tourists do, "What a Paradise is, or at least might be, this country [Brazil] if it were possessed by the English!"[20]

Foreign travelers often reinforced the urban elite's scorn for the capabilities of their own peoples. Charles Darwin observed of the indigenous peoples of Tierra del Fuego: "I believe if the world was searched, no lower grade of man could be found."[21] Moreover, "their language does not deserve to be called articulate. Capt. Cook says it is like a man clearing his throat; to which may be added another very hoarse man trying to shout and a third encouraging a horse with that peculiar noise which is made in one side of the mouth. Imagine these sounds and a few gutturals mingled with them, and there will be as near an approximation to their language as any European may expect to obtain."[22] G. F. Masterman, an English army doctor, had the ill fortune to be imprisoned and tortured by the government of Paraguayan dictator Francisco Solano López in 1868. He wrote of his sufferings from the torrid sun and from the rain when he was tied down with pegs and left in the open air with no shelter. Still clothed and with a blanket, he wondered how his fellow captives, many of them naked, were faring. Answering his own musing, he wrote, "Some of them were natives, some Brazilian negroes; they could bear it without much inconvenience; but the majority were foreigners, and it was pitiable to see the expression of mute agony their faces bore."[23] In the same sentence he indicted the Solano López government for its inhumanity, and he callously assumed that blacks would not suffer the same pain as foreigners.

Few travelers displayed the good temper and humor that Edmund Temple did in Bolivia in the 1820s. One night, lodged amid numerous Indians on the floor of the curate's house in Caracolla, Temple was awakened when "an old wizened, winter-apple looking creature [laid] her bones beside me as closely as she could well do without becoming the actual partner of my bed."[24] He wrapped himself tightly in his poncho and squirmed as far away as he could among all the sleeping bodies. When he awoke, he found that he had miraculously wandered far from the old crone and was nicely wedged between two beautiful young *cholas* (mestizas) whom he had earlier admired, although observing that their luxuriant locks could use a good washing. Explaining how he could have made such an unconscious pilgrimage while sleeping, he observed, "I merely abandoned the chill sterility of winter for the genial luxuriance of summer—that I had fled from a bleak inhospitable desert, to repose myself in the delightful regions between the tropics."[25] A true and happy traveler was he.

After the 1860s, sooner in some areas, a new liberal generation appeared, influenced by the 1848 revolutions in Europe and intent on claiming the optimistic promise of the independence period. Slowly, things fell into place. New capital came to revive mining and plantation agriculture. Cities grew in population and boasted trolley cars and streetlights. The advent of steamships forced investment in the modernization of port facilities. New roads were built. A telegraph and the transatlantic cable connected formerly isolated cities with each other and with the world. Immigrants came in search of land or opportunity or simply from curiosity. The politically ambitious made accommodations with each other. National revenues saw a mild increase and were used to pay for professional training and salaries for the military and for a modest expansion of government jobs.

The activity and show of prosperity impressed Latinos and foreigners alike. Some saw only the surface, and usually urban, reality of improved roads, ports, and trade, as well as the new immigrants, and they gloried in the modern hustle and bustle. Other travelers, and some Latin Americans, saw the darker side of progress. They observed Indians pushed from ancestral lands, or nearly exterminated in the Indian wars of the late nineteenth century in Argentina, Chile, and northern Mexico. They saw that the highly praised educational improvements did not reach rural areas or benefit the poor. They also experienced the rising cost of living as export crops replaced subsistence food crops and imported goods flooded countries to cater to the tastes of the new immigrants, small middle sectors, and the elite.

British historian and statesman James Bryce made an extended trip through South America in 1912 and responded to both the excitement of the quickening pace he found in the Atlantic cities and the stagnation he saw on the Pacific side. How much more ground he could cover in four months than Humboldt could at the beginning of the nineteenth century! Still, Bryce counseled other travelers not to expect roads fit for driving in most places, to be prepared to travel by mule in the Andes, and to expect high prices, especially in Buenos Aires and Montevideo, acknowledged to be "the most expensive places in the world to live in."[26] Basil Hall would have been much shocked to hear his delightful Guayaquil described as "the pest-house of the continent, rivalling for the prevalence and malignity of its malarial fevers such dens of disease as Fontesvilla on the Pungwe River in South Africa and the Guinea coast itself."[27] Had Hall seen the city through rose-colored glasses in 1821? Or had the city's growth and a century of poverty turned the pleasant Ecuadorian town into a "pest-house"?

More knowledgeable than most travelers after Humboldt, Bryce understood the devastating effect of the Spanish conquest upon the indigenous peoples and also recognized that the hemisphere was home to a wide variety of Indians. He asserted that the indigenous majorities of Bolivia and Peru had contributed nothing to their nations and remained isolated from the urban governing classes. "He [the Indian] neither loves nor hates, but fears, the white man, and the white man neither loves nor hates, but despises him, there being some fear, at least in Bolivia, mingled with the contempt. They are held together neither by social relations nor by political, but by the need which the white landowner has for the Indian's labour and by the power of long habit which has made the Indian acquiesce in his subjection as a rent payer."[28] If only someone had listened to Humboldt!

Bryce's optimism revived in Santiago, Chile, which he thought modern, confident, and prosperous in contrast to the old-fashioned cities of Cuzco, La Paz, and Lima. If Santiago reassured him, Buenos Aires surpassed his expectations. "Buenos Aires is something between Paris and New York. It has the business rush and the luxury of the one, the gaiety, and pleasure-loving aspect of the other. Everybody seems to have money, and to like spending it, and to like letting everybody else know that it is being spent."[29]

In Buenos Aires, Bryce summarized his impressions.

Loitering in the great Avenida de Mayo and watching the hurrying crowd and the whirl of motor cars, and the gay shop-windows, and the open-air cafes on the sidewalks, and the Parisian glitter of the women's dresses, one feels much nearer to Europe than anywhere else in South America. Bolivia suggests the seventeenth century and Peru the eighteenth, and even in energetic Chile there is an air of the elder time, and a soothing sense of detachment. But here all is twentieth century, with suggestions of the twenty-first.[30]

Brazil rather overwhelmed Bryce, and he echoed Mansfield's reaction.

The first thought that rises in the mind of those who are possessed, as in this age we all more or less are, by the passion for the development of natural resources, is a feeling of regret that a West European race, powerful by its numbers and its skill, say the North American or German or English has not, to use the familiar phrase, "got the thing in hand." The white part of the Brazilian nation—and it is only that part that need be considered—seems altogether too small for the tasks which the possession of this country imposes.[31]

As Humboldt had done over one hundred years earlier, Bryce deplored the lack of both depth and breadth in education. Although fascinated by the visible signs of progress, he concluded that even in the cities cultural life frequently was shallow and boring. Worse still was the prospect of spending time in the countryside.

The traveller in South America who confines himself, as many do, to the larger cities, finds them so like those of Europe and North America in their possession of the appliances of modern civilization, in their electric street cars and handsome parks, in their ably written press, in the volume of business they transact—I might add in the aspect of the legislatures and in the administrative machinery of their government—that he is apt to fancy a like resemblance in the countries as a whole. But the small towns and rural districts are very far behind, though least so in Chile and Argentina.[32]

IV

As we leave our travelers and embark on our own journey to meet some city and country folk of nineteenth-century Latin America, a question arises: What do the people whom we shall meet along the way have in common? Febvre argues that projecting individual lives in some detail upon the screens of our imaginations can help us to understand a period and perhaps discover its prevailing attitude. But are these people typical? If so, in what ways? Are they atypical? Can we tell the difference? Can we learn about Latin America in general from a single example?

For over one hundred and fifty years, Latin American history has teemed with a variety of stories. The life of Emilio Coni in Buenos Aires of the 1890s will relate a different tale from that of Atanasio Tzul in Guatemala of the 1820s. For that matter, the neighbors of Coni and Tzul might rip up our notes and insist that we listen to them in order to get the stories right. Unfortunately, we do not have the luxury of interviewing the people who knew our subjects. Few were important enough to receive more than a mention in "regular" history books. After all, most were neither politicians nor military leaders. Were liberal, urban historians to grant them a line, the writers would shape their stories to fit their own views of national progress and civilization. Calfucurá no doubt would appear as a "savage," and Agustín Marroquín as no more than a "bandit." Carlota Lucia de Brito would be a *sinverguenza* (shameless one), or a *pobre mujer* (poor woman). Most probably, however, these individuals would not be considered part of "real history."

These silhouettes do not constitute a random sample of all the possible types we might encounter. They provide, rather, an idiosyncratic cross section of social types. The individuals included differed greatly from each other, but each was prominent enough—or deviant enough—to have left sources, or "tracks" as French historian Marc Bloch would have it. Perhaps none of them was entirely "average." Still, we can learn from both the nearly average and the deviant as well as from persons who were combinations of the two.

The Italian historian Carlo Ginzburg, for example, states that the sixteenth-century miller Menocchio was an atypical person who provides clues to a speculative understanding of his more "ordinary" neighbors. The miller's literacy, his familiarity with the written treatises of his time, his ability to synthesize and discuss theories about the cosmos, and even his brush with the Inquisition set him apart from the average peasant. Ginzburg carefully probes Menocchio's ideas, tracing some of them to contemporary books and philosophers. The residue, Ginzburg argues, may represent a consciousness that Menocchio shared with many of his illiterate friends. Indeed, some of these ideas even go back to a pre-Christian *mentalité*. In almost geologic layers of consciousness, Ginzburg finds values, beliefs, and superstitions that expand our understanding both of Menocchio's contemporaries and of his forebears. The speculation is logical, provocative, and, ultimately, unprovable, for the origin and direction of mental artifacts puzzle even more than do those of physical artifacts.[33] Ginzburg, however, provides us with an example of how the life of one unusual, although probably only mildly so, person can illuminate the lives of the more ordinary. We, like curious foreign travelers, merely have to ask the right questions.

While a mildly unusual person can offer clues to the average, how can someone who is clearly deviant—a sociopath, for example, or a mystic—reveal anything about "normal" society? The historians Robert Forster and Orest Ranum suggest that "the moral and social values of a society, especially on the level of collective mentalities and community behavior, are clarified by the study of those who reject those values and are cast out of society."[34] In fact, much like the drawings in children's books that reveal either of two faces depending on whether the observer focuses on the black or on the white space, a silhouette is a profile that can be comprehended only by looking at the interaction between the substantive and the surrounding space. We can learn from the way that their contemporaries treated deviants and from the way that laws and institutions regarded them. The sociopathic Marroquín was lauded when he assisted the "right" side in the Independence War. Nicolás Zúñiga y Miranda represented both a fool and a savant to Mexicans who lived under the Porfirian dictatorship. And when we study the life of Carlota Lucia de Brito, we see what Brazilian society considered deviance and what it considered appropriate punishment. If our silhouettes are carefully outlined, and their surrounding contexts sharply defined, we indeed can reach some conclusions about the typical and the deviant.

In our magic-lantern show—the projection of individual silhouettes from the nineteenth-century history of Latin America—we will meet each subject as an individual. Yet the particular silhouette might be common enough in some cases so that hundreds, even thousands, of people at the time might have cast roughly the same shadow. For some of our people, we are fortunate to have an inkling of their internal lives as well as of their behaviors and the reactions of their contemporaries. Can a silhouette, then, be three-dimensional?

By and large, these essays will not discuss explicitly the fleshless abstractions of class, ethnic group, and gender. However, we may employ our historical imaginations to ask questions. To what extent is Soledad Román de Núñez representative of her gender and class? Does Mandeponay's story tell us anything about Indians in general, or does Calfucurá's? Can we say that we understand the role of the church on the frontier better from knowing something about the career of José de Calasanz Vela? Our answers no doubt will vary with the individual portrait and with the confidence that we feel in the characterization of the group to which he or she belonged.

We must be alert to the possibility of committing an ecological fallacy when we consider individuals. No one person truly can "stand for" his or her group. Our noting that Francisco de Paula Mayrink behaved in a certain way or believed certain things does not enable us to assert that all Brazilian entrepreneurs thought the same way. Yet we also must comment that any aggregate portrait of a group—of Indians, for example, or of the bourgeoisie—similarly cannot allow us to make assumptions about the beliefs or behaviors of an individual who is a member of that group. If we concede that it is equally fallacious to argue from the particular to the general as it is to argue from the general to the particular, then we may conclude that a full understanding of a historical era may require us to study both the particular and the general. A textbook generalization or a theoretical model of modernization needs to be looked at as a context within which we may place both the deviant mystic Teresa Urrea and the artisan José Leocadio Camacho. These two examples—like most of the other persons portrayed in this book—represent part of Latin America's rich and varied "aristocracy of the sensitive, the considerate and the plucky." They are a vital part of Forster's "true human tradition."

Judith Ewell

NOTES

1. Quoted in David Lowenthal, *The Past Is a Foreign Country* (Cambridge, 1985), p. xvi.

2. Paul Fussell, *Abroad: British Literary Traveling between the Wars* (New York, 1980), p. 39.

3. Lucien Febvre, *Life in Renaissance France*, ed. and trans. Marian Rothstein (Cambridge, MA, 1977), p. 3.

4. Ibid., p. 2.

5. Ibid.

6. Louis A. Pérez, Jr., "Vagrants, Beggars, and Bandits: Social Origins of Cuban Separatism, 1878–1895," *American Historical Review* 90 (December 1985): 1121.

7. Richard W. Slatta, "Rural Criminality and Social Conflict in Nineteenth-Century Buenos Aires Province," *Hispanic American Historical Review* 60 (August 1980): 450–75.

8. Rebecca J. Scott, *Slave Emancipation in Cuba: The Transition to Free Labor, 1860–1899* (Princeton, 1985).

9. Frank Safford, "Politics, Ideology and Society in Post-Independence Spanish America," in *The Cambridge History of Latin America*, ed. Leslie Bethell (Cambridge, 1985), 3:405.

10. Eric R. Wolf, *Europe and the People without History* (Berkeley and Los Angeles, 1982), p. 5.

11. Florencia Mallon, "Nationalist and Antistate Coalitions in the War of the Pacific: Junín and Cajamarca, 1879–1902," in *Resistance, Rebellion, and Consciousness in the Andean Peasant World, 18th to 20th Centuries*, ed. Steve J. Stern (Madison, 1987), pp. 233–34.

12. Steve J. Stern, "New Approaches to the Study of Peasant Rebellion and Consciousness: Implications of the Andean Experience," in ibid., p. 10.

13. Frank MacShane, ed., *Impressions of Latin America: Five Centuries of Travel and Adventure by English and North American Writers* (New York, 1963), p. 86.

14. Alexander von Humboldt and Aimé Bonpland, *Personal Narrative of Travels to the Equinoctial Regions of the New Continent during the Years 1799–1804*, trans. Helen Maria Williams (1826; reprint ed., New York, 1966), pp. 231–32.

15. Alexander von Humboldt, *Political Essay on the Kingdom of New Spain*, edited and with introduction by Mary Maples Dunn (New York, 1972), p. 212.

16. Ibid., p. 240.

17. Charles Blachford Mansfield, *Paraguay, Brazil, and the Plate: Letters Written in 1852–1853* (1856; reprint ed., New York, 1971), p. 50.

18. Ibid., p. 97.

19. Ibid., p. 29.

20. Ibid., p. 26.

21. MacShane, *Impressions of Latin America*, p. 119.

22. Ibid., pp. 116–17.

23. Ibid., p. 144.

24. Ibid., p. 100.

25. Ibid., p. 102.

26. James Bryce, *South America: Observations and Impressions* (New York, 1913), p. 588.

27. Ibid., p. 40.

28. Ibid., p. 185.

29. Ibid., p. 318.

30. Ibid., p. 346.

31. Ibid., p. 420.

32. Ibid., p. 580.

33. Carlo Ginzburg, *The Cheese and the Worms: The Cosmos of a Sixteenth-Century Miller,* trans. John Tedeschi and Anne Tedeschi (New York, 1982).

34. Robert Forster and Orest Ranum, eds., *Deviants and the Abandoned in French Society* (Baltimore, 1978), p. viii.

I
The Independence Generation: Between Colony and Republic, 1780–1830

Most Latin Americans had been content to be part of the great Iberian empires, even as those empires were in decline. They did have a number of specific grievances against the colonial administrations, but only a few individuals, such as Simón Bolívar and Francisco Miranda of Venezuela, advocated independence for Latin America before 1808. European events provided the shock that allowed republican ideology to spread. When Napoleon I invaded the Iberian Peninsula in 1807, he drove the Portuguese and Spanish kings into exile. Napoleon's brother, Joseph Bonaparte, ruled Spain until 1814. Six years of a French king, whose reign was considered illegitimate by Spanish Americans, sufficed to allow the seed of independence to grow in America. Dom João VI, the Portuguese king, fled to Brazil and ruled his empire from there between 1808 and 1820. He raised the status of Brazil to that of co-kingdom with Portugal, and when he reluctantly returned to Portugal in 1820, he left behind his oldest son, Pedro I, as regent of Brazil. In 1822, Pedro I declared the nation's independence from Portugal almost without any bloodshed.

The wars for independence in Mexico and Central America were long and drawn out (1808–1821) and were tinged with social and ethnic tensions. Thousands of Indians and mestizos followed two priests, Miguel Hidalgo and José María Morelos, between 1810 and 1815 in a campaign for independence and social justice. The threat of class warfare scared the white creole elite and generally turned them against independence. In the essays that follow, we see that the Mexican Creole Antonio López de Santa Anna initially sided with the royalists (Chapter 1), whereas the bandit Agustín Marroquín (also a Mexican Creole) joined Hidalgo's forces (Chapter 2). Marroquín's earlier life, however, suggests that Hidalgo's ideals attracted him less than did the opportunity to pillage and to get even with his enemies. After the uprising of the lower classes had been quelled, the white creole elite more readily embraced independence.

Although we are concerned here only with Santa Anna's early years, he subsequently joined another famous royalist, Agustín Iturbide, to fight for independence, which came in 1821. The careers of Santa Anna and Marroquín also tell us much about the life of early nineteenth-century soldiers and how the Spanish system of justice worked.

In distant Chiapas, at that time part of the viceroyalty of Mexico but attached to the Central American captaincy general of Guatemala, Atanasio Tzul and Lucas Aguilar's revolt a few years later in 1820 (Chapter 3) resembled a traditional Indian rebellion against the hated tribute tax more than it did a skirmish for political independence. The term "Indian rebellion" calls for reexamination, however, for the rebellion divided more than it united the indigenous population.

In South America the year 1810 marked the beginning of the white Creoles' movement toward separation from Spain. Conventional history highlights the activities of Bolívar or of Mariano Moreno and José de San Martín of Argentina as well as the constitutions and grand military campaigns of the era. Beneath the surface of the South American march to republicanism existed some of the same ambiguities, albeit muted, of the Mexican wars. Argentines and Brazilians fought each other over the flat grasslands between southern Brazil and the Plata River. Yet patriotic zeal appeared to drive the combatants less than did the desire to build up and protect personal empires of land and cattle. The essay on Maria Antônia Muniz (Chapter 4), who lived for over one hundred years on that harsh frontier, suggests that life there was much the same before, during, and after the Independence Wars. Muniz's family history further reminds us that not all Latin American extended families helped and supported each other.

Clearly, the Independence Wars (1810–1825) did not provide the sharp break between a colonial past and a republican future that idealists hoped for and loyalists feared. Creole society, values, institutions, patterns, and habits persisted. Still, independence did soften the rigidity of colonial class and ethnic divisions, thereby providing greater opportunities for talented individuals, if not for the majority. Some of those who worked hard, moved quickly, and avoided political conflicts could begin to acquire wealth, just as Maria Antônia did. The quickest route to success was through military prowess and forceful leadership. Santa Anna's thirty-year political dominance of Mexico derived at least in part from the military role he had played during the wars. Tzul and Marroquín met fates more common to leaders of colonial rebellions. The experiences of these four Latin Americans can help us to imagine better their complex world while also inviting us to reconsider the meaning of abstractions such as patriot, royalist, and independence.

1

The Young Antonio López de Santa Anna: Veracruz Counterinsurgent and Incipient Caudillo

Christon I. Archer

That the victors write history is a truism. Thus Mexican historians have praised men like Father Miguel Hidalgo, José María Morelos, Vicente Guerrero, and Guadalupe Victoria who fought for independence between 1810 and 1821. We might well ask how and why the royalists differed from their patriot colleagues.

Some royalists, including Antonio López de Santa Anna and Agustín Iturbide, later became patriots. Iturbide signed the Treaty of Córdoba, which sealed Mexican independence in 1821, and shortly thereafter had himself crowned emperor of Mexico. His unhappy empire fell to a republican uprising in 1823, and he was executed in 1824. The wily Santa Anna bided his time and was a force in Mexico for over three decades. A royalist from 1810 when he entered the infantry until 1820 (the period portrayed in this essay), he joined Iturbide in 1821, served him, and then became part of the republican rebellion that unseated the emperor. A Liberal from 1823 until 1833, Santa Anna then turned to the Conservative party, which he dominated until his final exile in 1855.

Santa Anna's early career casts light on those who fought in the Mexican Independence Wars. How important were political principles such as republicanism or royalism to Santa Anna? Was he simply an opportunist?

Santa Anna's experience also adds to the historical debate on the role of colonial militias in Latin America. In some areas, including Mexico, the late eighteenth-century concern for imperial security and the long wars for independence increased the importance of creole military officers. Christon Archer offers an explanation for the respect accorded creole officers and the strength of royalism. Santa Anna, for example, provided the only government, protection, and services that the civilian population around Veracruz ever saw. Patriotic historiography usually overlooks the possibility that the royalists had strong grass-roots support, just as most historians dwell on Santa Anna's later irresponsibility and corruption rather than on his earlier popularity.

As occurred in the rest of Latin America, the Independence Wars in Mexico gave birth to the feisty caudillos who dominated nineteenth-century politics. As politicians, caudillos had to provide favors for their followers in order to survive. A leader such as Santa Anna may well have learned more about politics from personal wartime experience than from any of the writings of political philosophers.

Christon I. Archer is professor of history at the University of Calgary. His prize-winning book, *The Army of Bourbon Mexico, 1760–1810* (Albuquerque, 1977), and numerous articles have established him as an expert on eighteenth-century Latin American military history. He currently is at work on *The Eagle and the Thunderbird: Spanish-Indian Relations on the Northwest Coast in the Eighteenth Century* (1989) and on a study of the royalist army and counterinsurgency in Mexico during the wars for independence.

There is no good biography of Antonio López de Santa Anna. While he cast a broad shadow over much of the Mexican nineteenth century and was a central figure in almost all of the major crises of the period, historians of Mexico continue to grapple with his enigma. How could a leader survive despite overwhelming defeats as a military commander and apparently inexplicable personal political shifts from liberal to reactionary conservative, not to mention in the face of Mexico's economic stagnation, social chaos, and near fragmentation? If he was an incompetent fool, how could he endure crisis after crisis to regain power? If he was a traitor, how did he avoid the firing squads that terminated the lives of others? Clearly, Santa Anna contained within himself an indefinable elixir that made possible the nineteenth-century caudillo. However, natural talent, charisma, ambition, and guile do not alone explain his successes and failures. For a Santa Anna figure to exist in Mexico's regions or provinces or as leader of the nation, special conditions and background were essential. The War of Independence in his home province of Veracruz was a perfect laboratory, or incubator, for Santa Anna, the aspirant caudillo with national ambitions.

Until 1812 the province and port city of Veracruz escaped the "devouring flame of rebellion" that first broke out under the leadership of Padre Miguel Hidalgo in September 1810. After Hidalgo's death, Padre José María Morelos and his followers spread the revolution south and east toward Veracruz province.

By April 1812 the village and rural populations joined the insurgency, and revolution swept from the temperate interior towns of Jalapa, Córdoba, and Orizaba to the sweltering tropical lowlands and walled port city of Veracruz. Even though the power of the regime to punish rebellion was well known, there were grievances that compelled elements of the population to accept the risks. Fishermen, smugglers, artisans, traders, stock raisers, small agriculturalists, and other villagers of the thinly settled coastal and interior communities resisted the royalist army's military mobilizations, which grabbed men from their normal occupations and exposed their families to poverty and starvation. Peasant farmers rejected oppressive rents, control by absentee landowners, and the corruption of district administrators.

In contrast to the Mexicans from the highland interior or the Spaniards who arrived in the tropical lowlands, indigenous Veracruzanos—often *pardos* (mulattoes) and free blacks—were immune or resistant to *vómito negro* (yellow fever), malaria, and other tropical diseases. They knew how to deal with the biting insects, thorny vegetation, and torrid temperatures that soon felled those unaccustomed to their region. They possessed intimate familiarity with the dense bush, almost impenetrable mountainous terrain, and treacherous swampy coastline. Given leaders and a cause, Veracruzanos were excellent insurgents, who could maintain a near-permanent albeit low level of guerrilla activity, punctuated by bursts of energy when they would assemble forces to blockade essential roads inland and levy their own tariffs on commerce and transit. During some months and even years, these rebels managed to isolate the commercial entrepôt of Veracruz port and to interdict communications between the metropolis and Mexico City, the capital of Spain's most valuable American possession.

Because highland Mexican and Spanish expeditionary troops could not function in the unhealthy climate and there were insufficient acclimatized local forces available to patrol the roads and garrison the towns of Veracruz province, counterinsurgency planning confounded almost all of the royalist army commanders. Heavily protected military convoys succeeded in opening communications momentarily but left control of the country in the hands of the rebels. Moreover, merchants could not adjust to army schedules designed primarily for communications and the transit of precious metals rather than for the movement of bulk products such as flour, tobacco, and grain from the interior to provision the port city and supply its commerce. Gradually, the long war suffocated the city of Veracruz and atomized many of the province's smaller centers. The civilian populations abandoned their villages and rural haciendas to found new "escaped" communities in the impenetrable mountainous barrancas and isolated coastal swamplands beyond the reach of army patrols. To root them out, the royalist forces had to anticipate expeditions and sieges of rebel fortresses. In eight years the population of Veracruz city declined 40 percent, from 15,000 in 1810 to 12,075 in 1812 to only 8,934 in 1818. The port merchants clamored for military assistance to restore commerce while most senior army commanders plotted to escape the climate and insoluable insurgency to reside in temperate Jalapa or Orizaba.

As might be expected, the war offered a variety of new opportunities both to rebels and to royalists. New Orleans traders sold guns, munitions, manufactured goods, and provisions to the Veracruz insurgents, who opened new commercial networks reaching inland to the highland populations. In some regions, legitimate trade in Mexican textiles and other goods simply ceased to exist. While the insurgents subsisted by charging transit duties and running contraband trading networks, royalist officers and soldiers profited by selling protection, confiscating so-called rebel possessions, and engaging in a variety of other illegal activities.

The city of Veracruz was too strong for the lightly armed guerrillas to take in a frontal assault, but its defenses were porous and wide open to the activities of insurgent and royalist contrabandists. In 1816, Brigadier Fernando Mijares y Mancebo declared that the city "presented a truly melancholic look." He expressed doubt that the crumbling walls and bastions could withstand a five-day siege by a proper army. Heavy artillery pieces rusted, and even with liberal treatments of pitch, the gun carriages rotted in fewer than three years. Sands blowing from surrounding dunes banked up against the walls, creating natural ramps that invited smugglers to import bales of merchandise. In 1819, Brigadier Pascual de Liñan complained that there was a breach in the palisade at the bastion of Concepción "through which an entire house might be introduced." The garrison force was too small to provide adequate pickets or to patrol the walls continuously. With much of the population, including the army patrols, in league with the contrabandists, the one military engineer and a few pathetic companies of ragged forced laborer *presidarios* could not maintain the defenses.

Corruption, bitter disputes between officials, and frustration with the interminable insurgency made Veracruz unstable and dangerous to the Mexican royalist cause. In 1815 guerrilla successes in cutting off communications compelled the imperial government to divert an expeditionary force of over seventeen hundred Spanish troops under Brigadier Mijares, destined for Panama and Peru, to Veracruz with orders to smash the insurgents, open communications, and construct a *camino militar* (military road) and telegraph system guarded by a line of forts reaching from the port into the interior. The Spanish regulars won temporary victories, dispersed the guerrillas led by Guadalupe Victoria and other chiefs, and made possible the construction of some fortified posts along the road inland.

Despite Mijares's belief that generous dosing of his men with fiery *aguardiente* (cane alcohol) accorded them protection from the tropical climate, yellow fever and other diseases consumed the inebriated European soldiers as fast as they did the sober ones. Even with full power to dismiss corrupt or useless army commanders and civilian administrators, Mijares failed to achieve much in the way of meaningful reform. After a few months of hectic campaigning, he himself fell ill and abandoned Veracruz, which sank back into chronic insurgency. By 1818–19 political and administrative chaos, widespread guerrilla attacks, and blockades preventing communications forced Viceroy Juan Ruíz de Apodaca (conde del Venadito) to appoint the subinspector general of the Mexican army, Brigadier Marshal Pascual de Liñan, to try his hand at pacifying Veracruz. Everyone agreed that a major key to suppressing the insurgency lay in somehow recruiting acclimatized locals who could bear the burden of counterinsurgency duties that devastated the health of European and highland troops.

Given the crisis over suitable manpower, it was little wonder that in 1815 young Sublieutenant Antonio López de Santa Anna of the Fixed Infantry Regiment of Veracruz received a transfer from duty in the Mexican north to his home province for counterinsurgency operations. Born in Jalapa, Veracruz, in 1794 or 1795, Santa Anna became an officer cadet in the Fixed Infantry Regiment of Veracruz in 1810 during an expansion of the unit from two to three battalions.

Unlike other Mexican infantry regiments, the Veracruz regiment was designed to be a climate-hardened unit stationed permanently in the tropical environs of the port city. From the 1790s forward, the regime planned to recruit officers and soldiers locally so that highland battalions would not have to suffer from the ruinous climate, disease losses, and unacceptable levels of desertion. In reality, however, the regiment was little more than a holding tank for Mexican criminals and vagrants who were sentenced to military service at Veracruz rather than to even less appetizing punishment as forced laborers in the port, Manila, or Havana. Recruits included a large number of chronic deserters and petty offenders from other army units, as well as common murderers, robbers, and other assorted criminals. For many highland Mexicans, transfer to the Veracruz infantry was tantamount to a death sentence—except that their executioners were the mosquitoes that carried the fearful *vómito negro*. At Veracruz, the infantry continued to pursue their violent habits, and when yellow fever swept away their comrades, the survivors attempted to desert and flee inland. Frequently, they fell into the hands of the insurgents and ended up serving in the guerrilla bands.

Santa Anna's education among these cutthroat soldiers and officers, whose chronic drunkenness, laziness, illegal activities, and addiction to gambling-fiestas-fandangos-and-fornication had caused them to be dumped into Veracruz, may only be imagined. Many of his fellow troops engaged in contraband trade and even used the proximity of their barracks to the outer city walls to lower goods and coined silver from the roof of their building into the city. Although he was sent north in 1811, away from some of these evil influences, young Santa Anna was charged with embezzling regimental funds to pay off his gambling debts. Like many young officers unable to control their personal lives, he appeared to be headed for a less than exemplary military career. Fortunately or unfortunately, Santa Anna's transfer to counterinsurgency duties in Veracruz province separated him from the nefarious influences of his comrades in the Fixed Infantry Regiment and gave him scope to build on his strengths.

After years of useless violence, some royalist commanders realized that the occasional application of superior armed force against the Veracruz insurgents did not end rebellion. Ambushes, skirmishes at river crossings, and difficult passages through many miles of roads obstructed by felled trees and camouflaged pits to hinder cavalry, exhausted and frustrated regular soldiers. Royalist

garrisons were insufficient to protect rural landowners, who cooperated with the insurgents in order to prevent the burning of
their houses, rustling of their livestock, and destructive raids into
local towns. Communities such as Boca del Río and Antigua near
Veracruz, which normally provisioned the port with meat, vegetables, and other necessities, became permanent war zones in
which both sides practiced scorched-earth tactics that made agricultural production impossible. The government lost much of its
vital income from the interior tobacco-growing zones when the
unprotected farmers moved to safer locations under insurgent
control. Blacks from the sugar haciendas abandoned the cane-
fields and occupied lands to engage in subsistence agriculture.
Although the royalists garrisoned Veracruz and the major interior
towns of the province, the population was insurgent in its loyalties
or at least acquiescent under their direction.

In 1816, after employing companies of the Spanish expeditionary Infantry Regiment of Barcelona to pursue rebel bands
into the rough backcountry bisected by rivers and mountains,
Brigadier Mijares fully understood the impossibility of fighting
guerrillas with regular infantry. The Spanish soldiers suffered
exhaustion, succumbed to disease, and even deserted to save their
lives. When the Barcelona infantry failed, Mijares recruited a
militia force of locals, most of whom were recently amnestied
insurgents, which he called the Realistas del Camino Real. In
addition, he advocated introduction of a general policy to con-
centrate the civilian population *bajo campana* (within hearing of
the community bells) in order to separate the guerrillas from
civilian support and to restore law-abiding communities. Assisted
by Viceroy Apodaca's generous amnesty program for insurgents
who would give up rebellion, the royalists developed a carrot-
and-stick approach designed to reward renewed loyalty and make
continued insurgency as unpalatable as possible. Dynamic young
officers such as Sublieutenant (now brevetted to captain) Santa
Anna were perfect candidates to lead search-and-destroy expeditions into the backcountry to obliterate agriculture, round up
civilians, and chase down guerrilla bands. Santa Anna enjoyed
an advantage over other officers in achieving these objectives
since he knew the country intimately, understood the population,
and could appeal to the insurgents in a variety of ways.

Field Marshal Pascual de Liñan added the final elements to
the royalist counterinsurgency policy. From 1818 to 1820 he
encouraged the royalist forces to maintain intense pressure upon

the guerrillas so that the insurgents would be forced to seek amnesty. Even though many of the bands appeared to be beaten, Liñan feared that relaxation of pressure by the army would permit them to reorganize. He calculated that since 1812 there had been three distinct cycles of insurgent aggression in the province of Veracruz. Liñan believed that unless pacification were consolidated, the rural rancheros could develop a fondness for the unregulated guerrilla life-style or for the lands that they now occupied in the most isolated districts.

Liñan understood that land was the key element in pacifying the province and in achieving the resettlement of the insurgents. Without agrarian reform to distribute agricultural land to the uprooted population, the cycle of insurgency would continue without end. Liñan noted that in the past amnestied rebels desiring land on which to raise crops were left without employment, to hang about the royalist garrisons. Since these individuals knew how to fight and did not have much other training, many of them either were taken into the militias or simply drifted back into insurgent or bandit gangs. Liñan argued that to make pacification permanent, royal amnesties had to be followed by a program to resettle the former insurgents. The question was where to find suitable land. In Veracruz province, there were no unoccupied crown lands available and suitable for agriculture. While expropriation was not even considered, Liñan did ask landowners to permit resettlement on their property and to charge no rent for a five-year period. He pointed out that hacienda lands had been ravaged for years during the insurgency without any possibility of profits for the owners. His program, at least, had the long-term prospect of restoring agriculture, the economy, and the wealth of the agrarian elite. Liñan decided to implement his agrarian policy with the resettlement of the abandoned towns of Xamapa and Medellín near Veracruz.

It was against this background that Santa Anna emerged as an effective counterinsurgency commander and royalist land reform administrator as well as a highly controversial figure in Veracruz. In 1818 he became commander of a militia unit, composed of amnestied insurgents and residents of the small communities located just outside of the port city, called the Realistas de Extramuros de Veracruz y Pueblo de la Boca del Río (literally, royalists from outside the walls of Veracruz and the town of Boca del Río). At the time, the insurgent bands were enjoying a definite edge over the royalist forces. Garrison commanders at Veracruz refused to pursue the well-mounted insurgents, who rode right up to the walls to mock the royalists. Santa Anna could not dispatch his militia force instantly to take on the rebels because his unpaid troops had to work at their regular jobs in and around the city. By the time the militia could assemble after the first alarm, the guerrillas often already had run off livestock, kidnapped persons for ransom, and killed anyone who resisted. On December 10, 1818, for example, over two hundred mounted insurgents raided the plain just outside of the walls of Veracruz where they burned two houses, stole livestock, and left proclamations, including one threatening Santa Anna. The Realistas de Extramuros, assisted by pickets from the Fixed Infantry of Veracruz and the Infantry Battalion of Asturias, opened fire, but the rebels withdrew in good order. The timidity of the governor of Veracruz on this occasion made Santa Anna furious. He was positive that if the governor had sent out the main force of the Asturias infantry, all escape routes might have been closed. Santa Anna found it particularly galling that a woman who sold vegetables in Veracruz had warned officials of the rebels' plans to raid the area.

Santa Anna wrote to the viceroy condemning the governor both for his indifference to the constant attacks and for exhibiting little willingness to punish the insurgents. Bitter that he could not engage the enemy in his own territory, Santa Anna requested fifty regular soldiers from the Fixed Regiment of Veracruz, who would form a rapid response force available at any time to strengthen his one hundred militia troops. In addition, he believed that the regulars would serve to train the militia and inculcate in them greater fighting courage. Given the quality of the soldiers in the Fixed Regiment, the feasibility of this plan was suspect. In any event, the governor rejected Santa Anna's complaints and his request, arguing that there were not enough soldiers to garrison the city, let alone to spare for possible chases through the countryside.

Santa Anna's boldness contrasted with the timidity of senior military authorities and earned him considerable notoriety as well as some grudging respect from other royalists. In a raid on Venta de Arriba, near the port city, in November 1818, Santa Anna's force surprised and captured a particularly sanguinary guerrilla chieftain, Francisco de Asis, along with his band, horses, and baggage. Rather than follow normal procedures, Santa Anna conducted his prisoner to a point immediately outside the walls of Veracruz where he ordered Asis executed by firing squad. There were no formalities such as an indictment, other judicial niceties, or the permission of the governor of Veracruz. While no royalist shed tears for the dead guerrilla leader, the governor interpreted the incident as an act of great disrespect for his position and a major breach of military discipline. He reported Santa Anna to the commander general of Puebla and Veracruz provinces, Brigadier Ciriaco de Llanos, who suspended Santa Anna immediately from his militia command.

Given his personality, it is not surprising that Santa Anna rejected his superiors' attempt to discipline him; he claimed that he deserved praise and reward for his labors, not punishment. Remarkably, Subinspector General Liñan intervened in the case on Santa Anna's behalf, describing him as "active, zealous, indefatigable in his service, and of very good military knowledge." He pointed out that Santa Anna had received special recognition from the regime for his contributions to the pacification of the country. Liñan argued that given this background and Santa Anna's age, "it is not strange that on some occasions he may have exceeded his powers." The execution of Asis was one of these occasions. To draw attention to his cause, Santa Anna broke another army regulation and without permission from his commanders traveled to Mexico City, where he laid his case before Viceroy Apodaca. He described Asis as a "pernicious and sanguinary chief" and stated that at the moment of his suspension from command, he had been extremely close to capturing or killing the principal insurgent leader, Guadalupe Victoria. Several priests and alcaldes from Veracruz wrote testimonials praising Santa Anna for terminating "the infamous ringleader Francisco de Asis̩ who was the terror of these districts." With Liñan's intervention, the viceroy returned Santa Anna to his command without pursuing further legal action.

His star now ascending, Santa Anna led a series of reckless search missions in early 1819 to root out guerrilla bands and track down the elusive Victoria, whose arrest truly would have brought great fame and rewards. During January, Santa Anna commanded a small force of 70 horsemen, 50 recently amnestied from the guerrilla band of Marcos Benavidez and 20 of his own Realistas de Extramuros. Already, Santa Anna's success as a counterinsurgent commander drew amnestied former rebels to his side. During five hectic days of marches and countermarches, Santa Anna searched the districts of Campos de Baja, Banderas,

Tamarindo, Paso de Fierro, Soyolapa, and Paso de Naranjo. Hounded from point to point, three guerrilla leaders, Manuel Salvador, Félix González, and Mariano Cenobio, with a priest and 230 armed men, presented themselves on different days to beg for amnesty. As Santa Anna informed Liñan, "All of them explained to me that they are exceedingly repentant for having belonged for so long to such a detestable and unjust cause."

In February 1819, Santa Anna continued the pursuit of Guadalupe Victoria into the Sierra de Masatiopa with seventy newly amnestied cavalry. They began by way of Soyolapa, Río Blanco, and Rincón Papaya, using machetes to open trails through the thick bush toward Masatiopa and La Laguna and into the region surrounding Aguas de Asufre. At Chilapa they encountered another royalist force and learned that Victoria was not in the region. The Indians of Masatiopa had eschewed rebellion to present themselves for pardons. Only one guerrilla chief, Pomoro, accompanied by fifteen to twenty poorly armed men, remained at large. Santa Anna tracked him for three days through very rugged country before exhaustion of the horses and lack of provisions forced him to discontinue the chase. Checking at the town of Córdoba for information, Santa Anna learned from an insurgent deserter that Guadalupe Victoria was almost alone, in poor health, and with little to eat other than roasted papayas. Although Santa Anna felt sick himself after the lengthy pursuit, he decided to track down the subordinate chiefs Cleto, Casas, and Bonilla who, like Victoria, had been reduced to wandering with few followers in the forests. Santa Anna's cavalry served loyally and without complaint; as he put it, "They all are anxious to prove their true repentance with their own hands and to distinguish themselves in the service of their sovereign."

Liñan, assigned by the viceroy to assume the interim governorship and intendancy of Veracruz in the first months of 1819 because of serious mismanagement and quarreling between senior officials, advanced the career of Santa Anna, whom he described as "this gallant officer." Aware of the need to settle over three hundred amnestied insurgents and others who were turning themselves in daily, Liñan assigned Santa Anna to reestablish the abandoned towns of Medellín and Xamapa and to organize a brand-new community at Loma de Santa María. Liñan underscored the suitability of Santa Anna for the commission, pointing out to Viceroy Apodaca that no other officer possessed his "energy, intelligence, and dexterity in the management of these people and knowledge of the country." What was even better, the Veracruzanos placed their confidence in him and surrendered to him so that they could seek amnesty. Santa Anna assumed responsibility for selecting the sites of the settlements, organizing the communities, and implementing a special military-political system of governance. Within a few months, he established four agricultural communities near Veracruz at Medellín, Xamapa, San Diego, and Tamarindo. They became models of constructive counterinsurgency planning and established Santa Anna as a regional leader with a significant following outside of the port city.

Liñan granted Santa Anna broad powers to establish the communities and then to watch over every aspect of their development. According to his instructions, Santa Anna was responsible for everything, from architectural planning to almost every area of governance. The villages were given a distinctly military orientation, with the settlers responsible to serve in a royalist militia company enlisting all healthy males between sixteen and fifty years of age. In addition to defending the communities against insurgent raids, these forces were to patrol and to maintain peace in nearby barrancas and mountainous districts. Arms and munitions were to be stored in a small fort, or blockhouse, constructed to house the garrison. Each family was instructed to produce surplus food to sustain the militia detachment. Moreover, Santa Anna and his designated subordinates received power to monitor the movements of community residents; their permission was needed by any person wishing to visit Veracruz or to go into the nearby mountains to harvest grain or corn. Finally, local garrison commanders and Santa Anna could override the decisions of appointed magistrates in any matter concerning military affairs.

In fact, Santa Anna created an even tighter system of controls than his instructions proposed. At Tamarindo, for example, he ordered the construction of a strong, octagonal-shaped fort to protect the new community and access to the road to Veracruz. In each of the four settlements, residents had to construct and maintain sheds that would house 100 soldiers so that passing units would not be billeted upon the population. Each community was laid out in a circle so that in case of a raid the people could be called in quickly from the fields. To avoid possible relapses into insurgency, residents could not leave the community without an official written license from the military commander. When they did receive permission, their document had to indicate the exact direction they expected to take, the time they needed to be absent, and the reasons for the trip.

Although control of amnestied insurgents and suppression of remaining guerrilla bands were primary factors, Santa Anna introduced other policies that improved community living standards and, at the same time, advanced his own reputation as an effective provincial leader. In all of the communities except Medellín, where a church building had remained standing, he ordered the construction of churches and residences for the village priests. One of his major objectives in 1820 was to hire suitable schoolteachers to educate the children and instruct them in the responsibilities of good citizenship. Concerned about living conditions, he obligated each family to build its house with an adequate kitchen and to erect corrals. He made certain that the community assigned sufficient land to each family for an adequate subsistence. For each resident, pasturelands were designated for livestock and fields set aside in which to grow corn, beans, bananas, and, in some cases, rice.

By 1820 the communities were able to market large quantities of garden vegetables and other crops in Veracruz. San Diego, the largest of the new settlements, enjoyed heightened prosperity because of its location on the *camino real* (highway), its fertile soil, its river setting, and its good climate. All of the communities achieved success in resettling former insurgents and in converting previously indomitable enemies into what the governor of Veracruz described as "civilized society." For two years, up to the end of 1820, there were no incidents of residents returning to insurgency, and the communities enjoyed unbroken peace. The governor attributed the success of the settlements to Santa Anna's "energy, hard work, and vigilance." By July 1820, Medellín had a population of 112 families, Xamapa 140, San Diego 287, and Tamarindo 54.

Although land resettlement programs administered by Santa Anna and other royalist officers had pacified many of the Veracruz insurgents by 1820, renewed upheavals began in 1821 with Agustín Iturbide's Plan de Iguala. Throughout Mexico the idea of independence attracted creole army officers. Santa Anna glimpsed new possibilities to enhance his power by replacing Spanish commanders and administrators. His Veracruz militia ensured him a solid core of support in expanding his base of operations. He had inherited a strong force of former insurgents and had learned how to appeal to his compatriots in order to advance his personal interests. By changing his allegiance in March 1821, to join Iturbide's associate José Joaquín de Herrera, Santa Anna achieved instant promotion to colonel and received command of Veracruz province. Backed by the soldiers of the *tierra caliente* (hot lowlands), he was ready for an even greater role as a caudillo on the national stage. Even in defeat, he could fall back upon the support of the people of the *tierra caliente*.

SOURCES

Almost all of the material used in this study came from primary sources in the Archivo General de la Nación in Mexico City. For published work on Santa Anna, see William Hardy Callcott, *Santa Anna: The Story of an Enigma Who Once Was Mexico* (Norman, 1936); Oakah L. Jones, *Santa Anna* (New York, 1968); and Ann F. Crawford, ed., *The Eagle: The Autobiography of Santa Anna* (Austin, 1967). For recent studies of the period, see Brian R. Hamnett, *Roots of Insurgency: Mexican Regions, 1750–1824* (Cambridge, 1986); and Stanley C. Green, *The Mexican Republic: The First Decade, 1823–1832* (Pittsburgh, 1987).

2

Agustín Marroquín: The Sociopath as Rebel

Eric Van Young

The Mexican struggle for independence was especially complex. As Prussian scientist and traveler Alexander von Humboldt pointed out in the early nineteenth century, Mexico enjoyed the richest and most diversified economy of all the Spanish possessions. Its population in 1814—at 6,122,000 the largest in Latin America—consisted of Spaniards, Creoles (American-born Spaniards), mestizos, mulattoes, blacks, and Indians. Mexico City was the second largest in the Spanish empire, after Madrid, and there were also other major cities in the colony, such as Guadalajara, Puebla, Guanajuato, and Valladolid (Morelia). The majority of the Mexican population, especially the Indians, lived in the countryside. Law and order in the countryside and small towns frequently was erratic at best. The Spanish simply did not have the resources to police adequately all of their extensive domain, although some would argue that the relative lightness of administration was a calculated imperial policy to defuse resistance. In fact, rebellions had been few and those usually directed at specific abuses, but ethnic tensions smoldered beneath the surface of this dynamic society.

Father Miguel Hidalgo's "Grito de Dolores" of September 16, 1810, ignited the Independence Wars and attracted "patriots" who responded for many reasons, personal as well as political. For example, Agustín Marroquín began his career as an outlaw in the 1790s, landed in jail several times, and finally was executed in 1811 as one of Hidalgo's patriotic followers. Marroquín forces us to question again what independence meant to the soldiers who fought for it (or against it). Ironically, he was a Creole and not part of the colored masses generally thought of as Hidalgo's followers. As he examines Marroquín's life, author Eric Van Young keeps in mind historian Eric Hobsbawm's theory of social banditry. Van Young concludes, however, that Marroquín committed his crimes for his own satisfaction and wealth and not because he was playing the role of a Robin Hood pleasing the poor with crimes against the rich.

This essay also allows us to examine Spanish administration and criminal justice in the last days of the empire. From what we find we might characterize colonial justice as either ineffective or surprisingly generous to common criminals. Retribution came more swiftly—and with fatal results—to Marroquín for his role as a patriot (or traitor, as the royalists would have it) than it did for his crimes as a robber and murderer.

Eric Van Young, associate professor of history at the University of California at San Diego, is one of the most accomplished social historians of late colonial Mexico. His *Hacienda and Market in Eighteenth-Century Mexico: The Rural Economy of the Guadalajara Region, 1675–1810* (Berkeley, 1981) will soon be followed by a work in progress, "Rural Discontent in Latin America, 1750–1850." Professor Van Young received his Ph.D. from the University of California at Berkeley.

A SHOOT-OUT IN GUADALAJARA

On Monday morning, November 11, 1805, the chief magistrate of Guadalajara, don Tomás Ignacio Villaseñor, one of the most important citizens of one of New Spain's most important provincial capitals—a major landowner and the scion of an illustrious family of ancient, conquistador lineage—sat down to write an account of a police action the previous night and to initiate formal criminal proceedings against the bandit Agustín Marroquín and several accomplices. Informed that a highly suspicious group of men were living in a house in the city's *barrio* (quarter) of the Colegio de San Diego, and that the men never ventured out of the house during the daytime but only at night, Villaseñor had resolved to investigate the matter, as was his duty. Around midnight of Sunday, November 10, he had gone to the house with a large detachment of armed soldiers and constables, whom he prudently placed around it. After repeated knockings on the door and injunctions to open in the name of the king, all of which failed to produce any response from the darkened house, Villaseñor ordered the soldiers to break down the door with their rifle butts. Forcing their way into the house, they were greeted with a hail of bullets, and in the ensuing shoot-out two of the soldiers were wounded. Marroquín and an associate, half dressed, were pursued into the patio of the house by several soldiers. Urged by one of these to give himself up to the king's justice, Marroquín replied, "I'll give myself up, you bastard!" and shot the man at point-blank range, although not fatally. Throwing down their pistols, Marroquín and his confederate were arrested along with five unarmed men encountered hiding in various parts of the house and stable, and three women and the landlord found cowering in one of the bedrooms of the house. A number of witnesses to the incident attested that Marroquín had said openly that if he had stayed at his original post in the living room when the soldiers invaded the house, he would have been able to kill six or seven of them. The bandit also inquired ominously of one young officer the name of the magistrate who had commanded the party "in case some day we meet again."

Agustín Marroquín was to remain imprisoned in Guadalajara almost exactly five years to the day of his capture. He was freed in November 1810 by Father Miguel Hidalgo's talented and loyal lieutenant José Antonio ("El Amo") Torres when Torres took the city for the rebel cause and almost immediately emptied the local jails. Hidalgo made Marroquín a captain in the rebel army within a matter of days, and he apparently held the priest's confidence until both were captured by royalist forces the following winter and executed in the early summer of 1811. Marroquín's name is that most commonly associated, besides Hidalgo's own, with the mass executions of European Spaniards that took place in Guadalajara during December and January 1810–11. How had Marroquín come to be in Guadalajara, and what were the outlines of his career prior to 1810? In attempting to answer these questions we can gain insight into the nature of late colonial Mexican society—a sense of its color and texture— as well as into the nature of the social space created by rebellion, and of at least one of the types of men that erupted into that space. While the social matrix of Marroquín's life is less clear than that of some other secondary leaders, and his short revolutionary career in some ways less representative of the era of rebellion as a whole, his personal story is nonetheless a kind of metaphor for an entire aspect of the period and worth the retelling in and of itself.

A LIFE OF CRIME

Marroquín's life is largely a blank until we encounter him at the age of about twenty, under prosecution for a number of serious offenses and already with a full-blown criminal career of some years behind him. An American Spaniard (Creole), he was born in about 1774 in the provincial city of Tulancingo, to the northeast of Mexico City, the center of an extended rural jurisdiction embracing a population of about thirty-five thousand.[1]

Although nothing is known of his parentage or early life, there are strong cumulative indications that he came from much the same type of middling rural background as many other provincial revolutionary chieftains, or perhaps even a cut above. For one thing, he was literate. For another, what we know of his family, his marriage, at least some of his personal associations, and possibly his wider social connections tends to indicate a middling status in provincial society. His uncle, don Francisco Marroquín, was a priest in the Tulancingo area who enjoyed good relations with local land-owning Creoles and sheltered his errant nephew on at least one occasion, when Agustín was recuperating from an illness. Marroquín's wife, doña Dolores Saldierna, was the daughter of a local estate administrator. One of Marroquín's best friends was a local schoolteacher from a small village in the Zempoala district, a Spaniard named Joseph Diosdado. At one point Agustín worked as a mule driver for a Mexican nobleman resident in Mexico City, a post it is unlikely he would have obtained without some personal connection, however minimal. Furthermore, the fact that Marroquín held the position of sergeant in the provincial militia of Tulancingo, and was by virtue of his position immune from civil prosecution because of the military *fuero,* also indicates a certain social cachet.[2]

As far as Marroquín's personal characteristics are concerned, one has the impression of a man at once devious and ingenuous, charming but inconstant and, on occasion, sadistic, capable of being ingratiating with authorities but prone to challenge authority figures, personally fearless and even reckless, generous and acquisitive, petulant, intelligent, and given over entirely and without conscience to a life of idleness when he could manage it and of undiscriminating crime against individuals and the state whenever his resources dwindled. In short, Agustín Marroquín probably can reasonably be described as a sociopathic personality.[3] He had at least two mistresses recorded in the documents relating to him, and he was strongly implicated in the alleged murder of one of their husbands. He was a notoriously good judge of horseflesh, enjoyed some fame as a bullfighter, and obviously liked to live well. Marroquín was openhanded with his confederates and others; he enjoyed the reputation in his bandit days of being "generous" and of having an easy, intimate manner. He was an object of not unsympathetic curiosity among people whom he had not victimized, and one witness in an 1805 robbery case involving Marroquín attested that he and a local woman had wanted very much to meet the famous highwayman in person.

We first pick up Marroquín's criminal trail in 1795, by which time he was already a robber of considerable notoriety in his hometown of Tulancingo. At the age of twenty he was known as an habitué of *pulquerías* (pulque shops),[4] games of chance, and cockfights. He was a well-known figure on the streets of Tulancingo and was obviously the central member of a little group of criminal associates. He made himself persona non grata among the decent citizens of Tulancingo not only by his swaggering wantonness but also by his preying upon businesses in the town through extortion and robbery, a pattern he was to maintain, as circumstances allowed, over the next decade. Given his obvious intelligence and the equally obvious counterproductiveness of thus fouling his own nest, his local criminal activity suggests a studied defiance and insouciance, a provocative "catch-me-if-you-can" attitude borne out in the impression conveyed by his own statements and later activities.

Marroquín apparently had served at least one term in jail by the age of twenty, probably for tobacco smuggling. In this same year of 1795 he was brought up on charges (the nature of which are vague) and, after briefly attempting to claim sanctuary in a church, was sent to jail in Mexico City and then in Tulancingo. After serving more than two years he escaped in December 1797, smashing through the half-open door of the town jail while several Indian laborers were cleaning out the night soil of the inmates. He was not reapprehended until February 1799. In the meantime, he went to the Gulf Coast, near Veracruz, where he was taken on as an employee by a prominent local hacendado on the recommendation of Marroquín's uncle, the priest. Here Marroquín contracted a serious fever and was forced, after only a short time, to return to the upland area of his hometown in order to recuperate in its more salubrious climate. He remained in his uncle's house in Tulancingo for several months. His health recovered, Marroquín went to the nearby pueblo of Santo Tomás, where he occasionally stayed with his schoolmaster friend Diosdado, a bachelor about forty years old. It was in this man's company that Marroquín was arrested by members of the Acordada (New Spain's rural constabulary) at the beginning of 1799.

Marroquín's movements, apart from his sojourn near the coast and his return to the Tulancingo area, are somewhat difficult to trace during the thirteen months between his escape and recapture. During this time he was accused of a number of crimes and of different criminal associations, and the incomplete record of his trials is typically vague on which charges were resolved in his favor and which against him. Then, too, he was married by now and probably had children, but his wife remains a shadow playing across the background of his career. She was to continue so for the rest of his official, documented life, her place usurped by Marroquín's mistresses and criminal accomplices.

What is clear from the records is that, at the very least, Marroquín and Diosdado had stolen about one dozen oxen from a hacienda in the area of Zempoala, a small town near Tulancingo, sometime shortly after the former's escape from jail in 1797. These oxen Marroquín had hidden for a time on the estate administered by his father-in-law (without the man's knowledge), selling some of the butchered meat locally and the rest of the animals to some Indians on the road to Texcoco and in the town of Texcoco itself. Marroquín was accused of a variety of crimes putatively committed over the course of the next year or so, including a number of robberies, a murder, several assaults, and cattle rustling. During the course of the investigation in 1799, several crimes for which Marroquín had been under indictment during his imprisonment from 1795 to late 1797 surfaced again, including the robbery of some silver at the mining town of Zimapan, a house robbery in Zempoala (on which occasion, when a little girl laughed at him, he swaggeringly told her that "he was a man capable of even bigger things"), the theft of some horses that he attempted to sell to the district magistrate of Zempoala, and unspecified crimes in and around Puebla.

Three features of Marroquín's style as a criminal emerge clearly during this 1795–1799 period. First, there was his strong tendency to associate with groups of criminal confederates rather than act alone. At one point his cohorts included several men of "ill fame," and later still, upon his arrest in Guadalajara in 1805, he headed a large group of people. While group banditry was by no means unusual, given the necessity of substantial armed force in such encounters, Marroquín's clear leadership role among his confederates indicates a certain gregariousness (perhaps even charisma?) and a first-among-equals status, which he took with him, as we shall see, even into the prison environment. Second, there was about Marroquín's doings a certain self-conscious panache, alluded to earlier and emphasized by his tendency to engage in criminal acts in his own hometown as well as by his attempt to sell stolen horses to one of the local magistrates. Although many small-time local criminals and village incorrigibles preyed on their neighbors, Marroquín's geographic range (across most of central Mexico) and his general predilection for assault and robbery on the highways and in rural areas tend to indicate that his crimes in and around Tulancingo were not committed out of a lack of alternatives or professional imagination but were an active choice. Third, and related, Marroquín insisted on violently resisting arrest on at least three occasions, thus putting himself at considerable risk of injury or death and aggravating the crimes for which he was being apprehended.

Marroquín had demonstrated his tendency to resist arrest first in 1795, when he was captured by armed Acordada constables. Upon his reapprehension in early 1799, he led the constables a chase on horseback, and when his horse fell under him he grabbed his own two carbines (one of which was found to be heavily charged), planted himself squarely in the road, and faced his pursuers defiantly, although no shots were actually exchanged. As we have seen, his capture in Guadalajara six years later involved a Bonnie-and-Clyde-style shoot-out that miraculously cost no lives. Furthermore, on all three occasions Marroquín insisted on using threats and provocative language against his captors after he was in custody. In 1795 he threatened that his confederates would free him on the road or break him out of jail; in 1799 he called his captors "cabras" (shegoats); and in 1805 he made fairly explicit threats of vengeance against the arresting magistrate, Villaseñor.

These latter two characteristics particularly—the criminal panache and the defiant provocativeness—suggest that Marroquín's style was, in part at least, a public statement, a conscious stance of some kind. While it is true that Marroquín's career gives absolutely no sign of what we have come to think of, following the work of the English historian Eric Hobsbawm, as social banditry—that is, of Robin Hood-style crime: of any sense of a social inequity to which Marroquín saw his actions as a corrective, or of any shred of a notion of redistributive justice— his criminal activities as theater probably had a wide audience. No less a personage than the viceroy himself once referred to Marroquín as "el famoso reo" (the famous criminal). It seems likely, therefore, that Marroquín's activities were widely known, although what those actions may have meant to people other than his victims (who apparently never included the very poor, it should be noted) is a matter of speculation. Nonetheless, it is difficult to believe that the highly visible clashes of Agustín Marroquín and other such men with the police, the state, and the comfortable citizens of provincial society had no impact on popular awareness or lacked any resonation with popular discontent. What had a highly personal tone and significance to the criminal, then, may have had quite another kind of meaning for a society under stress as a whole.

Marroquín's own declaration, made in Mexico City shortly after his arrest in early February 1799, betrays a certain ingenuous quality beneath an understandable effort to exculpate himself from the various crimes of which he stood accused. He was, he stated, a native of Tulancingo, twenty-six years of age, and a rural laborer; he made no mention of his wife or of his position in the Tulancingo militia. He acknowledged that he was under suspicion for a robbery and murder but denied complicity in the crimes (he was shortly vindicated), saying he was at the home of his ecclesiastical uncle recuperating from fever and praying with his wife when the murder was committed. He admitted the jailbreak in 1797 and the theft of the oxen in company with Diosdado but denied guilt in any of the other crimes ascribed to him or involvement with his alleged band of accomplices. The jail escape he justified by claiming he had grown desperate over the delays in his case (not implausible given the slowness with which the machine of royal justice ground), and his bearing of arms as a necessity for one making his living in the countryside. In general he portrayed himself with some skill as a simple rustic, guilty at worst of poverty and a few mistakes in judgment.

In the meantime, during the years of his imprisonment and illicit freedom, something of a legal controversy had erupted among the viceregal authorities in Mexico City, officials of the Acordada and the militia, and local authorities over which jurisdiction had the right to try Marroquín, whose membership in the militia regiment of Tulancingo presumably entitled him to certain legal immunities and protections. Because of the political delicacy of the question, Viceroy Branciforte summoned an extraordinary commission sometime in 1797, which advised that despite Marroquín's military status, he should be tried by the civil authorities. The case was thus kicked back to the latter at just about the time Marroquín was escaping from the Tulancingo jail, his fatigue at the protractedness of his case undoubtedly relating to just this question.

After his reapprehension at the beginning of 1799, Marroquín was jailed in Mexico City, where he remained until early 1802, presumably on charges of escaping jail and of rustling and, possibly, on the basis of one or another of the outstanding indictments against him. When the case was reviewed sometime in 1801, the crown attorneys of Mexico City's chancellery court pointed out that Marroquín had served about five years during his two imprisonments, had been completely absolved of the murder charge, the most serious accusation, and had "established in the service of the jail distinguished merit." In a sanguine tone the prosecutors asserted that Marroquín, "finding himself chastened in this way, it is prudently hoped will mend his ways because of what he himself, his wife, and his children have suffered over more than six years, and with his separation from those companions who corrupted him." In early January 1802 he was freed from jail by order of Viceroy Marquina.

The sanguine, pious hopes of the crown prosecutors and judges were not to be fulfilled. Although Marroquín's movements during early 1802 are not known, by the summer he was living in the provincial town of Apam, to the northeast of Mexico City, about midway between the capital and Tulancingo, working in some capacity on a local hacienda. During 1802 and the first months of 1803, Marroquín managed to establish a kind of reign of terror in Apam, engage in theft and extortion (or so it was alleged), and carry on an affair with the wife of a local innkeeper.

Specifically, the royal magistrate of the district, reporting to the viceroy, asserted that Marroquín was well known to the principal citizens of the town for his "violent resolution and daring" in crime. The official continued: "This man has made himself so feared, and has the town so terrorized, that the more comfortable citizens are forced to render as tribute whatever he asks of them as loans, since were they not to do so they would be the victims of his violence." In other words, he was shaking people down. He habitually rode through the town streets heavily armed and openly defiant of local officials and the Acordada, and he said of the latter that it would require an army of constables to capture him. More than one merchant of the town claimed that Marroquín extorted money from him in his store at night. In addition to these incidents of strong-arm extortion,

Marroquín was accused by the local tithe collector of having stolen a number of horses and mules from him. Finally, Marroquín had become amorously involved with María Nava, the wife of an Apam innkeeper. Marroquín eventually took her with him on the crime spree that ended in Guadalajara, where she was arrested with him. Nava, witnesses testified, was much given to putting noxious herbs in people's food and drink (an inauspicious habit, one would think, for her husband's establishment). Induced by her involvement with the famous highwayman, she did the same thing with her husband's chocolate, it was generally believed, thus driving him insane, into brief residence in the asylum of San Hipólito in Mexico City, and to a premature death.

Aware of the impending move to arrest him (his apprehension having been the subject of a "very secret" correspondence between the Acordada administrator and the viceroy in Mexico City), Marroquín, in one of his disarmingly ingenuous actions with an apparently disingenuous motive, brought the matter into the public domain, as it were, by writing directly to Viceroy Iturrigaray in an attempt to exculpate himself. "This is not the first time I have been slandered in this way," he wrote, and then detailed his tranquil life in Apam and his innocence. Realizing that protestations of injured innocence would probably not suffice, Marroquín voluntarily presented himself before the viceregal authorities and was jailed on May 7, 1803. From prison he again wrote directly to the new viceroy, protesting his innocence and demanding that his alleged crimes be proved against him:

> There will perhaps be some accusation against me, because in this world no-one is without enemies; but if I am a perverse and delinquent man, let it be specified what crimes I have been accused of in which I am culpable, and what people I have harmed, because it is not enough to say vaguely that a man is bad: the facts and occasions of that badness must be specified and proved. What, then, are the facts that make me feared, bold, and delinquent? I have provoked no-one, nor injured or mistreated anyone; I have not committed kidnapping or robbery; so that, if I am bad, there should have been proof of my excesses.

The crown prosecutor once more found compelling reasons to urge Marroquín's release and substantial exoneration. He believed that the crimes that could be proved against Marroquín were not of any gravity; that María Nava was (only temporarily, as it turned out) happily back with her husband; and that Marroquín's voluntary surrender argued strongly in his favor. Furthermore, his long-suffering wife and her father testified to his innocence, and Marroquín was able to obtain a bondsman in Mexico City. Then, too, the admittedly exaggerated, nearly hysterical notoriety attaching by this time to Marroquín's doings (apparently every highway robbery in the Valley of Mexico was ascribed to him) may have had, paradoxically, a deflationary effect on his criminal stature in the eyes of the central authorities. In any case, in June 1803, Agustín Marroquín was released on bond by the viceroy but admonished to keep away from Apam and carry no dangerous weapons.

By the end of the year Marroquín, probably through some personal connection, had secured a position as a mule driver for the marquis of Jaral de Berrio, one of the wealthiest of Mexico's titled aristocrats. The employment provided an occasion for yet another scrape with the law. Returning from the marquis's estates in the interior of the country in February 1804, Marroquín was driving a mule train on the road ahead of his master's coach and other entourage. Upon reaching the pass of Barrientos on the way into Mexico City, Marroquín had an encounter with a group of mule drivers and their animals heading in the opposite direction. Heated words were exchanged, tempers flared, and a fight ensued in the road (the marquis, from his coach, was a witness). The strangers pelted Marroquín with rocks, and he drew a long knife and attacked the group, severely wounding one of their number, Juan José Mendoza. The wounded man brought a complaint before the royal authorities, who jailed his assailant. Marroquín was again out of jail shortly, his bond posted by a merchant of Mexico City and influence exerted in his behalf by his powerful employer. But the following spring (April 1805) Mendoza died, apparently due to complications (an infection, one imagines), from the wound inflicted by Marroquín. This mischance resulted in Marroquín's being jailed once again by the Mexico City authorities. A small monetary settlement with the victim's family (possibly underwritten by the marquis) secured Marroquín's release from jail within a short time.

Marroquín was to remain free only until his capture at Guadalajara the following winter. What impelled him to embark on the crime spree that eventually took him west to the capital of New Galicia and into his (in every sense) fatal encounter with insurrection—whether lack of means, boredom, disillusion with his chances in Mexico City, or some change in personal circumstances—can only be guessed at, but by the summer of 1805 he apparently had left the viceregal capital (although not, for the moment, others of his old haunts) behind forever, and, *sans famille,* had begun to make his way across central Mexico.

Most of what can be pieced together about Marroquín's activities between June and November 1805 is based on testimony and accusations that surfaced after his capture at Guadalajara, so that although some of it is very credible and vivid, much of the material in the record is at worst apocryphal or garbled, and at best lacks immediacy and specificity. His first move had been north and west, into the Bajío region, where he was the major suspect in a highway robbery that netted some ten thousand pesos, committed near the Villa of San Felipe, in the district of San Miguel el Grande (later San Miguel Allende), on June 29, 1805. By this time he was the leader of a group of brigands estimated at twenty men. The royal treasurer of Sombrerete also accused Marroquín and his band of having stolen about seven thousand pesos of royal funds on their way to the mining town in late June 1805 and of having robbed a local merchant of a lesser amount. Although Marroquín denied any knowledge of or complicity in either crime, the evidence for his having masterminded the San Felipe robbery brought a conviction. A crime to which he did confess, although he minimized his role in it, was the theft of some three thousand pesos from a house in the village of Acaxochitlan, near Tulancingo (he had doubled back on his own trail), in September 1805. The victim of the robbery, don Nicolás Pastrana, clearly identified Marroquín, stating that the highwayman "attempted only to disguise his voice by trying to talk like a [European] Spaniard." Other witnesses also placed Marroquín at the scene of this robbery. During the incident two men were nearly killed, and a gunfight ensued in the town cemetery between several armed locals and the fleeing robbers, one of whom was later captured and implicated Marroquín as the leader of the bandits. At this same time other witnesses came forward with the accusation that Marroquín had been involved in large-scale tobacco smuggling, the crime for which he had first been sent to jail a decade previously.

Apparently at this point Marroquín, in the company of at least some of his habitual accomplices, returned to the Bajío area and made stops in Salamanca, León, and other towns on his way to

San Juan de los Lagos. With him in the party were María Nava and another young creole woman, María Vicenta Partida, who testified later that Marroquín had bought her a house in Apam and that she had been his mistress for two years or more. Arriving at San Juan de los Lagos in early October 1805, the party of seven to ten people stayed at first in an inn and then rented a house for a month. María Nava posed as Marroquín's wife and prayed daily (perhaps for the elimination of her amorous rival) to the local manifestation of the Virgin, while Agustín posed as don Francisco Villaseñor, a buyer of horses and mules from Cuernavaca. In the rented house in Lagos the highwayman set up an illegal card game, which he kept going at all hours of the day and night. His continual winning of large amounts in cash and jewels (the sum of ten thousand pesos was later mentioned, but it is not clear whether this was recovered when he was arrested) became the talk of the town. Although one witness in Lagos asserted that no "distinguished" citizens of the town gambled with the new arrival, apparently a priest and several local estate owners did play. Wanting to avoid being recognized by anyone at the huge annual livestock and trading fair that was to begin in Lagos on November 1, Marroquín and his party moved on via Jalostotlan and Tepatitlan to Guadalajara, where, as we have seen, they were shortly captured and jailed.

DE PROFUNDIS[5]

The lengthy parenthesis in Agustín Marroquín's criminal career constituted by his five-year imprisonment in Guadalajara was filled with complex legal argument and controversy, further accusations, and development by the protagonist of an unusual but, one imagines, for him characteristic modus vivendi to ease the rigors of his captivity. Immediately upon the news of his capture becoming generally known, a flood of accusations came to the attention of the Guadalajara authorities, ascribing to Marroquín numerous unsolved crimes in several different towns. Prosecution of Marroquín's case and of that of his associates was entrusted to don José Pérez de Acal, a veteran sergeant major of the provincial militia of Guadalajara, and *alcalde ordinario* (magistrate) of the city in 1805. Pérez de Acal, much given to public questioning of his own competence in legal affairs and to lamenting the complexity of the charges at the same time as he expressed moral and civic outrage at Marroquín's criminality, stated his position strongly, if rather extravagantly, from the beginning:

> All these excesses, judged juridically, give unequivocal proof of the crimes committed by Marroquín and his accomplices, and of the notoriously disorderly life of this man, always with the object of oppressing humanity, of scandalizing and terrorizing all these towns to the point of plunging them into mourning ... and gaining by these impious means not only the money to support himself, but also making his name famous, as he has accomplished by these reprehensible means, so noxious to public society.

The thicket of jurisdictional and legal complications, the necessity of having local officials and witnesses from distant towns make depositions, and the strictly observed rights of the accused in reviewing and responding to those depositions in various ways led to interminable delays in the case and generated an enormous pile of documentation that had to be reviewed by prosecutors and judges at every stage of deliberation. Notwithstanding the general scrupulosity with which Pérez de Acal and other royal officials handled the case, Marroquín's previous notoriety established in the minds of such functionaries a strong prima facie case for his guilt and that of his associates. Added to this was the perceived need to make of the famous highwayman an example in order to discourage the wave of brigandage prevalent in central New Spain in general, and in the Guadalajara region in particular, at the end of the eighteenth and the beginning of the nineteenth centuries, characterized by one high judicial official in Mexico City as a "flood of evildoers."

In finally summarizing his case, in a statement dated the last day of 1808, Pérez de Acal referred to Marroquín as "famous and singular in the present epoch for his boldness and temerity, and for the wantonness with which he has thrown himself into the commission of many very execrable evils." Reviewing Marroquín's criminal career, Pérez de Acal pointed to the brigand's own admission that by the age of twenty-two he had already committed so many crimes as to win for himself "renown for his wickedness," and that even when he was behaving well he gained his livelihood from gambling and smuggling. Having committed any number of crimes all punishable by death, Marroquín should be so punished, concluded the prosecutor: he should be hanged, and then his severed head displayed publicly in Acaxochitlan for two weeks and his right hand in Guadalajara. For the accomplices, Pérez de Acal recommended long sentences at hard labor and public floggings. A trained lawyer in Guadalajara, asked independently to review the prosecutor's findings and proposed sentence, suggested reducing Marroquín's punishment to public flogging and ten years at hard labor in a *presidio* (military prison). The intendant of Guadalajara agreed in April 1809, and the Mexico City military tribunal confirmed the sentence in September. The sentence for the bandit leader finally came down to ten years' hard labor at a military fortress in Havana, and two hundred lashes, but this punishment only applied to the charge of resisting the king's troops, since this was the only crime the military jurisdiction was competent to try. The crimes of a non-military nature—comprising the bulk of the outstanding charges—were left to the Audiencia of Guadalajara for sentencing, but owing to the necessity of gathering more testimony in these cases, the actions were still pending before the court in September 1810 when Marroquín was freed from prison by the rebels. The two hundred lashes were administered publicly to Marroquín, as to his chief accomplice, Felipe Rodríguez, on Wednesday, October 4, 1809. One has no difficulty at all in imagining that a *gachupín* (European Spaniard) later died for each lash.

In the meantime, while his judicial fate was being decided, Marroquín was not idle in prison but managed to build a small empire and alleviate for himself the discomforts of prison life. In October 1809, after Marroquín's sentence had been confirmed and the lashes administered, Intendant Roque Abarca, who had taken an interest in Marroquín's case because of the involvement of the viceregal authorities and the notoriety of the defendant, noted that the famous highwayman had done quite well for himself within a few days of his capture in late 1805. "The prisoner Agustín Marroquín entered jail with ordinary clothing and with no money; and within a few days it was noticed that he had purchased new clothing, that he was managing business interests [*que manejaba intereses*], that he was loaning money, and trading." Abarca further noted that during the past few years several employees of the prison had petitioned the intendant to release Marroquín, prompting him to comment that the prisoner had a "party" of supporters in jail. More recently, Abarca said, Marroquín, the conditions of whose confinement required him to be chained in a cell, was encountered by the intendant "free in the prison yard, dressed magnificently, and what drew my attention even more was that his baggage gave signs that he was ready to mount a horse." Apparently some prison employee, presumably having been bribed by the bandit, had forged an order with the signature of the royal prosecutor for the release of Marroquín. Abarca's chance arrival at the jail ruined the plot, but he was never able to determine who the accomplice had been.

An even more circumstantial description of jail life at the time gives a hint of Marroquín's position in the social hierarchy of the Guadalajara prison. In April 1810 a prison guard accused an inmate, Gabriel Mesa, before a city magistrate of having had homosexual relations with several other prisoners, an accusation of *pecado nefando* (unnatural crimes), which brought an immediate investigation by the authorities. Mesa, a young Indian (seventeen years old) from a nearby village, was an army deserter. In response to the serious charges against him, he said he had been the passive victim of yet another prisoner, Máximo Rivera, an older Spaniard, who was the only man with whom he had committed any *torpezas* (indecencies). Mesa testified that he had awakened one November night to find himself with an erection and Rivera on top of him "moving up and down upon the witness, thus penetrated." Mesa managed to withdraw himself before ejaculation (an important point in the judges' minds), struck Rivera several times, and told the older man to go back to his own bed in the communal dormitory. During the following weeks Rivera importuned Mesa nearly every night to repeat this performance, once or twice coming to Mesa while he slept and fondling him "with the object of putting [him] in a state so that penetration would be possible." Mesa consistently refused these overtures and acts, at one point reminding Rivera that he and several fellow inmates were in the midst of a course of spiritual exercises being conducted by a priest.

Rivera, in jail for stealing livestock, denied the charges, as did two other men accused by the prison guard of having relations with Mesa. Several other prisoners accused each other of varying degrees of homosexual involvement, but none of the accused admitted any culpability except Mesa, and he only with Rivera. In June of the following year (1811) medical examinations of the accused were ordered by the civil authorities, but several physicians agreed in detailed opinions that these would be inconclusive. Marroquín was dragged into the case by name when

Rivera requested that the bandit be questioned regarding Rivera's behavior in prison. This Marroquín asserted was blameless, but he accused another man, Guadalupe Silva, earlier involved in the accusations and cross-accusations of the prisoners, of involvement with Mesa.

Shortly after this testimony, Marroquín was released from prison with the former inmates, and the investigation was taken up again by the authorities only after Marroquín's death and the reapprehension of Mesa, Silva, and others in 1811. Silva's defense attorney in an 1811 deposition impugned Marroquín's testimony by suggesting that Rivera was his creature, that both "abhorred Silva and abused him because he would not submit to them," and that Marroquín had suborned the testimony of several witnesses against Silva. This charge drew forward a flood of testimony against the deceased Marroquín, painting him as the cruel, unprincipled, would-be kingpin of the prison. One witness affirmed that Marroquín indeed had tried to suborn him to testify against Silva, and another that Marroquín persecuted Silva because the latter "did not agree with [Marroquín's] twisted ideas and perverse faction; [Marroquín] hated other prisoners as well because they did not countenance his thefts and the discord he created, so that there was no other convict in the jail more troublesome [than Marroquín]." Yet another inmate affirmed that Marroquín's bad conduct in the jail was "notorious," and still another that Marroquín hated Silva because of his failure to "humble himself" before the bandit chieftain.

Making sense of the accusations and counteraccusations is a bit difficult, but it appears that Marroquín, in attempting to organize the inmates to suit his own ends, persecuted Silva, Mesa's friend, and that Mesa accused Rivera, Marroquín's cohort, out of revenge. This was substantially the finding of the advising attorney in the case, who also found sufficient circumstantial evidence that Silva and Mesa had been sexually involved with each other, however, to recommend moderate punishment for them (two years at hard labor on public works projects for Silva, and remittance to the military authorities for Mesa).

THE REBEL

The next-to-last item in Marroquín's voluminous dossier, which opens the most well-known chapter in his career, is a laconic note from Father Hidalgo's famous Lieutenant José Antonio

Torres to the effect that the notary of the Audiencia should give back to Marroquín any property that had been impounded at his capture five years earlier. Marroquín, who had been freed when Torres took the city and emptied the jails in mid-November, duly signed the receipt on November 25, 1810, and received back his property.

The following day Hidalgo arrived in the city at the head of an army of some seven thousand men. What Marroquín had been doing during the preceding few days is not clear, but presumably he was sufficiently visible so as to come to the notice of the insurgent chief, who probably knew something of him from years before. At some point during the next two weeks, most likely toward the end of November, Hidalgo drew Agustín Marroquín into his inner circle of trusted lieutenants and commissioned him a captain in the insurgent forces. A Guadalajara ecclesiastical official, Dr. Velasco, later described the scene with a pen dipped in acid, referring to Marroquín as Father Hidalgo's "repugnant bodyguard"

> whom Hidalgo made a Captain in an officers' staff meeting, and by the most theatrical act declared him free of any ill fame [*libre de toda nota*], receiving from him an oath of loyalty, and blessing him placed the epaulets upon shoulders which still bore the two hundred lashes placed there by Justice in our streets fourteen months before such a quixotic scene.[6]

The freeing of Marroquín and his rapid absorption into the inner circle of Hidalgo's cohorts almost certainly helped to alienate prominent creole commanders in the insurgent forces, such as Ignacio Allende and Mariano Abasolo, who abhorred the marginal social elements attracted to the movement and deeply mistrusted its popular base, and with whom in any case the priest was already on very bad terms.

Whatever Marroquín's relationship to Miguel Hidalgo or the insurgent movement as a whole, and whatever his other activities at Guadalajara and after, it is certain that he was centrally involved in the infamous mass executions of several hundred European Spaniards that took place in the city during the latter two weeks of December 1810. The evidence for this is his own confession and the accounts of witnesses and subsequent writers on the period. Precisely why Hidalgo ordered the executions has never been made clear. Hidalgo himself claimed that the executions were ordered to placate his Indian followers. Later historians claimed that Hidalgo did it out of simple viciousness, or alternatively that he essentially overreacted to continual rumors and some evidence of plots against his life by Creoles and *gachupines.* On the whole, Hidalgo's own argument of pressure from the popular sectors of his supporters is the most credible explanation.

The executions began on the night of December 12 and continued for the rest of the month. Although the chronology of the executions and of Marroquín's role in them is difficult to reconstruct with any precision, it seems likely that he was involved in them at the start and intermittently thereafter. Marroquín himself, in brief testimony after his capture with Hidalgo and others in the spring of 1811, claimed that he had carried out the execution of one contingent of forty-eight Europeans, on a date unspecified, as he was on his way out of the city to scout the approaching enemy forces. Apparently this was done in conjunction with another insurgent commander named Alatorre, who had received a warrant from Hidalgo's own hand with the names of European prisoners being held in the Colegio de San Juan. Alatorre delegated the task to Marroquín who, with his men, conducted the prisoners to the *cerro* (hill) de San Martín, a few miles distant from the city, beheaded the prisoners, and left the bodies in a pit the insurgents had dug. The same Dr. Velasco who penned the disdainful description of Hidalgo's commissioning of Marroquín added to the account a lurid tableau of the executions in which the prisoners were naked and were "yielded up to the barbarous fury of the Indians, who killed them with lances, throwing their bodies into the depths of the canyon." Informed testimony implicated Marroquín in still more instances of mass executions, although he himself denied this, and several other incidents, some possibly apocryphal and some based on solid documentation, give a picture of Marroquín's relationship to these events and the apparent coolness with which he gave himself over to the political executions of European Spaniards in Guadalajara in these months.

On January 17, 1811, the enormous but untrained and unwieldy insurgent army led by Miguel Hidalgo met a quick and decisive defeat at the hands of a much smaller but militarily more effective royalist force led by Félix María Calleja, royalist commander in chief and future Mexican viceroy, at the bridge of Calderón, about thirty miles east of Guadalajara. Hidalgo and his lieutenants fled north from Guadalajara, hoping to regroup and eventually gain support from the United States, but these hopes were not to be realized. Betrayed by a one-time insurgent officer in the north of New Spain, Hidalgo and a large party were captured at Acatita de Bajan, between Saltillo and Monclova, on March 21, 1811. It is quite clear from accounts of the capture that Hidalgo's twenty-man mounted escort, which surrendered without resistance, was commanded by Agustín Marroquín, another indication of the confidence the insurgent leader had placed in the highwayman. In the meantime Marroquín, who apparently had been with Hidalgo since the flight from Guadalajara, had not been idle. He admitted under interrogation in Chihuahua that while the party was on the road between Matehuala and Saltillo they had encountered a carriage with two European Spaniards and their families inside, and that Marroquín himself had ordered the men executed on the spot. After the capture at Bajan, Marroquín was jailed in an improvised prison cell in Chihuahua's former Jesuit college. On May 10 he was led with two lesser officers to the city's Franciscan convent and executed by firing squad. A terse entry appended to Marroquín's criminal dossier in Guadalajara the following September acknowledged that it was well known that the highwayman had been brought to justice in Chihuahua the preceding spring, and that one of his former associates, Felipe Rodríguez, had been arrested as an insurgent and was at that time in jail in the city.

The career of Agustín Marroquín is a clear and particularly well-documented example of the way in which social deviance and marginality can overlap or conflate with rebellion. Moreover, whether crime or delinquency was antecedent to rebellion, or rebellion to crime or delinquency, is not always so clear in the Mexican context. Now, that acts of criminality or delinquency should occur within the context of revolutionary violence, or that criminals and delinquents should be injected into the insurgent moment, would by no means be unusual in the history of rebellion in general, or of collective violent protest in the early modern period in particular. And arriving at a quantitative assessment as to whether one set of such collective phenomena—say, the French Revolution, the classical European grain riot, or the uprisings of the common people in early modern Italian cities—was more characterized by nonprogrammatic criminal behavior than another would just as obviously be impossible. Nonetheless, one is left with the impression in the Mexican case that there was an even greater than usual characteristic fluidity between the two types of social phenomena.

This leads us to ask to what degree Marroquín and other insurgents were organically a part of the collectivities in whose names they took up arms against the constituted authorities. In the case of some, their embeddedness in the matrix of family, clan, town, and region, despite the signs of their delinquency and the evidence that they and their families availed themselves of the rebellion to enrich and advance themselves socially, lends some credibility to the view that their actions as insurgent chieftains resonated with the thinking of the rebels they led. In the case of Marroquín, however, it is exceedingly difficult to imagine, and there is no evidence to indicate, that he had even the faintest ideological formulation in his head when he participated in the mass executions in Guadalajara or the other actions ascribed to him, any more than did the plagues sent by God to scourge the Egyptians in the biblical account of Exodus. Certainly his career shows no hint of social banditry, or of connectedness to any community, except possibly a criminal one, or to any interest other than his own; indeed, this is one of the essential characteristics of the sociopathic personality. That there were a great many other individuals similar to Marroquín in their relationship to the collective behavioral and ideological phenomena of the independence rebellions, even if their activities were not so egregiously magnified, is evident from the documents of the time.

NOTES

1. Unless otherwise indicated, "Spaniard" as used here connotes a person of Spanish ancestry born in the New World.

2. The *fuero,* an ancient corporate charter extended to the military and the church, entitled its members, among other privileges, to trial by their own rather than by civil courts.

3. *Sociopathy* is generally defined in psychiatry as an antisocial personality disorder characterized by (1) inability to sustain consistent work behavior; (2) failure to accept social norms with respect to lawful behavior; (3) inability to form an enduring attachment with a single significant other; (4) aggressiveness; (5) impulsivity, or failure to plan ahead; (6) disregard for the truth; and (7) recklessness.

4. Pulque is a traditional Mexican intoxicant made from the fermented juice of a certain species of cactus.

5. *De profundis,* "from the depths," is taken from the prison memoirs of the same title (1897) by Oscar Wilde.

6. Quoted in José Ramírez Flores, *El gobierno insurgente en Guadalajara, 1810–1811* (Guadalajara, 1969), pp. 95–96.

SOURCES

The documentation on Agustín Marroquín was drawn overwhelmingly from unpublished archival sources in Biblioteca Pública del Estado, Guadalajara, Mexico—sec. "Criminal," bundles 1, 6, 9, 18, 21, 25; and in Archivo General de la Nación, Mexico City, Mexico—sec. "Operaciones de Guerra," vols. 4A, 145; and "Historia," vol. 584. A vast literature in Spanish, English, and other languages exists on the Mexican independence struggles, although only occasional references to Marroquín occur in it. The most important recent historical treatments in English are Hugh M. Hamill, Jr., *The Hidalgo Revolt: Prelude to Mexican Independence* (reprint, Westport, CT, 1981); John Tutino, *From Insurrection to Revolution in Mexico: Social Bases of Agrarian Violence, 1750–1940* (Princeton, 1986); Brian R. Hamnett, *Roots of Insurgency: Mexican Regions, 1750–1824* (Cambridge, 1986); and Timothy E. Anna, *The Fall of the Royal Government in Mexico City* (Lincoln, 1978). On Mexican banditry in the nineteenth century, see Paul J. Vanderwood, *Disorder and Progress: Bandits, Police, and Mexican Development* (Lincoln, 1981); and the articles in *Bibliotheca Americana* 1 (November 1982), dedicated to the theme "Social Banditry in Nineteenth-Century Latin America," Paul J. Vanderwood, ed., particularly Christon I. Archer, "Banditry and Revolution in New Spain, 1790–1821," pp. 58–59; and William B. Taylor, "Sacarse de pobre: El bandolerismo en la Nueva Galicia, 1794–1821," *Revista Jalisco* 2 (1981): 34–45. The major works of Eric Hobsbawm are *Primitive Rebels: Studies in Archaic Forms of Social Movement in the 19th and 20th Centuries* (New York, 1965); and *Bandits* (New York, 1969). On the criminal justice system in late colonial Mexico, see Colin M. MacLachlan, *Criminal Justice in Eighteenth-Century Mexico: A Study of the Tribunal of the Acordada* (Berkeley and Los Angeles, 1974). The period of insurgent control of Guadalajara is treated in detail in José Ramírez Flores, *El gobierno insurgente en Guadalajara, 1810–1811* (Guadalajara, 1969).

3

Atanasio Tzul, Lucas Aguilar, and the Indian Kingdom of Totonicapán

David J. McCreery

Chiapas was part of the captaincy general of Guatemala, which included all of Central America down to Panama and was a dependency of the viceroyalty of New Spain, or Mexico. Central Americans by and large did not join in the early stages of the Mexican independence struggles led by Fathers Miguel Hidalgo and José María Morelos (1810–1815). When Agustín Iturbide signed an independence treaty with the Spanish viceroy in 1821, Central Americans chose to remain part of an independent Mexico. As emperor (1821–1823), Iturbide unwisely proved insensitive to their local concerns, and Central Americans seized the opportunity of the 1823 revolt against Iturbide to declare their independence from Mexico. The province of Chiapas, however, remained with Mexico rather than join the other Central American republics.

Atanasio Tzul's history allows us to examine the role that the indigenous population played during the independence epoch. A member of the Indian aristocracy, Tzul had been confirmed by the Spanish as a leader of his town. As such, he shared with Spanish officials responsibility for collecting taxes and tribute. Increasing resistance by the Indians to paying tribute led Tzul and Lucas Aguilar, an Indian commoner, to rebel against the Spanish in 1820. Over the years, their rebellion gained fame as part of the independence struggles and as an example of an indigenous people who established their own king and nation.

In his essay, David McCreery points out that the Indians who named Tzul as their king did not necessarily intend to reject their other, more distant, king in Spain. Their rebellion resembled a colonial uprising against a specific grievance more than it did a revolt for independence. The pardon of Tzul and Aguilar in 1821 may have reflected Spanish uncertainty, as McCreery argues, but it also was consistent with the imperial policy of dispensing justice mildly to Indians in order to avoid creating martyrs. The lack of unity among Tzul's Indian villages reveals that, like the Creoles, Indians had different reasons for becoming royalists or patriots. Perhaps this disunity is another clue to Spain's ability to dominate millions of Indians with a minimum of force. Their divisions meant that whether they fought to uphold the Spanish empire or to forge a creole republic, indigenous peoples would continue to be despised and granted only limited citizenship privileges.

David McCreery is associate professor of history at Georgia State University and director of the Latin American Studies Consortium in the University System of Georgia. He has published numerous articles on indigenous communities and the social and economic history of nineteenth-century Guatemala. McCreery is the author of *Development and the State in Reforma Guatemala* (1983). He is at work on a study of rural Guatemala from 1760 to 1940.

> It was on the Friday after the arrival of the papers of the Constitution that they celebrated the coronation of Atanasio Tzul. There were public displays of joy, . . . nine days of bull fights, the music of drums and salvos of rockets. Tzul presented himself in public dressed as a Spanish soldier, with a three-pointed hat such as the Spanish use, a sword, a medal at his throat, and a staff [*vara*] of office taken from the *gobernador*. The town hall was adorned with hangings, and he and Lucas Aguilar watched the festivities from a throne set under a canopy taken from the church.

With the possible exception of the Tzotzil-Tzeltal uprisings that swept highland Chiapas in the years 1708–1713, the *tumulto* (uprising or riot) at Totonicapán in 1820 is the best known of the colonial Central American Indian revolts. In the past, interest has focused on Atanasio Tzul, "the Indian King," and on possible connections between the rebellion and the events that led the next year to independence from Spain. In fact, Tzul, while not a minor actor, was never the "motor" of this revolt, and the *tumulto* itself stemmed less from aspirations to political independence than from demands for relief from the abuses of the Crown and of Indian officials. If it stands out from among similar protests for its duration and for the crowning of a "king," it is otherwise not untypical of a number of late colonial uprisings among the area's indigenous populations. The turbulent conditions of the times and the nature of the rebels, despised and illiterate Indian peasants, limit the detail available about individuals. But an examination of what the historian can recover concerning the people, the communities, and the conflicts that resulted in the Indian kingdom of Totonicapán reveals much about the social and political tensions surfacing in the last years of Spain's American empire.

By spring 1820 almost all of Spanish America was in turmoil. Independence movements raged in Mexico and in South America, and this violence lapped the borders of a still peaceful but hardly tranquil Central America. To a large extent, events in Spain had set these American uprisings in motion. Following its defeats in the Seven Years' War (1756–1763), the Spanish Crown initiated sweeping reforms in the New World meant to tighten control of its empire and raise revenue to finance improved defenses. State agents had managed to put these reforms only partially in place, however, when Spain found itself again sucked into war after 1793, this time as the somewhat reluctant ally of revolutionary France. When the alliance threatened to crumble under the pounding of British guns, Napoleon, in May 1808, kidnapped the Spanish king, invaded Spain, and put his brother Joseph on the throne. The Spanish people fought back. They established a regency for the abducted king and called a meeting of a representative assembly, the Cortes, which, for the first time, included delegates from the American colonies.

In 1812 the Cortes, dominated by an urban bourgoisie under the influence of the Enlightenment and aware that the survival of the Spanish state rested on New World loyalty, produced a constitution that limited the king's power and offered equal status to most Americans and Spaniards. King Ferdinand VII swore obedience to the constitution from his exile in France, but when the British finally restored him to the throne in 1814, he reneged. Like the Restoration French Bourbons, he learned nothing and forgot nothing. Yet the drama continued, for in January 1820 an army revolt led by Liberals forced him to accept for a second time the 1812 constitution. As each twist in Spanish politics intersected with the peculiar local conditions of different areas of the Americas, individual colonies opted for independence.

Central America appeared to be an exception to this general movement toward independence. The Spanish called the isthmus "Guatemala," and it was a subdivision of the viceroyalty of New Spain (Mexico) to the north. The Hidalgo revolts, which mingled race war and desire for independence, broke out in central New Spain in 1810 and simmered for a decade but did not spread to Guatemala. In Guatemala a series of strong governors, aided by a tiny Spanish and *criollo* (whites born in the New World) elite, struggled successfully to keep a lid on the discontent of the Indian and *casta* (mixed blood) majority. The immediate conflict was not so much about independence as the reluctance of the lower orders to pay the taxes that supported the regime. Guatemala's indigenous population by law was liable for a head tax called tribute. So too, in theory, were the *castas,* but most ignored the tax, and the state made little effort to collect from them. Tribute in Guatemala took a number of forms in the three hundred years following the conquest in 1521. For example, until 1738 Indian women as well as men had to pay the tax, and then, for a time, unmarried and married men paid, but by the late eighteenth century, tribute fell chiefly on married Indian men aged eighteen to fifty. If by law tribute was a tax on individuals, in practice the state assessed it by community, on the basis of rough, and often out-of-date, population counts. Local Indian leaders had the responsibility for collecting and delivering the levy in twice-per-year installments to the Spanish. The Indians originally paid the tax in kind, using cacao or cotton or whatever else was the local product of commercial value, but in 1747 the Crown commuted all such payments to coin, which had an important, if unanticipated, effect. Over the course of the centuries following the institution of tribute, the money value of many of the commodities used by the communities to pay the tax had changed. When the new law converted these items to their eighteenth-century cash equivalents, some villages found themselves owing much more, often by two or three times, than that paid by other towns of similar size. Whole regions saw taxes go up dramatically. Not surprisingly, this produced complaints and calls for reform.

Crown officials began to study the problem in the 1780s and, with customary dispatch, in 1801 adopted a plan for the *nivelación,* or the leveling, of tributes. This involved new censuses and a standardization of the amount due at sixteen reales, or two pesos, per year for each Indian male. In fact, "leveling" was not exactly what occurred. Those communities already paying more than two pesos per tributary continued to be liable for the larger amount; those paying less had their taxes "leveled" up to the new figure.

The increases that resulted from *nivelación* were quite substantial in many instances, especially among the Indians of the western highlands and the Verapaz. According to calculations by the Guatemalan historian Manuel Fernández Molina, these increases amounted to:

District	% Increase	District	% Increase
Suchitepéquez	9.21%	Chimaltenango	30.29%
Chiquimula-Zacapa	10.84%	Totonicapán- Huehuetenango	37.57%
Quezaltenango	26.25%	Amatatitlán- Sacatepequez	40.08%
Sololá	28.91%	Verapaz	104.23%

Government efforts to implement the leveled taxes touched off a storm of protest. A major riot broke out in Cobán in the Verapaz in 1803, driving crown officials from the town and requiring regular troops and *ladino** militia from the capital to put it down. Few towns ever had paid tribute promptly, and most now dragged their feet even more. In these years, too, they came under other, extraordinary demands on their limited resources. Between 1801 and 1807 the state took over and called in loans owed to town *cajas de la comunidad* (community reserve funds) and to the church and sent the proceeds to Europe to help finance the wars. This *consolidación* forced individuals to sell properties or liquidate businesses, often at a loss, to make good their debts, and it drained more than 1 million pesos from the local economy. Repeatedly, too, crown officials simply *hecharon la mano* (stuck their hand) in community reserve funds, to meet real or manufactured emergencies, and on several occasions they demanded "voluntary" contributions to the war effort. In these years as well, disastrous locust plagues swept up the west coast and into the highlands, devastating wide areas of export and food crops.

In March 1811 the Cortes abolished tribute. Official notice of this did not arrive in Guatemala until more than a year later, but unofficial news circulated much sooner and filtered into the highlands. Resistance to the tax grew apace. Confronted by

*In Guatemala, a *ladino* is someone of European or "national" culture, whatever the individual's racial makeup. The word carries, however, and this was particularly the case in the late colonial period, the connotation of less than pure Caucasian heritage.

growing protests from the communities, in April 1811 the Audiencia, or high court, of Guatemala ordered a reduction in tribute to pre-*nivelación* levels. This response satisfied no one. Indians were certain, not without reason given their past experience, that the Spanish tax officials, often in conjunction with some of their own leaders, meant to cheat them. Unrest finally forced crown officials to suspend collections in January 1812. In May of that year the new constitution arrived in Guatemala. Two of its provisions were of particular interest to the Indians. One provision decreed that, henceforth, all native-born residents of Spain and the empire not of African ancestry were full citizens with equal rights. Gone was the Indian's legal situation as a second-class citizen or perpetual "minor" before the law. And, article 339 of the constitution provided that all citizens be taxed only according to their ability to pay. This provision confirmed, or so it seemed at the time, the abolition of tribute. The Cortes had key sections of the constitution translated into Indian languages and circulated these in the communities. Victoria Bricker, in *The Indian Christ, the Indian King*, renders part of this explanation as:

> Now there is no one
>   Who has thought to say
> That we are not Spaniards
>   all of us. . . .
> Beloved sons!
>   Open the pupils of your eyes
> Now your tribute is gone

The Indians would now be liable for "Spanish taxes," such as the *diezmo* (tithe) and the *alcabala* (sales tax), from which they had been exempt, but the hated tribute was gone.

The fortunes of war, however, soon reversed the situation yet again. In May 1814, Ferdinand returned, tore up the constitution, and reinstituted tribute at the higher *nivelación* rates. The Audiencia published news of this in Guatemala in January 1815 and began attempts to collect the tax in November. It is hardly to be wondered that the Indians suspected a trick. Many refused to pay. The highlands rustled with rumors. Resistance seems to have been particularly strong in the villages around San Miguel Totonicapán, chief town of the Totonicapán-Huehuetenango province (much of present-day northwestern Guatemala) and residence of the province's *alcalde mayor* (governor), which had suffered large increases in the *nivelación* reforms. A savage riot, linked to land disputes with the town of Sololá and to tributes, had exploded in 1813, resulting in the wounding of the *alcalde mayor*. In 1816, in San Miguel itself, town officials, led by the *primer alcalde* (chief town council member) Atanasio Tzul, flatly refused to collect tribute. Tzul had long been a leader in efforts to resist the tax. At the time, he was about fifty-five years old, a peasant farmer, and in addition to being *primer alcalde*, was head of the important local clan of Lincag. Tzul and his fellow officials took up per tributary only four reales for the community fund and 2.5 reales to support the priest.

By 1818 the new governor of Totonicapán-Huehuetenango, Manuel José Lara, was finding himself under increasing pressure from Guatemala City to collect overdue tribute. The towns of his district were some fifteen thousand dollars in arrears; this debt jumped to almost thirty thousand dollars by 1820. Most obstinate were San Miguel, which had paid practically nothing, the nearby towns of San Francisco el Alto, San Cristobal Totonicapán, Momostenango, and Santa María Chiquimula, and, to the north, Sacapulas, Cotzal, and Chajul. When his superiors instituted legal proceedings against him, Lara protested that he was powerless. Unceasingly, he claimed, he had crisscrossed the highlands exhorting and threatening, but the towns either appealed to the Audiencia or simply ignored his demands. Furthermore, he complained, the Audiencia, worried about touching off a general revolt, refused to allow him to punish offending officials or communities. In Sacapulas, a severely frustrated Lara pulled a knife on a threatening crowd and had to flee for his life. *Ladino* troops restored order but could not collect tribute either. In Santa María Chiquimula a mob assaulted the local priest for urging them to pay. The crisis, the Audiencia feared, threatened to get out of hand and spread Totonicapán's "noxious example" to other areas of the highlands. Without the tribute, government revenues, particularly the salaries of crown officials, would dry up.

Despairing of Lara, the Audiencia in late 1818 turned to a former governor of Totonicapán, Prudencio de Cozar, and appointed him special *comisario de orden* (commissioner of order) to bring the Indians to heel. Cozar's career in Guatemala was typical of that of many officials in the late colonial period. A Spaniard, he entered the military as a cadet in 1775 and in

1780 advanced to officer. The early 1800s found him serving as governor of Totonicapán-Huehuetenango. Following this governorship, he reorganized and commanded the militia of the region until 1813. After leaving royal service, Cozar filled various offices on the city council of Quezaltenango, the largest town in the western highlands and located some twenty miles southwest of San Miguel Totonicapán. All of his activities since 1811, as he repeatedly pointed out, had been without official salary.

Comisario Cozar visited town after town in Totonicapán-Huehuetenango to explain and threaten, but he met with no more success than had Lara. This already unpromising mission became next to impossible with the arrival from Spain of the first news of the 1820 liberal revolution and reinstatement of the 1812 constitution. Even after official publication of the document in Guatemala in July 1820, however, disagreement continued among crown officials (as it has among writers on the topic since) as to whether this ended tribute for a second time. The Audiencia argued that, in the absence of a specific ruling, restoration of the constitution did not end tribute and continued its attempts to collect the tax. The Audiencia's interpretation only reinforced Indian suspicions and resistance, convincing many that tribute probably had not been reinstated in 1815. Delegation after delegation from the highland towns visited Guatemala City to ask the truth of the Audiencia; each received the same answer and went away dissatisfied. San Miguel Totonicapán sent three delegations to the capital in the first months of 1820, at least one of which was headed by Atanasio Tzul and by an individual named Lucas Aguilar. Aguilar, about the same age of Tzul and, like him, a small farmer, was also a longtime activist in antitribute agitation and once had led a *tumulto* against the local priest over the tax. But whereas Tzul was a member of the town's hereditary aristocracy, Aguilar was a *macegual* (commoner). He figured, nevertheless, as an individual of considerable local importance because of his wealth, his position as *mayordomo* (head) of the important *cofradía*, or religious brotherhood, of Santisimo Sacramento, and his evident leadership qualities. The Audiencia told Tzul and Aguilar that, as far as it knew, tribute remained in effect and that even if it were to turn out that the constitution did abolish the tax, back tribute for the period 1815–1820 would still be due.

To understand the conflict about to turn violent in Totonicapán, it is necessary to understand the political organization of the highland Indian towns. Several overlapping and interconnected but distinct groups and institutions, commonly lumped together by the Spanish as *justicias* (justices), ruled the villages. The titular, if rarely de facto, head of the community was the *gobernador* (governor), an Indian appointed by the *alcalde mayor* to oversee the town in the interests of the colonial state. For this position the Spanish selected, or claimed to select, individuals from among the survivors of the preconquest hereditary town aristocracies, identifiable remnants of which have existed in some communities into the twentieth century. In these elite families, males called *principales* (principal men) headed kinship groups called *parcialidades* (clans), members of which commonly lived in the same area and held property together. *Parcialidades* continued to be particularly strong institutions in the Totonicapán area; the town of San Miguel, for example, according to testimony at the time, had five. In 1820, Tzul was first *principal* of the large *parcialidad* of Lincag, but he was not the *gobernador*. Whatever the supposed qualifications for this position, Spanish colonial officials, in reality, made and unmade *gobernadores* with such little regard for local sensibilities that by the late colonial period most were obvious creatures of the Spanish rulers and commanded little respect among the indigenous population.

Colonial law provided that each Indian or Spanish community have a *cabildo* (town council) presided over by elected *alcaldes* (council members). Although in theory these posts might be filled by any male of the community, much more powerful *costumbre* (custom) dictated that the hereditary *principales,* where they persisted, dominate both the selection process and in the membership of the town council. The *alcaldes* handled day-to-day administration and justice within the village, collected taxes, apportioned labor for community needs and to meet the demands of the Spanish, and generally mediated contacts between the town and the outside world.

Also important in the village structure were the *cofradías.* Each was a lay religious brotherhood devoted to a specific saint or religious figure. Men occupied the major offices, although women assisted their husbands and sometimes held minor or subordinate posts. In 1820, San Miguel Totonicapán had eighteen Indian *cofradías.*

Cofradía	Capital	Cofradía	Capital
Santisima Trinidad	$50	Las Animas	$24
Santa Cruz	$50	de la Llagas	$46
Santa Catarina	$53	Santa Ana	$28
Rosario	$46	Guadalupe	$80
San Francisco	$37	San Nícolas	$52
San Antonio	$31	Chiantla	$100
Señor de Esquipulas	$65	Santisimo Sacramento	$64
Mereceedes	$45	Concepción	$45
Santa Cecilia	$132	Archangel	none

Members joined voluntarily and contributed their time and money to adorn the saint's image and to celebrate its fiesta with church services, firecrackers, music, and ritual drunkenness. *Cofradía capitales* (funds) served too as reserves to help meet community emergencies or expenses, such as sending delegations to the capital to inquire about tribute. Service to a *cofradía,* especially as the *mayordomo,* brought an individual prestige in the community, and *maceguales* as well as hereditary *principales* might hold the post as head. The important qualifications were devotion to the cult and the time and the money necessary to undertake the often elaborate ceremonies and ritual connected with a given image.

Taken together the offices of the *cabildo* and the *cofradía* made up, and still make up, the much-studied *cargo* system, common throughout much of Mesoamerica, in which different *cofradías* assume the financial responsibility for sponsoring various religious festivals. Those persons who served successfully in a series of civil and religious offices entered in their advanced years into the category of "elder" of the town. The usual name for these elders in Guatemalan indigenous communities is also *principales.* A self-selecting and self-perpetuating institution, the body of elders had responsibility, along with the hereditary *principales,* if these existed, for selection of the *alcaldes,* for advising on all aspects of community life, and, in general, for the preservation and perpetuation of values and customary practices. The double meaning of *principal* would have confused no one in Totonicapán, as the specific content of the word would be obvious in the context of a given individual. A number of men, including Atanasio Tzul, had the status of *principal* in both senses.

Such were the *justicias* with whom *Alcalde Mayor* Lara and *Comisario* Cozar had had so little success. The Audiencia finally ordered Cozar to "pacify" the towns and put an end to the resistance. In March and again in April 1820, Cozar ordered Tzul, Aguilar, and the other rebellious authorities of San Miguel to appear in Quezaltenango to explain themselves. They refused, saying that if Cozar wished to talk to them he could come to Totonicapán, but they threatened to cut off his head if he did! Clearly, the *alcalde mayor* had little control over even his chief town.

In the early months of 1820 it was, in any event, not so much San Miguel but the neighboring town of Santa María Chiquimula that took the leading role in actively resisting tax demands. Most of the towns around Totonicapán were land poor, but Santa María's situation was particularly difficult. With a growing population and few resources, the aggressive Chiquimulas invaded or rented the lands of their more fortunate neighbors, migrated to distant townships in search of land and work, and engaged in long-distance trade. They were not about to pay unnecessary taxes.

After repeated clashes with their own town authorities, on March 17, 1820, some two hundred inhabitants of Santa María Chiquimula descended on San Miguel Totonicapán to inquire yet again of *Alcalde Mayor* Lara about tribute. They claimed to know that a paper recently had arrived from the capital supporting their position and demanded to see it. Because Lara was out of town, the Chiquimulas, soon joined by a large number of Indians from San Miguel led by Lucas Aguilar, congregated in front of the lieutenant governor's house, yelling that Lara was a robber and demanding to see the document. The lieutenant governor, with a howling mob at his door, ordered the scribe of the town council to read the only newly arrived order he could find, which dealt not with tribute but with taxes for the support of the priest at Santa María Chiquimula. Not satisfied, Aguilar "took the voice of the crowd" and threatened the lieutenant governor, and the mob roughed up the scribe, saying that he either was lying or could not read. Several *justicias* who sought to calm the Indians found it necessary to take refuge in the lieutenant governor's house. The crowd then dispersed, the Chiquimulas returning to their village, and the residents of San

Miguel going to Aguilar's house to discuss what to do. When the lieutenant governor learned, or so his informants warned him, that the Indians planned to kill him that night "because they wanted no *ladinos* in the town," he bundled himself and his family out of San Miguel.

The conflict simmered. Cozar, with little force available to back up his threats, adhered to the standard axiom of Spanish colonial government: do little, and that slowly. Aguilar and Tzul, for their part, continued to meet with groups from other towns to discuss the situation, and, periodically, they clashed openly with Lara; neither side, however, seemed able or willing to force the issue.

Suddenly, in early summer, the situation at Totonicapán exploded, touched off by the July 5 arrival in San Miguel of "the papers of the constitution." Apparently, the villagers were expecting something, for they went out to meet the mail carrier arriving from Guatemala City and brought him into town accompanied by "riotous" celebrations. One of the most intriguing, unanswered questions about the rebellion concerns the exact nature of these "papers," to which various participants refer but never describe. The Spanish at the time, and some writers since, believed that the leaders of the outbreak had contact with proindependence agitators in the capital and that these papers might have been such a link. But crown officials who questioned the leaders of the uprising after its repression, although clearly aware of the existence of the papers and interested in connections to Guatemala City, failed to pursue the topic. Who sent the papers? Of what did they consist? One source speaks of five printed items. Probably the papers were copies of the constitution, together with the explanations of key passages earlier translated into Indian languages. Individuals or a group of proindependence enthusiasts in the capital may well have sought to stir up trouble for the Spanish authorities in the countryside by encouraging the Indians' just complaints. What Tzul, Aguilar, and their supporters said the papers were (remember, only the scribe of the *cabildo* and perhaps a few others among the Indians, but not Tzul or Aguilar, could read) was confirmation of the end of tribute.

The papers proved too, the leaders argued, and here they more clearly erred, that the Crown never had reestablished tribute. To the cries of "thief," *Alcalde Mayor* Lara fled the town the next day for Quezaltenango and the protection of *Comisario* Cosar. Aguilar and Tzul, with their supporters, cornered several *justicias* who had counseled cooperation with the Spanish and upbraided them for stealing from the people. When the *justicias* denied the charge, the rioters beat them and threatened to "rip out their guts." Tzul took the staff of office of the *gobernador* for himself and gave that of the second *alcalde* to Antonio Sitalan. Later, Sitalan recalled, under interrogation, that he had tried to turn down the "honor," but when Aguilar questioned his manhood, asking whether "he was a man with balls," he had had to accept the post.

The power and pretensions of the rebels grew quickly. Groups of Indians came from the surrounding towns to confer with Tzul and Aguilar; armed with clubs, they stayed to guard the leaders' houses. Aguilar ordered the *justicias* of San Francisco el Alto, San Andrés Xecul, and other villages to appear in Totonicapán and explain why they had continued to collect tribute. Surrounded by bodyguards, Aguilar berated these officials and demanded that they return the money to the people. He had them hung up and whipped "until they passed out." Most of Aguilar's victims later claimed that they had had no intention of obeying his orders but that upon returning to their towns they were threatened by mobs and forced to give up what tribute funds they possessed. Aguilar also instituted a tax of two reales each on all married men, to repay, he claimed, community and *cofradía* funds spent pursuing the tribute question.

While all agreed that Aguilar was "principal head" of the uprising, and several witnesses even labeled Tzul his "pawn," it was Atanasio Tzul who took the crown of "king." Or did he? Tzul, not surprisingly, later denied that any coronation had occurred. Bricker, in her treatment of the revolt, accepts this statement, arguing that since the Indians never wavered in professing loyalty to the Spanish king they could not very well have raised another king. Yet Bricker's interpretation presumes an elaborated theory of unitary kingship, which the Indians almost certainly did not have. Rather, they seemed to find no difficulty with the idea of "subkings"; for example, while Tzul ruled Totonicapán, Justo Rainos claimed to be "king" of San Francisco el Alto. As head of one of the largest *parcialidades* in the town, as a hereditary noble (even if not, as some have suggested, in any identifiable sense a direct descendant of the Quiché kings), and with a long history of leading resistance to tribute, Tzul was the logical candidate. Almost certainly, then, Tzul did put on "the crown of Saint Joseph," borrowed from the saint's statue in the town church; his wife, Felipa Soc, donned that of Saint Cecilia, obtained from the image of the *cofradía* of that name. Tzul's regalia—Spanish three-cornered hat, pants, shoes, and sword— he took, with no apparent conscious irony, from an available costume for the Dance of the Conquest, a dance performed by Indians on festival days and that commemorates the defeat of the Indians by the Spanish conquerors.

Real power, however, lay with Lucas Aguilar. It was Aguilar who "raised the *cofradías*" and led the crowds; his son carried his invitations and orders to the neighboring towns and his messages to Guatemala City. Delegations from other towns visited him chiefly, and it was at his house that meetings took place and that doubting *justicias* and *ladinos* were interrogated and punished (one claimed to have had his ear cut off). It is of interest, and probably indicative of their perspective, that Aguilar, Tzul, and others spent one evening trying to repair a paper picture of King Ferdinand. Aguilar took the title of "president" under Tzul, the king. This, of course, followed the pattern of titles within the Spanish imperial system in which the president of the Audiencia of Guatemala served under the king of Spain. President was the highest title to which Aguilar, as a commoner, might logically aspire, and it was an office, within the experience of the Indians, of great day-to-day power. The king might rule, but like God, was far away, whereas the president was an all-too-concrete reality.

The flight of Lara and the coronation of Tzul forced Cozar to take more active steps. Even so, he could not act precipitously because he lacked an adequate armed force to move against the towns. The colonial government of Guatemala maintained few regular army troops. Most of these it stationed in the capital to maintain order and on the north coast for defense against the British and pirates. To control the countryside the state relied on a militia made up of some Spanish and creole officers but filled out mainly with small-town and rural *ladinos* and *castas* drawn to the units by *fueros* (legal privileges granted to those connected with the military). The core of the forces available to Cozar were four battalions of town militia from Quezaltenango. These he claimed to have organized, or reorganized, himself between 1811 and 1813, but, he now lamented, they had been allowed to fall into disarray in subsequent years. It took time to get the troops into shape and to arm them with muskets from state warehouses. To reinforce these battalions, Cozar called up the militia of the nearby towns of Santa Cruz del Quiché and Sololá and from the *ladino* settlements of Salcajá and San Carlos Sija. These soldiers came with what arms they had on hand, typically pikes, swords, and machetes, and a few shotguns. In all, Cozar put together a force of some one thousand men.

After several weeks of preparation, Cozar moved on San Miguel on August 3 from four directions simultaneously. To cover his flank and provide an avenue of retreat if necessary, he left a detachment of fifty men of the Salcajá and Sija militias at the junction of the road to San Francisco el Alto. Entering San Miguel, the militia troops encountered hostile crowds but little active resistance. Their commander went to Tzul's house first and then Aguilar's, where the Indians waited. Most of the Indians spoke no Spanish, so the commander could not make himself understood, and he dared not enter the leader's house for fear of being cut off from his men and killed. Instead, the Spanish recruited the town priest, who seems to have remained in San Miguel throughout the uprising without any problem, to get up on a table in front of the crowd and explain to the Indians in their own language that they did have to pay tribute. This news was not well received; one witness spoke of a shower of rocks. At that moment, news arrived of an attack by the rearguard.

The militia left at the road junction had taken up position in a strategic pass. Soon, however, hundreds of Indians from San Cristobal Totonicapán and San Francisco el Alto congregated on the hills above them and then attacked, hurling rocks down on the soldiers. Soon all of the militia members were wounded. The attacking villagers forced them to give way, falling back toward Totonicapán until they met reinforcements rushing to their rescue. With these the militia counterattacked and captured several of their tormentors. Why San Francisco and San Cristobal had attacked the troops when the Indians of San Miguel and of other communities did not is a mystery. The incident does make clear, however, the lack of coordination between the towns and the indigenous population's evident failure to prepare for what they must have realized would be the Spanish response to their rebellion.

The events that followed were later hotly disputed by the parties involved. The troops "denuded" San Miguel, its inhabitants claimed, carrying off "pots and pans, wheat, corn, pigs, and chickens." They dragged people from their houses and put nooses around their necks to terrorize them into revealing hidden weapons or, of probably greater immediate interest to the troopers, more loot. Militia members bayoneted one woman repeatedly, reportedly because she attacked them with a stick of firewood. She later died, but Cozar denied any necessary connection between the two events. The Indians protested that at least three villagers died from such abuse and complained that the priest had refused them "the holy oils."

The militia whipped dozens of Indians, as exemplary punishment and in pursuit of hidden animals and goods. They "gave them the leather," one soldier recalled, for two days, and some Indians were said to have received as many as three hundred lashes. Few of the leaders tried to escape, and Tzul and Aguilar fell prisoner without resistance. Either they did not understand the gravity of their offense, which, given their past experience and in spite of their protests of innocence, seems highly unlikely, or, as Severo Martínez Peláez suggests in his book *Motines de Indios*, they accepted responsibility for their actions and the punishment that would certainly follow as an inevitable consequence of their role as community leaders. The purpose of the uprising was to call the Crown's attention to the real and perceived abuses of Spanish and Indian officials. In this the villagers succeeded but, that done, someone had to "take the fall" in order to maintain the legitimacy of the system. One individual who did escape was the town's scribe, one of the few people who could have read and testified to the contents of the famous papers.

The following day on August 4, Cozar sent thirty-four prisoners, including Tzul and Aguilar, in chains to Quezaltenango for trial. What is striking in the leaders' testimony is their willingness to incriminate each other. Each claimed to be ignorant of his supposed offenses, and each sought to shift the blame for the disturbances to others. Aguilar, the first to be interrogated, said that he did not know why he had been arrested but guessed that it had to do with the soldiers finding some papers, about which he knew nothing, in his house. He allowed the use of his house for meetings at the request of the *principales* because it was large, he said, but he had nothing to do with any whippings of Indian officials or attacks on *ladinos*. Tzul, for his part, protested that it was not he but Aguilar who had ordered the other towns to stop paying tribute and who had had the *justicias* beaten. Tzul denied crowning himself and said that he and others of the *principales* had taken the staffs of office from the *gobernador* and second *alcalde* only because they had failed in their duties. It was Aguilar who had stirred up the towns; they sent delegations to him with money, for what purpose Tzul did not know. Aguilar's son professed to know nothing of his father's activities, and although he admitted calling the *alcalde mayor* a thief, he claimed he had been drunk when he had done so. In part, Aguilar's son's denial played to Spanish prejudices, which assumed a childlike and stupid Indian. But, as Severo Martínez points out, it may also reflect the relatively unpremeditated, spontaneous nature of the outbreak itself, which limited the opportunity for "revolutionary solidarity" to develop.

During the *tumulto,* class conflict bubbled to the surface in several of the communities. Aggrieved *principales,* abused by Aguilar and his accomplices, had hastened to tell the Spanish after repression of the uprising that the *maceguales* of their towns had supported the *sedición* enthusiastically: "the very same commoners held the bull fights and shouted 'Long live Lucas Aguilar who is our king.'" The appeal of the Totonicapán uprising for the masses of the community had been abolition of tribute, a tax from which *justicias* not uncommonly had exempted themselves. Indeed, some *justicias* had profited from skimming the tribute before turning it over to the Spanish or had cooperated with Spanish officials in coerced labor schemes and the *repartimiento de efectos* (forced sale of unneeded goods at inflated prices). It is hardly to be wondered that given the opportunity the populace had beaten the *principales* of San Cristobol Totonicapán "with sticks" or that these officials had reported the attacks to the Spanish with relish, in hopes of revenge. Not all local officials had worked for the community as singlemindedly as Tzul; even in the case of Aguilar there remain questions concerning not only abuses of power but also what happened to the monies collected from the two-reales head tax.

Crown officials at the time, and a number of writers subsequently, have attempted to link the events in San Miguel to designs for political independence from Spain. Daniel Contreras, in one of the first studies of the *tumulto,* concluded that "the rebellious Indians of Totonicapán in 1820 ought to be understood as part of a whole process, the process that culminated in the proclamation of independence." He has a point but a limited one. Certainly the decade-long conflict over tribute contributed to the general unrest that prefaced independence. The events at

San Miguel thus were both a product and a cause of this unrest. But the uprising clearly did not have independence from Spain as its goal. It was in most ways a typical colonial riot against the abuses of Spanish and Indian officials. The idea of a "king" seems to have emerged chiefly because the uprising lasted much longer than was normal in these cases. And it lasted longer because of the unsettled condition of the colony brought on by the situation in Spain, by the independence revolts under way to the north and south, and by the decade of resistance to tribute collection. Whereas tax rebels in the early part of the century found themselves quickly rounded up and shipped off to serve stiff sentences in the penal fortresses at Omoa on the Honduras coast and in the isolated Petén, between 1818 and 1820 Guatemala's Audiencia moved slowly, fearing a race war and independence movement such as had erupted to the north. Most witnesses remembered that the festivities in Totonicapán included *vivas* for King Ferdinand. Indeed, and only slightly disingenuously, the *tumulto's* jailed leaders claimed not to understand why they had been imprisoned simply for celebrating the king's constitution.

Why did Totonicapán's revolt not develop into a broader Indian and *casta* uprising such as had occurred in Peru in the 1780s or in Mexico from 1708 to 1713 and during the nineteenth century? Certainly the leaders tried, sending out calls to join them not only to the towns of the district of Totonicapán but also to Indian communities in Sololá and Quezaltenango. However, the Indians themselves were a product of the Spanish colonial system or, more accurately, a product of the interaction over several centuries of this system with indigenous institutions and values. In Guatemala, this limited the Indians' perspective to the *pueblo de indios* (local community) and regularly blocked or destroyed any institution above the municipality not under direct Spanish control. Indian villages of highland Guatemala remained isolated from each other by language and dialect, by costume, by custom, and by the hostilities engendered in centuries of conflict, chiefly over land, among themselves. What drew a broad range of Indians to the 1708–1713 Tzotzil-Tzeltal revolt in Chiapas and the nineteenth-century Caste War in Yucatán, for example, and, more importantly, what held them together over time, was messianic religion. This unifying element was lacking in Totonicapán. Contreras suggests as a possible substitute Tzul as a descendant of the last Quiché kings. A similar claim seems to have been effective in eighteenth-century Peru, but there is scant evidence that the Totonicapán rebels thought in such terms and even less that the other towns found the idea appealing or convincing. In any event, only the villages in the immediate vicinity of Totonicapán answered Aguilar's call, and even several of these exhibited doubts about an Indian "king."

What happened to the leaders jailed in Quezaltenango? Tradition has it that they either paid with their lives or gained release only after independence. In fact, their fate was less dramatic. Late in 1820 and again in March 1821, the prisoners applied for pardons. They denied any intention of disloyalty, and they put forward a calculated explanation of their actions, claiming, "[As we were] born in the countryside and raised accustomed only to the crudest circumstances and like our parents used only to being with animals, it is not possible that with this sort of upbringing we could distinguish right from wrong and for this reason we should not suffer the fate of a civilized man." On March 22, 1821, the Audiencia granted pardons to Aguilar, Tzul, and various of the others still in jail. This is in dramatic contrast to the harsh penalties passed out to earlier tax rebels and obviously reflects the uncertain climate of the last year of the Spanish colony of Guatemala. *Alcalde Mayor* Lara protested bitterly, saying that the Indians sought their freedom only in order to return to San Miguel Totonicapán to seek revenge against him. Cozar expressed fear for his life if he had to return to Totonicapán to try again to collect tributes. And the inhabitants of the town openly threatened that, once the troops left, they would wreak vengeance on any of their fellows who had cooperated with the Spanish.

SOURCES

The chief sources for this chapter are original or primary documents in the Archivo General de Centro América in Guatemala City. These include the interrogation records of Tzul, Aguilar, and their compatriots and the reports of Cozar and Lara to the Audiencia. Given the usual bulk of colonial judicial records, the court proceedings are surprisingly sketchy, perhaps yet another indication of the weakened condition of the state.

Victoria Reifler Bricker includes a useful account of the uprising in *The Indian Christ, the Indian King: The Historical Substrate of Maya Myth and Ritual* (Austin, 1981); and in Spanish there is J. Daniel Contreras's *Una rebelión indígena en el partido de Totonicapán en 1820* (2d printing, Guatemala, 1968). Severo Martínez Peláez treats the rebellion topically, together with a dozen others, in the first chapters of *Motines de Indios (la violencia colonial en Centroamérica y Chiapas)* (Puebla, n.d.) and promises in the future a chapter specifically on the events at Totonicapán.

Good treatments and bibliographies in English of late colonial Guatemala include those in W. George Lovell, *Conquest and Survival in Colonial Guatemala: A Historical Geography of the Cuchumatan Highlands, 1500–1821* (Kingston, Ontario, 1985); Thomas Thorstein Veblen, "The Ecological, Cultural, and Historical Bases of Forest Preservation in Totonicapán, Guatemala" (Ph.D. diss., University of California, Berkeley, 1975); and Miles Wortman, *Government and Society in Central America, 1680–1840* (New York, 1982). William B. Taylor's *Drinking, Homicide, and Rebellion in Colonial Mexican Villages* (Stanford, 1979), although it does not deal specifically with Totonicapán, sets the rebellion in perspective.

4

Maria Antônia Muniz: Frontier Matriarch

John Charles Chasteen

As noted in the introduction to Part 1, Dom Pedro I proclaimed Brazil's independence from Portugal in 1822 with a minimum of conflict or bloodshed. Yet the imperial ambitions of Dom João VI (1808–1820) and Dom Pedro I (1820–1831) caused considerable trouble for the inhabitants of the region far to the south, the *banda oriental,* or eastern bank, of the Plata River. Both the Spanish and the Portuguese coveted control of this magnificent river system. During the colonial period the Spanish saw the river as a vulnerable path to the famed *plata* (silver) mines of Potosí in Bolivia. The Portuguese saw the Plata River as the most convenient way to reach their western inland regions of Mato Grosso. After Argentina's independence in 1816 and Brazil's in 1822, the two Latin American behemoths continued to press for advantage in the area; both ignored the challenge of the Uruguayan caudillo José Artigas, who fought for independence of the region. In 1828 the British forced Argentina and Brazil to recognize an independent Uruguay as a buffer state between them, but for years both of the larger nations continued to intervene in Uruguayan politics.

The people who lived in the disputed territory suffered and profited in their no-man's-land. Maria Antônia Muniz lived in the region for an incredible ten decades, from her birth in 1762 to her death in 1870. She married, brought up thirteen children, and, after the death of her husband in 1824, indirectly managed the family estates.

John Chasteen's essay raises various historical issues. For Maria Antônia, the frontier was a land of opportunity, much as the U.S. frontier was portrayed by the historian Frederick Jackson Turner. Frontier families, like most families in Latin America, were large and extended. Maria Antônia's experience suggests, however, that among family members competition may have been as common as the more idealized notion of cooperation. The Indian and mestizo gauchos, or cowboys, contrast strongly with members of more settled indigenous communities under Atanasio Tzul in Guatemala. Did they have more personal autonomy and opportunity than their Guatemalan counterparts? Issues of royalism or patriotism, of empire or independence, seem to have been less intense in this region, overshadowed by the competition between Brazil and

Argentina and by the harshness of day-to-day life. Political independence per se apparently affected Maria Antônia's family only slightly. We might ponder also the lives and roles of women on the frontier. Chasteen paints Maria Antônia as a tough survivor, but he leaves open the question of whether she ruled over her family like a strong-willed matriarch, or more passively allowed her husband and sons to shelter and protect her.

John Charles Chasteen, assistant professor of history at Bates College, received his doctorate from the University of North Carolina at Chapel Hill in 1988. He has received Social Science Research Council and Fulbright grants to support field research in Brazil and Uruguay and is the author of articles on violence and machismo in that region.

In the summer of 1866 news from Paraguay arrived at a ranch house in southern Brazil. The allies (Brazil, Argentina, and Uruguay) had lost four thousand dead and wounded in an attempt to take the Paraguayan stronghold at Curupaití. The wife of the house learned, to her relief, that her two sons with the army were all right, and one of her nephews had become a hero. But another of her nephews had died. At the spinning wheel sat her mother, Maria Antônia Muniz, the grandmother of these four soldiers. She had lived already over one hundred years and had seen too many wars. She had presided over a family divided by the struggles of the period, the formative years of Brazil's southern borderland. Hers was a family that had turned upon itself, on one occasion family members killing one another before her very eyes. To her, the present carnage of Curupaití and the name of its hero were merely echoes of the past. As the wooden wheel whirred and the woolen yarn twisted between her calloused fingers, she sang to herself. Her children and grandchildren had often heard her songs, which she had made about her own life. "'Twas in the village of San Carlos that I was born and raised," she sang, "and it's noble blood of Portugal I carry in my veins."

Shortly before 1760 an aristocratic but impoverished ancestor had come to the vast no-man's-land between the New World empires of Spain and Portugal. The Portuguese Crown had built a citadel, Colônia do Sacramento, deep in territory claimed by the Spanish. This wide expanse of rolling and well-watered grassland was still a wild frontier, occupied only by dwindling tribal bands of nomadic Charrua Indians, by a few thousand drifting gauchos, and by tough longhorn cattle that had run wild and thrived, their herds numbered in the millions. A son of this noble ancestor had married the daughter of the garrison commander at Colônia do Sacramento, and the young couple went to claim land and cattle in no-man's-land at a place called San Carlos. Mario Antônia was born there in 1762.

Soon after Maria Antônia's birth, a Spanish army arrived to push the Portuguese out of San Carlos, which lay in the disputed territory. Her parents fled with the baby and three older children to the citadel at Colônia. The Spanish army besieged and captured the town, and Maria Antônia's mother died during the fighting. Within a few years, Spanish authorities allowed her father to resettle in San Carlos, where Maria Antônia and her three brothers grew up in the care of their unmarried aunts. Always in search of unclaimed land, the Muniz family left San Carlos about 1773 and occupied land farther north at a place called Herval, many miles from the nearest neighbor but much closer to the major Portuguese settlement at Rio Grande. In 1784 a mixed Spanish and Portuguese expedition passed by the Muniz house, surveying a strip of neutral territory between the competing empires. Once again, as in San Carlos, the Muniz claim fell in no-man's-land.

Life in no-man's-land was dangerous. Maria Antônia's father kept his blunderbuss loaded in case a party of Spanish soldiers, freebooting gauchos, or hostile Charruas should appear. But the land was there for the taking, and Muniz could have the meat and sell the hide of any longhorn he could catch. He could also brand all the cattle and horses that he found on his land and try to tame them, but for these operations he needed the help of gauchos.

The gauchos were mostly Guaraní Indians who had become Christians in the Jesuit missions on the edge of the disputed territories. The missions had sent men out to harvest the wild herds of no-man's-land, and these men had learned the skills of mounted herdsmen. When the missions were destroyed in the 1750s, many Guaranís had come to live on the rolling plains, where they could easily survive by killing wild cattle. Maria Antônia's father had lived on the plains for years, but he could never ride, rope, and brand the way a gaucho did. He probably never learned to throw a *boleadora* (the three tethered stones that a gaucho could send whirling through the air to entangle the legs of a running animal). Muniz knew that the gauchos might be enticed by the offer of good wages to come for a week or two and help him. Although it cost them nothing to live from the wild herds, they liked to have some silver coins to buy the few amenities they wanted, or to gamble, which they passionately enjoyed.

It was hard to get a gaucho to stay for long, however, even with good pay, so Muniz almost certainly had a few slaves. They would have sown wheat, which grew well in the soil of Herval. They also raised mules, which men from the north bought to take to the distant mines of central Brazil; in the fall, Muniz took some of the mules to carry his wheat and hides to a riverbank. There, twenty-foot sailing boats passed on their way to Rio Grande where Muniz could sell the wheat and hides to buy sacks of salt and sugar, cloth and ribbons for Maria Antônia's feast-day dress, a fine beaver hat, and a bottle of wine or two. He could also buy Paraguayan tea if he already had learned to appreciate its bitter taste and stimulating effects. Sooner or later, almost all newcomers did come to like this tea, and besides, Brazil did not yet produce much coffee.

By the 1780s, five or six other Portuguese families had settled within a few miles of Muniz. The Amaro da Silveira brothers were the first of these. They were sons of one of many poor Azorean families sent by the Portuguese Crown to populate the disputed lands. Maria Antônia married Manuel Amaro da Silveira when she was fourteen years old. To find a priest the wedding party had to ride to a Spanish outpost two days away, and when they did not return for a week, those who had stayed behind to prepare the wedding feast began to fear a calamity. Almost a century later, Maria Antônia still enjoyed telling the story of how the wedding party had waited at the outpost, delayed for days by the absence of the priest, who finally appeared to perform the ceremony.

Manuel built a house for his bride on one of the highest hills in no-man's-land. From there, one almost could see Portuguese territory to the north and Spanish territory to the south. Manuel set about rounding up and branding the wild longhorns on his claim, and Maria Antônia spun and wove, washed clothes and cooked (almost certainly with the help of one or two slave women), and began to bear and raise children. Her first son, José, was healthy, but the second died in infancy. Then she had two more sons, Hilário and Jerônimo, and a daughter, Maria Antônia. João, Vasco, Dionísio, Manuel, Balbina, and Francisca followed. The last of these was born in 1788, and Maria Antônia then stopped having children for ten years, but when her son Dionísio died in adolescence, she began again. She had three more girls, and a boy, whom she named Dionísio. In all, thirteen children survived to become adults.

A large family brought advantages in the early days of settlement. The Amaro da Silveira girls helped their mother and eventually married sons of the families settled nearby. The boys learned to ride and rope and throw the *boleadora* better than their father or grandfather ever could. They also learned to use guns. In 1801 there was a war, and the oldest three boys learned to use a sword and a lance as well. José and Hilário were captured by the Spanish in that war, but relatives of their grandfather in Spanish territory managed to win their release. The war had gone very well for Portugal. The Portuguese army had captured all of the no-man's-land where Herval lay and had pushed the Spanish far to the west. From now on, Herval would be part of Brazil. Families that were already well established there got title to the property they claimed, especially if the family had aristocratic pretensions like Maria Antônia's. The Crown rewarded the officers of its victorious army with more grants of land. The Amaro da Silveira family profited in both ways.

The half-century that Maria Antônia spent raising her thirteen children (roughly from 1775 to 1825) were the formative years of the Brazilian borderland. During this time, families of settlers were brought in from the Azores, virtually all the pastureland was distributed and settled, and the settlers were able to push the Spanish out of land that they had claimed for three hundred years. The strength of the Portuguese settlement in the borderland was its homogeneity and greater sense of attachment to an imperial purpose. Although they acquired the gauchos' skill and eventually abandoned the cultivation of wheat altogether, families like Maria Antônia's maintained a strongly European community life that distinguished their society from that of their Spanish-speaking neighbors. Symptomatic was the greater importance of the state religion in the Brazilian borderland. Maria Antônia had a heavy Bible bound in leather and wood, and on Friday evenings it was customary for one of her sons to read aloud from it. Occasionally, she led family and slaves in singing a repetitive *terça*, one third of the rosary. Churches were more frequent on the Brazilian side of the border, and periodically they sent traveling revivals through the countryside. Three-day caroling trips were popular for January's feast of the Three Wise Men.

By contrast, the Spanish borderland remained less populated, and its inhabitants had more diverse racial and geographic origins. Land title there was not granted to the occupants but was sold in huge tracts to speculators at the viceregal court, and conflict frequently arose between the absentee landlords and the actual occupants of the land. Spanish authorities envied the thriving settlements of the Portuguese borderland and recommended the adoption of Portuguese methods. But they had accomplished little when the Spanish-American wars of independence began in 1810.

Turmoil in the Spanish borderland meant opportunity for the Portuguese borderlanders. Herval became a permanent military camp, the starting point of repeated invasions of Spanish territory. These expeditions brought back hundreds of thousands of cattle as the spoils of war. Finally, in 1820 the Brazilian borderlanders conquered the entire area of present-day Uruguay. The families of Herval and other borderland areas of Brazil flooded into the occupied territory and acquired large areas of land there. Maria Antônia's family profited in this way, too.

The Amaro da Silveiras received at least four royal grants in the names of various family members. They used their income to buy more land, cattle, and slaves, and with the added income they bought still more. By the year 1824, when Maria Antônia's husband Manuel died, their family owned about one hundred and fifty square miles of pasture, seventeen thousand semiwild longhorns, four hundred tame longhorns, almost one thousand horses in various stages of domestication, and fifty-four slaves. (By now, fifty years after Maria Antônia's father had come to Herval, the slaves had learned all the skills of the gauchos.) The widow's house, described for the purposes of the probate inventory, was solid but plain, and the family had few luxuries of any kind despite their large holdings. For the Amaro da Silveiras, cattle and land were not means to an end but an end in themselves. Like most of the lords of the borderland who would follow them in the nineteenth century, Maria Antônia and her children had lived in the backlands all their lives, and their aspirations were those of rural people in a traditional culture.

Maria Antônia was sixty-two years old when her husband died. She was proud of the wealth she and her family had built. But troubled times lay ahead for the family. To begin with, this huge collection of pasture and animals was the work of more than one generation. Maria Antônia's oldest sons, José and Hilário, were in their fifties by the time they inherited legal title to the land on which they lived. And there were problems with the distribution of the inheritance. After her husband's death, Maria Antônia's sons and sons-in-law quarreled so terribly that she preferred to entrust the administration of her remaining property (half of the total at Manuel's death) to a neutral party: Domingos Amaro da Silveira, her husband's son by a slave woman. Manuel had always taken a special interest in Domingos, who could read and write (something Maria Antônia could not do), and the old man's will had manumitted him and left him land and cattle. The other Amaro da Silveira men liked and respected Domingos but did not feel they had to compete with him. He managed the huge estate for eight years, sending his sons to study in Rio Grande and eventually becoming a slave owner himself.

When Domingos retired in 1832, Maria Antônia had to find a new administrator for her property. These were conflictive times in the borderland. The Uruguayans had recently broken free from Brazil (itself now independent from Portugal), and they repaid their old enemies by raiding destructively into the Brazilian borderland. No more could Uruguayan cattle be extracted by the thousands with impunity, and the Brazilian government itself exacted a tax on the animals imported legally. In addition, passions ran high throughout Brazil as Conservatives and Liberals disputed key questions of the country's political organization. When Firmina Amaro da Silveira married Juca Teodoro Braga, a famous war captain from the glory days of 1811–1827, old Maria Antônia thought her new son-in-law was just the man to defend the family's interests, and she made him administrator of her property.

Braga stopped the fighting over land, but the family found oher things to fight about. One night in 1833, Maria Antônia's eldest daughter (who had always been her favorite) knocked on the door in the middle of the night with her crying children. Her husband had just been killed by a group of men who came in the night to cut his throat. This death was the third in a series of revenge killings among the Amaro da Silveiras and their in-laws. So that her daughter's family would not have to return to the house where this episode occurred, Maria Antônia moved her own household to a new residence a couple of miles away, and the young widow occupied the original hilltop homestead. The old woman had barely gotten accustomed to her new house when another disaster struck. Enraged by her preference for Juca Teodoro Braga, her pampered youngest son, Dionísio, had awaited his chance and finally shot Braga in the back on a hunting trip.

The murder happened only days before the whole borderland was convulsed by the beginnings of the Farrapo War, a ten-year secessionist attempt led by the radical Liberals. In Herval, people held divided loyalties. The Farrapos championed an open border favorable to the borderlanders, but a tradition of military service to the empire pulled the sentiments of the people of Herval in another direction. Maria Antônia's sons and grandsons enlisted on both sides. Her son Vasco became a Farrapo leader so devoted to the cause that he refused to spare the property of the family when the Farrapos ordered requisitions. Her recently widowed daughter, who maintained outspoken loyalty to the empire, soon suffered these requisitions. In 1839 men arrived to tell the old woman that her son Vasco had died at the hand of one of her grandsons, the eldest son of her favorite daughter and the future hero of Curupaití.

The Farrapo War dragged on, ravaging the family's herds and exacerbating old resentments. Maria Antônia's sons José and Hilário had become deadly enemies because of a dispute over their inheritance. Neither could tolerate the presence of the other without threat of violence. One day in 1844, Hilário went to visit his eighty-two-year-old mother at her house. After the midday meal, he and the two men with him lay down in a bedroom for a nap, and while they were asleep José arrived with his son João Pedro. Awakened by voices from the other room, Hilário arose and walked out to greet the visitors. The two brothers were stunned at having come unexpectedly into each other's presence in their mother's parlor. They mumbled a greeting and then sat down dumbly in front of Maria Antônia and the others. Later, the old woman recalled the terrible silence that fell over the room and the words that José cried when he suddenly leaped up: "Because of this heartless fiend I am ruined and miserable!"

The fight that ensued before her very eyes was a confused nightmare. Afterward, even the participants did not know quite what had happened. By that time José was on his horse, calling repeatedly for his son João Pedro. But João Pedro and his uncle Hilário lay dead in a pool of blood on Maria Antônia's parlor floor. Before Hilário's companions could reload their guns, José rode away and fled south into Uruguay where he would remain for many years.

Finally, in 1855, Maria Antônia gave up the matriarchal household that she had maintained for thirty years and went to live with her daughter Francisca. There she spent her last fifteen years, spinning wool and singing about her long life. She continued to grieve over the deaths of her children (she survived eleven of them) but could rejoice in the fertility of her eighty-four grandchildren. One of her multitudinous great-grandchildren, born in the year of Curupaití, listened with special attention to the stories of his family. These were the stories that Maria Antônia had loved to tell about an aristocratic ancestor or about a wedding party that disappeared for one week, as well as the tragic stories the old woman seldom told but that could be collected from uncles and aunts on the long winter evenings of the borderland. Finally, during the first quarter of the twentieth century, this great-grandson wrote down these stories, more or less as they appear here.

SOURCES

The great-grandson who collected the family's oral traditions, and supplemented them with court documents and other archival materials, was Manuel da Costa Medeiros. His manuscript was published, many years after his death, as *História do Herval: Descrição, física e histórica* (Porto Alegre, 1980). The historical context for Maria Antônia's life was drawn from Chasteen's research on the nineteenth-century social and political history of the Brazilian-Uruguayan borderland in the nineteenth century, conducted at the Arquivo Público do Rio Grande do Sul and the Arquivo Histórico do Rio Grande do Sul, both in Pôrto Alegre, Brazil; and the Archivo General de la Nación, with its Sección Judicial, in Montevideo, Uruguay.

II
The First Republican Generations: Between American Barbarism and European Civilization, 1825–1875

The generation that dominated the independence era bore confusion and hardships, but their prevailing mood was one of hope and expectation. In contrast, Latin Americans who experienced the first fifty years of independence suffered from dashed hopes and frequent pessimism as the glories of the late Bourbon period faded into memory while the promises of republicanism seemed a chimera. The security, certainty, and prosperity of the enlightened monarchy gave way to poverty, stagnation, insecurity, and civil conflict. What had appeared to be a single society during the colonial period proved after independence to be an archipelago of peoples, regions, and conflicting interests.

Elites in the cities struggled to develop an active cultural life and to reconcile their ideals of European civilization with the realities of American discord. They had the advantages of leisure time; of relative tranquility; of access to universities and to other intellectuals and their libraries; and of the opportunity to meet and exchange views with foreign visitors. Authors wrote about and discussed their own work and European poetry and novels and groped their way toward an authentic American voice. Some writers, such as Juana Manuela Gorriti of Argentina, had to flee political unrest at home. Gorriti, safely in Lima, Peru, after a brief and unhappy marriage to a Bolivian president, joined other writers in *tertulias* (discussion groups) where they read and talked about their work (Chapter 8). Music, even opera, had wide popular appeal. Mexicans took pride in Angela Peralta's fame as an interpreter of the great European operas and in her efforts to write and perform truly Mexican works (Chapter 11).

Although shaken by conflicts between anticlerical and conservative forces, the Catholic church still dominated education and retained its colonial aura of grandeur and formality in major cities. In the countryside or on the frontier, priests like José de Calasanz Vela in Colombia might be found who emulated the selfless dedication and devotion of early sixteenth-century friars (Chapter 10). The small circles of educated elites sometimes felt alienated from their own nations and from the Europe they so admired. The mestizo Juan Bustamante longed for his fellow Peruvians to become more modern, more like Europeans, but he also criticized the inhumane conditions that had accompanied industrialism (Chapter 6). Many Latin American urbanites were, like their famous contemporary Domingo F. Sarmiento, author of *Life in the Argentine Republic in the Days of the Tyrants; or, Civilization and Barbarism,* simultaneously attracted to and repelled by their crude compatriots.

Most people in Latin America lived in rural areas and small villages, distant from the few comforts and amusements offered by the cities. In the countryside, nature—and human beings—remained untamed and relatively untamable. Political rebels as well as bandits commandeered horses, cattle, and crops. The new republican governments, based in major cities and allied with urban elites, struggled to replace imperial justice and administration in the volatile countryside. They had little success. Political and family feuds could poison an entire region; the feuds intensified whenever they became linked to national political parties or leaders. Carlota Lucia de Brito's story demonstrates how in Brazil a local feud intersected with Liberal and Conservative politics, leading to violence and tragedy in the untamed northeastern state of Pernambuco. Punishment ultimately came from the distant imperial government in Rio de Janeiro, and a temporary order was achieved (Chapter 7). In Paraguay, a relatively homogeneous and compact nation dominated by a traditional caudillo president, a judge drew on Hispanic legal tradition to defuse the conflict between Rosa Dominga Ocampos and her Spanish lover. In this case, the judge ensured social harmony by seeing that neither party lost face before the community (Chapter 5).

Sometimes the country, towns, or indigenous peoples rose up against the capital cities and the political and economic control they represented. By the 1870s most Latin American countries had experienced at least one major conflict pitting the provinces against the capital city. In Peru the rebellion that Juan Bustamante reluctantly headed had regional as well as indigenous roots since indigenous communities had strong agricultural and familial ties to their regions. Even when the provinces won, as happened in 1852 in Argentina, the cities proved too strong to be dominated. Ultimately, the cities triumphed over their captors, suggesting either that the outsiders had fought primarily to join the elite or that urban culture, with its ties to Europe, was too powerful to be overcome.

What of the special regions called frontiers? On the fringes of empire— to the far south in Argentina and Chile, in the Amazon or backlands of the Brazilian *sertão,* in the Venezuelan Orinoco or Guayana highlands, in the Colombian llanos, to the far north in Mexico—there frequently remained groups of unconquered Indians. Unlike indigenous settlements nearer to the European and mestizo population cores, the Indians who lived on the fringes dwelt in relative peace for the early part of the century. But as commercial agriculture and mining expanded, and as settlers fanned out from more populated areas, soldiers and priests began pacification of the frontier peoples. On the Argentine pampas, Calfurcá and his son Namuncurá, like their Indian counterparts in the trans-Mississippi west in the United States, at first lived unmolested by the national government. By the 1880s, however, they had succumbed to the rush of soldiers, speculators, and ranchers into their homeland (Chapter 12).

One's chances in life varied with residence in city, town, country, or frontier; with personal or family connections; with access to land or skills; with race; and with gender. Although many independence leaders espoused the liberal goal of freedom from servitude for all peoples, practical political and economic concerns meant that many blacks remained either enslaved or apprenticed until midcentury (or later, in the cases of Cuba and Brazil). Racial discrimination was more subtle than it was in the United States, but it existed. Most Creoles and persons of more European appearance looked down upon blacks, *castas,* and Indians as less civilized than themselves and perhaps incapable of improvement. The elite's political principles followed from their misguided social assumptions.

It is more difficult to generalize about what changes women experienced in the first decades after independence. At times, and in some places, it appears that wealthy or elite women were able to escape some of the restrictions enforced against their sisters. Some women, such as Soledad Román de Núñez, even could wield power and influence in national politics, acting through their husbands or fathers (Chapter 9). Soledad's history reminds us too of the power and influence of Encarnación, the famed wife of the Argentine caudillo Juan Manuel de Rosas. Of course, presidents and their wives could more easily escape the restrictions that constrained other, less grand individuals. Juana Manuela Gorriti and, for a while, Angela Peralta seemed to enjoy unconventional lives of freedom and ease. Yet they also suffered for their freedom, and they achieved their greatest happiness when they refrained from straying too far from cultural norms. In other cases, notions of family honor and pride seem to have limited wealthy women more than they did their poorer sisters. Rosa Dominga Ocampos, a nonelite woman of Paraguay, apparently enjoyed a good deal of personal and sexual freedom.

Some studies have suggested that women found their opportunities and status in 1850 reduced from what they had been under the Bourbon monarchs. Other researchers have pointed out that after independence *tertulias,* charitable organizations, and political conflicts may have given women some space in which to increase their experience, autonomy, and influence. It is difficult to determine the extent to which gender affected people's lives quite apart from questions of class, residence, race, and education.

What was the relationship between the social history as seen in these essays and the turbulent political history of the period? Perhaps the bitter civil wars reflected, in part, personal ambitions (Carlota Lucia de Brito), ethnic or regional frustration with central governments (Juan Bustamante), or, even, a kind of anomie and confusion that followed the erosion of the Iberian colonial order. Liberal and Conservative parties advanced and defended their rival political programs, but historians have suggested that overt ideological cleavages represented only one level of what really was at stake.

In some ways the nineteenth-century conflicts meant a continuation of the hopes of the Independence Wars. In the very broadest terms, people fought over whether to recreate the enlightened Iberian society of the late eighteenth century or the liberal, western European society of the nineteenth century. In more personal terms, people struggled to keep or to expand any small advantage that they possessed, sometimes by calling on old traditions, sometimes by embracing modern ways. By the 1870s, after fifty years of struggle, the issue had been resolved largely in favor of the liberal European modernizers. The excitement and appeal of these early years of national life are in that one can see real alternatives competing for control of the future. How might Latin America be different today if Juan Bustamante had won, or if all judges had been as wise as one Paraguayan jurist and all communities as closely knit as that of Rosa Dominga Ocampos in Paraguay?

5

Rosa Dominga Ocampos:
A Matter of Honor in Paraguay

Thomas L. Whigham

Historians have paid scant attention to Paraguay. An isolated colonial backwater, this peaceful agricultural region, populated by friendly Guaraní Indians, developed into a mestizo society that generally lacked the extremes of wealth and poverty found in more important parts of the empire. The Jesuits chose Paraguay as a hospitable field in which to develop an extensive and idealistic mission area. Paraguayan leaders, much like the Central American elites who scorned union with Mexico, chose autonomy over absorption into the Argentine confederation at the time of independence.

The early republican history of Paraguay often has been dismissed as a simple tale of backward caudillos (José Gaspar Rodríguez de Francia, 1816–1840; Carlos Antonio López, 1840–1862, and his son, Francisco Solano López, 1862–1870). The inland nation seemed oblivious to the liberal European values that represented progress and that were beginning to penetrate some of the other Latin American countries. Historians cite the disastrous War of the Triple Alliance (1865–1870), which robbed Paraguay of 60 percent of its male population, as further evidence of the irresponsibility of traditional caudillos. Yet if Paraguay's splendid backwardness is examined more closely, one finds that its caudillos tried to reconcile economic development with the maintenance of traditional communal values. Some of these Hispanic and mestizo values even may have offered a more effective, and less costly, development model than that provided by Europeanized urban society.

The progress of the 1847 legal suit in which Rosa Dominga Ocampos sued her Spanish lover for breach of promise reveals both positive and negative aspects of López's Paraguay. A woman's honor was analogous legally to a possession that could be stolen, and even a woman of modest social background could go to court and insist on compensation. Women had limited legal and civil rights, but Rosa could appear before the court alone without the intercession of a male relative. Paraguayan society, although tightly knit, was no egalitarian utopia, however. Whereas Paraguayans accorded their former Spanish masters high status and respect, even though they sometimes resented them, they discriminated against people of darker skin and considered them to be inferior. Perhaps most significantly, Thomas Whigham's essay demonstrates the tension between the community's desire to compensate an individual for his or her grievances and its longing to guarantee community harmony by encouraging a truce or reconciliation between litigants.

Thomas Whigham received his Ph.D. from Stanford University in 1986 and is an assistant professor of history at the University of Georgia. He joins a new generation of historians in directing attention to the uniqueness and creativity of Paraguay in the critical transitional period from 1750 to 1880. Whigham has published several articles on commerce, cattle raising, the tobacco trade, and industry in the Upper Plata River region during this time.

A visitor to Paraguay in the midnineteenth century would discover a land that was quiet and isolated in the extreme. The great muddy rivers that surrounded the inland republic gave it a picturesque appearance as they bathed its verdant landscape, rich with flowering trees and all manner of exotic plants and animals. Yet these same waters had long served as a barrier, as a warning sign that Paraguay wanted no truck with the outside world. Nearly thirty years had passed since the taciturn dictator and doctor of theology José Gaspar Rodríguez de Francia first elaborated a policy of nonintercourse with neighboring states, a policy well justified by the violent political realities of the day. Both Francia and his corpulent successor, Carlos Antonio López, faced the threat of foreign expansionism and both adamantly refused to accept anything less than recognition of national independence. Paraguayan society might prosper or decline, they believed, but only on terms that were specifically Paraguayan in context.

The authoritarian nature and staunch isolationism of Paraguay's government encountered no resistance in the countryside. There the tiny landed elite pursued its traditional interest in stockraising, while the small farmer, or *kokuejara*, occupied himself with the cultivation of maize, tobacco, and manioc root. Social life was in every way limited to the family, the church, and the *pulpería* (general store). And if infusions of information and new habits from beyond the frontier were few, they were not much missed in a rustic world dominated by Hispanic values. The dictators in Asunción might periodically take advantage of foreign contacts in commerce, but rarely did any outside influences trickle down to the average Paraguayan, whose passive acquiescence in this unchanging pattern of life was generally taken for granted.

So it had always been for Rosa Dominga Ocampos, a young woman of modest background from the interior farming village of Capiatá. Until the late 1840s she contented herself with the usual pursuits of girlhood in the Paraguayan countryside. These included domestic chores, babysitting, tending animals, rolling cigars, and preparing the maté gourd in which was drunk yerba maté, the fragrant green tea so popular throughout the southern third of the continent. As she matured, her thoughts probably focused more and more on marriage, perhaps with a wealthy older man who could provide for both her and her mother. This is where the trouble started. In 1847, now at age twenty-four, Ocampos became the victim of mean-hearted local gossips who claimed that she was about to bear a child out of wedlock. The squabble that ensued might have gone unnoticed were it not for her reaction. Rather than meekly accept the damage that malicious rumor might cause her reputation, Ocampos decided to fight back through legal means.

Estupro (seduction or breach of promise if the woman consented voluntarily to the sex act) was a serious offense under Spanish legal precepts. An individual's reputation was central to the scheme of balances within the community, and a charge of *estupro* could upset all of these balances. Only a woman with a good reputation could bring such a charge before the authorities since known prostitutes and "women of loose morals" had no legal recourse against mistreatment. Nonetheless, in the Paraguay of the 1840s it was still odd for any woman who felt wronged by her lover or betrothed to appeal to the law.

The judicial system available to Rosa Dominga Ocampos inherited much from the colonial past, including an array of vaguely defined rural judgeships. In some districts, municipal *delegados* (military commanders) fulfilled judicial as well as administrative functions. Regardless of the nomenclature, all judges were responsible to and appointed by the central government in Asunción.

Ocampos, in testing the legal waters, first met in a short session with a *juez territorial,* the Paraguayan equivalent of a circuit judge, and he evidently advised her to drop the matter. She flatly refused. In early 1848 she decided to bypass intermediate levels and recorded her complaint with the interim vice president of the republic, Juan José Alvarenga. The latter had been an important jurist even during the colonial period, and perhaps Ocampos expected him to give her case a careful and sympathetic analysis.

In the *demanda* (complaint), Ocampos maintained that life in Capiatá had become difficult for her. Having lost her father at an early age, she now faced the shameless gossip of local busybodies. Specifically, she had become romantically linked with a Spanish resident, Martín de Abazolo, who had taken full advantage of the "weakness of her sex." Having plied her with assurances of his love and a promise of marriage, Abazolo had slept with her on several occasions, or so she claimed.

Ocampos swore that she had taken Abazolo at his word—for he was a gentleman—and that the two even had gone so far as to petition Carlos Antonio López for permission to wed. Government consent was needed because Dr. Francia earlier had outlawed marriage between Paraguayans and the hated Spaniards. Although in dealing with foreigners López often acted with as much caprice as Francia, he nevertheless recently had seen fit to alter the marriage law on a case-by-case basis. Perhaps López thought to curry the favor of individuals who, although no longer a threat to the state, could potentially strengthen the regime through their support. In any case, on this occasion, as with other elderly Spaniards marrying their local paramours, López evidently offered no objections, and Ocampos began to plan her trousseau.

Almost overnight, however, the relationship began to turn sour. Abazolo appeared at the Ocampos residence less and less and, when confronted with these absences, made a startling accusation: he claimed that his now former fiancée had become pregnant by a mulatto who worked in her household. This was indeed a serious charge. As in other areas of Spanish America, Paraguay maintained a culture that was deeply conscious of race. Any mention of a possible dalliance with a mulatto could spell social ruin, even for someone from a relatively poor background. This explains the eagerness with which Ocampos sought to clear her name, as well as her willingness to pay the high fees for stamped paper (on which all state petitions had to be written) and for the services of legal advisers and professional scribes. Given the gravity of the issue involved, Ocampos had no intention of allowing her own illiteracy to stand in the way of vindication. She knew that a relationship with a European, even an illicit one, might bring considerable advantages, but with a mulatto, never!

In her plea to Alvarenga, Ocampos presented herself as the aggrieved party. She was not, in fact, pregnant, as a visit to a midwife in nearby Pirayú had confirmed, nor had she experienced a miscarriage. Abazolo's betrayal and false public utterings, she maintained, made it impossible for her to remain silent. As her reputation was irretrievably tarnished, she demanded some kind of compensation from the Spaniard. Ocampos emphasized that she acted not out of malice "but only to obtain vindication, to satisfy her gravely offended honor."

Even if her portrayal of these events was basically accurate, Ocampos clearly stood to gain from any xenophobic feelings she might encounter in Alvarenga. Since late colonial times, when they controlled the all-important Asunción *cabildo* (city council), Europeans had been regarded in Paraguay with some distrust. Although always a small minority in the country, they possessed a commercial acumen that brought them success even in bad times, and Paraguayans envied as much as hated them.

The local Spaniards proved the obvious victims of the 1811 *cuartelazo* (barracks revolt), which brought independence to Paraguay. Given the uncompromising spirit of the times, it was no surprise when the new revolutionary junta sought to wrest control of the bureaucracy from the Spaniards. But the Paraguayans went even further, casually stripping their former colonial masters of any influence in commerce and in the church. Abandoning the idealistic platitudes of equality and brotherhood for a less lofty expediency, the government erected stiff precautionary measures against all Spaniards, from the lowliest day worker to the highest member of the mercantile elite. In this manner, the Paraguayans gave vent to their hatred.

Dr. Francia, himself the son of a foreigner, was no exception. As supreme dictator, he strove to dismantle those institutions most visibly connected with the Europeans, not excluding the priesthood, which he reshaped to suit his own needs. Inclined to suspicion by his temper and situation, Francia took no chances, and beginning in the late 1810s, he exiled those Europeans whom he considered dangerous and harassed those who remained in Asunción with massive fines and forced contributions. Adding humiliation to contempt, he also forbade them from riding horseback, a traditional perquisite of gentlemen. In response to such pressures, many Spaniards fled into the countryside, where they hoped to lead quiet lives until the advent of a more sympathetic regime. There Europeans like Abazolo invested their capital in land and cattle, kept their heads low, and secured informal alliances with Paraguayan women.

In his own account before Alvarenga, Abazolo protested his complete innocence and sought to portray Rosa Dominga Ocampos as little more than a common gold digger. He had been the victim throughout and not Ocampos, toward whom he had always shown the proper decorum. After all, had he not been the one to formulate the marriage contract in the first place and to seek the appropriate licenses from the president of the republic? Abazolo was at least in his midfifties at the time and in all of his years in Paraguay had never made trouble for the government. Now a village hussy had made a fool of him by charging him with *estupro*. He was in no mood to be generous.

According to Abazolo, the real trouble had started when word reached him that Ocampos had boasted publicly of being pregnant, a great surprise to him indeed since, despite her claim to the contrary, they had never shared a bed. The Spaniard stated that the woman refused to confirm or deny her pregnancy, which was, to his way of thinking, a tacit confession of wrongdoing. Moreover, she declined to return any of the gifts he had given her, although he had tried on several occasions to reclaim them.

Still further evidence of Ocampos's illicit behavior soon came to light. Her mulatto lover, Domingo Benítez, actually visited Abazolo and confirmed the nature of his relation with Ocampos. Other citizens of Capiatá then stepped forward to swear that they also had knowledge of her pregnancy. As for the midwife's report, this Abazolo dismissed out of hand. The woman might conceivably have miscarried at some point in the recent past, but that she had been pregnant by Benítez was beyond doubt.

If anyone's honor had been offended, Abazolo concluded, surely it was his own. He stood accused of seduction and breach of promise, both completely specious charges, and the woman who denounced him had been manifestly unfaithful and was therefore unworthy of the government's consideration. Her "lack of morals had corrupted the neighborhood," and Abazolo begged the interim vice president to silence her once and for all.

At the distance of over 140 years it is difficult to choose between the merits of the different charges and countercharges. Standards of evidence in 1840s Paraguay allowed for the admission of hearsay, and sifting through the many layers of rumor would present a formidable task in any event. On the surface, Abazolo's case is the weaker. His litany of witnesses is not supported by sworn affidavits in the extant documentation. At the same time, an alleged pregnancy should have offered easy opportunities for confirmation, but no record exists to show that this was done. For her part, Ocampos was hardly a disinterested party, but a preponderance of evidence does seem to favor her position.

In the end, Alvarenga's approach to the whole matter proved less than Solomonic. Falling back on his legal prerogatives, he passed all of the paperwork on to lower officials and requested a judgment from a district-level justice of the peace, José de la Paz Berges. Although only in his midtwenties, Berges already had made a name for himself as an efficient functionary of the López government and had risen quickly in the state bureaucracy. His later career was likewise notable and included service as Paraguayan delegate to a mixed-claims commission in Washington, DC, and a stint as foreign minister of the republic before and during the disastrous Triple Alliance War (1865–1870).

In his resolution of the Ocampos-Abazolo difficulties, Berges rendered a judgment in keeping with common sense and with Paraguayan social reality. The small society of Capiatá would be rife with intrigue and jealousy in any case and what the present situation called for was maximum toleration and flexibility. Therefore, Berges ordered the two parties to attempt a reconciliation, to forget their past differences and recriminations, and to work out a solution that could salvage honor on both sides. He granted them five days in which to present a plan.

On May 15, 1848, Berges approved the final terms of reconciliation between Rosa Dominga Ocampos and Martín de Abazolo. The latter agreed to pay the young woman thirty-four pesos in silver as a token of sincere regret over the whole affair, and in accepting this rather generous sum—enough to purchase a small herd of cattle—Ocampos effectively brought the relationship back full circle. In closing the case, Berges declared both parties essentially blameless. True, they had fallen victim to malicious gossip, but none of this loose talk had any basis in fact. No *estupro* had occurred. If they now desired, they were free to continue their lives together with their reputations intact. And this is exactly what Berges advised them to do; the government had spoken.

The judicial records do not indicate whether the couple continued on the path to a happy marriage. One suspects that Abazolo was angry for having lost so much cash, but he could have regained the money simply by marrying the woman. No matter—from the viewpoint of the state, it was enough that order had been restored to the community and that Berges had mandated a "Christian reconciliation." Whether that really ended the matter or not is something we doubtless shall never know.

The case of Rosa Dominga Ocampos and Martín de Abazolo illustrates much about Paraguayan society in the midnineteenth century. For one thing, it shows how a small-town environment easily transformed idle gossip into a heated legal feud. To be sure, Paraguay was not alone in this regard; a similar chain of events might well be imagined in rural areas of the United States or Europe in precisely the same historical period.

What, then, is specifically Paraguayan about this whole affair? The answer lies in the unusual degree to which Hispanic legal tradition retained its force within the independent republic. Certain social theorists have mistakenly argued that the process of nation building ripped apart much of the older sense of community, leaving little more than a void in its place. This phenomenon, it is supposed, explains the nearly desperate search for identity that Latin Americans experience in the present day. In Paraguay, however, traditional values clearly lived on after independence, with the state periodically intervening, as in this instance, to reinforce established standards of behavior. Elsewhere, French, and to a much lesser degree North American, models already had begun to erode the old patterns. Paraguay was different. As an absolutist in the Bourbon mold rather than a Bolívar-style revolutionary, Dr. Francia modified only those elements of the colonial system that might restrain his authoritarian leadership. In almost all other respects, the tenor of the colonial past remained fixed in Paraguay, even years after Francia's death. Changes did occur under Carlos Antonio López, but only very slowly.

For Rosa Dominga Ocampos, there was something beneficial in all this, since the conservative traditions permitted a direct appeal to the highest authorities for advice as well as judgment. Alvarenga and Berges acted as manifestations of the paterfamilias principle, each guiding the litigants with a fatherly hand in the direction of a satisfactory reconciliation. That Ocampos should turn to the state for help might surprise those who view Hispanic culture as a sort of prison for women. Ocampos knew differently. Primitive and isolated though it might be, Paraguay still afforded her ample opportunities to press for restitution of her honor.

SOURCES

Documentation on Rosa Dominga Ocampos, including all affidavits and pleas, can be found in Asunción's National Archive, Sección Nueva Encuadernación, vol. 2680. This archive, especially its Sección Judicial Criminal, also provided many details as to legal procedure in 1840s Paraguay.

6

Civilization and Its Barbarism: The Inevitability of Juan Bustamante's Failure

Nils P. Jacobsen

Indian relations continued to trouble the new republics, especially in regions such as the Andes where indigenous populations were the majority. Peru, rich in minerals and administered by a large colonial bureaucracy, spawned a conservative creole elite anxious to protect its wealth and privileges. Such self-interest, coupled with colonial tradition, provoked perhaps the greatest failure of the new republics: their inability to develop a creative and humane pattern of Indian-European relations. Critics veered between well-meaning reformist efforts to turn the Indians into Europeans and periods of equally well-meaning paternalistic protection that often isolated and ignored the indigenous communities, except during times of tax and tribute collection.

Juan Bustamante, born in Peru in 1808 of a creole father and a mestiza mother, grew up to be a politician, a writer, an advocate for Indians, and, reluctantly, a leader of the Indian rebellion in 1867. His own complex view of civilization and barbarism was derived not only from his Peruvian experience but also from his travels around the world.

Bustamante found the roles of social critic and reformer nearly impossible to play. Like most liberals, he was both ambivalent about the value of indigenous traditions and frustrated by the entrenched elites who rejected all reform. At the same time, he tortured himself with the belief that reform would provoke an irreconcilable clash between anarchy and authoritarianism, for, if Indians were allowed to do as they wanted, would not they be idle or constantly threaten society with rebellion, the definition of *anarchy*? On the other hand, officials and hacendados clearly abused and exploited Indians in ways that brooked no possibility of individual or community advancement. Perhaps the greatest tragedy for individuals such as Bustamante was that a critic could neither entirely betray his own class nor wholeheartedly join the indigenous communities.

We might consider, too, the means by which a critic could have his voice heard. Should it be through writing? election to congress? working within the system for gradual change? promoting armed rebellion? What factors might dictate the choice of tactics?

82

Nils Jacobsen, assistant professor of history at the University of Illinois, Urbana, has studied land tenure and society in the Peruvian altiplano between 1770 and 1920, the long nineteenth century. His interest has been especially in the region's agricultural, economic, and social history, topics on which he has published widely in Spanish, German, and English. He is coeditor with Hans-Jürgen Puhle of *The Economies of Mexico and Peru during the Late Colonial Period, 1760–1810* (1986) and, with Joseph Love, of *Guiding the Invisible Hand: Economic Liberalism and the State in Latin American History* (1988).

Juan Bustamante was born in Peru in 1808 in the small altiplano hamlet of Vilque some twenty miles northwest of the departmental capital of Puno. The altiplano is the vast Andean grassland plain that surrounds Lake Titicaca. Since pre-Hispanic times the wealth of the region had consisted in herds of llamas, alpacas, and, after the Spanish conquest, cattle and sheep. In a region with over 90 percent Indian peasants and estate laborers, Juan was born into a family of relative privilege and wealth. His father, a Creole from the city of Arequipa, served as junior officer in royal Spanish militia units in the altiplano. His mother had been born in Vilque where she inherited several livestock haciendas. Family lore has it that she was a descendant of Túpac Amaru I, the last Inca, executed by order of the Spanish Viceroy Francisco de Toledo in 1572. Whatever the veracity of this claim, it is clear that Juan's mother was a mestiza and that Juan considered himself of mixed racial ancestry. A portrait fashioned of him in Paris when he was forty years old shows an elegantly dressed, dark-skinned man with well-groomed hair and a prominent nose. But it is Bustamante's large, black eyes that most captivate the viewer. They are penetrating and intense, yet at the same time melancholic and sad. They lend his demeanor a gentle but disturbing seriousness.

Juan's restlessness was evident from his earliest childhood. He was happiest when he was roaming the wide pampas and exploring craggy cliffs and mysterious pre-Hispanic ruins together with his Indian playmates. His propensity to run away from home exasperated his parents so much that they kept Juan tied to a chair "for one fourth part of my childhood," as he later recalled. A stern upbringing that also relied upon flogging as an educational tool was as unexceptional in Peru as in many other societies during the nineteenth century. Yet the harsh discipline may go a long way toward explaining why Juan later felt merely respect for his father, whereas he deeply loved his mother with her "angelical temper."

Later in life Juan also held a grudge against his father because "he did not procure [for] me an education commensurate with his middle class income." To be sure, schools were few and far between in rural Peru during the waning years of Spanish rule and the early postindependence period. But most sons (and a very few daughters) of respectable families were sent to secondary schools in the departmental capital or to Arequipa or Cuzco, where some might even go on to take a degree at the university in law, theology, or medicine. Juan received primary instruction with a priest in Cabanilla, a hamlet only a few miles from his native Vilque. There he learned basic reading, writing, and arithmetic, along with a heavy dose of religious instruction. The religious teaching reinforced the strong, if somewhat conventional, sense of religiosity that his father sought to imbue in him, probably the major paternal legacy that would stay with Juan for the rest of his life.

After four or five years of formal education, there occurred a strange hiatus. During his teenage years, Juan seems to have led "the crazy life of a local town bohemian": endless public and private parties with his peers, amorous adventures, wild races across the pampas and through rivers to prove his prowess in horsemanship, and searching, late-night discussions over candlelight about the state of a world apparently coming apart at the seams with the end of Spanish rule. To escape the boredom of Vilque, he spent weeks or months with relatives and family friends in the provincial capital of Lampa or in the splendid city of Arequipa. This pleasant, aimless life was occasionally interrupted by business deals or by more purposeful activity on the family's livestock estates. Before he was twenty years old, Bustamante did attend secondary school in Puno for a few years, but he apparently failed to complete the course of studies.

This was to be the sum total of Juan's formal education. Perhaps his own restlessness and unease at conforming to other people's rules accounted for his limited schooling more than his father's neglect did. Bustamante would later write of himself that "in nature's distribution of attributes and talents my share has been somewhat scarce." Yet he was anything but dull. Throughout life he eagerly tried to understand anything new, whether a machine, a social institution, a government policy, a monument, or a work of art. He acquired some, albeit unsystematic, knowledge of European literature and history. By middle age, he could write acceptable romantic-style prose. In short, Juan Bustamante showed all the marks of an autodidact.

During the late 1820s, Bustamante began his working life in earnest. He set up shop as a wool trader in Cabanilla, site of his early lessons. He sold wool from his family's estates and from peasants and other estate owners in various parts of the altiplano. The purchasers usually were European merchants who had established themselves in Arequipa after the Spanish defeat in late 1824. Juan dispatched strings of mules or llamas loaded with bales of sorted wool over Andean passes to the entrepôt city. The muleteers, either laborers from his estates or independent entrepreneurs, returned with alcohol, dried peppers, raisins, sugar, or a few European imports, which Bustamante offered to his business friends in the altiplano. He himself traveled from one end of the altiplano to the other, from the valleys around Cuzco to La Paz and to the eastern escarpment of the Andes, in order to establish new business contacts and to find new sources of supply of wool or other regional commodities. He attended the annual trade fairs, the most important of which was held in his native Vilque. For three or four weeks each year around Pentecost in late May, the little town would be filled with thousands of merchants, hacendados, peasants, and muleteers selling everything from Manchester cottons to Argentine mules, quinine, wool, and gold.

By all accounts Bustamante did very well as a wool trader. Having entered the market in the late 1820s during the slump that had followed the brief initial European euphoria about trade with hitherto inaccessible Spanish America, he saw his business grow with the rapid increase in wool exports from southern Peru between 1835 and 1840. Bustamante earned money well in excess of what he needed for his modest life-style in rural Peru. Throughout his life he always considered making money "a good thing," to be encouraged for Peru's progress as long as the profits were based on honest work. He repeatedly remarked, with a sense of pride and satisfaction, that his Peruvian silver pesos spoke loudly and clearly during his journeys abroad whenever some haughty foreigner tried to snub him for his uncommon appearance.

Business success in southern Peru during the midnineteenth century was unthinkable without establishing an extensive web of personal ties of trust and mutual obligations with business associates, transport entrepreneurs, local and provincial authorities, and Indian peasants. Bustamante's successful wool trade thus can be read as a measure of the respect that he earned for himself in the region. Before he was thirty years old he had held local offices in Cabanilla, where he spent personal funds for public works, such as construction of a bridge and canalization of a river to provide potable water, to benefit the little town. His behavior in all his subsequent administrative and elective offices was marked similarly by probity, complete lack of self-interest, and dedication to securing some positive benefits for his constituency. These were unusual qualities in Peru during a time when many worthy individuals treated the national revenues as pigs would a trough of slops. Graft and opportunism were rampant. Bustamante viewed himself as somewhat of a "gentleman politician" for whom public service was a sacrifice for the good of the *patria*. He chose to serve the country rather than to advance his own personal fortune through private business.

In 1839, Bustamante was elected deputy to the national congress for his native province of Lampa. By then he was disgusted with the early republican government in Peru, in particular, with its domination by military caudillos. He had grown up as a true child of the country's independence struggle. Born a year before the popular struggles against Spanish domination reached the Andes, Bustamante came of age just as the conclusive battle of Ayacucho sealed Peruvian independence in December 1824. Six months later during Simón Bolívar's triumphant tour through the southern Andes, the notables in Puno eulogized him as if he were a deity. That brief era of emancipatory, nationalistic liberalism gave Bustamante's political orientation its first powerful imprint. The equality of the Indian—now called "Peruvian" under the law—the removal of restrictions on trade, the abolition of many privileges, and the ambitious plans for a broad-based laicized educational system were all sanctified by legislation in the 1820s and remained crucial goals in Bustamante's own political agenda throughout his life. As evidence of the importance he gave to the early republican legislation, in 1867 he reprinted, in both Spanish and Quechua, a key bolivarian decree of July 4, 1825, which outlawed personal services and forced labor by Indians.

By 1839 it was clear that the early liberal republican program had failed. Privileges, even without legal sanction, were alive and well. The Indians continued to be exploited as before. Schools, except perhaps in Lima and a few other cities, remained scarce, traditional, and ineffective. To be sure, Bustamante believed that under the short-lived Peru-Bolivian confederation, forged by Andrés Santa Cruz between 1836 and 1839, the Indians' situation briefly had improved. He considered Santa Cruz's regime the only one "that was good," that respected the property and dignity of its citizens, during the first quarter century of Peruvian independence.

Unfortunately, the congress that Bustamante attended in 1839 and 1840 was dominated by the adherents of the caudillo Marshal Agustín Gamarra, who with Chilean help had just defeated Santa Cruz's confederation. Not surprisingly, Bustamante found much of the congress's work "filled with absurdities" and "malintentioned." He disapproved of the strengthening of the powers of the executive, the undermining of the independent judiciary, and the extensive concessions to the military. He expressed disappointment with the ineffectiveness and lack of resolution of the congress, which had done "nothing, absolutely nothing for the good of the people, and from our deliberations only flow unjust approbations of pensions and unconstitutional pecuniary remunerations."

In good part Bustamante blamed the provincial deputies for their inability to resist the blandishments of the omnipotent executive. A deputy would leave his province full of civic virtue and enthusiasm; he had a hundred projects and plans in mind to benefit the country, and he knew exactly what he had to achieve for the good of his province. But once he arrives in the capital, "he takes his seat on the bench in the chamber, he makes out the staircase of the [government] palace, manages to climb it, the air of the high place obfuscates his senses, he forgets his propositions and from the first day he resolutely votes against the very ideas which he had planned to promote." In short, by hundreds of mechanisms, the president knew how "to domesticate" most congressional deputies, and still their home provinces continued to reelect them.

His bitter experience in congress contributed to Bustamante's decision to take a journey around the world between 1841 and 1844. Yet scarcely had he returned when, in 1845, Bustamante once more agreed to represent his province in the congress. He was elected subsequently to the important Constitutional Convention of 1855–1857. None of these congresses, however, approved any of his legislative proposals. He put forward the election of bishops, the establishment of free schools in every district, the construction of roads throughout the republic, limitations on the executive's power to grant military promotions, and the reestablishment of debtors' prison to enforce contracts at a time when debts routinely went unpaid. Bustamante, refusing to become a "domesticated" partisan of any political faction, attacked all factions without fail. It is not surprising that many of the politicians, pamphleteers, and newspaper writers of the day found it easy to isolate him by ridiculing him or declaring him crazy.

His travels and his rather unusual travel accounts also contributed to the elites' tendency to stamp Bustamante as an odd outsider and a nuisance. The elites were annoyed and incredulous at Bustamante's incessant hectoring about Peru's backwardness and corruption and at his audacious presentation of some of the dark side of European progress. Furthermore, European travel had long been a rare privilege for a few aristocrats. How could a provincial mestizo of scant education dare to spend five years exploring the world and interpreting it to them?

Juan Bustamante's *Viaje al antiguo mundo por el Peruano Juan Bustamante, natural del departamento de Puno,* printed in two editions in Lima in 1845, was the first travel account about the Eastern Hemisphere published by a Peruvian, possibly by any Latin American. Bustamante's much longer and more ambitious *Apuntes y observaciones civiles, políticas y religiosas con las noticias adquiridas en este segundo viaje a la Europa* appeared four years later in Paris.

His first journey, begun in May 1841, took Bustamante by way of Panama, Jamaica, and Cuba to the eastern seaboard of the United States. He was impressed by the bustle of New York, by the trains and stagecoaches running like clockwork, by model social institutions like the Philadelphia prison, and by the industriousness of the population. Yet he retained ambiguous feelings about the North Americans.

> The inhabitants show in their dress and customs a mixture of colonial liveliness and English gravity; they display urbaneness, joyfulness and hospitality; the ladies have a fresh look, are well formed and too well educated. Generally the North Americans are robust, educated mostly towards work; they have little compassion for others. Everyone is seeking his own well-being, and even the children are not treated with the same love which one notes in other countries. Parents educate them well until they can take care of their own subsistence and [the parents] believe they have no further obligations. After reaching puberty the children are separated from the paternal house.

From Boston, he journeyed to Liverpool, England, where he spent two months visiting every factory in town. He continued on to London, Paris, Madrid, Rome, Naples, Vienna, the Ottoman Empire, Athens, Damascus, Jerusalem, Cairo, and places in between. From the Red Sea, he took a steamer to Calcutta, Macao, and China and finally back across the Pacific to Valparaiso, Chile, and then home in March 1844 to conclude his four-year odyssey.

He visited and inspected factories, banks, post offices, cathedrals, and museums and attended theater productions and opera. He incessantly asked questions and made comparisons. Spain appeared poor and backward compared with France, but he praised Madrid and its people and recommended that Peru establish close commercial and cultural ties to its former metropolis. In spite of France's modernity, he criticized the French for the stagnant water in the bay at Marseilles, which he thought a danger to public health. He had an audience with Pope Gregory XVI and, after kissing the pope's feet, received indulgences down to the third generation.

Upon reaching the Ottoman Empire, the tone of Bustamante's observations shifted. He had held preconceived notions about the "despotism" and "semi-barbarism" of the Turks. In spite of continuing to believe that Peru was in "a better state of culture than Turkey," he saw all manner of parallels between his native altiplano and the rural landscapes and customs of the Balkans. The textiles were similar to the fine *cumpis* (high-quality woolen of Incaic origin); the Moldavians drank a fermented beverage very similar to Peruvian *chicha*; and the sad music of Vidin, capital of Bulgaria, reminded him of Peruvian *huayños*. He concluded that the parallels could be explained by the fact that "disgrace, misery and slavery, continued for various centuries, . . . can form very distant countries in the same manner, with the same character and customs." Just as with Peru, he concluded that only bad government and pernicious social customs kept the Ottoman Empire from progressing.

Along the banks of the Nile, he was struck with compassion for the Egyptian fellaheen. The captain of his boat told him that when the floods arrived the many people who lived in miserable villages along the Nile would drown, together with the few heads of their livestock that had survived a recent epidemic. Bustamante mused that "in my thoughts during that night I knew that, of the inhabitants of the world, not even one eighth can be called happy. The rest are extremely unfortunate. I plan to conserve this idea, to learn to overcome spells of bad fortune and suffer them with resignation."

Bustamante observed that the Chinese were extremely hostile to foreigners, and, in response, he characterized them as "the worst people" he had encountered. Still, typical of his sympathy for the underdog, he attributed the hostility in part to the efforts of the English to force China to trade.

> But, thinking about it calmly, one has to confess that [the Chinese] are right in abhorring us and labeling us the *foreign demon* [italics in original]; they have been provoked for no other reason than insatiable covetousness. They have lived peacefully without offending anybody for innumerable centuries. . . . To oblige them by force to enter into relations [with foreign nations] seems a barbaric thing. They now have to defend themselves and once they become ambitious, as is natural, and being so numerous, they will one day conquer the whole world.

Although he initially was happier than he had ever been to return to his home in Cabanilla, within a year Bustamante again became impatient with the course of Peru's public affairs. By mid-1845 the nation was in the midst of the most chaotic civil war period of its young history. Again Bustamante saw nothing good coming from the congress to which he had been elected. "It is impossible for me to stay with good humor in Peru," he wrote, "where I will never see anything but backwardness, decadence, ruin. . . . The actual state of affairs for me is a foreboding of a horrible future."

Three years later, in early 1848, he left Peru for his second journey abroad. He again visited England and France, where he witnessed the June revolution of that year. He traveled on to Belgium and the Netherlands, northern Germany, Denmark, Norway, Sweden, and Russia as far as Moscow. Bustamante stayed another six months in Paris—by then a magnet for Latin American expatriates—to write his second travel book and see it through to publication. In late 1849 he returned to Peru by way of Mexico.

Bustamante's travel journals are extraordinarily rich and important testimonies to the intellectual and emotional turmoil that Peruvians experienced as they confronted a rapidly modernizing Europe busily engaged in seeking to establish supremacy over the whole globe. Europe represented the epitome of progress and civilization, advancing its values and norms as universal ones.

Most well-educated Latin American writers and politicians by the 1840s were rapidly adopting the emerging European world view. Although selectively, they embraced notions of constitutionalism, a liberal social order, free trade policies, and the European concept of progress.

Like many of his countrymen, Bustamante had been powerfully influenced by European progress and modernization. Yet his provincial mestizo background apparently rendered the European influence on him more fragile and his views more contradictory and ambivalent than those of the more famous of Latin America's liberal writers of the period. He marveled at the railroads, the telegraph, the clockworklike functioning of large cotton mills, the cleanliness and functional layout of modern city streets, civilian supremacy over the military (in the United States and England), and, more generally, political systems that guaranteed order and the freedom of the individual. These impressions repeatedly led him to juxtapose the "civilized world" of the North Atlantic and the "ignorant world" of his native Peru. He worried that his motherland would never see "even a small imitation of these advances."

Still, Bustamante's conclusions often diverged from the conventional contrasts between European civilization and Latin American barbarism. His concern for the common people prompted him to notice that two thirds of the workers in the efficient Manchester cotton mills were children under twelve years old and women, that modern machines deprived innumerable laborers of work, and that many people in England's industrial cities were absolutely poor and saw themselves forced to emigrate to the United States, "where these unfortunate ones have to go begging until they find somebody who will employ them. Who would have thought that Great Britain, one of the wealthiest and haughtiest nations in the world, which is deemed to be happy, would have to cast off her own children, sending them to beg for bread in her former colonies!" Indeed, progress in England merely seemed to make the rich wealthier while many poor people died of starvation. In Peru, on the other hand, where "flowers and fruits flourish through all seasons, . . . it is impossible that somebody died from hunger!"

He had discovered the irreconcilable contradiction in Europe's civilized progress. It was the industrializing Europe that produced extremes of wealth and poverty; backward Peru, in spite of all its exploitation and inequities, had a more moderate income distribution. Indeed, by his second journey Bustamante had distilled such observations into a radical critique of progress and the "civilizing process." Humanity was divided into a small minority that received all benefits and the rest who lived in despair. Just like wild beasts, humans satisfied their appetite for the good things in life through deceit, ruses, skulduggery, brute force, or daring. Society had placed a premium on these base qualities and granted honors to those persons displaying them. What most disturbed Bustamante was that such means of advancing oneself were constantly refined and perfected through the daily progress of human knowledge and thus "wreaked much more havoc among those nations that pride themselves as being *civilized* than among the *savages* [italics in original]." "Should it be true," he wondered, "that, although enlightenment brings great benefits to people, it also corrupts and degrades them with defects of the most vile sort?"

Bustamante's thought fully expressed the contradictions that he found. He urged the adoption of many aspects of modern civilization to overcome Peru's backwardness, but he also deplored the dark side of this civilization, studiously overlooked by most of Peru's liberals. As a merchant, he believed that "trade is the life blood of towns" and that free trade and enterprise were crucial to the advancement of nations. Yet by the 1840s he had become convinced that Great Britain had reduced Spanish America "to the state of a poor trading factory of the British Empire," and he advocated protective tariffs on British goods to encourage Peru to build up its own modern manufacturing industries. He believed that a few wealthy people had exploited and brutalized the miserable masses, who fled from their desperation into alcoholism and a futile expectation of rewards in heaven. On other occasions, he suggested that many commoners were innately lazy, vagrant, and dirty, "preferring hunger to work." He personally was a devout Catholic, whose sense of compassion derived greatly from his religion, but he castigated the church and many individual priests for their abuses and called for reform. He hated despotism and caudillos, but he had a deep fear of anarchy. He believed that order was a prerequisite for the revival of trade and industry. During the June revolution that he witnessed in Paris in 1848, he supported the government and army against the revolutionaries, quite simply "because I like order."

His ambivalent ideas did not fit neatly into the scheme of political orientations that competed for dominance in midnineteenth-century Peru. He could not accept the position of clerical conservatives who wanted to safeguard every privilege of the church and to defend the hierarchical colonial social order. Nor could he fully embrace the position of Peru's liberals who increasingly espoused free trade, sought to modernize the infrastructure of the country, and tried to strengthen the central state for their own economic benefit. Upon returning from his second journey abroad in mid-1849, Bustamante again dedicated himself to his business interests in Cabanilla. Besides the wool trade and livestock, he briefly ventured into gold mining in the Eastern Cordillera of Puno department.

Between mid-1854 and early 1855, General Ramón Castilla led a successful rebellion against Peru's elected president, José Rufino Echenique. Soon after taking up arms, Castilla decreed the abolition of slavery and of the *contribución de indígenas,* the successor tax to the infamous colonial Indian tribute. These measures prompted Juan Bustamante to join Castilla. He raised a battalion of troops in Puno, received a commission as colonel, and fought on the side of the "Liberator of Indians and slaves" at the crucial battle that secured victory for Castilla.

After participating in the Constitutional Convention of 1855–1857, Bustamante was appointed to a series of high-level administrative positions, a result of his close ties to Castilla. As intendant of Lima he spent more than seventy thousand pesos of his own money on construction projects to increase the flow of the Rimac River, which provided the city with drinking water. During the early 1860s, he served briefly as prefect of Huancavelica and Cuzco, where he undertook similar public works. Yet the satirical press of the capital never stopped ridiculing him. Manuel Atanasio Fuentes, who under the pseudonym "El Murciélago" ("The Bat") published satirical articles similar to those in London's *Punch* or Paris's *Charivari,* repeatedly had fun with Bustamante. He called him "Don Burro Andante" ("Mr. Wandering Donkey") and suggested that since Bustamante talked funny (with the accent of the southern highlands) and smelled of llamas, this curious intendant surely came from Puno, reputed to be one of the "cevilized [!] countries," a gibe at Bustamante's limited education.

Castilla surrendered the presidency in 1862, and his immediate successors could not fill his shoes. In 1865, Bustamante found another politician to admire and support. The young army colonel Mariano Ignacio Prado, whom Bustamante had befriended during occasional business trips to Arequipa, rebelled against the regime in power because he was frustrated with its vacillation in meeting the challenge of a Spanish ultimatum and threatened invasion. Motivated by Prado's ardent nationalism, Bustamante promptly joined the rebellion. Prado took power as "Dictator" in late 1865 and organized Peru's defense against the Spanish naval squadron. Bustamante joined the Peruvian forces at the battle of Callao on May 2, 1866, which effectively ended the threat of Spanish invasion. Prado rewarded his loyalty and service by appointing him prefect of the department of Huanuco and, later, inspector general of the postal service for southern Peru.

Bustamante had become embroiled in Peru's partisan politics. To be sure, his motives continued to be high-minded. He had supported Castilla and later Prado not with the hope of personal gain but because he hoped to receive a chance to advance his own reformist ideas. He tried to combine the political realism of partisan politics with his personal vision of a Peruvian utopia of justice and progress for all. Bustamante's effort ultimately was to prove both futile and tragic.

Prado's administration, although daring and reformist, finally led the country into another cycle of rebellion and civil war. By 1866 the national debt had grown so large that its service absorbed most of the country's revenue. Finance Minister Manuel Pardo introduced a comprehensive package of taxes to put the treasury on a sounder basis. Among the new taxes was a *contribución personal*, a head tax to be paid by every male between the ages of twenty-one and sixty years. Although the rates were to be adjusted to regional levels of income, the tax clearly would be highly regressive, and the Indians would bear the major burden.

The arbitrary manner in which local authorities began to collect the taxes in October and November 1866 led to spontaneous peasant protests and revolts in various parts of the Sierra, but most seriously in Huancané, department of Puno. On top of a variety of traditional forced-labor services and fees, the Indians suddenly received orders to pay three new imposts: five pesos for a "national loan" to help defray expenses of the defense against Spain, "alms" of two reales to aid in the completion of Puno's cathedral, and a *contribución personal* of one and one half pesos. Upon the Huancané Indians' demand, the prefect of Puno abolished the taxes and tolerated the Indians' replacement of some local authorities with men of their own choice. By then the rebellion had spread to neighboring villages, but the bishop of Puno and several small military contingents had temporarily pacified the rebellious peasants by December 1866. Thus, the early stages of the uprising had been a spontaneous reaction to taxes, labor exactions by local authorities, and other local grievances.

Bustamante first became involved in the peasant revolts in February 1867, some four months after the first protests had erupted in Huancané. He found himself in a serious quandary. He recognized the justice of the peasants' demands, but he loathed the thought of uprisings and civil war, which he thought could lead only to anarchy. Moreover, he was a committed partisan of Mariano Ignacio Prado and could not condone the destabilization of his friend's administration. Bustamante chose a two-pronged approach to further his dual goals of justice and order. He contacted local authorities in the areas of the uprising and counseled them to remove abusive officials and grant redress to the peasants. At the same time, he pleaded with the Indians to halt any acts of insubordination or violence and to work with him for the legal redress of their complaints. In February he dispatched a manifesto to be printed in Lima's most renowned daily newspaper. The manifesto very generally stated the case on behalf of the Indians and more fully explained and justified his own conduct. He denied that he was trying to instigate a race war or plotting to lead the Indians for his own personal advantage. He knew, he asserted, of the dangers to "the civilized and progressive part of the nation" posed by "brutal uprisings of semi-barbaric masses."

On March 15 the Constitutional Convention abolished the *contribución personal,* but the conspiracies against Prado had begun. In Huancané local notables, dissatisfied with his government, took advantage of the peasants' agitation and tried to mobilize them against Prado. Large crowds appeared in the town plaza chanting "Long live Castilla! Death to Prado!" Bustamante, with a few allies, again intervened to calm the peasants. His efforts again met success for a brief time.

Between the end of March and late May, the rebellion spread over a wider area of the altiplano. Indian rebels once again removed district governors. They directed their protests against those who illegally continued to collect the head tax and to visit other abuses on them. Some anti-Prado forces also may have encouraged this phase of the rebellion, but the escalating confrontations took on a dynamic of their own in April and May. Prado's local authorities were losing control over events, and provincial landholders and authorities put together citizens' militias to defend the region against the Indian "hordes." Sensationalist and racist reports in the Lima press claimed that thousands of rebellious Indians intended to exterminate the whites and mestizos in the department.

In panic, three Puno deputies, themselves large landholders, introduced a bill at the convention that authorized draconian measures against the Indian rebels in order "to save civilization in the department of Puno." Although some Lima newspapers denounced the demand for generous application of the death penalty and deportation of communities of rebellious peasants to the rain-forest lowlands, the bill passed. Provincial militia units actually deported several hundred peasants. In the process of "pacifying" communities suspected of rebellion, the local troops carried out numerous brutal acts, such as executions, burning of peasant houses, and theft of livestock.

Bustamante's dilemma worsened. He still wanted the Indians to end the rebellion, but he could not support the "pacification." His ambivalence paralyzed him, and he probably limited his intervention at this stage to urging prudence and caution on the Indians. The situation improved, indeed seemed to be resolved, when General Baltasar Caravedo took control of the region. Caravedo understood that any cruelties committed by the Indians during the uprising were "minor compared with those that they have suffered since ancient times, and much smaller yet, if one keeps in mind the degree of brutalization to which these hamlets were subjected." Caravedo's troops remained for the time being the effective power in the department, and he saw that many of the officials were replaced with men more open to the concerns of the Indian peasants.

Once the area seemed to be peaceful again, Bustamante sprang into action. In June and early July he either personally visited communities that had participated in the rebellion, or he sent one of his allies, to ask all residents to assemble "in the most public place." He then explained to them that they owed a debt of gratitude and loyalty to the humanitarian actions of General Caravedo and to the government of Mariano Ignacio Prado, which had sent Caravedo. Bustamante asked all of those assembled to sign a solemn declaration that he had written. The *actas* reiterated their gratitude to Prado, whom they lauded as "our father and king, whom we consider of a stature equal to that of Manco Capac, founder of the Peruvian Empire," and their vow to defend the Holy Catholic religion. The cover letters with which these declarations were to be remitted to the Lima press did not fail to express the peasants' deep gratitude to Señor Colonel Juan Bustamante. If it had not been for him, "the blood of many victims would have flowed," and many would have been turned into beggars without bread for their children. "We shall spill the last drop of our blood in defense of the true republican man, Don Juan Bustamante."

Bustamante's words, put into the mouths of his Indian clients, integrated his liberal constitutionalist principles, his longing for order, and his strong Christian faith into a vision of a divine order on earth that sounded rather millenarian. The president is the contemporary just king, the modern Manco Capac. Bustamante here made a powerful appeal to Andean utopian thought that foresaw redemption through the return of the Incas. The militant fight for the Holy Catholic religion became synonymous with the fight for President Prado. Through this Andean redemptionist discourse Bustamante was forging a chain of loyalty tying the peasants to "King Prado" through the intermediation of himself and General Caravedo.

Juan Bustamante had crossed the Rubicon of his life. For the first time he saw a need to mobilize peasants, to plunge into a grass-roots campaign of armed struggle, in order to advance his goals. The repressive campaigns by Puno's notables had convinced him that they would institute a type of order that was tyrannical in nature and absolutely incompatible with his struggle for justice for the Indians. Signs were mounting throughout Peru of a broad-based political movement of dissatisfied elite sectors to overthrow Prado. All the contradictions in Bustamante's thought seemed to collapse. The maintenance of the only kind of order that was true to his liberal republican ideals no longer conflicted with militant action; rather, it might demand such action. Political partisanship, which he had rejected for so long, became necessary for the redemption of the Indian pariahs. The Prado administration must be saved.

Bustamante nonetheless made one final effort to prevent the Armageddon that he feared was necessary. In early July 1867 he traveled to Lima as the plenipotentiary of the altiplano peasantry and launched an energetic campaign to push the convention to adopt measures in favor of the Indians and to rally public support for their cause. While he labored in Lima, he directed a report and plea to the Indian communities in Puno. Writing in a blatantly paternalistic style, he urged them to refrain from further uprisings, and he exhorted them "to understand that you have to make payments in support of the nation." They should send their children to the cities to learn Spanish and other useful things. Once they knew Spanish, President Prado had promised to send them to secondary schools, after which they could return to Puno to instruct their brothers and become authorities in the villages. Had Bustamante again become so convinced of the viability of peaceful change that he would exhort the Indians to pay taxes? He may have foreseen the need to finance a campaign to defend the Prado administration in the event of a major movement to overthrow him. There is some evidence that he secretly may have instructed the communities to collect funds that were not passed on to the provincial and departmental authorities.

In August and September 1867, Bustamante brought together a number of respected citizens in Lima with whom he founded the Sociedad Amiga de los Indios, an association that was to work for reform laws in congress and protect the Indians against abuses and defend them in the courts. The Sociedad originally had some fifteen members, among them generals and former prefects who had served in the southern Sierra, the publisher of *El Comercio*, and a few Lima intellectuals and politicians. It was the first organization of its kind in Peru and, although its effectiveness was limited, it signaled the beginning of awareness among enlightened citizens in the capital of the serious problems faced by the Andean peasantry. Its paternalistic program failed to comprehend the need for state intervention to guarantee the Indians' landed property and to regulate the condition of labor tenants on haciendas, unthinkable state actions by Peruvian liberal principles. For these well-intentioned men the bolivarian laws of the 1820s had established the equality of the Indians before the law, had granted them individual title to their land, and remained the ne plus ultra in the struggle to emancipate the Indians.

Prado's political position was deteriorating rapidly. Serious conflicts with both radical liberals and conservatives in the convention, dissatisfaction with fiscal policy, rancor of displaced officers and bureaucrats from previous administrations, disgust over press censorship—all contributed to erode his support. The final straw came when the new liberal constitution, approved on August 29, weakened the position of the Catholic church by

abolishing *fueros* (privileges) and establishing freedom of instruction and freedom of the press. In Arequipa, the stronghold of
Catholicism in the country, the population organized tumultuous
demonstrations against the new constitution, and the city's
authorities refused to swear the oath of loyalty to it. First in
Arequipa, and then in much of the rest of the republic, generals
rose up to proclaim revolutions aimed at deposing the president.

Bustamante did his part to defend Prado when he traveled to
Arequipa in October and mobilized the Indian peasantry. Within
a week, he reported that he had raised an army of sixteen
thousand, confirming both the strong bonds of loyalty he had
forged in the district and the persistent state of alert among
Indians throughout the area. Most provinces in Puno, however,
declared against Prado. Only Huancané had remained loyal. A
provincial assembly there viewed antigovernment revolution as
harmful to the vital interests of the whole nation and appointed
Bustamante as "Superior Military Chief." Still, for the moment
the department remained quiet. The peasants wanted to finish
sowing their fields, and the antigovernment forces were sending
relief troops to their allies in Cuzco and Arequipa. Thus, the
following two months were a stand-off between the two hostile
forces in the altiplano. Anti-Prado notables from Puno vilified
Bustamante in the Lima papers as a madman who instigated the
Indians to adopt "savage communism" and to exterminate the
whites. One hostile writer insisted that Bustamante pursued "the
ridiculous idea" of having himself crowned as Inca.

In late December, Prado undertook one final, and futile, assault
on Arequipa. He resigned the presidency shortly thereafter in
January. Nearly simultaneously Bustamante, on December 30,
1867, took the city of Puno at the head of several thousand
Indian peasant troops. There was some minor looting, but by
and large his "hordes" must have behaved in a remarkably dis-
ciplined fashion, as even his enemies could not find any atrocities
to report. When news reached Puno on January 1 that Prado
had been defeated in Arequipa and had abandoned the siege,
Bustamante and his troops withdrew from Puno in the direction
of their redoubt Huancané. On the following day, the well-armed
anti-Prado forces under Colonel Andrés Recharte surprised Bustamante's forces close to the northern shore of Lake Titicaca.
For four hours the two sides engaged in an unequal battle: the
rifles of Recharte's troops against the clubs, knives, and rocks of

Bustamante's peasants. After suffering severe casualties the peasants were defeated, with hardly anyone able to escape.

Recharte's troops, notorious for their implacable repression, began to celebrate a blood feast. Many Indians were executed on the field of battle. The others were taken to the nearby hamlet of Pusi together with the handful of their non-Indian commanders. Recharte ordered some seventy-one Indian leaders to be locked up in one or two small thatch-roofed peasant huts, with just enough room to stand tightly packed. The next morning, January 3, 1868, the huts with the prisoners inside were put to the torch. Recharte's troops blocked any efforts by women from Pusi to extinguish the fire. The prisoners died a slow death of asphyxiation. Recharte's men finished off with sabers any who had not expired when the smoldering huts were finally opened.

For a century, Juan Bustamante's own death was shrouded in mystery. Recharte and his lieutenants spread false rumors about his end. As late as the 1960s, respectable writers claimed that after the battle of Pusi, Bustamante was stoned to death by Indians enraged at the tragedy that he had brought upon them. Some stories claimed that Indians hid his body in a cave where it remained in a perfect state of preservation. The truth, however, is more consistent with the events of the battle and the brutality that followed. After the massacre of the seventy-one peasant leaders, the victors ordered Bustamante to carry the bodies of his companions to the outskirts of the hamlet, where a pit had been dug to serve as a mass grave. Soon afterward he was stripped of his clothes, hung by his feet from a tree on the plaza, insulted, flogged, and then decapitated with a soldier's machete. His body, wrapped in a blanket, was interred close to Pusi's church.

Bustamante's enemies had probably long planned to kill him. Raising Indian troops for a partisan political movement occurred almost every day in midnineteenth-century Peru and normally met punishment no harsher than a brief exile, although implicated peasants could expect more severe treatment. For example, Bustamante's few white and mestizo associates suffered only brief imprisonment and fines, after which they returned to their homes and businesses. Bustamante's crime lay not in his partisan political alliance but in his far-reaching social goals. His advocacy of Indian rights led his enemies to consider him a madman who must be killed.

The rebellion did not end with the horrific events of Pusi. For months the communities in the border area between Huancané and Azángaro province continued a guerrilla campaign. Recharte roamed the department with his troops, meting out cruel reprisals against the peasants. The persistence of the rebellion made it clear that the Indians had an agenda of their own, quite apart from the paternalistic leadership of Juan Bustamante. What became known as the Bustamante rebellion was one of the two major peasant movements in Peru during the first century after independence. Both socioeconomic and partisan political developments, as well as both spontaneous peasant action and mobilization by members of the elite, were necessary to give it its extraordinary intensity and longevity.

Most tragically, the bloody conflagration did not improve conditions for what Bustamante had called in July 1867 "that historically unfortunate race."

> A shame to the Republic, to civilization and to Christianity, the Indians continue to suffer all the tributes, all the taxes and exactions reminiscent of the most horrible age of feudalism. The Indian has no family, no property, he even does not have a right to his own person. He is forced to die as a beast in a bull fight; his woman is violated, his children sold, his land devastated, as if it had no owner.

A tragic failure during his lifetime, Bustamante became an important precursor for later Peruvian *indigenistas*, or defenders of Indian rights and culture, such as Clorinda Matto de Turner, Manuel González Prada, and the Asociación Pro-Indígena.

The Pusi town council, decades after the rebellion, buried the remains of the seventy-one massacred Indian leaders and of Juan Bustamante together in a grave in the cemetery. In death, then, Bustamante was united with the Indians more than he could ever be in life. The grave is adorned with a withering cross of uneven timber and a cement structure, one foot tall and two feet long, in the shape of a vaulted house. It differs little from the surrounding graves, closely huddled together in this typical altiplano peasant cemetery. On the front of the vault, engraved by a shaky hand in the cement, the visitor will find the words: "Recuerdo del concejo para almas del mundo" ("the town council's memorial for the souls of the world").

SOURCES

The best, albeit a brief, account in English of the Bustamante rebellion is contained in Michael J. Gonzáles, "Neo-colonialism and Indian Unrest in Southern Peru, 1867–1898," *Bulletin of Latin American Studies* 6, no. 1 (1987): 1–26. An extensive and very informative but rather chaotic recent analysis of the rebellion, which also has much biographical data on Juan Bustamante, is Emilio Vásquez, *La rebelión de Juan Bustamante* (Lima, 1976). Three of Bustamante's own works remain crucial for understanding the man: *Viaje al antiguo mundo por el Peruano Juan Bustamante, natural del departamento de Puno,* 2d ed. (Lima, 1845); *Apuntes y observaciones civiles, políticas y religiosas con las noticias adquiridas en este segundo viaje a la Europa por el Peruano Juan Bustamante* (Paris, 1849); and *Los Indios del Perú, compilación hecha por Juan Bustamante* (Lima, 1867). There is a good chance that much unknown documentation on the rebellion exists in various archives that might make a more extended study well worthwhile.

7

Carlota Lucia de Brito: Women, Power, and Politics in Northeast Brazil

Joan E. Meznar

Brazil experienced less upheaval upon independence than did the Spanish-American nations. Under the 1824 constitution, Emperor Pedro I (1822–1831) allowed upper-class Brazilians to exercise some political influence, especially at the local and regional levels. Pedro I abdicated in 1831 in favor of his five-year-old son, Pedro II. A decade of disorder and uncertainty subsided in 1840 when young Pedro II began his official rule. His forty-nine-year reign represented political and legal continuity and generally was remarkable for its stability, moderation, and prosperity. Brazilian intellectuals worried less about the issues of civilization and barbarism, the conflicts between order and reform, than did their Spanish-American counterparts.

Still, rural areas and small towns in Brazil often experienced violence that belied the nation's reputation for tranquility. The central government, like the colonial Iberian administrations, could not control all of the vast national territory. Regional political leaders, allied with the rural poor and with backcountry bandits, enforced order with informal personal armies. Elites held together their networks of family, friends, and retainers by dispensing favors, protection, and jobs. Thus when Emperor Pedro II in Rio de Janeiro dismissed a Liberal ministry and called on the Conservatives to govern, the effects rippled far beyond the capital.

Carlota Lucia de Brito, an attractive young woman, was allied with her lover, a local politician, and his Liberal friends in a small town in the northeastern state of Pernambuco. In 1848, when the emperor changed ministries in Rio, the region erupted into a bloody feud between Liberals and Conservatives. Carlota ordered the assassination of a Conservative enemy and was condemned to life imprisonment by an imperial court for her role in the crime.

Carlota's story demonstrates not only that patron-client networks protected women but also that they sometimes allowed women, at least in backwoods areas, to act independently. The subliminal issues of family and individual honor often intersected with overtly political issues. Politics as practiced in midcentury Brazil was complex. So, too, was justice. Did

Carlota's sentence punish her for the crime of murder? for being a political
enemy of the party in power? or, perhaps, for being a woman who had
become too strong and independent?

Joan Meznar, assistant professor of Latin American studies at Mount
Holyoke College, has researched and presented papers on the world of
small farmers in northeastern Brazil from 1850 to 1900. She received
her Ph.D. from the University of Texas in Austin in 1986 and has held
numerous fellowships including a Tinker Foundation Summer Grant, a
Fulbright-Hays Study Abroad Grant, and a National Endowment for the
Humanities Travel to Collections Grant.

Politics in nineteenth-century Brazil centered primarily around
family. Patterns of power and deference within it prepared each
member for a role in the larger society. Families, by both por-
traying and reinforcing patron-client relationships, incorporated
and thus perpetuated the acceptance of a social hierarchy with
"protectors" at the top and "protected" at the bottom. The father's
responsibility lay in protecting and controlling the women and
children. To the fathers and older sons fell responsibility for
preserving the family's integrity, in particular, for safeguarding
the "honor" of female relations living within the household. The
virtue of the women thus reflected the control men had over
female family members. Men shaped the political world in which
women lived. Women's most important political role appeared
to be to acquiesce to the marriages that strengthened the extended
family alliances upon which local politics rested. But women, at
times, also acted as catalysts for political change. Some of the
women who most directly influenced politics were not bound by
traditional family roles; they exemplified an alternative to the
ideals of a rigidly hierarchical society while functioning under
the constraints of that very order. Carlota Lucia de Brito, the
mistress of a powerful Paraiban politician, had a dramatic impact
on political life in one Brazilian province during the midnineteenth century.

Carlota was a survivor. A refugee from catastrophic drought,
she rebuilt her life in a new community, battled prejudice, and
fought for her lover's political position. She survived a death
sentence (commuted to a life term in the penal colony on the
island of Fernando de Noronha) and finally died a free, very old
woman in Recife around the turn of the twentieth century. The
resilience that characterizes her story points to a strong, unusual
woman, but her struggles were shared by many other Brazilian

women. Carlota's story illuminates issues of class, gender, politics, and justice in nineteenth-century northeastern Brazil.

For those who lived in the backlands, in the northeastern *sertão*, periodic droughts severely disrupted normal life. About every thirty years the intensity of the drought would push men, women, and children from their familiar world, forcing them to begin anew in an area with more plentiful rainfall. All levels of society could be affected by the drought that scorched crops and destroyed fodder. The wealthy, bemoaning the loss of their cattle, often found refuge with relatives in the coastal region. The very poor, sometimes the last to leave because they had nowhere to go, died of hunger or exposure while searching for relief; the luckier of this group swelled the indigent contingent in the towns. The middling group, usually owning at least some portable property, also moved to the urban centers to rebuild their lives. For all, drought meant drastic change. Families, by and large, attempted to move together during droughts; the bonds of blood would help ease the transition and earn acceptance into a new community. Often, nonetheless, drought disrupted families as well. Fathers and brothers, insisting that women and children move immediately to healthier surroundings, might stay with the family goods until the last hope of salvaging crops and herds was gone. In the flight from the scorched backlands, adults and children succumbed to disease and death, destroying family balance. Lashing out against the hopelessness of their situation, men turned to banditry, abandoning their wives and children. And women who felt tied to undesirable marriages used the disruption to free themselves from unwanted husbands.

Drought years altered social conditions in both the countryside and the towns. Population exploded in the areas unaffected by the drought, pressuring the minimal social services available. The ties of familiarity and even of patronage and camaraderie that had bound backlanders to the city dwellers disintegrated. While the swelling mass of the poor frightened the staid urban society, many profited from the misery of others. Women and young girls from the backlands arrived in the towns laden with all their earthly possessions, trusting that the value of their gold jewelry would keep them clothed, fed, and sheltered until they found a new means of survival. The value of gold, in response to the sudden supply, always dropped precipitously. Townspeople bought up the cheap gold, saving it for the inevitable price rise when they would realize handsome profits. Once all their ornaments had been sold, women from the interior who had lost the protection of male kin might find in prostitution their only alternative for replenishing cash reserves and thus assuring survival.

In the drought of 1845, Carlota Lucia de Brito was among those who left the backlands of the province of Pernambuco and settled in the town of Areia. Situated in the humid *brejo* region of the province of Paraíba, Areia was not subject to dryness. An important market center in the midnineteenth century, it served as entrepôt for the coastal plantation region and the cattle-ranching *sertão*. Its merchant families also maintained close commercial ties with Recife, a major port and capital of the province of Pernambuco. The prosperity and wide-ranging connections of Areia's elite families placed the town among the most influential in provincial politics. Carlota arrived in Areia with a daughter, but no husband. She claimed to be a widow and later would be implicated in the murder of her husband. But in 1845 she was concerned primarily with building a new life. While hers had certainly not been a life of luxury, neither had it been one of penury. She had owned some land, she survived the move to Areia, and she quickly settled into a situation that seemed rather comfortable: she came under the protection of Areia's leading Liberal politician, Joaquim José dos Santos Leal. Apparently a woman of considerable beauty, Carlota did not possess the social status (nor did her family have the political ties) necessary to make her an acceptable wife for a member of the Santos Leal family. Nevertheless, she was soon installed in Joaquim José's town home and behaved as though the two had indeed legally married. She had found an important male protector, but in forfeiting the acceptable role of an "honest" woman, she became a target for accusations against her own and her lover's morality. While many sons of important Brazilian families enjoyed liaisons with women who were not their wives, these affairs were to remain discreet. Townspeople who readily accepted even frequent forays to the local houses of prostitution would pass harsh judgment on those men who, they believed, flaunted immorality by openly living with women they were unwilling to marry.

From 1844 to 1848 the Liberal party controlled the government ministries in Rio de Janeiro, the capital city of the Brazilian empire. Liberal ascendancy in the capital was reflected in the provinces. In 1846, Joaquim José dos Santos Leal, lieutenant colonel and commander of Areia's National Guard, was elected to and served in Paraíba's legislative assembly. His chief Conservative opponent was Trajano Alipio de Holanda Chacon, another illustrious citizen of Areia who had served as deputy in both the national and provincial assemblies, as president of the province of Paraíba (1839–40), and as municipal judge of Areia from 1840 to 1848. It was during the Liberal ascendancy that Carlota and Joaquim José set up housekeeping together. Townspeople, suspicious and envious of Carlota, could do nothing but murmur. Trajano Chacon (Joaquim José's neighbor in town), however, let it be known that he considered Carlota nothing more than a prostitute; neither he nor Carlota disguised the distaste each inspired in the other.

In 1848 the Liberal party fell from favor, and Conservatives once again occupied the chief imperial ministries. Three years after Carlota's flight from drought, the provinces of Pernambuco and Paraíba entered a period of serious political upheaval. In Recife, a newly formed party of the Praia (composed primarily of disgruntled Liberals) challenged the Conservative government for power. Armed rebellion ensued. Driven from Recife, Praieira leaders fled north, seeking adherents as they went, hoping to return with greater strength to Pernambuco. The movement did not gather much momentum in Paraíba, with the notable exception of the town of Areia. Politics there, as elsewhere, was closely tied to family interests. The Conservatives of Areia, led by Trajano Chacon, despised the Santos Leal Liberals. Their animosity in town and provincial government preceded the Praieira revolt and would survive the collapse of the Praieira movement. But the heightened tensions caused by the rebellion (the Santos Leal faction supported the Praieriros who were opposed by Trajano Chacon's Conservative allies) would bring sinister consequences to both families.

When loyal government troops quashed the revolt, members of the Santos Leal family suffered not only a defeat and prison terms but also the humiliation of losing to the Conservative faction. Liberals, potential traitors to the imperial government, were forced out of local public office. Even the family space of the defeated Liberals was violated. The home of doña Maria José dos Santos Leal (Joaquim José's mother) was requisitioned to serve as headquarters for the imperial troops that defeated the Praieira movement. The looting that accompanied the stay of government troops in the Santos Leal house was so thorough that even the diadems from images in doña Maria's home altar were stolen. When, that same year, Joaquim José dos Santos Leal (from the safety of his family ranch in the interior of Paraíba) ran against Trajano Alipio de Holanda Chacon for a seat in the national Chamber of Deputies, few in Areia doubted that Trajano Chacon would win the election.

After Joaquim José's flight from Areia following the defeat of the Praia, Carlota took charge of his business in town. She also took the initiative in expanding her role as benefactress to loyal Liberals. Among her duties was that of serving as liaison between her lover's more humble clients and the church. Much of local life was tied to the Catholic church. All the important passages from birth through marriage to death were channeled through the local church. Parish priests oversaw the spiritual well-being of their flock while also providing the framework in which temporal duties could be performed. Besides baptizing children, marrying couples, and burying the dead, the priests explained government decrees and collaborated with political authorities to ensure an orderly society. Just as the family imparted to its members the values of deference, so also did the church, while confirming the importance of families, instill values that contributed to an orderly, hierarchical community. Carlota, herself only a marginal member of the society that the church promoted, became responsible for helping her lover's supporters assume the role of upstanding citizens. She arranged, among other things, church baptisms and marriages for those who could not afford the parish fees.

In 1849 the town priest, Father Francisco de Holanda Chacon, was also Trajano Chacon's brother. One afternoon, while Carlota conferred with the priest about an upcoming baptism, Trajano arrived to pay his brother a visit. Furious at finding a "prostitute" in Areia's vicarage, and in an apparent effort to drive home his political and moral superiority over his Liberal opponent, Trajano openly confronted Carlota: he attempted literally to kick her out of his brother's house. For a woman who possessed a measure of social prestige, the accusation of leading an irregular life, coupled with the humiliation of being expelled from the vicarage, proved unbearable. In her anger at this affront, Carlota saw the opportunity to avenge both her own and her outlaw lover's honor. She decided to contact old relations in the *sertão* and commissioned Trajano's murder.

While Joaquim José (still avoiding a prison term for his role in the Praieira revolt by remaining far from Areia) probably knew little or nothing of Carlota's plan, his family in town supported her attempt to avenge his honor. Carlota charged Antonio Brabo, a cousin of Joaquim José's from the interior, with executing Trajano Chacon. Brabo, in turn, solicited the aid of one of the *agregados* (tenant farmers) of the Santos Leal family, a man named Antonio José das Virgens, locally known as Beiju, who lived by favor on Santos Leal land. Beiju refused Brabo, but, after Carlota herself intervened, he accepted his duty to his patron and, encouraged by her promises of reward and protection, agreed to cooperate. Carlota's extended family thus joined with the Santos Leal clan in the determination to execute Trajano Chacon.

After several unsuccessful ambush attempts, Brabo and Beiju finally succeeded in killing Trajano Chacon on September 5, 1849, the very day that Trajano defeated Joaquim José in the contest for a seat in the Chamber of Deputies. To many in Areia the murder seemed to be revenge for the electoral defeat; Joaquim José, of course, became the prime suspect for ordering the crime. With Conservatives firmly in power in Areia after the Praieira debacle, the quest for justice reflected party as well as family animosity. Conservatives determined to bring the Liberals to justice while the Chacon family sought to avenge the death of one of their own.

Carlota immediately sent messengers to her lover, who remained hidden in the backlands of the province, urging him to flee even farther from the justice to be dispensed by Areia Conservatives. Although Carlota had planned the crime, Joaquim José tacitly accepted responsibility, thus fulfilling his duty to protect his woman; he knew that if he stayed in Paraíba he would be held liable for Trajano Chacon's death. Carlota eventually joined him in his flight from the province. The Conservative thirst for vengeance, however, would not be satiated without bringing the criminals to justice in Areia. The deputy police chief of Areia, José Pereira Copque, relentlessly pursued leads concerning the Santos Leal group throughout the northeast. In March 1850 he finally tracked down Joaquim José, the latter's brother Manoel José, and Carlota in the interior of the province of Rio Grande do Norte, only to find them heavily armed and prepared to resist capture. Copque believed it imperative to seek reinforcements before engaging the fugitives in a gun battle, and in so doing allowed them to escape. The Santos Leal family had a wide network of friends throughout the northeast who gave the fugitives cover and provisions to help them in their flight.

For their part, the Chacons had influential ties to provincial authorities in the region and managed to circulate descriptions of the fleeing group to police chiefs in the surrounding provinces.

Early in 1851 those accused of the murder of Trajano Chacon were sentenced in absentia. By that time it had become clear that Carlota had planned the crime. She and Beiju were sentenced to death; Joaquim José to twenty years in prison, and Manoel José to twenty-three years and four months imprisonment (Antonio Brabo had been killed by a slave). The search for the accused continued; they were finally captured on May 16, 1851, in the province of Piauí and sent back to Areia.

Meanwhile, in May 1851 the emperor granted amnesty to those who had participated in the Praieira revolt, ordering that "an eternal silence enfold all the facts about which the amnestied group might be questioned regarding their complicity in the rebellion that recently took place in the province of Pernambuco." The Conservatives could no longer hope to punish the Praia group, but they could still make Joaquim José and his supporters pay for the murder of Trajano Chacon.

The outlaws were finally brought to Areia in early December 1851, only a few days before the yearly holiday honoring Our Lady of the Conception, the town's patron saint. What a contrast the criminal Carlota presented to the Holy Mother of God! The inhabitants of Areia took seriously their duties toward the town patroness; her feast day was always prepared with elaborate care. Devotion to saints in northeastern Brazil long had reinforced the importance of protection in a paternalistic society. As with human relations, there existed a large variety of degrees of power among the saints. In rural Brazilian society, personal relations of patronage and protection provided the surest guarantees of security and immediate improvement of living conditions. The same occurred in dealing with saints. A system of duties and obligations guaranteed supernatural action. Not all saints possessed the same power; some proved stronger by exerting more influence on their own patrons, and thus assured greater miracles for their devotees. Devotion to a certain saint indicated acceptance of that image as powerful to bargain effectively with the supreme patron, God.

Our Lady of the Conception, the patroness of Areia, was one of the representations of the Virgin Mary most closely associated with motherhood. Her devotees believed that as the mother of God, she would influence her son on their behalf and that as the town's chosen patroness, she dispensed special protection and favor to its inhabitants. The Virgin ranked second only to Christ in most Brazilians' perceptions of supernatural power. Some even believed that Mary's role as mother made her more powerful than her divine son, for in the family hierarchy children must defer to their parents. Yet, overall, the Virgin's role appealed to the populace not so much for her authority as for her maternal compassion: the same attitude Mary had displayed toward her son at the foot of his cross would also be manifested toward her "children" in Areia. Carlota's image as "murderess" and "prostitute" sharply contrasted with the image of Mary's compassion and virginal motherhood, which Areia was preparing to celebrate.

The townspeople well knew that the powerful Santos Leal family would attempt to keep its two sons from paying the legal consequences of the crime they had committed. Family responsibilities included protecting its members from the law. But political rivalry between Conservatives and Liberals had reached such a point by 1851 that it was impossible to protect Joaquim José and Manoel José from justice. At one time important local political leaders, they were brought into town chained to their mounts, in a humiliating display of power eroded. The president of Paraíba instructed Areia's deputy police chief not to release the Santos Leal brothers under any circumstances; they were to be considered prisoners of the state. Carlota, not a part of the Santos Leal family, did not enjoy the same attempts at protection as did her lover. She, however, also counted on family support. Her relatives in Pajeú das Flores, province of Pernambuco, attempted to have her removed to their town's jurisdiction in order to stand trial for the murder of her husband. But Father Francisco Chacon petitioned the president of Paraíba to guarantee that Carlota would pay for the death of his brother and not be sent to Pernambuco to be tried for the death of a less important man and, possibly, be released or sentenced to a less rigorous penalty. Father Chacon's petition, sent all the way to the minister of justice of the Brazilian empire, succeeded in keeping Carlota from benefiting from her family's attempt to protect her. Once again, she alone would be responsible for her survival.

With the accused finally captured and in Areia, a jury was assembled to try them. Most of the earlier sentences were upheld, with the exception of Carlota's, now changed from death to life imprisonment. Only Beiju, a poor retainer who at one time had enjoyed the protection of the Santos Leal family, was sentenced to death for the murder of Trajano Chacon. Despite petitions for imperial clemency, he was hanged in 1863. Carlota, Joaquim José, and Manoel José were sent to the island prison of Fernando de Noronha.

Escape from the island was practically impossible. The only recourse left the Santos Leal family was to request authorities to bring their boys back to the mainland. Once the brothers were on the mainland, the family could supply them with some amenities and even conspire to free them by force. In 1865, doña Maria, in a display of lofty maternal responsibility, petitioned the president of the province to transfer her sons to the prison of Paraíba, since they were blind and sick and suffering and she wanted to give them the aid she owed them as their mother. Her petition was not granted. Joaquim José died on Fernando de Noronha, and Manoel José eventually returned to Areia, blind and crazed from his prison experience.

Carlota, on the other hand, survived. She, who had accompanied Joaquim José in his flight through at least four northeastern provinces and stood trial with him in Areia, quickly abandoned him once they reached Fernando de Noronha. It was clear to her that her erstwhile lover needed protection far more than he was able to offer it and that she had to manage to protect herself. Once again, she sought the company of a powerful man, this time the director of the penal colony. For more than thirty years she lived as comfortably as possible on Fernando de Noronha. In 1889 the Brazilian emperor was deposed. The new republican government commuted life sentences to thirty years in prison. Carlota was free at last. In 1890 she left the island and settled in Recife where she spent her last days in charge of a boardinghouse for young men from influential families in the interior who came to Pernambuco's capital to study.

The Santos Leal family continued to play an important role in Areia politics. Carlota's crime did not relegate them to political obscurity or even political impotence, but it did exacerbate tensions at a particularly volatile time. Had Trajano Chacon not been murdered, Joaquim José dos Santos Leal probably would have continued to be a major political force in the town. Yet Carlota's story must be understood as more than simply the account of a woman who ruins one man's life. Carlota knew she would never be accepted as a full member of the community she entered when she moved to Areia in the drought of 1845. She had refused to confine herself to a role others sought to impose. She was not willing even to subject herself fully to the man with whom she lived. The self-assertion and independence of this woman, who moved beyond the boundaries of family hierarchy perceived as so vital to social order, contributed, in the final analysis, to the community's outrage against the Santos Leal family. It was bad enough that Carlota lived openly in concubinage with Joaquim José, but a man who could not keep his woman in check should suffer for that crime as well as for any others that grew from that inability. Ultimately, even though Carlota ordered the murder, Joaquim José was responsible for it. Only in the context of patriarchy can the political and family revenge against the Santos Leal brothers be fully understood.

Carlota well knew the options available to women without influential husbands. Rather than conform to the place reserved for her in a stratified world, she determined to move upward. It was, after all, impossible to maintain the ideal hierarchical society when nature and politics conspired to disrupt order. Those who understood the fragility of hierarchy, who individually survived its disruption by disaster, would chip away at the standards of accepted authority. But they remained subject to a system still gasping for survival. Carlota, for all her strength and independent ways, was fully dependent on men until the end of her very long life.

SOURCES

The most complete account of Carlota's crime is in Horacio de Almeida, *Brejo de Areia,* 2d ed. (João Pessoa, Paraíba, 1980), pp. 61–75. My account here is based also on manuscript documents from the Arquivo Nacional and the Arquivo Histórico da Paraíba. This research was made possible through a National Endowment for the Humanities Travel to Collections Grant.

8

Juana Manuela Gorriti: Writer in Exile

Gertrude M. Yeager

After winning independence in 1816, Argentina suffered from a series of civil wars often pitting the liberal elites of Buenos Aires against backlands leaders who wanted more regional autonomy. The caudillo Juan Manuel de Rosas ruled Argentina from 1829 until 1852. He allowed the Buenos Aires cattle ranchers to control the economic and political life of the nation, and he tolerated the autonomy of regional caudillos as long as they did not challenge him. Rosas persecuted his enemies unmercifully, sending a whole generation into exile during his long rule. After his fall the tensions between the provinces and Buenos Aires gradually abated. By the 1870s, Buenos Aires had secured uncontested control over the rest of the nation and had become a model of modernity and culture.

In 1831 the family of Juana Manuela Gorriti fled from the Argentine conflicts into exile in Bolivia. There Gorriti married the ill-fated Manuel Isidro Belzú, an army officer who later served as president of Bolivia. After her separation from Belzú, Gorriti moved to Lima, Peru, and began her career as a teacher and writer. She remained in Lima as part of an artists' circle until she returned to Buenos Aires in 1878.

Gorriti, an intelligent and educated woman of good family, both lived within as well as challenged the restrictions placed on women. She accompanied her husband on military campaigns, and she dared to separate from him and live independently. She took a lover and had his child while her husband was still living, apparently without incurring society's wrath. Gorriti's *tertulia* (discussion group) invited women as well as men to read and comment on each other's writing. Yet, in her own prose, Juana Manuela generally endorsed the traditional Hispanic view of women's roles. Did she escape censure for her personal behavior because she defended traditional values on some level, or because she was charming, talented, and attractive?

Some intellectuals seem to be citizens of cities rather than of nations. In Lima and Buenos Aires, Gorriti found kindred spirits and an opportunity to teach and write. The life of a political exile is filled with hardship, but, ironically, we might never have heard of Juana Manuela if her native country had been peaceful during her youth. Like many writers in exile she became a member of an international network that, in her case, provided the friendship and support that she had lost when she left her hometown. It is easy to see how so many Latin American intellectuals from small towns and rural areas became alienated from the customs, values, and "country bumpkins" that they left behind.

Gertrude Yeager is associate professor of history at Tulane University. Her current research concerns the international dimensions of the intellectual community in nineteenth-century Spanish America. Her work on Chilean historiography and schoolteachers in Chile and Peru has contributed to the development of her latest interest.

Juana Manuela Gorriti lived the type of life that romantic fiction celebrates. She grew up in a society noted for its barbaric, rustic nature. A child bride, she married a man best remembered as a demonic force in Bolivian history. Her name was linked to adultery and sedition, and she was exiled. After a divorce, she lived the life of an independent woman and had a child out of wedlock yet did not suffer social ostracism. She was a woman of great energy who was admired for her beauty, wit, grace, and elegance. She also was a talented and successful writer, teacher, and editor who presided over a salon and defended women's rights. When she died in 1892 at age seventy-four, she must have been pleased about and perhaps surprised at how extraordinarily full and vital her life had been.

Juana Manuela was born into a traditional society and a revolutionary family. Salta, the province in which she was born on June 15, 1818, was both culturally and geographically distant from Buenos Aires and from the pampas normally associated with modern Argentina. Salta's rugged, mountainous terrain and deep fertile valleys are reminiscent of Bolivia. The richness of the land and its proximity to the silver-mining complex at Potosí in Bolivia made Salta an attractive site for Spanish settlers, who established vast stock-raising ventures on the abundant land. The mule, the sixteenth-century equivalent of an all-terrain vehicle, became the basis of regional fortunes, and the annual Salta mule fair was the jewel in the crown of the local economy.

Gorriti's grandfather was one of those persons attracted to the region. Don Ignacio de Gorriti was an enterprising Basque merchant-rancher who acquired several estates and established the basis of the family's fortune and respectability. By 1810 the Gorritis were powerful and influential. Juana Manuela's father, José Ignacio de Gorriti, is remembered in Argentina as an intellectual, lawyer, statesman, warrior, and patriot.

When the wars of independence began in 1810, Salta, because of its location along trade and communication routes, found itself in a state of perpetual conflict lasting until the 1830s. The revolution and the civil wars that followed were a very real part of Juana Manuela's childhood as her father and uncles served in them as generals and statesmen. She wrote that some of her earliest memories were of gaucho armies bivouacked on the family ranch and of the famous caudillo Martín Güemes, who used the house as an office. Writing later of Güemes, she said that in Salta he was counted among the local heroes and martyrs but that he possessed the stature and nobility to become a truly national figure of patriotism. Güemes was a great warrior who used his sword for good and truth, and the nation owed its independence to him. Of nearly equal importance to Gorriti was another Salteño, Dionisio de Puch, to whom she was related by marriage. After Güemes's mysterious death, General Puch, like Güemes, fought for liberty and democracy. Puch lacked the spirit of a military man, however, a characteristic Gorriti admired, and took up arms only as a means to defend liberty; he was not interested in power and glory. For Gorriti the greatest battle Puch fought began in 1832 against the tyranny of Facundo Quiroga and Juan de Rosas.

The Gorritis were closely allied to the Güemes-Puch faction, and the family's fortunes rose and sank accordingly. In 1831 these fortunes sank so low that the Gorritis were declared prisoners of the fatherland by the ambitious and ruthless Quiroga and were forced into political exile along with some two thousand other souls; the family wealth was confiscated. Juana Manuela remembered the flight. All of the distinguished families who had served the nation honorably in the revolution were persecuted by the agents of Rosas, who seized their property. To her Rosas was an American Nero, a horrible and monstrous despot. When she packed her belongings in 1831, Juana Manuela did not realize that her life as a wanderer had begun and that she would not return to Argentina for some fifty years.

Like other girls of her class, when Juana Manuela was eight years old she was enrolled in a convent school, but the discipline depressed her, so she withdrew and continued her education with private tutors at home. The family evidently valued education because her father and uncles were trained in law and theology at the famous Jesuit university, San Francisco Xavier, in Chuquisaca, now Sucre, Bolivia. She was fortunate that her uncle,

Father Juan Ignacio, a respected intellectual, took an interest in her schooling. She spent her childhood on various *estancias* (ranches), which one depending on the proximity of the fighting. What she remembered most about those years was the natural beauty of her home, a delicious oasis of green, and its lush flower gardens, to which she could retreat whenever her life turned somber.

The life of a political exile was little better than that of a political prisoner, especially in the small, remote Bolivian town of Tarija. Despite the company of her family (there were eight Gorriti children) and the hospitality of local citizens, Juana Manuela was thirteen and bored. She read romantic novels and fell in love with love. Her life centered around domestic tasks. There were few parties, so socializing depended upon attending Mass.

Assigned to the local garrison was a young, twenty-two-year-old army captain, Manuel Isidro Belzú. Like Gorriti, Belzú had been exiled to Tarija, in his case for some breach of military discipline by General Andrés de Santa Cruz, president of Bolivia. Gorriti and Belzú were complete opposites in physical appearance, temperament, education, and background. She was tall, blonde, rather well educated for the time, and from an important family. Belzú was dark, strong, a soldier by training; he had scant formal education and an unimpressive genealogy. Little about him except his restless energy hinted at the man he was to become. Gorriti and Belzú fell in love, and despite initial resistance from her family, were married without pomp or ostentation in 1833 when she was fifteen years old. The match clearly surprised everyone; speaking of Gorriti, a contemporary noted that her only defect was her husband.

Gorriti stayed married to Belzú until 1848. During this time they moved about Bolivia as his military career advanced. While her husband participated in a series of barracks revolts, Gorriti bore three daughters (one of whom, Clorinda, died in infancy) and began writing; for a while she also taught school. But relations were not good between the couple. Belzú was a restless man, Gorriti wrote. He turned hard when confined with the family; his blood stirred, his mind was agitated in that sterile existence. Then, without looking back, without thinking of anything but his ego and his personal needs, Belzú abandoned himself to his destiny as a caudillo and left his home.

Gorriti had separated from Belzú first in 1842. She clearly did not approve of his conduct, which was opposed to her way of thinking and her love of order and true heroism as represented by the figures of Güemes, Puch, and her father and uncles. She was believed to be a supporter of José Ballivián, president of Bolivia and an enemy of Belzú, to whom she has been romantically linked. Gorriti's part in the Belzú-Ballivián rivalry is difficult to document. One version has it that when Belzú discovered Gorriti's ties to the Ballivián party, he escorted her to the shore of Lake Titicaca, took away her horse, and indicated the road to Peru. Another account states that while she was attracted to Ballivián, their relationship was innocent.

History has been much kinder to the memory of Ballivián as a political leader than it has been to that of Belzú. Ballivián is remembered as an enlightened caudillo, or strongman, who was smart enough to recognize his limitations and people his administration with experts. He is also remembered as a notorious womanizer whose sexual exploits jeopardized the virtue of all married women, and Belzú publicly denounced him as such in 1847. Given the size and nature of Bolivian society, Ballivián and Gorriti would have known each other; they would have frequented the same circles and attended the same dinner parties during the period when President Ballivián and General Belzú were allies. As something of an intellectual herself, Gorriti would have been naturally attracted to the people who surrounded Ballivián. And a tall, slender, green-eyed blonde with a quick wit and a gift for repartee would have been noticed in the salons of Sucre.

Belzú, on the other hand, has been depicted as a ruthless populist leader dominated by consuming ambition. His great gift was to have such a charismatic personality that the lower classes would have followed him anywhere. If Ballivián is associated with culture, reason, and responsible government, Belzú represents passion, crudity, and personal enrichment. In 1848, Belzú successfully toppled the government headed by Ballivián, and the deposed president, his supporters, and Gorriti went into exile. Once installed as president, Belzú was generous toward the Ballivián supporters, allowing many of them to return to Bolivia, but Gorriti chose to remain in Peru.

Penniless and alone, Gorriti established a school to support herself and her daughters while Belzú entered La Paz in triumph at the head of a military column; his presidency lasted for eight years. Despite his rough exterior, the Belzú legacy was not completely black, for he championed the cause of the poor, especially the Indian population. They called him "Tata" Belzú, an indigenous word for patriarch, or father, because he promised to end the *pongo* (forced-labor system) that obligated Indians to work, and he reduced restrictions on their movement. But most critics believe that Belzú simply manipulated the sentiments of the people without improving their lives and that during his administration political life became so vulgar that the word *belcismo* (to be a supporter of Belzú) became synonymous with blatant demagoguery and opportunism. Governments, however, have never lasted long in Bolivia, and Belzú went into voluntary exile in 1855, declaring the country to be ungovernable.

In the meantime, Gorriti established herself in Peru. Her spirits were good, and she refused to indulge in self-pity. She compared herself to a bird, which after a storm destroyed its nest found the inner strength to locate a new tree and build another nest. First, Gorriti lived in Arequipa, but in 1850 she moved to Lima where she remained for the next thirty years. She began her life again and took a new love, Julián Sandoval, with whom she had a son, Julio, in 1852. Lima was a large and sophisticated city compared to the other places where Juana Manuela had lived. In 1850 it still retained much of its former viceregal splendor. With its large multiethnic population, Lima also had an exotic quality. It was, for example, a city well known for its religiosity. It boasted of numerous churches, many with gold and silver altars built during the colonial era; and it was the home of the pious *beatas* (holy women) who patterned themselves after the mystic St. Rose of Lima.

It was also the home of the sultry *tapada,* a type of woman unknown in other Latin American cities. *Tapada* was a name given a woman who draped herself seductively in a *manta* and *saya* (mantle and long, flowing dress). The custom of veiling women was of Moorish origin and was introduced during the 1600s. Its intent was to make a woman invisible in the streets and, thereby, free her to go about her business unmolested by male advances. But in Peru, the costume was worn in such a way as to hide the woman's identity while enhancing her beauty and mystery, permitting her to flirt with the men she met on the street. Foreign visitors found the custom intriguing and commented on it regularly in their travel books. The shawl would be draped so as to cover a woman's face except for her eyes (which were always described as dark and beckoning), and it would be wrapped around her in such a way as to gather the shapeless dress and hold it close to the body. Any woman could don the *tapada* costume, and many did, because so dressed they could step outside of the narrow confines of acceptable social behavior. Sometimes women would employ the costume in order to spy on their husbands, attract lovers, or engage in flirtations. The openness of Lima was a refreshing departure from altiplano society, and in the mild coastal climate Gorriti's life and career blossomed.

Gorriti began writing in earnest when she moved to Lima. The city had a small but intense cultural life. A series of short novels and essays, based on her remembrances of life in Argentina, began appearing in the 1850s and established her literary credentials. Her school where she taught boys and girls also served as the site for her famous salon. Her first work was a short romantic novel, *La Quena*. The title, borrowed from the Quechuan language, meant "the pain of love." This work was followed by *El lucero del manantial* (The bright star of spring), an episode of political tyranny, and *El guante negro* (The black glove), a romantic thriller set in Buenos Aires in the 1840s. From the first, Gorriti's works were well received and critically acclaimed, and through their serialization in the press, her popularity spread throughout South America. Not only was her work popular, but it also was well respected, and she began to write for the leading literary reviews. Almost all of her works were autobiographical in nature; since her life was full of sorrow and pain, it made excellent copy for her romantic novels.

Gorriti did not identify with a specific literary or intellectual philosophy. Like most Latin American writers she was an eclectic; given her education, her writing lacked artistic and stylistic refinement. What impressed readers was the simple, natural quality of her prose and verse. Reflecting her upbringing, her novels were chaste and often contained moral lessons for her young female audience. As she once remarked, her novels could enter through the front door of the family home. Gorriti was never accused by critics of losing the feminine dimension, a deadly charge that was levied against some of her closest friends.

Gorriti further confirmed her belief in the importance of family ties by her close relationship with her two daughters, Eldemira and Mercedes, who had accompanied her to Lima. Eldemira returned to La Paz to live with her father and offer him moral support. She had had an affectionate relationship with her father from childhood, which turned into adoration when she became an adult. In 1854, Belzú married Eldemira to his political confidant and successor as president, General Jorge Cordoba, who assumed the presidency in 1855 and governed for two years. In 1861 he was assassinated. Mercedes, Gorriti's other daughter, continued to live with her mother in Lima, where she later married. Like her mother, Mercedes was a successful poet.

Surrounded by her students, her books, and her friends, Gorriti had settled into a pleasant and tranquil life by the 1860s. She began to travel and visited Eldemira in La Paz regularly. She developed correspondences with fellow writers and was particularly eager to cultivate the talent and friendship of other women who shared her interest in literature. Just as her life seemed to be sorted out, Belzú returned from his self-imposed exile in Europe.

After leaving Bolivia in 1855, Belzú roamed Europe from London to Constantinople for almost a decade. He traveled comfortably with the large satchels of money he had brought with him. Almost as soon as he returned to Bolivia in 1865, Belzú, who was addicted to politics, began to mobilize his supporters. His plan was to remove the tyrant Mariano Melgarejo from office. The goal was a reasonable one because Melgarejo was a hated, unpopular man. To the Bolivian masses he was "El Arabe" (the Arab) whereas El Tata Belzú was still the liberator. Riding ahead of his legions, Belzú seized La Paz easily. Magnanimous in victory, Belzú entered the presidential palace to accept Melgarejo's surrender. As a gesture of peace, he opened his arms in welcome and ordered his followers to do the same. Melgarejo responded in kind. He lifted his right arm to return Belzú's *abrazo* (embrace), but in his left hand Melgarejo held a pistol. When Belzú came into range, Melgarejo shot him in the head. Melgarejo then ran onto the balcony and shouted to the crowd: "Belzú is dead! The victor has been vanquished!" "Who lives now?" he asked, and the panicked crowd answered, "Viva Melgarejo!"

With Belzú's body lying on the floor in the presidential palace, Melgarejo descended to the central plaza where he mounted a horse and received the applause of his followers. Some of his troops went into the crowd and attacked and killed many of the dead Tata's supporters. After a triumphal tour of the city, Melgarejo returned to the palace and celebrated his victory with friends by emptying a large number of beer bottles.

Gorriti was in La Paz on March 27, 1865, the day Belzú died; she had been visiting her daughter. Eldemira's home was near the presidential palace, and when the women heard the commotion, they went outside to learn that Belzú, father and husband, was dead. The news created a tremendous popular outcry. The savior of the people was dead.

The last service Gorriti performed for Belzú was to collect his body and prepare it for burial. Given Melgarejo's temperament, Gorriti admitted that she was frightened to approach him, but after sundown she gathered her strength and presented herself at the palace to claim Belzú's body, which had been stripped of its valuables and medals. His supporters surrounded the cadaver and treated it with religious veneration. The parlors of the Belzú home, she wrote, were turned into a funeral chapel, and the mourners invaded the house and filled the patios and the stairways; everywhere for three days the multitude, estimated in the hundreds, mourned and threatened revenge.

Belzú's funeral was sumptuous, the likes of which had not been seen before. All types of people, rich, old, young, poor, donned black mourning clothes and accompanied the body to the burial site. The soldiers were grave and nervous; the women carried flowers, and the people, the masses, cried. Gorriti followed the hearse on foot; she was thin, pale, elegant in her grief, and as much of an attraction as was Belzú. At the cemetery the orators condemned the acts of Melgarejo while they remembered Belzú's superhuman qualities. By the end, according to one witness, the mob was delirious, with some believing that Belzú would miraculously return to life. Many feared violence, but violence did not erupt. At the burial Gorriti led the people in prayer and asked God to end the terrible drama, the horror, the violence that had consumed Bolivia since its origins and had claimed Belzú's life. Alive, Belzú was an agent of anarchy; perhaps his death could serve peace and order.

With Belzú resting in his tomb, Gorriti returned to Lima and resumed her life. But Lima was anything but tranquil. A Spanish fleet had entered the Pacific with plans to reconquer lost colonies. In May 1866 the war of words became an armed conflict as the Spanish first shelled Valparaíso, Chile, and then sailed up the coast and attacked Callao, a Peruvian port a few miles from Lima. With her adopted country under attack, Gorriti volunteered her services to defend Callao and, like Florence Nightingale, worked as a nurse during the conflict. Juana Manuela was heroic in this last battle between Spaniard and American, wrote a friend, as she tended the sick beside the Sisters of Charity. For her bravery,

Peru decorated her with the Star of the Second of May Award, honoring her noble and generous behavior.

In the 1870s, Gorriti played an important role in Lima's cultural life by opening her home to the local intelligentsia. In 1876 she began her famous *veladas literarias,* literary evenings essentially given to provide herself and other women writers with a place where they could read and discuss literature. In the 1800s in Latin America a favorite form of amusement was the *tertulia* (salon) held in a private home. A *tertulia* could be many things, ranging from a house party with dancing, games, and refreshments to a serious discussion of politics or literature. It could be a simple or lavish affair depending on one's social status and economic resources. *Tertulias* were particularly important to young people, especially young women, because they offered a chance for socializing and meeting members of the opposite sex.

Gorriti's *veladas literarias* took place in an informal and relaxed setting, which permitted and encouraged conversation and discussion. They attracted famous writers but also undiscovered talents and were hailed by the press as a success and a welcome addition to Lima's cultural scene. She also included her students in the proceedings, and they were happy to attend because the *veladas* were amusing and included music, singing, skits, and the latest jokes and gossip. From the beginning, what made the *veladas* unique was the inclusion of women, not only as observers but also as participants. Not a feminist in the modern sense of the word, Gorriti advocated redefining women's roles in society.

One person whose career Gorriti helped launch was that of noted Peruvian novelist Clorinda Matto de Turner. She was twenty years old at the time and had just received warm applause for her traditional tales of life in Cuzco, the royal city of the Inca, which had appeared in the regional press. With her own hands, Gorriti affixed "to the hair of the beautiful writer a crown of rich filigree, intertwined with the branches of the symbolic laurel and placed in her hand a pen and pad of gold, along with a magnificent bouquet of flowers." Such a dramatic honoring of talent was the signature of the Gorriti *veladas*. The party that followed the coronation was wonderful as the poets sang in honor of the young writer, and everyone pressed a flower in her hand in tribute of admiration and affection.

Gorriti was a published author and an editor when she began her *veladas* in 1876. In 1874 she had established a weekly women's journal, *El Album,* dedicated to literature, the arts, theater, education, and fashion. That same year she launched another journal, *El Alborada,* a family weekly. Gorriti, who once was hailed as South America's George Sand, dedicated her salon to progress and the intellectual development of Latin America. She arranged the program for each session and invited special guests but did not dominate the proceedings. The *veladas* also had a theatrical dimension; when new talents debuted they were solemnly christened and given literary *compadres* (godparents) in a mocking baptism ritual. The *veladas* were well known outside of Peru and were a stopping place for visiting intellectuals.

Each session included readings or performances by women of their compositions and a discussion of issues of interest to women. The topics discussed are not unfamiliar to the contemporary audience: the role of mother, the need for general education and for employment preparation, the management of households headed by females, and even how beauty affects perceptions of a woman's worth. Gorriti used her *tertulia* to showcase her friends and to introduce new talent.

Sessions began at 8:30 in the evening and ended about 3:00 in the morning. A typical evening included lots of music, especially new compositions, and singing but no dancing. Around midnight, refreshments, usually hot chocolate and pastries, were served. Gorriti's house occupied a corner lot, and it had a small side door so guests could leave unobserved. The *veladas* were enormously successful, and as many as fifty or sixty people attended on a regular basis.

During the 1870s in Lima, Gorriti continued to edit *El Album* and dedicated it to expanding the role of women throughout society. Her goals were modest, and she argued that the sexes had specialized roles. To make the review of interest to women she had sections that dealt with fashion, the local social scene, novels, and home management. Such an approach, she hoped, would secure greater access for women to professions such as teaching. She also reminded women of their moral superiority and their special responsibility in molding culture and values. The journal dealt too with more common questions, such as how to behave at a dance, or the real meaning of motherhood. Gorriti did not advocate suffrage because she believed that women could wield greater influence without the vote.

El Album was full of crosscultural comparisons of women's roles in Europe and the United States, and clearly the United States was considered to be an example worthy of emulation. It is interesting that Gorriti greatly admired Harriet Beecher Stowe, author of *Uncle Tom's Cabin,* and used Stowe as an example of what an educated and committed woman could accomplish through her writing. Rightly or wrongly, Gorriti attributed Stowe's immensely popular study with bringing about the Civil War and ending the dread institution of slavery.

Perhaps because of her own disappointment in marriage, Gorriti used the journal to counsel young women about marriage. One short story, "Los malos" (The bad ones), was about Eve's ten daughters and how nine of them married the wrong men. Unfortunately, young women are frequently attracted to what is novel and dangerous. Why is it, the story asks, that a woman becomes glacier cold and indifferent when in the presence of an honorable man who loves her, yet will willingly go off with the scoundrel who she fears will abandon her? Young women were very sheltered in Latin American society and had little opportunity to meet young men and develop friendships. Gorriti believed that their lack of experience contributed to their poor judgment of men.

Women also had little to say about whom they would marry because the arrangements usually were made by parents. Gorriti warned, for example, against the customary spring-winter wedding that might force a girl of sixteen to marry a man of forty. Parents approved of such marriages because they guaranteed their daughters' financial security, but such a difference in age generally left both parties unhappy and frustrated.

On a lighter note, she scolded girls about being overly flirtatious, insincere, and too concerned with appearances. She warned against idleness; the woman who breakfasted and stayed in bed until noon and cultivated useless, amusing friends garnered Gorriti's scorn. Probably because she worked and wrote, Gorriti hated useless women who depended on beauty and fashion to get attention. For such women, the nights were too short and the days did not exist, she said. But the single greatest vice of Peruvian women was their love for and consumption of luxury; too much attention was placed on fashion and expensive jewelry. Yet Gorriti believed that men were primarily responsible for the defect; it was they who spent money on their mistresses and wives, and women unfortunately learned this lesson quickly.

In 1878, when Gorriti was sixty years old, she abandoned Lima and settled for the last part of her life in Buenos Aires. With the death of her daughter Mercedes, she felt her ties with Lima severed and went to live among her relatives and friends in Argentina. She had made a preliminary trip four years earlier to visit relatives in Buenos Aires and decided she would like to live there. The city in the 1880s was recognized as the Paris of South America. If Lima exemplified America's Spanish heritage and grandeur, Buenos Aires was the symbol of an expanding, capitalist dream. A product of the nineteenth century, it boasted a European immigrant population that was industrious and educated. Foreign visitors to Buenos Aires expressed amazement at the enormous metropolis of nearly one million residents, which sprawled along the banks of the River Plate. The city's increasing wealth and cosmopolitan air put it on the schedules of touring celebrities. Foreigners applauded its numerous bookshops, its broad, new tree-lined avenues, its chic boutiques, its excellent opera and theater, and its ornate public buildings. The city was European in its construction, citizenry, and culture. It also had become the intellectual capital of South America.

When she arrived in the Argentine capital, Gorriti was greeted as the grande dame of national letters; recognition and status were heaped upon her. She continued to write, edited an international cookbook, and worked as an editor. Her home continued to be a meeting place for writers and the avant-garde. When she died in 1892, she was mourned throughout the continent. Gorriti is remembered in Argentina as a writer, an American heroine, and an admirable woman.

SOURCES

The life of Juana Manuela Gorriti has been reconstructed from the following sources (no adequate biography exists): Alcides Arguedas, *Historia de Bolivia*, vols. 1, 2, 4, 5 (La Paz, 1981); Alfredo O. Conde, *Juana Manuela Gorriti: Dolor, belleza, trabajo, patriotismo* (Buenos Aires, 1939); Juana Manuela Gorriti, *Oasis en la vida* (Buenos Aires, 1888); idem, *Páginas literarias: Leyendas, cuentos, narraciones* (Buenos Aires, 1946[?]); idem, *Sueños y realidades*, 2 vols. (Buenos Aires, 1909); idem, *Veladas literarias de Lima, 1876–1877* (Buenos Aires, 1892); Roger M. Haigh, *Martín Güemes, Tyrant or Tool?* (Fort Worth, 1972); Clorinda Matto de Turner, *Bocetos al lápiz de Americanos célebres* (Lima, 1890); Martha Mercader, *Juanamanuela mucha mujer* (Buenos Aires, 1982); José Riva Agüero, *Carácter de la literatura del Peru independiente* (Lima,

1905); and Augusto Tamayo Vargas, *Relatos limeños* (Lima, 1947). Also consulted were the following nineteenth-century newspapers from Lima, Peru: *El Album, El Alborada, El Correo del Peru, América Ilustrada, Ateneo de Lima, Perlas y Flores, Los Andes,* and *Revista de Lima.* The correspondence of Ricardo Palma, housed in the Biblioteca Nacional de Peru, contains letters between Palma and Matto de Turner concerning Gorriti.

9

Soledad Román de Núñez:
A President's Wife

Helen Delpar

In Colombia, as occurred in many Latin American countries, the competition between political parties became the grand theme of national history after independence. Those who called themselves Liberals gained the first advantage, from 1832 to 1837, after the breakup of Gran Colombia. In the early 1840s the Liberals divided; moderates, who called themselves Conservatives, split from the Liberal party, leaving it in the hands of those whom they considered to be extremists. As partisans did all over the Western Hemisphere, the two parties argued over issues of provincial autonomy, free trade, and the role of the Roman Catholic church.

In Colombia the fight over the church's role was especially intense. Conservatives defended all of the church's prerogatives whereas the Liberals wanted to enact anticlerical reforms to limit the church's wealth and influence. In 1863, Liberals came into power and, to the chagrin of the church and the Conservatives, wrote one of the most liberal constitutions in the Americas. Rafael Núñez first served as a Liberal president from 1880 to 1882. In 1885, during his second term, he shocked the nation when he allied himself with the Conservative party and promulgated a new, conservative constitution.

Soledad Román de Núñez was born in 1835 and grew up in a Colombian Conservative family. Although a fervent Conservative and Catholic, Soledad married Rafael Núñez in a civil ceremony in 1877. The church did not recognize the marriage, especially because Núñez's first wife still lived. Soledad's story, like that of many other "proper" women, suggests that even individuals who strongly defended the church and traditional values at times found it impossible to live by their inflexible codes.

The history of Liberals and Conservatives in Colombia leads us to consider once again the intense political rivalries of Latin America. Did the rivals represent cliques with different social or economic interests? If we dig more deeply would we find family and regional feuds at the heart of partisan competition? Whatever the sources of the loyalty, partisan identification was important and usually lifelong. People rarely changed parties as did Núñez.

Issues relating to the political influence of women necessarily must focus on their indirect role, for women could neither vote nor hold office. Soledad clearly had influence over her husband and even offered him military advice. Her loyalty to the church and the Conservatives, considered typical of women, must have contributed to the eclipse of the Liberals.

Helen Delpar, professor of history at the University of Alabama, is one of the foremost authorities on nineteenth-century Colombia. Along with numerous articles, she is the author of *Red against Blue: The Liberal Party in Colombian Politics, 1863–1899* (1981). She also performed a service to the profession by editing the *Encyclopedia of Latin America* (1974).

In July 1884 political and social elites in Bogotá were gripped by excitement as they awaited the arrival of the controversial president-elect of Colombia, Rafael Núñez, and his equally controversial wife, Soledad Román de Núñez. Politicians eagerly anticipated the arrival of Rafael. Not only had four months elapsed since the inaugural date set by law, April 1, but also his presence was required to deal with the pressing political and economic problems confronting the country. Prices for Colombia's leading exports, coffee and cinchona bark (used in making quinine), had been in a slump for several years, and the national government was virtually bankrupt. The incoming president believed that Colombia's economic woes were due in large part to the federalist constitution of 1863, which he thought weakened the national government to the point of impotence. His frequent calls for drastic reform of the constitution had alienated many members of the Liberal party, of which he had been a member since his youth. By 1884 he retained the support only of the so-called independent wing of the party, but he had been cultivating friendly relations with the rival Conservative party for years. Now everyone wondered whether he planned to mend fences with his erstwhile Liberal comrades or move toward a definite and permanent alliance with the Conservatives.

However enigmatic his intentions, Rafael was a familiar figure to Bogotanos, having already served a term in the presidency (1880–1882). There was more curiosity about his wife and about the welcome that she would receive from straitlaced Bogotá society. Soledad's notoriety stemmed from the circumstances of her marriage to the president-elect. She had married Núñez in 1877 in accordance with civil law. However, Rafael's first wife, Dolores Gallegos, whom he had married in a Roman Catholic ceremony in 1851, was still alive. Therefore, in the eyes of the church and of devout Catholics, his marriage to Soledad was invalid, and they were both living in sin. The fact that Rafael and Dolores had been divorced in 1872 made no difference since the Catholic church did not recognize divorce. Rafael had made efforts to obtain from the clerical authorities an annulment—that is, a formal decision that his marriage to Dolores had never been valid—but he had not been successful. So delicate was the situation that during Rafael's first term in the presidency, Soledad had remained in Cartagena, the Caribbean city where both of them had been born. Meanwhile, his political enemies had openly labeled him an adulterer and a bigamist because of his irregular marriage and had directed similarly unflattering epithets at Soledad.

Soledad's defiance of religion and conventional society is all the more surprising because she was a deeply pious individual whose devotion to Catholicism was never in doubt. Nor can her decision to marry Núñez be described as the impulse of youthful passion, for she was over forty at the time and her husband ten years older. But Soledad had always been a rebel of sorts; her unconventional marriage to Núñez was but one episode in a life that exemplified the ways in which some women could expand the constricted roles assigned to them in nineteenth-century Colombia.

The first of seventeen children, Soledad Román was born on October 6, 1835, to Manuel Román and Rafaela Polanco y Ripoll. Her father, a native of Spain and a pharmacist by profession, had been en route to Mexico when he was shipwrecked near Cartagena. Deciding to remain in Colombia, he supported himself at first by working as a tutor and married one of his students, Rafaela Polanco. Soon afterward he established a pharmacy on what is now Calle Román.

In the mid-1830s, Cartagena gave little evidence of the eminence it had enjoyed during the Spanish colonial period when the city had been a major gateway to South America, especially important as a port of entry for African slaves. Only the city's massive fortifications remained as a mute reminder of its former importance to the Spanish Crown. Cartagena's fortunes had begun to decline during the wars of independence, when the city's inhabitants had suffered great hardships, and it never fully recovered. In 1831 the population was only 11,900, little more than half of what it had been in 1815. Moreover, Cartagena would soon be eclipsed as Colombia's principal port by Barranquilla, its upstart rival to the east. Thus Cartagena, while experiencing some growth in the late nineteenth century, was destined to remain a sleepy provincial capital. Inhabitants of interior Colombia were wont to look down on Cartagena, and indeed the entire Caribbean region, as a place of tropical indolence and moral laxity. Contributing to their disdain was racial prejudice against the largely black and mulatto population of the Caribbean coast.

The struggle for independence had brought about the emigration or decadence of many families of the Cartagena elite, thereby producing a vacuum that was filled by enterprising newcomers like Soledad's father. His pharmacy prospered, partly because of the potions concocted on its premises, such as Curarina Román, which reportedly cured a wide range of ailments from indigestion to tuberculosis. Like other prominent residents, Manuel joined the city's Masonic lodge, the oldest in Colombia, and became a supporter of worthy causes. When cholera ravaged Cartagena in 1849, for example, he donated cash and medicines to poor victims of the epidemic.

Little is known about Soledad's formal education, but she is described as a voracious reader whose habit of reading in bed by candlelight once led to a fire. Like most Colombian females, she was very religious, being especially devoted to the Virgin of Las Mercedes, for whose statue the child Soledad embroidered a dress. By all accounts she was a high-spirited girl who enjoyed excursions, concerts, and the performances put on by a Spanish dramatic troupe. When Juan José Nieto, a rising Liberal politician and fellow Mason of her father, wrote a play, which was performed in the patio of his home, she had a leading role. She helped her father keep the accounts of the pharmacy and, as the eldest, looked after her younger siblings when their mother died. She also acquired some of her father's pharmaceutical lore, for she later described herself as effecting cures in Bogotá with the contents of the medicine chest she always carried. According to her memoirs, when she was about seventeen she became engaged to marry the son of a Spanish merchant.

Except for her reading and the help she gave her father, there is little to distinguish Soledad's life to the point from that of other young Colombian women of similar background. The slow pace of social and economic change in nineteenth-century Colombia and its isolation from foreign intellectual currents meant that there would be little alteration in the gender roles and relations inherited from Spain. During the nineteenth century the Colombian woman of the upper class, like her colonial ancestors, was expected to be virtuous, submissive, and self-sacrificing and in general to emulate the Virgin Mary. Confined to the domestic sphere, she ventured out-of-doors only in the company of servants or family members. Marriage and motherhood were her destiny.

Upper-class women received little schooling in comparison with their male counterparts. They learned to read and write and to supervise the household tasks that eventually would be their responsibility. Although they might operate a home-centered business, such as the preparation of food for sale, they rarely sought gainful employment, in contrast to women of the lower classes, who often worked as domestic servants, laundresses, or food vendors. Thousands of women were also employed in cottage industries until they fell victim to foreign imports: as late as 1870, 70 percent of those classified as artisans in Colombia were women. By the end of the decade, however, a women's journal edited in Bogotá was advising its readers that the woman who was absorbed in domestic chores to the exclusion of other interests would become tedious to family and friends.

The editor of this publication, Soledad Acosta de Samper (1833–1913), was one of Colombia's outstanding nineteenth-century women. The daughter of a distinguished historian and public figure and his North American wife, she lived in Europe, the United States, and Peru and was the author of numerous literary and historical works. *La Mujer,* which she founded in 1878, was the first women's periodical in Colombia to be edited by a woman. Here she printed articles on the role of women in history and on the feminist movements of Europe and the United States as well as information on fashion and the home.

Soledad Acosta de Samper is sometimes credited with encouraging the conversion of her husband, historian José María Samper, from liberalism to conservatism. Although denied the right of formal participation in the country's political system, upper-class women frequently held strong political beliefs. This had become evident during the era of independence. Manuela Sanz Santamaría de González had presided over a *tertulia* (literary circle) where ideas of revolution were discussed. Policarpa Salavarrieta became a national hero after she was hanged as a spy by Spanish authorities in 1817. Another female martyr to the cause of independence was Antonia Santos Plata, who was shot by the Spanish in 1819 for financing a guerrilla force in the northeastern province of Socorro. Once independence had been achieved, women often identified themselves as Conservatives or Liberals, either in secret or in open defiance of their fathers or husbands. One memoirist recalled how his Conservative mother suffered in silence as his father indoctrinated him with Liberal ideas, but it is interesting to note that the author followed his mother's political inclinations rather than his father's.

Soledad Román also developed strong political convictions and became a fervent supporter of the Conservative party at an early age. The origins of her conservatism can only be surmised. Since she was so religious, it was perhaps only natural that she was drawn to the party that saw itself as the defender of Catholicism from the assaults of the anticlerical Liberals. Soledad's father did not take an active part in politics, but persons of his social standing in nineteenth-century Cartagena were likely to be Conservatives. On the other hand, Soledad's younger sister Rafaela became an ardent Liberal who supported the anti-Núñez, or radical, faction of the party; Núñez, who was very fond of her, jokingly referred to her as "la Radicala." It might be noted here that party loyalties in nineteenth-century Colombia were usually lifelong and intense, and individuals like Núñez who shifted party allegiances were rare. However, parents, spouses, and siblings often had conflicting partisan ties.

Despite its conventional beginnings, Soledad Román's life would take unexpected turns. Her engagement dragged on to the point that it became a subject of popular ridicule. After five years, for reasons that she does not explain in her memoirs, she broke the engagement and remained unmarried. One historian has suggested that, given her strong personality, it may have been difficult for her to find a husband to whom she could be properly submissive. Her father evidently respected her judgment for he made her the executor of his will despite the fact that he had at least one grown son. At the time of his death in 1874, he left her some urban property as well as two thousand pesos in cash. She used her legacy to open a tobacconist's shop, which she ran herself for many years. In short, as she said in her memoirs, she was a woman of great energy.

As a girl Soledad knew Rafael Núñez, but the nature of their early relationship is not clear. Rafael, although ten years her elder, frequented the same social circles as she, such as the home of Juan José Nieto, where they probably met. In 1846, Rafael, a fledgling lawyer and poet, fell in love with a local girl, identified by one author as a relative of Soledad's. For some reason the romance was objectionable to Rafael's father, who packed his son off to Panama, then a Colombian province. There Rafael met Dolores Gallegos, sister-in-law of Juan de Obaldía, a prominent landowner, politician, and future vice president of Colombia. Rafael returned to Cartagena in 1848, but three years later he went back to Panama to marry Dolores. His enemies later charged that he had wed Dolores only to further his political career under the patronage of Obaldía, but that seems unlikely. It is true that he was soon elected to the congress as a representative from Panama, but he already had made a name for himself in Cartagena and was a protégé of José María Obando, soon to be elected president of Colombia. Dolores, moreover, invariably is described as an attractive young woman. Despite the birth of two sons, the marriage did not prove to be a happy one, and the couple was often separated because she remained in Panama while he was in Bogotá serving in the congress and in the cabinet.

In 1859, Dolores and Rafael parted for the last time as he left Panama to take a Senate seat in Bogotá. There he met Gregoria de Haro, the accomplished young wife of Dundas Logan, a British merchant many years her elder. Gregoria and Rafael became lovers in 1860 just as Colombia was about to be engulfed in civil war. In 1863, Gregoria left her husband and traveled to New York; Rafael followed a few months later. They continued their affair in Le Havre, France, where Núñez had been named consul. However, in 1868, Gregoria sailed alone to New York while Rafael remained in Europe until 1874, when he returned to Colombia to make an unsuccessful bid for the presidency. He was elected in 1876 for a two-year term as governor of his native state of Bolívar.

In her memoirs, Soledad reported that Rafael always had been attracted to her and that he had proposed marriage in 1857 soon after she had broken her engagement. This seems unlikely, however, as he was already married to Dolores in 1857. In any event, he renewed his friendship with Soledad upon returning to Colombia in 1874. He visited her when he was in Cartagena and was a regular correspondent while away. By mid-1876 he was talking about linking his life with hers, although he expressed reluctance to take such a step because of his belief that happiness is a mirage. Within the next year, Soledad accepted his marriage proposal. Many years later she said that she had decided to "sacrifice" her religious beliefs and marry Rafael in order to advance the cause of conservatism by exerting influence on him. It is also clear that she was deeply in love.

Even so, the decision to marry Rafael must have cost her a great deal of uncertainty and anguish. The divorce that Dolores Gallegos had obtained from him in 1872 in no way invalidated their marriage in the eyes of the Catholic church. Not only would Soledad be violating her deepest religious beliefs by marrying Núñez, but she also could be certain that a civil marriage would scandalize Colombian society. It was this situation that probably accounts for the way in which the marriage took place. Accompanied by two of her brothers, Soledad traveled to Paris, ostensibly to consult a famous French heart specialist. Rafael, meanwhile, sailed to New York to make arrangements for equipment to be used in dredging a vital canal near Cartagena. On June 28, 1877, the Colombian consul in Paris performed the marriage, with Soledad's brother Eduardo standing in for Núñez. She returned to Cartagena the following December to join her husband, who had preceded her.

The story of this marriage provides insight into the divergent patterns of sexual behavior expected of males and females, at least among the upper classes, in nineteenth-century Colombia. Despite his church wedding in 1851, Rafael always had been a freethinker, and his civil marriage brought him no pangs of conscience. Shortly after his marriage to Soledad he wrote a friend that after condemning theocracy for years, he was not about to bow down before it in his private life. In any case, as a man he enjoyed much more sexual freedom than any similarly situated female. His relations with Gregoria de Haro and Soledad raised eyebrows mainly because they were open and involved women of the upper class, not because he had violated his marriage vows to Dolores. A discreet liaison with a woman of the lower class would have produced little if any tongue-wagging and would not have seriously affected his social life or political career.

Soledad, on the other hand, had been expected to remain chaste while unmarried; if she had been married, an extramarital affair would have brought the most severe censure. Gregoria de Haro, it will be recalled, left Colombia during her affair with Núñez and never returned. Since Soledad's civil marriage flouted Catholic teaching and social convention, she could well expect to be snubbed by polite society in Colombia. For this reason the couple considered living abroad permanently but decided not to abandon their home and families. In these circumstances, it is not surprising that Soledad chose to stay in Cartagena during Rafael's first presidential term. There she could look after her business and be near her family, which remained supportive despite her unconventional marriage. There is some evidence that members of Rafael's family, especially his mother, were unhappy about the marriage. The bishop of Cartagena, Monseñor Eugenio Biffi, made no secret of his disapproval, although he acquiesced in a young seminarian's visit to the Núñez home because he was a kinsman of Soledad. Bogotá, however, was more puritanical than Cartagena. Now that she was accompanying Rafael to the capital, as one of his political foes put it, "we shall see what results from this challenge to the cream of Bogotá society."

As it turned out, politics rather than religious principle dictated the conduct of Bogotá's leading citizens. When Rafael and Soledad arrived at the railroad station, the welcoming committee included both Liberals who were his political adversaries and Conservatives with whom he had been developing closer relations. The Liberals came without their wives while the Conservatives brought theirs. The irony lay in that the Liberals, most of whom were anticlerical, should have been indifferent to the irregularity of Rafael and Soledad's marriage. It was the Conservatives, as defenders of Catholicism, who should have been offended.

What the wives themselves thought is difficult to determine given the near-invisibility of Colombian women in the historical record. Liberal women in Bogotá are said to have been adamantly opposed to establishing social relations with Soledad. At least one prominent Conservative had similar scruples. The wife of one of Núñez's closest Conservative collaborators and sister of another, she could not bring herself to visit Soledad for nearly two years.

By that time, however, the First Lady had received the approval, if not the blessing, of the archbishop of Bogotá himself. The date was September 28, 1885, and the occasion was Núñez's sixtieth birthday. The archbishop, José Telésforo Paúl, not only attended the banquet held to celebrate the event, but he also gave Soledad his arm when it was time to go into dinner. Many were shocked by the archbishop's action, but others dismissed the criticism as being politically motivated and pointed out that Núñez, whatever his personal beliefs, was proving a friend to the church in Colombia.

A second reason for the banquet was to celebrate Núñez's recent triumph over his Liberal political enemies, an event that would soon redound to the benefit of the church. Late in 1884 the Liberals had risen in revolt against the Núñez administration, and in the ensuing emergency the president had called upon the Conservatives for support. By September 28 Núñez and his Conservative allies had defeated the Liberals and were about to reorganize the federal government in accordance with Conservative prescriptions. Just two weeks earlier the president had convoked a constituent assembly to draft a new constitution for the country. The resulting charter, the constitution of 1886, reflected its Conservative origins by restoring centralism, strengthening the powers of the chief executive, and making Catholicism the official religion of the nation.

It is generally believed that Soledad played a major role in the events of 1884–85, first, by encouraging Rafael to join forces with the Conservatives, and second, by taking an active part in the direction of the war against the Liberals. For this reason she is sometimes known as the Colombian Deborah, after the biblical prophet and judge who led the Israelites into battle against the Canaanites. As mentioned earlier, Solidad once said that she had married Rafael to advance the cause of the Conservative party. Such an assertion implies that she thought that she would be able to nudge her husband away from the Liberal party, with some of whose members he already had quarreled in 1877, and toward conservatism.

In her memoirs she denied that Núñez ever had adopted any course of action because she demanded it, but she did admit giving him advice when her feminine intuition gave her insight that had escaped her husband. Several historians claim that it was she who persuaded Núñez to make the crucial decision to turn over the government's arms to the Conservatives in 1884. She herself reported that while he was ill during this period, she averted a strike by telegraph operators by ordering the secretary of the treasury to pay the back wages owed to them. On another occasion, she recalled, she twice countermanded an order of her husband to one of his generals. Núñez grumbled but followed her wishes, and events proved her to have been correct.

Under the new Conservative-dominated regime Núñez was elected to a six-year presidential term beginning in August 1886. Ironically, the improved relations between the Catholic church and the Colombian government made the marital status of Núñez and his wife even more murky. Not only did the Roman Catholic marriage rite become the only one with any legal validity, but the law was applied retroactively, thereby throwing into question the legality of Rafael and Soledad's civil marriage. This vexatious situation eventually was resolved, however. Dolores Gallegos died in Panama early in 1889, and Rafael and Soledad were married a month later in a religious ceremony performed by Bishop Biffi in the Church of San Pedro Claver in Cartagena. Soledad's conscience could rest easy now that her marriage had received the blessing of the church. According to a fulsome article published in the diocesan weekly, the wedding had also soothed the consciences of four million Colombians, that is, the entire population.

Soledad and Rafael had moved permanently to Cartagena in 1888, retiring to a modest home that she had inherited from her father in the suburb of El Cabrero. Núñez remained titular president and was reelected to another six-year term in 1892, but he preferred to leave the day-to-day operations of the government in the hands of others and confined himself to guiding his followers by means of letters and of articles written for local newspapers. Soledad continued to play a political role by controlling access, as it were, to Rafael. It was she who received the mail and decided which letters he would see. She was also the one who greeted the many persons who came to call upon the president. Among the latter was the Nicaraguan poet Rubén Darío, who visited El Cabrero in 1892. He described Soledad as affable, intelligent, and obviously devoted to her husband. If she had intellectual interests, the poet wrote, she did not allow the cook to spoil the soup on that account.

Núñez was equally devoted to his wife and expressed the hope that God would call him before her. She could live without him, he wrote, but he would not know how to make the time pass without her company. His wish was granted, for he died in 1894, thirty years before Soledad. It is not clear whether he ever became a Catholic believer, but Soledad was convinced that he had been reconciled with the church on his deathbed. His remains were placed in a chapel in El Cabrero, which Soledad had erected in 1889 in honor of the Virgin of Las Mercedes.

After Núñez's death, Soledad rejected a pension offered by the government, despite the fact that she was in straitened financial circumstances, and lived on in El Cabrero tending the songbirds and flowers of which she was so fond. In her old age she was comforted by the presence of many friends and relatives.

She regarded one niece as an adoptive daughter, and she remained close to her sister Rafaela, who lived nearby. Her brother Enrique, who headed the family business and served three times as provincial governor under the Conservative regime, was known as one of Cartagena's most progressive citizens. Soledad died on October 19, 1924, soon after her eighty-ninth birthday.

Recent studies of women in colonial Latin America have shown that the stereotype of the cowed and subservient daughter and wife needs qualification, for there were numerous upper-class women who wielded great economic power and moral influence. While we still know very little about the lives of women in nineteenth-century Latin America, the story of Soledad Román de Núñez shows that it may be inaccurate to see them as completely under the domination of fathers and husbands. Still, it is true that, as in Victorian North America, the upper-class woman was assigned to a domestic sphere separate from the public sphere occupied by males. Thus, women received little education and were barred from public office, the clergy, the professions, and most forms of business enterprise. A double standard in sexual behavior also prevailed. Only in the late nineteenth century did feminists begin to challenge these conditions in Argentina, Chile, Brazil, and other Latin American countries undergoing rapid social and economic change.

In Colombia, Soledad Román was able to expand the boundaries of the domestic sphere by taking part in business and, albeit indirectly, in politics. She was perceived by contemporaries as an exceptionally strong and capable woman. Future researchers may be able to tell us the extent to which she was an aberration, or whether similarly strong women existed in significant numbers throughout nineteenth-century Latin America.

SOURCES

There are few published sources relating to the life of Soledad Román de Núñez, and they are not always reliable. Daniel Lemaitre, *Soledad Núñez de Román: Recuerdos* (Cartagena, 1927), is a memoir based on Lemaitre's conversations with Soledad shortly before her death. A more recent work, Juan Pablo Llinas's *Soledad Román* (Bogotá, 1986), came to my attention too late to be consulted for this essay. Other works by individuals who knew her and Rafael in their later years are Julio H. Palacio, *Núñez: Recuerdos y memorias (1893–1894)* (Barranquilla, n.d.); Fernando de la Vega, "Doña Soledad," in *Letrados y políticos* (Cartagena, 1926); and Pedro María Revollo, *Recuerdos del Doctor Rafael Núñez* (Barranquilla, 1951).

10

José de Calasanz Vela:
Frontier Priest

Jane M. Rausch

One of the most troubling issues in nineteenth-century Colombia, as noted in the essay on Soledad Román de Núñez, involved the power and influence of the Catholic church. Conservative Colombians believed that the church restrained the passions of the colored masses by advising the poor and miserable to wait for their rewards in Heaven. Liberals, on the other hand, imbued with the individualistic and anticlerical philosophy of the Enlightenment, resented the church's influence in national politics, especially because the church hierarchy usually allied itself with the Conservatives.

Simple folk, however, merely saw the sacrifice and devotion of priests in rural areas. In an era when national governments had neither the will nor the resources to assume responsibility for the welfare of their citizens, the church and its servants remained a source of aid and solace to many.

Father José de Calasanz Vela, born in 1840, became an outlaw of sorts when he and some of his fellow Dominicans defied the anticlerical laws of the Colombian Liberals in 1861. An exile to the southern frontier, Calasanz Vela extended the reach of the church into areas where national authority scarcely existed. In the conflict between civilization and barbarism, he stood squarely on the side of civilization as conventionally interpreted, but he did not turn his back on the people of the provinces. He ministered to the frontier population between 1861 and 1895. Once the Conservatives returned to power and restored the church to its preeminent position, Father Vela undertook a mission to explore and chart the unknown frontier territory for the government.

In many ways, Father Vela resembled a rural caudillo. He dispensed favors, tried to maintain order, and interceded with the authorities on behalf of his parishioners. A close study of his story might provide some clues both to the abiding strength of the church and to the way in which a patron-client network gradually developed.

Like other Latin American countries as well as the United States, Colombia began to push into its frontier regions in the late nineteenth century. The settlers, desiring to escape the civil conflicts that wracked more populous regions, were attracted by promises of land and economic opportunity. In contrast to what occurred in the United States, however, in Colombia private investors and the government were slow to commit the capital needed to build the roads or railroads that would ensure the economic future of the llanos frontier. In the absence of either government or investors, caudillos or priests like Vela exercised extraordinary influence.

Jane M. Rausch's *A Tropical Plains Frontier: The Llanos of Colombia, 1531–1831* (1984) has become the preeminent socioeconomic history of the Colombian llanos. Rausch is at work on a second volume to bring this study up to the 1980s. A professor of history at the University of Massachusetts at Amherst, Rausch has published widely on the horsemen, the church, the ecology, and the rebellions of the llanos region and also on Latin American films for classroom use.

Fray José de Calasanz Vela was a Catholic priest in the territory of San Martín (present-day Meta), Colombia, in an era when church and state were at war, and the Liberal government in Bogotá had eradicated all religious orders. Vela was born on August 27, 1840, in Gámbita, Santander. He joined the Dominicans in 1859, just two years before President Tomás C. Mosquera issued a decree suppressing religious communities throughout the republic. Rather than renounce his vows, the young monk followed several of his Dominican brothers into exile in the remote Llanos Orientales (eastern tropical plains) that were cut off from the highland capital by the 18,000-foot-high Andean Eastern Cordillera. Many of his companions succumbed to deadly fevers endemic to the llanos, but Vela overcame that peril to fall in love with the rolling grasslands, swift rivers, and tropical forests that formed the homeland for a few thousand *llaneros* (mestizo cowboys) and seminomadic Achagua, Mítua, and Guahibo Indians. For the next thirty years, Vela ministered to the people of the territory, explored the wilderness, and urged Bogotá authorities to foster the region's growth. This essay recounts his eventful life against the backdrop of troubled church-state relations and the early history of a unique Colombian frontier region, the llanos of San Martín.

With the exception of Mexico, nowhere in nineteenth-century Latin America was the church-state question so bitter as in Colombia. The long war of independence inculcated in the patriots a fervent anticlerical spirit that made them resolve to challenge the legal structure of power and privilege enjoyed by the church under the colonial regime. National political parties coalesced in part around conflicting ideas about the role that the church should play. The Conservatives, backed by the Catholic hierarchy, sought to retain the institution's prewar privileges, while the Liberals hacked away at the special legal status of the clergy, their monopoly over education, and their sources of wealth. When they were dominant in the 1820s, the Liberals enforced a rigorous *patronato real* (secular authority over ecclesiastical affairs), limited ecclesiastical *fueros* (special privileges), cut sources of clerical income, and abolished the Inquisition. Convinced that religious orders were obsolete and parasitic, they passed laws closing all *conventos menores* (convents having fewer than eight members) and requiring that novices be at least twenty-five years old before taking religious vows. The Conservatives aggressively opposed these measures, resorting to violence as in the case of the civil war of 1839 and revoking them whenever they were able to gain hegemony.

The accession of Liberal General José Hilario López to the presidency in 1849 brought a renewed attack against the vestiges of colonialism. López expelled the Jesuits (who had been invited back to the country ten years before), abolished church tithes, extinguished the ecclesiastical *fuero,* and legalized divorce. After quashing a revolt sparked in protest by the clergy, the Liberals went on to enshrine these acts in the constitution of 1853, which separated church and state and guaranteed freedom of religion to all citizens.

In these uncertain times the Dominicans, Franciscans, Augustinians, and Recoletos struggled to keep their communities alive while their membership steadily decreased and complaints were legion about their relaxed discipline. Despite repeated demands by the government, the superiors of these orders were unable to find missionaries to convert Indians on the frontier. In 1839, President José Ignacio Márquez informed the congress that the regular orders had suffered grievous losses in personnel, and the remaining monks were too old or too sick to go out to the missions. "If the trend continues," he warned, "all convents may disappear because monastic rules were the creation of another era, and today they are not reinforced by public opinion nor favored by prevailing ideas."

Between 1835 and 1861 the number of Dominican priests declined 27 percent, from seventy-two to fifty-two. In 1836 the government closed the order's monastery in Chiquinquirá because it had fewer than eight members. The remaining monasteries in Bogotá, Tunja, and Pasto continued to support a handful of missionaries in the llanos of Casanare and Cuiloto north of the Meta River. In 1838, Fray Francisco Granados, *cura* (priest) of Tame, reported that there were still four active missions in Casanare serving 634 Indians and 176 whites, but he predicted that isolation and poverty would undermine these numbers if the government did not send more supplies and raise the stipends of the priests. Such help was not forthcoming, and the missions slowly disintegrated. Historian Fray Andrés Mesanza sadly notes that Padre Fray Manuel Murillo, who died in 1855, was the last Dominican missionary in Casanare.

The worst was yet to come. After a devastating three-year civil war, fought in part over religious issues, Liberal General Tomás C. Mosquera vanquished the Conservative armies to take control of Bogotá on July 18, 1861. Determined to bring the church, which had backed the Conservatives, to submission, the flamboyant provisional president issued on July 20 the law of *tuición* (inspection), which stated that no cleric could exercise his ministry without permission from the national or state government. On July 26 he dissolved the Jesuits (who had been invited back in 1858 from their most recent expulsion). On September 9 he decreed the law of *desamortización* (disentailment) authorizing the government to seize all property belonging to religious orders except church buildings actually used for services. When Archbishop Antonio Herrán protested, Mosquera clapped him in prison. Two days later, on November 5, he suppressed all convents, monasteries, and religious houses of both sexes. The order stated that professed clergy who accepted *tuición* and *desamortización* might continue to live in their communities and receive a small income from the government; those who refused would be imprisoned or expelled from the republic.

The arrival of soldiers at the Dominican monastery in Bogotá to enforce the decree of November 5 plunged the community into turmoil. Provincial Fray Benedicto Bonilla and some of the monks took the course of least resistance and swore allegiance to the government. Others, fearing exile, went into hiding. The rest, consisting of Prior Fray Antonio Acero, five priests, and José de Calasanz Vela and five other choir monks openly defied the order. The soldiers arrested the resisters, who were sentenced to exile in Villavicencio, capital of the Cundinamarcan canton of San Martín. Five days later, escorted by soldiers, they set out on the hazardous journey over the Andean Cordillera to begin their residence on the llanos frontier.

In 1861 the road linking Bogotá with Villavicencio 20 leagues (103 kilometers) away was little more than a rough mule trail. Leaving the capital in a southerly direction, it climbed up the mountain rim of the *sabana* (savannah) of Bogotá to pass through the Boquerón of Chipaque at 12,313 feet above sea level and then descend the cordillera to the town of Chipaque at an altitude of 7,977 feet. From here the trail followed the Cáqueza River through the villages of Cáqueza (altitude 5,520 feet) and Quetame (altitude 4,789 feet), where travelers had to cross a deep gorge cut by the Río Negro by riding in a basket suspended from a cable. From Quetame the trail continued in an easterly direction to Villavicencio (altitude 1,492 feet). Up and down ridges, blocked by fallen trees and landslides, the trail wound over dizzy precipices that were heavy going even for mules. Torrents of water fell off the mountain slopes, precipitating rock and mud slides. During the rainy season, nearly all the *quebradas* (canyons) were unpassable. In the best of conditions during the dry season, the trip took five days. Nevertheless, when the weary Dominicans reached the last outcropping of the Andes at the Alto de Buenavista, just above Villavicencio, they were rewarded by a breathtaking sight. Stretched out before them was the splendid panorama of the tropical plains with their varied colors, their hills, their palm forests, and their rivers flowing into the distant horizon. As one visitor exclaimed, "The vista of the immense pampa is majestic and imposing. In the Llano all is great, and in the physical as well as the moral order, everything takes on gigantic proportions."

Dwarfed by lush surroundings, the village of Villavicencio was hardly of "gigantic proportions." Founded in the 1840s by settlers from Cáqueza and Quetame, in 1861 it was a motley collection of thatched huts on streets laid out at right angles. Most of the six hundred inhabitants raised subsistence crops of *yuca, plátano,* and rice and tended the cattle that roamed the unfenced plains beyond the town. Villagers traded with Quetame, Fosca, and Cáqueza in the highlands, with the town of San Martín in the llanos to the south, and with the Achaguas who lived along the banks of the rivers. Every year the *llaneros* rounded up cattle near San Martín and drove the herds through Villavicencio and up the cordillera for sale in Bogotá.

Although not especially religious, the people of Villavicencio valued the services of Catholic priests, who were rarely seen in their isolated town. For that reason and in spite of their solidly Liberal loyalties, they welcomed the Dominican exiles. The local militia *jefe* (chief), on the other hand, was eager to humiliate them. He approached Fray Acero and threatened to shoot him if he did not swear allegiance to the new laws. Acero refused, and the *jefe*, drunk and angry, ordered his soldiers to set up a scaffold in the plaza. As the horrified townspeople looked on, Acero was marched to the place of execution. The soldiers raised their muskets, and the *jefe* gave the signal to fire, but, wonder of wonders, the guns did not go off. The soldiers, so impressed by the courage of the prior, had loaded them without powder. Now beside himself with rage, the *jefe* ordered the soldiers arrested. He drew his sword to cut off Acero's head, but before he could reach his victim, the spectators fell upon him, seized his weapon, and took him to the jail. The Dominican historian who recounted this incident in a biography of Fray Acero did not omit its extraordinary denouement. Having escaped death, the prior immediately went to the prison to talk to the *jefe*. He obtained his release, converted his former persecutor, and heard his confession!

The Dominicans were assigned as parish priests to towns throughout the canton of San Martin. In the next few months, José de Calasanz Vela watched helplessly as his companions contracted malarial fevers. Three died by March 1862. Fray Félix Penagos died later that year in Surimena, and Deacon Fray José María Silva died in 1863. Fray Buenaventura García was sick for weeks but escaped death by convincing the local officials to allow him to go to the healthier climate of Cáqueza where eventually he recovered.

Most of the survivors took advantage of easing political tensions to return to Bogotá after the promulgation of the constitution of 1863 and Archbishop Herrán's proclamation permitting clergy to submit to the government except in matters relating to dogma and discipline, but Vela stayed on. Undeterred by fevers or rudimentary living conditions, he was enchanted by the llanos and felt intuitively their enormous potential. As he explained to the minister of the treasury in 1890:

> Twenty-eight years ago by virtue of the ideas triumphant then and in obedience to the decrees on religious communities, I had to come, because I belonged to one of the extinguished orders, to the Llanos of San Martín. On becoming acquainted with this very beautiful region, passing through its pampas, navigating its rivers, getting to know some of its savage tribes

and practicing out of necessity some uses and customs inherent to the wilderness, the idea came to me that it was and is today, the principal place for the republic to convert the savage Indians that would be a logical consequence of the colonization of its vast wilderness and the clear and stable demarcation of its borders.

The 1860s brought dynamic changes to Villavicencio and its environs. In the aftermath of the civil war of 1859–1861, the Dominicans were not the only immigrants to seek their fortunes in the llanos. Dozens of young men arrived from the highlands and staked out their claims. In 1860, for example, Manuel Fernández appeared in Villavicencio without one real in his pocket. He worked hard, purchased two *hatos* (ranches) with one thousand cattle, and made enough money to educate his numerous children at the best *colegios* in Bogotá. Sergio Convers left his store in the Calle Real of Bogotá and settled in Villavicencio in 1864. He cleared seventy-five hectares of forest and planted eighty thousand coffee trees. Narciso Reyes and Frederico Silva also planted coffee on their estates, and Ricardo Rojas R., who came penniless to the llanos in 1862, was one of the leading landowners by the end of the century.

Chief among the *empresarios* (entrepreneurs) who lobbied in Bogotá for government-sponsored development of the region was Emiliano Restrepo E., an Antioqueñan lawyer who made his first trip to Villavicencio in 1868. Convinced that the llanos would become the center of "a rich, civilized and populous nation," Restrepo acquired three cattle *hatos* and a cacao plantation. As congressman for Cundinamarca in 1870–71, he used his considerable debating skill to win support for improvements in the Bogotá-Villavicencio road. His book, *Una excursión al territorio de San Martín,* published in 1870, perhaps more than any other treatise won for the region its nickname "the future of Colombia."

By this time the Liberal government in Bogotá had accepted the cession of the canton of San Martín from Cundinamarca and declared it a "national territory." Under Law 39 of June 4, 1868, the Colombian president appointed a prefect as the chief administrative officer who was empowered to enforce legislation, settle disputes, create towns, civilize Indians, and defend the borders of the territory from foreign encroachment. The national government agreed to pay the salaries of local officials, priests, missionaries, and schoolteachers. It promised to build a primary school in each *corregimiento* (district), to raise a census, and to provide mail service and police protection. Finally, Law 39 authorized the president to award up to ten hectares of *baldíos* (public land) to any colonist who would settle in the territory, and it exempted from military conscription Indians who accepted civilized life.

As the only cleric in the new territory, Vela attended to the spiritual needs of the settlers and visited the Indian villages along the Humadea, Guatiquía, and Meta rivers. Isolated from Bogotá by the cordillera, he was not affected by Tomás C. Mosquera's renewed persecution of the church on his reelection to the presidency in 1866. Supported by the most extreme faction of the Liberals, Mosquera prohibited the collection of tithes and exiled Archbishop Herrán and the bishops of Pasto and Santa Marta. He confiscated Nuestra Señora del Rosario, the Dominican church in Bogotá, had the altars and religious ornaments torn down, and converted the building into a meeting room for the congress.

In 1867 the mercurial Mosquera was himself exiled, and his successor, Santos Acosta, attempted a reconciliation with the Catholic hierarchy. Archbishop Herrán returned to Bogotá but died in February 1868 and was replaced by Vicente Arbeláez, who called a Provincial Council in June during which he urged the bishops to do everything possible to aid the professed clergy and enjoined the monks and nuns to remain loyal to their vows while living outside their convents. In 1869, Vela took advantage of the lull in hostilities to return to Bogotá to complete his education. He received Holy Orders on September 26, 1870, and was ordained a priest in 1872.

The passage by the congress of the Organic Decree of November 1, 1870, which established free, compulsory, and secular primary education, inflamed once again the church-state issue. Although Archbishop Arbeláez gave qualified support to the plan, which removed all Catholic religious instruction from the public schools, Conservatives and right-wing Catholics led by the bishops of Popayán, Medellín, and Pasto denounced the law variously as unconstitutional, impractical, a step toward socialism, a Liberal conspiracy, and a Masonic plot to destroy the church. In July 1876 the Conservatives launched a major revolt that capitalized on popular opposition to secular education. Taking on the mantle of a religious crusade, rebel troops carried the white and yellow flag of the Papal States and banners calling for

"Liberty of Conscience," "Toleration of All Cults," "Christian Education," and "Respect for the Beliefs of the Majority."

The devastating war lasted two years, left hundreds dead, cost over 10 million pesos, and brought the economy to a standstill, but the Liberal government persevered. After the rebels surrendered, the congress took immediate reprisals against the Conservatives and their Catholic allies, exiling the bishops of Popayán, Pasto, and Medellín and strictly enforcing the more obnoxious anticlerical laws. Thus, as church historian J. Lloyd Mecham has pointed out, in spite of occasional respites in the preceding decade, the position of the Colombian church in 1880 was unique for a Catholic country of that time. Church and state were separated. Ecclesiastical *fueros* were abolished, the government did not enforce the payment of tithes, religious orders were abolished, ecclesiastical property was expropriated, and the government controlled purely spiritual matters through the law of *tuición*. These restrictions, eased to some extent after the election of Rafael Núñez in 1880, were not completely repealed until the Conservatives ousted the Liberals from power in 1885 and promulgated the constitution of 1886.

In 1873, José de Calasanz Vela returned to the llanos after serving for one year as parish priest of Cájica, Cundinamarca. He found Villavicencio recovering from a devastating fire that had broken out on February 9, 1871, in a house on the corner of the plaza and that within hours had reduced to ashes the church, parish house, school, jail, and entire southeastern portion of the town. The people had rebuilt their houses along a single street laid out toward the mountains to catch the evening breezes and constructed a makeshift church with a dirt floor and thatched roof.

Despite the disaster, the territory teemed with action. Improvements in the road to Bogotá encouraged immigration from Cundinamarca. Peasants were moving into Uribe to the south along a road built between the state of Tolima (present-day Huila) and the llanos by a company engaged in extracting quinine from the cinchona trees that grew on both sides of the Andean Cordillera. From the east came a steady influx of Venezuelans seeking refuge from the civil wars that convulsed their country. The population of the territory grew from 1,677 in 1843 to 4,056 in 1870 and continued to expand in the years that followed. Coffee plantations and cattle *hatos* multiplied between Villavicencio and San Martín. By 1874 there were over five hundred thousand coffee trees and one hundred twenty thousand head of cattle in the region, and every year the ranchers drove thirty thousand steers up the cordillera to sell in the markets of Bogotá.

A top government priority in establishing the territory of San Martín was to incorporate the thousands of Indians living in the wilderness into the Colombian nation. Three hundred years of white domination had gradually assimilated the Achaguas and Piapocos. On the other hand, during the nineteenth century, new groups such as the Mituas migrated into the llanos from the Orinoco region, and the nomadic Guahibos, fiercely hostile to white encroachment, had absorbed other Indian societies to become a formidable adversary to Colombian rule. Local officials and settlers pleaded with Bogotá to send soldiers and missionaries to protect them from Guahibo raids. In response to these demands, the congress passed four laws between 1868 and 1874 authorizing the president to promote the conversion of the Indians by sending missionaries, awarding land to those who would settle permanently, establishing white colonies in Indian areas, and appointing a civil commissary who would be responsible for improving Indian relations. These well-intentioned acts were stillborn, for the congress neglected to fund them, and the president could not find priests to assign to the llanos because of the dissolution of the religious communities.

As a result, for most of the time between 1873 and 1895, José de Calasanz Vela was the only priest in the territory. He administered the parishes of Villavicencio, San Juan de los Llanos, Jiramena, Uribe, San Martín, Cabuyaro, Sebastopol, and San Pedro de Arimena, traveling between them by horse, foot, and canoe to baptize children, perform marriages, and say Mass. Some insight into his activities can be gleaned from a report that he sent to Archbishop Arbeláez on March 31, 1884, which describes a three-month *visita* (inspection) that he had just completed of the missions along the Meta River.

Vela wrote that he left Villavicencio on January 4 and went by canoe to Cabuyaro, where he was greeted warmly by Achaguas who had not seen a priest for six years. The Dominican baptized the village children and those brought by parents from miles away. He heard many confessions and witnessed eleven marriages. After two weeks, some Indians from Sebastopol arrived to escort him to their town five days farther away along the Meta. Vela was surprised to find Sebastopol in ruins. The Indians explained that some years before, its inhabitants, believing that the world was about to end, had fled to Vichada, and only recently had they returned, disillusioned, sick, and hungry after wandering from place to place unable to find a home. An attack of fever prostrated the priest for several days, but after his recovery, he urged the Indians to rebuild the town, baptized more than fifty children, and witnessed many marriages. He stayed with them one month and promised to return the following January.

Continuing down the Meta, the Dominican marveled at sighting ruins of missions built during the eighteenth century. At Casimena he found covered by thick jungle the remains of a large chapel and walls made of rocks that could only have been transported from great distances. He told the archbishop, "The ruins of these towns can not be explained in any other way except by the lack of a priest who is everywhere the basis on which rests the future of the towns." Some Indians living near Casimena asked Vela to help them get supplies from the government and a schoolteacher, but, he confessed, "My efforts have been sterile because my weak voice finds no echo from the officials."

Later he was approached by a group of Guahibos who were grieving because disease had carried off their captain and many other members of their community. At once Vela appointed a new chief and ordered the Indians to build a town at a site between Giramena and Cabuyaro. He promised to instruct them in Christianity and waited while the Guahibos built their houses and moved into them with their few belongings. On completion of the work, he shared with them "a rustic but very clean lunch that I accepted with the same sincerity with which they offered it. I said goodby to them among demonstrations of the purest pleasure that my visit had brought to them."

The Dominican went back to Cabuyaro to hear more confessions and witness twelve marriages. He spent the first two weeks of Lent in Jiramena and would have gone to San Martín where a "multitude of disorders and diseases" beset the people, but learning that a malignant fever had appeared in Villavicencio, he decided to return there immediately. On Palm Sunday he traveled to Cumaral to hear a confession and then made the ten-hour trip back to Villavicencio to conduct Holy Week services. He concluded his account noting that Easter Mass was well attended. "All the town was joyful which shows that each day the influence of the Gospel is being felt more—a gratifying result."

Throughout his report Vela criticized government neglect of the region that "because of its topographic situation can not enjoy an efficient and healthy administration," and he stressed the need for more missionaries.

> Illustrious Señor: The priest in these regions, it can not be denied, is too much in demand; his presence would make a complete transformation because what other magnet would attract to social life so many people who wander through these immense and great deserts without more shelter than Providence. They all miss the priest and with much reason, because it has been well said that a people without a pastor never will find its happiness.

Vela's authority as parish priest and his attractive personality made him one of the leading citizens of Villavicencio. Travelers to the territory seldom failed to mention him. Nicolás Pardo, for example, who came to Villavicencio in November 1874 to defend a relative accused of murder, wrote that among the officials who welcomed him was "Fray Calasanz Vela, a man who by his regular and pure customs and his mild and peaceful character, lacking in hypocrisy and fanaticism, appears to be a creature born of the gospel itself." In 1887, Rufino Gutiérrez, a government inspector from Cundinamarca, observed that

> few priests can be found who are so appropriate for those extensive regions as this notable religious man, since Reverend Padre Vela, who is still young and of strong constitution, unites to his great zeal for the propagation of the faith and for all that relates to the moral and material progress of that territory, a fertile and tireless activity, a great knowledge of the Llanos, exquisite tact to dominate his baptized flock and to reduce the savages on the banks of the Meta and the Ariari. He is generous, hospitable, charitable, of good practical sense and no little wisdom.

The most complete description we have of Vela was set down by Ernst Röthlisberger, an Austrian professor, who visited Villavicencio in December 1883 and was greatly impressed by the parish priest.

> "El Pater" as he was affectionately called, was a Dominican friar, tall and robust and in his forties. He had an expressive, kindly face, red cheeks and a beautiful, thick beard worn with the permission of his superiors. Padre Vela, in his white and black habit, was a splendid and masculine figure. But almost never, because of the fierce heat of that region, did he wear the habit of the order; in civilian clothes he looked more like a stout miller. He liked very much to ride horseback and to share the life of the Llaneros. He was a Llanero in the best sense of the word. He had

also a small *hato*; he raised cattle and sold it. He had to do this because the government did not pay his salary punctually and because the inhabitants of the Llanos do not show any special largess with their clergy. The priest there was of a different type, since the people passed most of the year without the counsel of the church and were accustomed even to bury the dead without help from the clergy when the priest was absent, so their submission and respect for the clergy was not very marked. For this reason, any kind of fanatic and any priest who always had religion in his mouth might soon have been thrown out of the Llanos. Padre Vela, on the other hand, with his natural uprightness, had won the complete confidence of the people. Also on his trips along the Meta River, he learned how to inspire the respect and veneration of the savage Indians so that there [were] always some who came to him to be baptized. Diligent and tolerant at all times, El Pater could be considered a counselor and educator of Villavicencio and its environs.

By the time of Röthlisberger's trip to Villavicencio, church-state relations on a national level had begun to improve. In 1880 a coalition of Conservatives and moderate Liberals elected Rafael Núñez president on a platform that called for religious toleration. The Regenerator, as Núñez came to be called, negotiated with a special papal envoy, Monseñor Juan Bautista Agnozzi, for the restoration of the religious orders, and in 1882 the Dominicans, Franciscans, and other communities were reincorporated. The congress repealed most of the anticlerical regulations enacted after the civil war of 1876–77, including the hated law of *tuición*. In 1884 the radical Liberals revolted in a last effort to regain control of the country. Their defeat in 1885 opened an era of Conservative domination that would continue until 1930.

With Núñez again serving as president, a new constitution was adopted in 1886 declaring Roman Catholicism to be the religion of Colombia and empowering civil authorities to enforce respect for the church. The new charter stated that public education must be organized in accordance with Catholic teaching and guaranteed the right of the church to conduct its affairs without government interference. A concordat signed by Núñez and the Holy See in 1887 amplified these privileges and awarded compensation to the church for its property expropriated in 1861. These measures paved the way for a renewal of missionary activity that would take place in the next decade.

In the meantime, José de Calasanz Vela embarked upon the greatest adventure of his career. Over the years his frustration had grown at Colombia's systematic neglect of its eastern territories and its failure to promote the conversion of their native inhabitants. Hoping to direct the attention of Bogotá to the untapped human and economic possibilities of the region, Vela approached Núñez's minister of the treasury in 1887 with a plan to explore by canoe the Ariari and Guaviare rivers as far as San Fernando de Atabapo on the Colombian-Venezuelan border nearly one thousand miles away. He proposed during the trip to keep exact navigational records, report on the geography and climate, and catalog the natural products that might be exploited profitably. Most important, he would visit the Indians along the rivers, bringing them the Gospel and extending to them a welcoming hand from the Colombian government. Upon his return to Villavicencio, Vela pledged to submit a full report of the voyage with detailed recommendations for the future evangelization and development of the region.

The minister of the treasury was receptive to Vela's project, especially since Colombia and Venezuela were in the midst of interminable negotiations over where their common boundary should be drawn. Recognizing that it would be prudent for Colombia to make its presence felt in the disputed territory, he signed a contract with the Dominican on December 23, 1887, authorizing him to explore the Ariari, Guaviare, Maquiriva, Teviare, Vichada, Muco, and Meta rivers and to proselytize the Indians living along their banks. Two and one-half years later, in June 1890, Vela delivered to the minister the report of his odyssey, eventually published under the title *Desde Villavicencio hasta San Fernando de Atabapo,* which spurred the reassessment of national territorial policy and the arrival of Salesian missionaries to the llanos.

As Vela noted in *Desde Villavicencio,* he had planned to start in March 1888, sailing from a port on the Ariari River south of San Martín, but the necessity of cutting a road between San Martín and the Ariari delayed his departure for one year. By March 1889 he had assembled his little fleet on the river. It consisted of *La Misionera,* which was a large pirogue with a crew of five *bogas* (oarsman); a medium-size dugout canoe with two *bogas*; and two small canoes paddled by Mituas who were to act as guides. He loaded the boats with provisions for the crew—meat, rice, flour, and salt; gifts of knives, axes, fishhooks, harpoons, and clothes for the Indians; and trade items such as coffee and medicine. Other indispensable equipment included a compass for navigation and firearms for hunting game and subduing the Indians, who, Vela wrote, "are inoffensive and even cordial when they recognize the superiority of others."

The expedition set out at the beginning of the rainy season, and most of the problems encountered on the trip to San Fernando were related to the torrential storms that raised the height of the rivers fully four meters above their dry season levels. While the canoes sailed easily with the current, a constant watch had to be kept for barriers formed by fallen trees. Near San Vicente a sudden squall whipped up the waves of the Ariari, capsizing the canoes. The men scrambled back to safety before the menacing eyes of an "infinity of fat crocodiles." Widespread flooding caused animals who lived along the banks of the Guaviare to withdraw to higher ground, making it difficult for the crew to supplement their diet with fresh game or fish. By the end of April, the explorers had exhausted their supplies and were living on what they could barter from the Indians. Often after sailing all day, they could not find a safe place to anchor and continued traveling through the night with the crew sleeping in hammocks on board. Throughout the trip they were tormented by voracious mosquitoes, and the constant rain did not relieve the sweltering heat that averaged around 84 degrees Fahrenheit. Vela gave thanks to God on reaching San Fernando on May 2, having covered some 927 miles in nine weeks (see map). He presented himself to the local authorities, apologizing for his ragged clothes and for his bare feet so swollen by mosquito bites that he could not get on his shoes.

San Fernando de Atabapo, founded in 1756, was the capital of the Venezuelan province of Amazonas. It consisted of forty-six *bahareque* (mud brick) houses notable for their poverty and lack of comfort. The population, in addition to government officials, was mostly mestizo and Indian merchants and sailors. The town was also the headquarters of the Compañía General de Alto Orinoco, a French firm that had been granted by Venezuela a monopoly on the export of rubber from Amazonas.

Vela rested in San Fernando for two months. While he collected supplies for the return trip, some of his Colombian crew deserted. He hired Venezuelan replacements and acquired a second pirogue, which he christened *La Vencedora*. The Dominican pleased the authorities by offering a special Mass on July 5 to mark Venezuela's Independence Day. He visited extensive cacao plantations owned by the Compañía General and noted that it was exporting six hundred tons of rubber per year to Ciudad Bolívar.

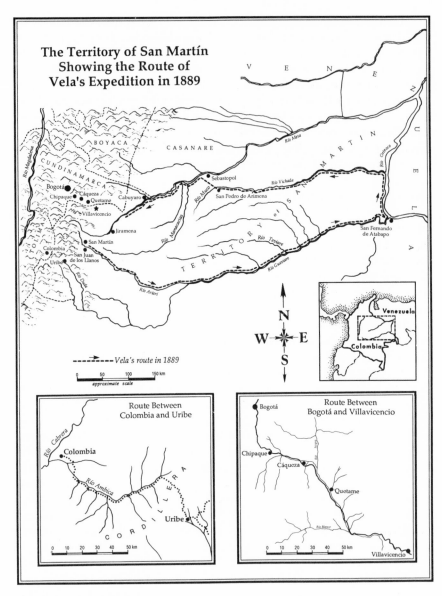

Courtesy of Patricia Cutts.

The return voyage up the Orinoco River and westward along the Vichada was more difficult. Now the crew had to pole the boats against a strong current. They toiled all day to make headway while during the night they were pelted by rain and beset by an "immense plague of mosquitoes who stuffed themselves on our flesh and tormented us with their buzzing." By early August some of the Venezuelan recruits were in a rebellious mood, and several abandoned the expedition as soon as it reached the Indian village of Tamaracoco on the Vichada.

Vela persuaded some Tamaracocans to work the canoes as far as San Pedro de Arimena on the Meta. Sailing up the Muco River to reach that town, the fleet had to pass through a channel completely clogged with fallen trees. The crew stripped the decks of the boats to reduce their height to a minimum. Then they hacked away with axes at the dense forest that blocked the path. Vela wrote, "To all these difficulties was added the abundance of snakes and wasps that at every step we found in the branches and that to avoid danger it was necessary to kill the first and endure the second."

On September 27 they came to San Pedro de Arimena. The worst part of the trip was now behind them, for the route along the Meta was familiar and relatively uneventful. On November 14 *La Misionera* and *La Vencedora* anchored at Villavicencio's port, La Cruz, ending a ten-month journey that had covered more than two thousand miles.

On each leg of the voyage, Vela visited Indian villages along the rivers. To all he distributed knives, harpoons, and clothing— presents that the natives accepted "without a word of gratitude" because they regarded gift-giving as an obligation. Among Indians already Christian, Vela baptized children, said Mass, and prayed the rosary. With the unconverted, he explained the advantages of Christianity and urged them to settle in towns where missions could be established. Everywhere, he listened patiently to Indian complaints of mistreatment by Colombian and Venezuelan settlers and promised to intercede with the government on their behalf.

Vela was a keen observer. *Desde Villavicencio* contains lengthy descriptions of the customs of the Mítuas, Guahibos, and other Indians. Ethnologists find his comments useful today, since they show that many native customs already had been altered due to contact with whites. The Dominican estimated that there were 21,531 Indians in the areas he had explored, of which approximately 84 percent were Guahibos. Vela believed that missionaries were essential to convert these nomads and to preserve the dwindling number of Achaguas, Mítuas, and Piapocos. He recommended that the government found a college in Villavicencio to prepare priests to work with Indians and locate colonies of white settlers with military protection in San Pedro de Arimena and San Vicente on the Ariari to expand Colombian presence into these remote areas and control white exploitation of the Indians. Alarmed by the scale of Venezuelan activities in San Fernando de Atabapo and the ominous presence of the Compañía General, he urged the minister of the treasury to take energetic steps to delineate the international border in order to prevent Venezuelan encroachment on Colombian soil.

Finally, Vela wrote passionately of the need to develop the economic and human potential of the llanos of San Martín and Vichada, for the *llaneros,* isolated as they were by the cordillera, could not progress without the "decided support and special protection of the national government." He recommended that the region be restored to the status of a "special territory" (an arrangement abrogated by the constitution of 1886) and that the government lower the price of salt to encourage cattle ranching, extend the telegraph line from Villavicencio to San Martín, build a road between Villavicencio and La Cruz, and promote steam navigation on the Meta. Only these measures, he concluded, would ensure "the rapid material, intellectual and moral colonization of our *llanuras orientales.*"

Vela's report struck a responsive chord in Bogotá. In 1892 the congress reclaimed the canton of San Martín from Cundinamarca and reorganized it as a national intendancy on January 17, 1893. The Spanish Queen Regent María Cristina mediated the long-smouldering boundary controversy between Colombia and Venezuela in 1891. With the settlement of the border, known as the Laudo Español, relations improved, and Venezuela permitted a Colombian entrepreneur, José Bonnet, to begin regular steamboat travel on the Meta between Orocué and Ciudad Bolívar in 1893. On February 3, 1896, the first Salesian priests arrived in Villavicencio. One year later they had founded missions in San Juan de Arama, Jiramena, Güejar, San Martín, and Uribe.

Padre Vela did not live to see this day, and his last years were clouded by a contentious dispute with local authorities in Villavicencio. On January 28, 1890, shortly after his return from San Fernando de Atabapo, a devastating fire once again leveled

Villavicencio. The following October the congress awarded eight thousand pesos to rebuild the church and parish house. Vela was a member of the junta created to oversee the reconstruction, but an argument arose between him and the others over how to proceed. By December 1893 the church was still in ruins, and Ricardo Rojas R., Manuel Fernández, and Cesareo A. Santos formally complained to the minister of government in Bogotá that Padre Vela "with character of absolute imposition is taking charge of distributing and ordering at his whim and against our unanimous will the investment of the existing capital causing arguments and sharp differences." The minister referred the matter to Archbishop Bernardo Herrera Restrepo, who pointed out that Vela could not dispose freely of the money since he was no longer the *cura* of Villavicencio. Herrera ruled in July 1894 that the funds must be handed over to the current priest and the president of the junta to be administered jointly.

The documents do not reveal the name of the new priest or the year he came to Villavicencio, but it is clear that Vela continued to minister to the *llaneros* until his tragic death in 1895. Archaeologist Carlos Cuervo Márquez, who met him in Villavicencio about the time of the dispute with the junta, described Vela as "a worthy and valiant priest" who was "the center around which moves all the religious, political and social organization of the immense territory comprehended between the Meta and Guaviare." Cuervo Márquez asserted that "Rev. Padre Vela is irreplaceable in the Llanos and what is to be regretted is that he does not have a young companion whom he can educate in the employment of the sacred ministry of this special region." Soon after this meeting, on December 9, 1895, Vela was crossing the Duda River to visit Uribe when his horse threw him, killing him instantly. He was buried under the main altar of the Uribe church where a marble stone was appropriately inscribed: "Fr. José C. Vela was born 27 August 1840. He received Holy Orders on 28 September 1870. He served disinterestedly the parishes of the Llanos of San Martín for twenty-four years. R.I.P."

SOURCES

This biographical sketch is drawn from a larger study of the history of the llanos of San Martín, Casanare, and Arauca as a Colombian frontier region from 1831 to 1931. The best sources about Vela are his own two reports, "Visita de las poblaciones del Meta," *Anales Religiosos* (Bogotá) 1 (1884): 351–53; and *Desde Villavicencio hasta San Fernando de Atabapo,* published by install-ments in *América Española* (Cartagena), 1935–36, and edited by Andrés Mesanza. Mesanza's history of the Dominican Order, *Apuntes y documentos sobre la orden dominicana en Colombia (de 1680 a 1930)—apuntes o narración* (Caracas, 1936), contains several references to Vela. Of the various travelers who describe their meetings with him, this essay cites the following: Carlos Cuervo Márquez, "El Llano," in *Una excursión al territorio de San Martín,* ed. Emiliano Restrepo Echavarría (Bogotá, 1870; reprint, 1955); Rufino Gutiérrez, "Villavicencio," *Monografías* (Bogotá) 1 (1920): 56–70; Nicolás Pardo, *Correría de Bogotá al territorio de San Martín* (Bogotá, 1875); and Ernst Röthlisberger, *El dorado,* trans. Antonio de Zubiaurre (Bogotá, 1963).

11

Angela Peralta: A Mexican Diva

Ronald H. Dolkart

The usual view of nineteenth-century Mexico stresses political and civil upheavals: the strife-ridden age of Antonio López de Santa Anna (1832–1855), the equally violent era of Benito Juárez and the Reforma (1855–1862), the French invasion and imposition of the foreign emperor Maximilian and his wife Charlotte (1862–1867), the return of Juárez (1867), and, finally, the process of settling into the order and progress of Porfirio Díaz's long reign (1876–1910). The study of these political earthquakes encourages us to forget that daily life continued all the while. Some Mexicans shaped tortillas, others played cards, danced, or sang, and some even went to the opera.

The singer Angela Peralta was born in 1845 in Mexico City, studied voice and opera in Europe, and, thereafter, divided her life as an opera star between Europe and Mexico. She ventured into composition and also organized and directed her own opera company, displaying considerable entrepreneurial skill.

Love of music and drama had long been part of Mexican culture. The folk culture borrowed instruments and music from indigenous traditions as well as from African and Hispanic traditions and rhythms. Carnival and other religious holidays provided opportunities for people of all social classes to stage sometimes elaborate dramas and masquerades. High society tended to admire and emulate European musical styles and tastes. Nevertheless, Peralta's career suggests that the melding of European and American traditions continued even in the sophisticated genre of opera. We might ask, though, whether Angela Peralta would have been as popular in Mexico if she first had not gained fame in Europe.

Peralta's career reminds us that artists, even those who are not necessarily apolitical, can transcend politics. Peralta could perform equally well under Juárez's rule or Maximilian's. We see, too, that a few talented women like Peralta (or Juana Manuela Gorriti) were able to find the social space they needed to excel in artistic fields. Yet in the end Peralta could no more escape the conventions that dictated a woman's proper behavior than could Rosa Dominga Ocampos in Paraguay or Carlota Lucia de Brito in Brazil. Why, then, did Peralta receive more criticism for her unconventional behavior than did either Soledad Román de Núñez or Juana Manuela Gorriti?

Ronald Dolkart, professor of history at California State College at Bakersfield, received his Ph.D. from the University of California, Los Angeles. He has long had an interest in opera in Latin America and has published several articles on that topic. His first love is Argentine history, and he coedited and contributed to *Prologue to Perón: Argentina in Depression and War* (1975).

O Patria, quanto mi costi!
Aida, act 3

Maria Callas, the most influential opera singer of recent times, gave her first performances in Mexico City in 1950 at the height of her vocal prowess. The director of the National Opera, Antonio Caraza Campos, brought her a copy of *Aida* that had belonged to Angela Peralta; this score was remarkable for a high, sustained E-flat at the end of the "Triumphal Scene" instead of the usual note indicated by Giuseppe Verdi. Indeed, Callas followed this version to honor Peralta and the Mexican opera-going public, and it can be heard on recordings made during her performance at the Palacio de Bellas Artes.

Who was this Angela Peralta, so highly regarded in Mexico and by Callas? She was born in 1845 and died in 1883; during this short span, her life had the same melodramatic quality as the operas in which she brilliantly performed. A woman bereft of physical attractiveness, Peralta was immensely popular because of the beauty of her voice. She grew up in modest circumstances but earned significant sums of money, received expensive gifts, and achieved international fame during her transatlantic career. Condemned to a loveless marriage, Peralta was freed by her husband's madness and death to enter into a scandalous liaison. Tirelessly singing her way across Europe and Mexico, she died of a terrible disease, precisely as did so many heroines of nineteenth-century opera. In the end, this great figure of Mexico's cultural history, at times widely praised by her country's leaders, was rejected and abandoned. Peralta's fate was not unlike that of the Egyptian princess Aida, her foremost role, who herself was destroyed by the choice between love and duty.

Most important for us, the career of Angela Peralta shows the constraints on and opportunities for women living a century ago in a Mexican society that was typically patriarchal, a society in which wives and daughters were relegated to completely subservient roles. Even though Mexico began a process of gradual modernization after the middle of the nineteenth century, females shared little if at all in the social advances. The theater, however, and particularly opera, did present one chance for women to gain renown because the soprano voice was the core of contemporary lyric drama. Peralta not only performed, but she also became known as a creative composer of popular songs and as an enterpreneur running her own opera companies. That her abilities were notable in her time has been overshadowed by the tragedy of her final years.

What allowed Peralta her success was the great passion for opera in Mexico, which lasted from independence in the 1820s through the 1920s, when it gave way, as it did everywhere, to the public's love affair with films and other mass media. Musical drama initially appeared in Italy at the beginning of the seventeenth century and progressed through baroque and classical expressions to reach a high point of public adoration in romantic opera of the nineteenth century. It was the preferred entertainment of the bourgeoisie in European cities who constructed the Continent's great opera houses as their temples to the lyric art.

What began in Mexico in frank imitation of European taste became a national obsession, especially in Mexico City but in provincial cities as well. To a very great degree, Mexico's opera resulted from the arrival of traveling companies from Europe. The most famous early visitor was Manuel García, who arrived with an entire company. García introduced to Mexico the type of opera that would continue to fascinate the Mexicans—bel canto, a florid style often seen in the compositions of Vincenzo Bellini, Gaetano Donizetti, and Gioacchino Rossini. In the 1830s opera became a common occurrence in Mexico, and Frances Calderón de la Barca, a famous observer of the capital's society, called it "decidedly the best public exhibition."

Thus by the time Angela Peralta was born on July 6, 1845, in Mexico City, the capital was decidedly opera-mad and willing to spend its money to see the world's most renowned singers. One of these was Henrietta Sontag. The German soprano enjoyed immense popularity throughout Europe and had come on tour to the United States, ending up in New Orleans where she boarded ship for Veracruz. When she reached Mexico City in 1854, Sontag was greeted with wild enthusiasm by a society dedicated to its own amusement in the final months of Antonio López de Santa Anna's dictatorship.

It was while Sontag was in Mexico that the career of Angela Peralta began. The story goes that the German artist was told of an amazing child singer and that she insisted on seeing her. The appearance of the tiny mestiza only made Sontag laugh, until Peralta sang a resplendent aria. Sontag embraced the child and predicted a great future for her if she went to Europe. This tale, however, may be only a legend such as appears in the biography of many opera stars. But Peralta's meeting with Henrietta Sontag, whatever its true nature, contained a grim irony: the European was soon to die tragically of cholera in Mexico, foreshadowing Angela's own dark fate.

Peralta has been described as growing up in very humble circumstances, and some versions of her life even discuss her employment as a maid. Yet she was probably from the lower middle class in the context of midnineteenth-century Mexico. As one indication, she received a good education, which permitted her to understand the several languages and worldly romantic operas in which she performed.

By the 1850s, when Peralta was still a child, Mexico had started to build its own, albeit Europeanized, musical tradition. Students were sent abroad to study, a conservatory was established, phil-harmonic societies were formed, and orchestral and operatic works were composed. One of the most active figures in this movement was Agustín Balderas, an impresario, a conductor, and a teacher. He undertook the training of Angela, always under the close supervision of her father, Manuel Peralta, and sponsored her debut, at the age of fifteen, in Verdi's immensely popular opera *Il Trovatore*. The major role of Leonora requires a wide range and a mature technique in a vocalist, but Peralta proved herself immediately. A refrain soon made the rounds of the capital that "Mexico owes something to the world for the death of Henrietta Sontag and so it has replaced her with Angela Peralta." Such instant success brought forth a donation of one thousand pesos to send Peralta to Europe. Accompanied by her father and Balderas, in 1861, at the age of sixteen, she left Mexico.

Angela's party disembarked in Cádiz, and a concert in the Spanish city produced a favorable report that quickly made its way back to Mexico. But the Mexican public would have to wait a long time to see Peralta again. For the next five years she received the operatic training and seasoning only Europe could provide. This process began in Italy, the center of the operatic world, where she studied with Francesco Lamperti, the most famous vocal coach in Europe, at the Milan conservatory. His judgment would follow her everywhere—"Angelica di voce e di nome" ("Angelic in voice and in name"). Her appearance, however, was anything but heavenly. Contemporary accounts describe her as short, almost dwarfish, obese, coarse-featured, and Indian-looking, far from the European ideal of a *prima donna assoluta* of an opera house. Nevertheless, Peralta learned to carry herself with great style and was always handsomely gowned and covered with jewels.

Peralta's debut in Italy took place in the country's most venerable operatic theater, La Scala in Milan. The title role in Donizetti's *Lucia di Lammermoor* is notable for its famous "mad scene" requiring the coloratura style, with its elaborate ornamentation, that Peralta had thoroughly mastered. Although she was understandably nervous and somewhat hesitant at her debut, it marked the beginning of what would be a triumphant European career. The singer from the New World was a novelty in Europe. She won an unqualified ovation for her performances in Bellini's *La Sonnambula* in Turin. The engaging tale of a sleepwalker whose adventures have a happy outcome was a perfect showcase for Peralta's somewhat limited acting but mellifluous vocal talents, and this opera became identified with her in Italy. Her travels carried her as far east as Alexandria, Egypt, and west as Lisbon, Portugal. Her fame grew and the critics' reviews became ever more ecstatic. One frequent comment indicated that Peralta remained one of the best exponents of a bel canto technique, typical of the earlier part of the nineteenth century, just at the time that opera was changing to a more dramatic ideal. The great tenor Lorenzo Salvi, who preferred the same repertoire, exclaimed, when he sang with her, "You belong to a school which no longer exists."

As Peralta's reputation spread throughout Europe, the news of her activities created great interest in Mexico, despite its preoccupation with continuing civil war and foreign intervention. The struggle between Liberals and Conservatives, which had divided the country deeply, gave rise to a French invasion in 1861, the same year that Peralta left for study abroad. The emperor of France, Napoleon III, in league with Mexican Conservatives, decided to place a monarch on a throne, and thus, in 1864, Maximilian von Hapsburg and his wife Charlotte arrived to form their court in Mexico. Naturally, opera would play a significant role in the royal plans not only because it was a favorite European entertainment but also because it represented the European view of the greatest artistic and civilizing achievement of the nineteenth century. Maximilian was surprised to find an operatic tradition already established in far-off Mexico, and he praised the Teatro Nacional as a beautiful auditorium, promptly renaming it the Teatro Imperial. In addition, he decided to foster opera in every way; he subsidized its performance as well as a school to train local talent. Maximilian's most significant contribution, ironically, was that he, a foreign prince, cultivated operas by Mexican composers. Even though Mexican musicians had written some operas in the Italian style (usually on European historical subjects), their operas had had difficulty competing with those that came from abroad. The monarch's attendance at *Agorante, Rey de la Nubia,* by Miguel Menenses, and *Pirro de Aragón,* by Leonardo Canales, boosted the prestige of local composers.

During their reign, Maximiliano and Carlotta (to use their Hispanicized names) needed a star attraction in order to raise imperial esteem and forge links with Mexican culture. Angela Peralta would be brought back in triumph. Her return was organized by Annibale Biacchi, an Italian bass who had come to Mexico as a performer and remained as an impresario. He put together the company that was to appear for a long season in the imperial capital, and he issued the announcement of Peralta's appearance. In Biacchi's glowing terms, she was someone "who has brought glory to Mexico throughout Europe . . . this shining star of her profession." The announcement of Angela's arrival in Veracruz on November 19, 1865, caused an exodus of dignitaries and populace from Mexico City to meet her party. The outpouring of emotion, the cries and shouts, went on through the late afternoon and into the night as the returning carriages reached the city and Angela's home: it had become apparent that the reception represented a patriotic demonstration against the French and that Mexicans had invested the singer with a symbolic role as victor over Europeans.

Peralta opened in her favorite opera, *La Sonnambula,* and descriptions of the evening of November 28 give every indication of a tumultuous event. Whenever she came onto the stage the audience broke into "frantic applause," which continued for a long time while papers with verses on them and bouquets of flowers rained down. The season continued with the usual Italian favorites, but a premiere by a Mexican composer took place as well—Melesio Morales's *Ildegonda,* a story of the medieval crusades, with Peralta in the leading role. So great was the demand to see her that employees of the opera house got most of the tickets and sold them at an enormous profit. In the midst of this euphoria, Peralta made a decision that would taint the public's view of the twenty-year-old diva. When a singer had had great success, a benefit performance marked that popularity. Angela's came on the night of January 29, 1866. She appeared in acts from three different operas, and during the intervals verses of praise were read. The difficulty grew out of a proclamation from Maximiliano naming her court singer and presenting her with diamond jewelry. Her acceptance connoted collaboration with the ever more despised emperor. Ignacio Altamirano, one of Mexico's distinguished writers and Liberal partisans, declared that all the honors gained in Europe by the Mexican singer had been "shamefully" thrown away.

Peralta was able to mute criticism in the capital by leaving for a tour of Mexico's other cities, bringing them opera on a professional scale, often for the first time. She also sought to counter prejudice against her single life as a theatrical woman by marrying her cousin, Eugenio Castera, a match that would result in great anguish for her. The opera company's journey proved exceedingly arduous; in this period, before the construction of railroads, scenery, costumes, and personnel had to travel by wagon and coach. From Querétaro to Guanajuato to Durango to San Luis Potosí to Zacatecas and, finally, to Guadalajara, where a magnificent new auditorium, the Teatro Degollado, was inaugurated, she was greeted with unbounded enthusiasm and received as a national heroine. In Zacatecas she accepted a large golden eagle brought on stage by four men. In Guadalajara she was carried in triumph back to her hotel. The tour proved very profitable, earning the sizable sum of one hundred thousand pesos.

While Mexico was caught up in the death throes of the empire as the French withdrew and the Liberals closed in on Maximiliano, Peralta announced that she would depart for another extended European tour. A final benefit took place for her, and the newspaper account underscored her unique talent: "It seems incredible that this incomparable woman is able to emit so many notes without taking a breath . . it seems like she has a bellows in her lungs . . . her delicious voice trills as never before; she ascends and descends chromatic scales as she has never done it."

On her way to Europe, Angela Peralta and her husband stopped off to appear in Havana's Teatro Tacón because the desire for opera in Cuba was also very great. From Havana she went to New York where she was presented in concerts by Max Maretzek, a colorful impresario who for many years had taken singers to Mexico. Most of 1869 she spent in Italy, especially the northern part of the peninsula, and again she had great success in the various opera houses before the most discerning audiences and knowledgeable critics of her chosen repertoire. An article in the Milan daily offered an extensive analysis of her art, including the significant point that, while other singers used an opera score as a point of departure for their own, often meaningless, embellishments, Peralta sang the music precisely as the composer had written it, with a performing musician's deep understanding of its meaning. She now found herself being compared favorably to Adelina Patti, certainly the most famous European singer of the last half of the nineteenth century. They shared the same type of voice and many of the same roles, and Patti herself would make a sensational appearance in Mexico in late 1886 and early 1887.

Angela had one more series of European performances, in Madrid, before returning to Mexico. Audiences and critics alike praised her operatic talent and her voice for its agility, purity, and security. While Mexican-Spanish relations had been strained during most of the years since Mexico's independence, approval from the former mother country for an artist from Latin America went far in helping to build cultural bridges. Her performances in her favorite operas, such as *Lucia di Lammermoor,* were particularly distinguished because in these she was paired with the tenor Enrico Tamberlick, the reigning male voice in Europe through the middle years of the century. Tamberlick's style fit Peralta's exactly, and they prepared to return to Mexico together for a season that would be arranged by Peralta herself.

Meanwhile, in Mexico, Peralta had been the object of constant news, much of it sensational. Stories reported her association with various crowned heads of Europe, even the empress of Russia. But more accurate rumors also had begun to circulate, rumors that her husband suffered from mental illness and often acted in irrational ways. The most exciting news Mexicans received, however, was of Angela Peralta's imminent return in 1871. In this era of the restored republic, with Benito Juárez as constitutional president, stability had at last returned to Mexico even if economic conditions remained difficult. The death of Juárez in 1872 resulted in the peaceful succession of Sebastián Lerdo de Tejada, and although he was ousted by a brief revolt in 1876, the Liberals maintained their dominance. The long reign of Porfirio Díaz during the last quarter of the nineteenth century and into the twentieth linked rapid economic development to the greatest period of operatic opulence in Mexico's history.

This resurgence of opera could not have had a better beginning than the "Great Season of Opera Peralta-Tamberlick" announced for the again-renamed Teatro Nacional. Opening night was fixed for the anniversary of the battle of Puebla, May 5, and the subscription series sold out immediately despite the relatively high prices. For example, a box of eight seats for a group of operas cost well over one hundred pesos, but it was possible to obtain a seat in the gallery for five or ten pesos for the same ten to twelve performances. Peralta received some three thousand pesos per month for her efforts, and Tamberlick twice as much. When this large company of artists from Europe arrived, they were eagerly received, and the first series of operas was such a great success that a second, third, fourth, and even fifth was given so that the entire season lasted almost five months.

These evenings became spectacular events. Before the curtain went up on the productions, military bands on stage would play the national anthem, marches, and various fanfares. When the principal singers appeared, there would be showers of bouquets and verses. Sometimes, after the performances, the artists would be carried back to their residences by the fans. The most grandiose night was August 28 when a gala benefit took place. This event was the topic of conversation everywhere, and the boxes and main floor were filled with men in full-dress suits and women in fashionable imported gowns and expensive jewelry; hundreds of poems were composed to honor the singers. Just before the end of the season, Tamberlick expressed his desire to appear in an opera by a Mexican composer. The result was *Guatimotzín* by Aniceto Ortega, unique as one of the first works composed on a pre-Hispanic Native American theme and given a lavish production with costumes based on ancient pictorial documents. Peralta was cast as the Aztec princess Malintzín.

The return of Enrico Tamberlick to Europe left a Mexican public demanding more opera, and Angela Peralta saw her opportunity to fill the gap. Her earlier tour of the cities of Mexico, which Annibale Biacchi had sponsored, and her investment in the Tamberlick venture, made it apparent that Peralta herself henceforth should reap the rewards as an impresaria. This entrepreneurial activity meant raising financing, recruiting singers and an orchestra, and acquiring scenery and costumes as well as arranging transportation, lodging, and advance bookings while on tour. The vocalists, of course, were the key to success, and many of these were Europeans whom Peralta induced to come to Mexico through the many contacts she had formed in Italy. However, aside from Angela herself, this company remained relatively weak, and the critics often turned strident in their censure. But for most Mexican opera fans the star and their favorite diversion proved enough. The "Italian Opera Company of La Peralta" opened on July 27, 1872, after a delay caused by the sudden death of Benito Juárez, with *Lucia di Lammermoor* again. Angela triumphed in the "mad scene" with her soprano voice echoing an agile flute. As the journal *El Teatro* noted: "Angela Peralta challenges the soft sounds of the flutes of the orchestra. . . . The flutes rise, Angela rises even higher; the notes give out in the instruments and still there remains in the throat of the Nightingale many more scales."

The season was a long one, lasting for the rest of the year. Its most interesting aspect lay in the introduction of several new operas, an indication of Peralta's close connections with the most up-to-date events on the stages of Europe. Musical drama began to change after the middle of the nineteenth century: the Italian principle of beautiful melodic music above all, with the story line, or libretto, as mere framework, gave way to an emphasis on theater that integrated music and text more fully. This transformation owes most to Richard Wagner in Germany and Giuseppe Verdi in Italy. Verdi's later operas were creating a sensation everywhere, and one of them, *La Forza del Destino,* Peralta now produced but with little success. The Mexican taste still remained unreservedly fixed on the bel canto style of the previous decades, the type of singing most associated with Angela herself. She attempted fewer novelties, however, as her company set off on a tour of the provinces in early 1873, to Celaya, Guanajuato, Morelia, San Luis Potosí, and Zacatecas, and to a special event in San Miguel de Allende where a newly opened theater was named after her, a rare honor for a woman. Then, in August of that year, she left Mexico once more for her last trip to Europe.

This period away from Mexico marks a low point in Peralta's activity; although she gave occasional performances, much of her time was devoted to the care of her husband whose mental condition was rapidly deteriorating. His abusive and irrational behavior finally forced her to have him committed to an institution near Paris in 1876. Seeking a distraction for her personal troubles, she found an outlet for her creative talents in composition, a traditionally male-defined endeavor. The result was the 1875 publication of the *Musical Album "Angela Peralta."* The volume itself remains interesting because of its elaborate lithographic illustrations of an idealized domesticity, expressive, no doubt, of Angela's frustrating marriage. The songs are written in Italian, a language she knew well enough to write carefully structured poetry; the tone reflects the conventional romantic longing of its time. Several pieces deal with Mexico and demonstrate Peralta's obviously strong feelings for her country. Her musical output certainly cannot be held up as original, but it demonstrates her multifaceted talent and ability to see herself as more than just the Nightingale.

The drive she possessed as an entrepreneur, who now felt the decline in her fortunes, induced Angela to put together another opera company in Europe to take to Mexico. She returned, accompanied by her deranged spouse, in 1877, in the early part of the long reign of Porfirio Díaz; her country was indeed changing under the spell of late nineteenth-century modernization, which finally induced a slow evolution in taste away from the earlier staples of the operatic repertoire. This new Mexican public, dedicated to novelty, became progressively disenchanted with the Peralta opera company's repetition of the standard works, a reaction that prompted the verse: "No more *Normas,* for God's sake, nor another indiscreet *Masked Ball;* let *Rigoletto* sleep awhile and *Ruy Blas* rest from his abuse." And despite the Europeans she brought over, the casts proved uneven and were often unpopular, even if Peralta herself still moved her fans to endless "bravas."

One new opera that Peralta introduced in this season was Verdi's *Aida.* Commissioned by the ruler of Egypt and given its premiere at the Cairo opera house at the end of 1871, the work found its way to Mexico only a few years later. *Aida* is the archetype of the grand opera, lavish in sight and sound, and its exotic setting in ancient Egypt fitted precisely the taste of the nineteenth century. But it seemed to have a special appeal in Mexico. The story of Egypt's conquest of Ethiopia and of Princess Aida's sacrifice for her country mirrored the conquest of the

Aztecs and the struggle to defend Mexico. Who better to portray the protagonist than Angela Peralta? In fact, the role represented a notable departure for her because it required much more dramatic singing and a heavier voice than her usual roles. Yet she made it her own by following a practice she had formerly scorned and changing the score to suit her particular abilities, as she did in the "Triumphal Scene." The Mexican audiences demanded that she perform *Aida* again and again.

She had hoped to take her company on tour. However, the decline of her mentally, and now physically, ill husband prevented her from leaving Mexico City; she was released from this burden in October 1877 when Eugenio Castera died. Shortly thereafter began the scandal that would ruin her reputation and cause the public to ridicule and abandon her. Her transgression was to offend a nineteenth-century ideal of Mexican womanhood; a young widow, custom dictated, should not soon remarry. Peralta had for some time maintained a professional relationship with a poet and journalist from Yucatán, Julián Montiel y Duarte. Flaunting gender constraints and social convention, she now began to live openly with Julián. The reaction of Mexican society was immediate; they refused to attend her performances. Worse still, although in her early thirties, the age at which most opera singers reached their full abilities permitting a career that might continue into their sixties, Peralta began to lose her voice. She not only had started singing very young but also had undertaken a repertoire of heavier roles, like Aida, in recent years that proved disastrous. Manuel Gutiérrez Nájara, writing under his favorite pen name, "El Duque Job," in his poetic style noted:

> I do not have the glory of counting myself among the last candles on the altar which makes up the recalcitrant admirers of the ex-Mexican Nightingale. . . . Between that feverish reception in which the carriage of the diva was conducted in triumph from the Buenavista station to the house in which she lived, and her latest failure in the Nacional, a long time has elapsed. Yet, La Peralta is a glory that has survived. Nevertheless, it is impossible, even sacrilegious, to compare her greatest period with her decadence.

Although ostracized from elite society, Angela Peralta remained a woman of determination and dedication to her art. Her personal and professional problems only energized her to continue forming her own companies and putting on operas.

The season of 1879 was particularly difficult, with almost empty houses and productions often whistled at (the sign of disapproval in Mexico), despite attempts to stimulate excitement with the premiere of Fabio Campana's *Esmeralda* (based on Victor Hugo's *Notre Dame de Paris*) and arrangements with the tram system to bring ticket holders directly to the theater and then wait to take them back to their connections. But she soon returned with another "Opera Company of Angela Peralta" in January of the following year, then off to Veracruz, and back to Mexico City for a traditional opening on the night of Easter Sunday, all without much success. Her last complete opera performance in Mexico City was, appropriately, in *Aida*; she returned to the stage in the capital one final time, in 1882, for a patriotic concert at which the then president, Manuel González, presided.

Peralta's career before her fellow Mexicans was now effectively at an end. Shunned in the federal capital, she could make only some attempts to visit the provincial cities where her traveling companion Julián Montiel did not stir up gossip and where her vocal decline did not arouse the denunciation of music critics. These tours took her to the most remote parts of Mexico, until finally, with some eighty personnel, mostly down-on-their-luck Italian musicians, she went off to the distant Pacific coast. From Guaymas she went to La Paz in Baja California to perform in an open-air patio. She then hired a ship to take the company across the Sea of Cortez to Mazatlán in the terrible summer heat of August 1883. Far from the cultural centers of Mexico, she was received avidly and a performance of *Il Trovatore* was put on, but so suffocating was the evening that few attended. *Aida* was announced for the following night. However, members of the company were already coming down with the dreaded illness yellow fever, a mosquito-borne plague of tropical cities. Little hope could be held out for its victims.

On August 30, 1883, a few days after her own symptoms appeared, Angela Peralta died in agony at the age of thirty-eight. In an ending to her life worthy of an opera, she married her one true love, Julián Montiel, just minutes before death claimed her. She was buried immediately. Yet interest in Mexico's most famous opera singer persisted so that in 1937 her remains were exhumed and reinterred in Mexico City. The stone reads: "The Mexican Nightingale. She sang like no one has ever sung in this world and was our outstanding emissary in the highest circles of musical art." Perhaps she would have preferred the last words for the dying Princess Aida after her similarly difficult and brief life—a simple "Pace, Pace" ("Peace, Peace").

SOURCES

Angela Peralta's public career can be studied best through the daily newspapers published during her lifetime. These carried stories about her, advertisements for her appearances, and reviews of her performances. Major publications in Mexico City were *El Imparcial, El Monitor Republicano, El Siglo XIX,* and *La Voz de México,* all of which covered the operatic stage, although not with great consistency; the best times for opera reviews were the years of the Porfirian regime. Opera material is also to be found in satirical journals, such as *La Orquesta* and *El Pájaro Verde,* and in theater magazines, which usually did not last more than a season or two.

A full biographical treatment of Peralta based on primary sources is still to be written, but one study is A[rmando] de María y Campos, *Angela Peralta: El Ruiseñor Mexicano* (Mexico, D.F., 1944). María y Campos based much of his work on the excerpted newspaper reviews in Enrique de Olavarría y Ferrari, *Reseña histórica del teatro en México, 1538–1911,* 4 vols. (México, D.F., 1895). Further information on Peralta is found in music histories of Mexico such as Julio Estrada, ed., *La música de Mexico,* vol. 1, *Historia,* pt. 3, *Período de la Independencia a la Revolución (1810–1910)* (Mexico, D.F., 1984). In addition, ephemera published about the singer during her lifetime, such as *Una tarde en casa de Angela Peralta* (Mexico, D.F., 1873), are useful in illuminating her private life.

12

Calfucurá and Namuncurá: Nation Builders of the Pampas

Kristine L. Jones

Most Latin American histories assume for convenience that the national boundaries that we see today had meaning for nineteenth-century Latin Americans. In fact, many people of the time considered national boundaries less important than a hospitable political or social climate. The Araucanian, or Mapuche, Indians were not swayed by abstract entities such as "Chile," "Argentina," or the nation-state whenever they sought reliable allies and economic opportunity.

Calfucurá, who was born in the 1770s, led the Mapuche in making treaties with the new Argentine government. He found the conservative caudillo Juan Manuel de Rosas (1829–1852) willing to sign treaties with the Indians to achieve peace on the frontier. Rosas, rather like the caudillos in Paraguay who, although conservative and backward in some ways, did manage to reinforce communal ties and values, left some space and autonomy for the indigenous peoples of Argentina. However, Rosas could not be characterized as an unambiguous Indian advocate since he also led military invasions into the southern pampas between 1829 and 1832.

Calfucurá and his son Namuncurá, who succeeded him after his death in 1873, encountered less tolerance when the liberals dominated the country. The population and economy of Buenos Aires had expanded, and Argentinians such as Presidents Bartolomé Mitre, Domingo Faustino Sarmiento, and Julio Roca believed that the frontier had to be conquered and the Indians either eliminated or assimilated. Like their U.S. contemporaries, these political leaders regarded the Indians as barbaric hordes standing in the way of civilization. In the name of progress, Argentine leaders broke treaties with and marched against the Indians, with the struggle culminating in General Roca's "Conquest of the Desert" in 1879–80.

Still, the history books' recital of the conquest leaves the reader with an erroneous impression. The military conquest of the Mapuche did not eradicate either their culture or their historical memory. Calfucurá's son and grandson, among others, bore witness to the durability of the cultural tradition of the original Americans.

Kristine Jones is an independent historical consultant who lives in Maine. She is the author of an essay on Indian warfare and reorganization on the margins of the Spanish empire for the *Cambridge History of the Native Peoples of the Americas* (forthcoming, 1992) and is at work on a book on commerce between Indian and creole societies in Argentina and Chile in the nineteenth century. Jones earned her doctorate from the University of Chicago and has received Fulbright and Social Science Research Council grants.

One day in 1835, according to the nineteenth-century Argentine chronicler Estanislao Zeballos, a "criminal horde" of treacherous Chilean Indians swept into the camps of the peaceful and pacified Vorogano Indian followers of Mariano Rondeau, a loyal supporter of the Argentine Rosista cause. As Zeballos recounts, "The throats of many chiefs, elders, and wise men were cut, and among the terrorizing clamor of the criminal horde, the name of the conquering caudillo Calfucurá sounded for the first time in the deserts, . . . the name of the Cacique General of the immense empire of the pampa." Zeballos's exciting and nationalistic tale *Callvucurá and the Dynasty of the People of the Stone* justified the famed War of the Desert of 1880, carried out "with Prussian precision" against hostile Indian invaders in southern Argentina. It celebrated the superiority of the conquest of Indian territory, "territory, in sum, where the future of the Republic will cast the civilization of twenty federal states upon the completion in time in the incalculable evolution of the Argentine nationality."

What is this "immense empire of the pampa"? Is it merely a literary glorification of a regionally limited development? We all have heard of the Aztec empire of Mesoamerica and the Incan empire of the Andean highlands, but what was this empire of Calfucurá? Like most stories about great Indian leaders, Zebellos's tale of Calfucurá and his successors follows a familiar heroic form in describing the ultimate defeat of a respected enemy. Like most stories of conquest told by the conqueror, it obscures another reality.

A simple shift in perspective permits a very different view of Calfucurá's "criminal horde." This angle casts light on the story of a persecuted and pursued Araucanian society, which moved out of the Chilean cordillera in an attempt to maintain its sovereignty and ensure cultural survival. In this view the "loyal" Mariano Rondeau appears an unreliable pawn of the Argentine army of Juan Manuel de Rosas, and the violence of Calfucurá's

immense empire the only option for a successful pantribal con-
solidation of an Indian resistance movement that had lasted nearly
half a century and, some say, continues even today to influence
social and political resistance to authoritarian and military rule.

Araucanian resistance to the conquest of their territorial stronghold began with their successful defense against Incan forays
beyond the southern corner of the Tihuantisuyo empire. Settled
in the mountain valleys, lake regions, and high pastures of the
southern cordillera, the Araucanians, known more correctly as
the Mapuche, continued to resist conquest and settlement in the
sixteenth and seventeenth centuries as Spanish colonists moved
into the central valley of Chile and the fertile orchards and
farmlands of Cuyo in western Argentina. Effectively maintaining
and defending a boundary throughout the eighteenth century,
the Mapuche of Chile and their relatives the Pehuenche on the
eastern slopes of the cordillera adapted many of the ways of the
new colonists to their own purposes. Traditional scattered Indian
settlements organized by exogamous lineages turned easily to
raising crops of wheat, tending apple orchards, and husbanding
flocks of sheep, all introduced by the Europeans. This cultural
receptivity to innovation translated into the political sphere as
well, and the Mapuche soon became masters of Spanish military
tactics, often bettering the Spaniards at their own game in successful defense of Mapuche sovereignty.

By the early nineteenth century population growth in creole
society increased pressure for Mapuche and Pehuenche lands in
Chile and Cuyo. Following independence for the Spanish colonies, the shift of focus in international trade stimulated local
economies in the central valley of Chile and, more markedly, the
economy in the rural environs of Argentina's port city of Buenos
Aires, creating even greater demand for territorial expansion.

Mapuche resistance took a new turn. A combination of the
pressure for creole settlement of Mapuche territories in Chile
and the attractions of the rich resources of the scarcely inhabited
grasslands to the east of the cordillera had the effect of drawing
the organized hunting and warrior societies of several Mapuche
lineages into the deserts, pampas, and patagonia of Argentina.
These excursions, which date from the eighteenth century,
became less transitory as different Mapuche lineages and intertribal amalgamations began to take up permanent residence in
these Argentine plains. The Ranqueles (a coalition of Mapuche,

Pehuenche, and creole military deserters) settled south of Córdoba in the late 1700s, and the Voroganos (allied bands of Mapuche and indigenous Pampas Indians) of Mariano Rondeau established themselves around the Salinas Grandes deeper south in the pampas in the early 1800s. Although now permanently residing in these deserts, these groups changed their traditional lifestyles dramatically to exploit effectively the riches of the pampas.

Foremost of the attractions for these Indian settlers were the vast *cimarrones* (unhusbanded herds of horses and cattle) that ranged in these ecologically ideal grasslands. The farming people of the cordillera gave up their sturdy pitched-roof *rucas* (huts) for more mobile dome-shaped skin tents in order to follow the seasonal patterns of the herds. They developed very quickly a complex of rituals centering on the horse, much as had the Plains Indians of North America when they moved out of the settled river valleys to follow on horseback the buffalo over the high plains. Also, much as had occurred in the North American plains, the new settlers of the deserts and pampas competed for resources with the autochthonous peoples of the region. Through a process of alliance, intermarriage, and warfare the settlers assimilated most of these native groups in a process known as the "Araucanization of the Desert."

When Calfucurá led his followers (ten thousand warriors and at least four times as many dependents) from their homelands in the region of the Imperial River and Cautín to take the Salinas Grandes in 1835, his intent, however, was not simply to partake of the attractions of pastoral life. By this time a more complicated and modern principle organized intertribal relations. The simple trading parties that had met seasonally and served to regulate and ease temporary local shortages were now replaced by important commercial ventures involving tremendous quantities of goods—goods upon which the sovereign Indian societies of most of the southern cone were dependent. Throughout most of the eighteenth century a steady trade between creole settlers and neighboring Pampas Indian allies had established an Indian demand for the *vicios* (vices) of tobacco, alcohol, and sugar, while the Indians had supplied the settlers with tack for livestock, with weavings, and, most important, with salt for curing hides and meat. When the free-trade policies following independence created an explosion in demand for cured meat and hides in Argentina and for livestock in Chile, Indian traders quite naturally were drawn into this burgeoning market.

In the 1810s and 1820s, Argentine ranchers in the southern frontier moved to institutionalize this market with Indian traders through a series of alliances, treaties, and, ultimately, annuity payments that pushed the Indians out of the commercial networks and into a pattern of dependency. Because these new alliance networks and annuity settlements effectively closed off a lucrative and growing commercial market to the nonallied groups farther west, hostilities and raids intensified. By now, a complex trans-cordilleran trade route depended upon access to the market economy.

When Calfucurá moved into this arena, he met with resistance from Indian warriors armed and organized by Juan Manuel de Rosas. One of these "pacified" groups followed the orders of Mariano Rondeau, settled near the Salinas Grandes. After a brief but violent struggle (only after peaceful overtures had failed) that ended in the death of Rondeau, Calfucurá emerged as leader of the Araucanian forces that dominated frontier relations for the rest of the century. By taking control of the Salinas Grandes, Calfucurá had consolidated his position as a major player in the rapidly growing market linking livestock production in Argentina and sales in Chile. At the same time, Calfucurá consolidated the political sovereignty of his people and used this position to build an effective intertribal confederation that not only resisted subjugation but also improved temporarily the living standards of his people.

Calfucurá's was a native movement not only born of resistance but also ushering in new pantribal cultural and political configurations, the growth of confederations, the rise of syncretic religious ceremonials, and the accumulation of wealth and improved living conditions as Indians built their business in the trade of livestock and *cautivas* (captives). To the Creoles in Argentina, the arrival of Calfucurá heralded a new epoch, an era in which old treaty and alliance networks with the indigenous Pampas and Tehuelche Indians broke down, organized raids threatened the livestock and property of frontier settlers, *cautivas* were carried away by the hundreds, and Argentine society turned to gaucho soldiers for help.

Contemporary accounts reveal that the nature of Calfucurá's government contrasted sharply with the harsh realities of Rosas's government. Mapuche society was organized along democratic principles, and leadership depended upon consensus and election in ceremonial gatherings. Resolutions of peace or declarations of war also depended upon collective decisions. Militarization of society meant a demand for a new hierarchy within the democratically selected leadership. The increasingly complex *parlamentos* (gatherings) organized graded societies of *caciques* (chiefs), *loncos* (warriors), and *subalternos* (soldiers) subordinate to Calfucurá. In another transformation of traditional government, Calfucurá inculcated in his followers the idea that his leadership was of divine origin. This explanation established legitimacy for his lineage and created a dynastic rule over the pampas in the following decades. As in the past, cultural adaptability and receptivity to change resulted in societal transformation that protected and enhanced political sovereignty.

Between 1834 and 1856, Calfucurá struck uneasy bargains between neighboring societies of Pampas, Araucanian, and Tehuelche Indians and Ranqueles. These decades of relative calm allowed Indian and creole caudillos to consolidate their political legitimacy through treaties and patronage. Most notably among the Argentines, Juan Manuel de Rosas had transferred his negotiating successes at the local level in the southern frontier to the national level. His administration drew upon the national treasury to institutionalize a system of annuity payments to dozens of Indian *caciques* and their followers in exchange for protection of the southern frontier. Calfucurá entered into this structured alliance network in 1838, formalizing the pacification agreement through the requisite political kinship of *compadrazgo*.

Unlike other *caciques,* Calfucurá escaped the trap of dependency through his control of the important salt mines (Vuta Chadihue) of the Salinas Grandes. Without salt the dried horse meat called *charqui,* which was an increasingly important staple in the Indian diet, could not be prepared. The growing Chilean market for the *charqui,* produced and traded widely throughout Indian and creole territory, as well as the trade in livestock herds along well-established *rastrillados* (trails) linking the Voroganos, Ranqueles, Pehuenche, and Huilliche (people of the south) and extending into Mapuche territory in Chile, motivated fierce competition for the resources of the pampas. As the Argentine economy became more and more geared to livestock production, Indian demand for what once had been wild herds likewise expanded. Pushed out of the commercial networks, the Indians responded by raiding except when an annuity agreement satisfied their demands. Control of the salt flats meant that Calfucurá enjoyed a competitive advantage in the commerce in salt along with the benefits he derived from the livestock obtained in raids and the tobacco, alcohol, and sugar received from annuity payments.

In a typical expression of caudillo politics of the time, Calfucurá's alliance with Rosas in Buenos Aires province did not preclude excursions, in 1844 and 1845, into Santa Fe and Córdoba, not coincidentally strongholds of Unitarian opposition to Rosas. The latter moved to harness the military expansion of his ally, who by now controlled more territory than the Creoles, according to a British observer traveling through the area. By this time, however, Calfucurá understood the annuity agreements for the limited palliatives that they were, and he began to negotiate with opposition Indian and creole caudillos, including General Justo José de Urquiza, Rosas's former ally turned enemy. Between 1847 and 1852, Calfucurá consolidated his position, taking advantage of any military distraction to carry out raids in undefended regions.

Building his empire, Calfucurá made diplomatic overtures to a number of Argentine caudillos, sending ambassadors to meet with Urquiza in Paraná, with another caudillo in San José, and even establishing an embassy in Buenos Aires. His official correspondence carried a diplomatic seal, bearing insignia depicting the sacred circle of *colihue* (a sturdy reed used for weapons and symbolically surrounding ceremonial gatherings) and the crossed *lanzas* and *boleadoras* of warfare. Calfucurá had learned that it took skill and intelligence to deal with his neighbors. He encouraged the education of his dependents, sending his own son to learn to read and write in mission schools in Chile.

In 1852, Urquiza finally defeated Rosas and sent him into exile, and the annuity structure guaranteeing peaceful relations in the Buenos Aires frontier disintegrated. In 1855 rebellion and uprisings spread among the allied tribes bordering the southern frontier in reaction to the betrayal of the treaty agreements. In a surprise turnabout, the Pampas Indian leader Catriel joined his forces with those of Namuncurá, the favored son of Calfucurá, in a raid into Sierra Chica. Raids against Tapalque, San Benito, and Juárez followed. The Ranqueles, led by Yanquetruz, a Mapuche chief newly arrived from the southern cordillera, joined forces with "el señor de las Salinas Grandes" (Calfucurá) in an even wider sweep along the frontier. Creole settlers lost hundreds of thousands of head of cattle and horses to the raiders, had hundreds of their women and children taken captive, and saw their settlements burned to the ground.

The raids did not come simply out of vengeance; they stemmed from necessity. Annual consumption of horses obtained by annuities had reached over one hundred thousand head. Argentine refusal to meet treaty obligations precipitated a crisis among the Araucanians. Ending the annuities was seen as nothing less than overt hostility, and the Indians responded accordingly.

Raids continued into 1858, and, among the complicated political struggles of the civil wars of the time, Calfucurá forged a peace agreement with Urquiza, who took office in the newly formed constitutional Argentine government. The civil war among the Creoles had contaminated the Indian confederations as well, and at the local level alliances and agreements broke down and re-formed. Catriel returned his Pampas followers to their isolated autonomy in the south. The Ranqueles looked inward to mourn the loss of their leaders Yanquetruz and Painé. Calfucurá cooled his ties with Urquiza.

The Indians regrouped in order to defend their interests more effectively. Much as had the Argentines, who had consolidated and centralized their government, the Indians responded to the new conditions. In the next decade the Indians organized and planned their raids for livestock and captives almost like military campaigns. While Argentine military efforts were diverted to resolve the costly War of the Triple Alliance in Paraguay (1865–1870), the Araucanians stepped up their raids into the undefended frontier. The professionalization of the Argentine army was mirrored in Indian warrior societies. Once again, the Indians adopted their opponents' military tactics in order to protect their own culture and sovereignty.

The accumulation of livestock and *cautivas* acquired in raids improved living conditions for inhabitants of the new "empire of the pampa." Following decades of relative calm, the intensified renewal of raids took on commercial dimensions, with commoditization not only of livestock but also of captives.

The "capture" of women and children characterized much in gender relations in creole frontier society. The Iberian tradition that equated male honor with the control of wives and daughters meant that an elopement could most honorably be explained as a kidnapping, and local justices of the peace recorded dozens, if not hundreds, of such events. To the Araucanians, on the other hand, marriage traditionally involved a mock kidnapping, with the warrior later providing recompense to the woman's family. When these two traditions began to merge as a result of friendly trading contacts in the late 1700s, the exchange of women as well as goods was not rare. However, more hostile encounters also led to less politically satisfactory results. When Juan Manuel de Rosas "redeemed" 634 *cautivas* as a consequence of the pacification treaties of 1833, the majority of these individuals spoke no Spanish, and many protested with great sadness at being separated from their Indian families.

When the dynamics of the old intercultural frontier society declined into a situation of barricaded mutual distrust, the treatment of captives appears to have grown harsher. As demand for livestock increased, so too did demand for a labor force to tend to the herds, and the *cautivas* performed those duties. While the status and wealth of warriors improved with the acquisition of military honor, livestock, and wives, the balance in the sexual division of labor required more and more women to tend to the horses and spin the wool from the flocks.

Calfucurá reportedly had dozens of wives, including some from among those thousands of creole women and children adopted by the Araucanians in the last half of the nineteenth century. Contrary to the sensational captivity literature that developed later in the century, many contemporary accounts indicated that most of the *cautivas* lived as well as or better than they had in frontier *ranchos* and often developed affection for their new families. While this may seem unlikely, by all indications Calfucurá's Voroganos and his strong allies the Ranqueles especially attracted thousands of Creoles into their ranks. Argentine officials decried the perfidy of these "criminals, deserters, and bad characters," but Indian society nevertheless held promise for a sizable proportion of rural gaucho society, which resisted the squeeze of taxation and the limitations imposed by the expanding state.

In 1873, having lived more than one hundred years, Calfucurá ended his days surrounded by his family in his Salinas Grandes *tolderías* (camps). Within hours of his death, dozens of leaders from among his allies arrived to pay their respects, and on the fourth of June a *parlamento* convened to decide his successor. According to one record, the chiefs of 224 tribes attended this ceremony, probably one of the most impressive spectacles in many decades. Music played on the portentous six-foot-long *cultún* (a trumpetlike instrument) intoned a somber note throughout the many long days of the meeting, and singing, dancing, feasting, and prayers filled the days as the leadership turned to its diviners for guidance.

The elders averted factionalism and civil war by deciding on a triumvirate for Calfucurá's successor, to be composed of three of his sons. Of the three, Manuel Namuncurá emerged as the most effective and talented in organizing the hegemony of Indian societies.

The election of Namuncurá coincided with new Argentine efforts to direct military attention to resolving what was now called "the Indian problem." After the Paraguayan war and the subsiding of civil unrest, the only impediment to progress, or "civilization" as the Argentines called it, remained the conquest of the "empire of the pampa." The army turned its attention to outfitting expeditions organized by the central government against Namuncurá's forces. They met a formidable enemy in the Indians, also well organized, supplied with contraband Remington rifles, and fiercely committed to the defense of their empire.

During the next five years the confederation of Namuncurá maintained its line of defense and continued to plague frontier populations, which, for the first time, outnumbered Indian forces. In one notable instance, in 1875, Namuncurá organized raids against several *partidos* (counties) in one concerted move that resulted in the loss of lives and the taking of captives and hundreds of thousands of cattle. The loss in livestock in one *partido* amounted to the total yearly production of eight counties combined. Argentines demanded action.

Following the military operations of General Adolfo Alsina in 1877 and General Julio A. Roca in 1878 and 1879, Araucanian resistance finally gave way. Namuncurá's confederation started to crumble, and surrendering groups complained of his arrogance and cruelty. When the combined national efforts of the Argentine and Chilean governments at last resulted in agreement over their boundaries, their attention turned to controlling those boundaries, and the extralegal commerce over the mountain passes was ended. Pushed deeper into the south, Namuncurá and his dwindling forces continued to resist in a few skirmishes, but they finally surrendered in 1883.

When the "pacified" leader died in 1908, the Argentine press paid patronizing homage to Namuncurá, couching their praise in self-congratulatory prose extolling the virtues of civilization.

In the comfort of even greater historical distance, however, it becomes easier to acknowledge the significance of the "empire of the pampa." Calfucurá and Namuncurá not only led their people in one of the longest struggles for sovereignty in the Americas, they also drew upon a rich tradition of pride, receptivity, and adaptability to bring about a cultural renaissance and to build a mobile, horse-borne empire that incorporated the majority of Indians in the southern cone.

An educated man, Namuncurá looked to his children to carry on his heritage. He took great interest in the schooling of his son Ceferino, who was educated in the Salesian missions established near the *reservas* set aside for the subjugated Indians. Ceferino Namuncurá excelled in his studies, pursuing his vocation in Rome, where he died of tuberculosis while in his early twenties. Today, many *paisanos,* as the descendants of the "vanquished" Indians call themselves, have established a religious cult around their heroes, and beatification of Ceferino Namuncurá is being discussed. Images of Ceferino hang in country kitchens and local buses and sometimes are even braided into the elaborate harnesses of horses belonging to *paisanos.* Even conquered, the Indians appear to have turned their cultural adaptability and openness to the continuation of cultural sovereignty.

SOURCES

This biography is part of a larger research project focusing on Indian-white commercial relations in the southern cone in the nineteenth century. The following archives, among others, have been consulted for this study: the Archivo General de la Nación, Buenos Aires, Sala 9, Comandancia de fronteras; and the Archivo Histórico de la Provincia de Buenos Aires, La Plata, "Negocio pacífico con el Indio." The following secondary sources are considered classics in Argentina: Adalberto A. Clifton Goldney, *El Cacique Namuncurá: El último soberano de la pampa,* 2d ed. (Buenos Aires, 1963); Lucio V. Mansilla, *Una excursión a los Indios Ranqueles, estudio preliminar de Mariano de Vedia y Mitre* (Buenos Aires, 1959); Dionisio Schoo Lastra, *El indio del desierto, 1535–1879* (Buenos Aires, 1977); Juan Carlos Walther, *La conquista del desierto* (Buenos Aires, 1970); and Estanislao S. Zeballos, *Callvucurá y la dinastía de los Piedra* (Buenos Aires, 1961).

For the Chilean perspective, see José Bengoa, *Historia del pueblo mapuche siglo XIX y XX* (Santiago, 1985); Pascual Coña, *Testimonio de un cacique mapuche, texto dictado al padre Ernesto Wilhelm de Moesbach*, 2d ed. (Santiago, 1973); and Ricardo Ferrando Keun, *Y así nació la frontera . . . Conquista, guerra, ocupación, pacificación, 1550–1900* (Santiago, 1986).

III
The Fin de Siècle
Generations: The Tension
between Decadence and
Progress, 1870–1910

A new spirit pervaded the last quarter of the nineteenth century in Latin America. In most areas the Europeanized urban liberals had defeated the traditionalists and were strengthening the new order, which would finally replace the old Iberian one. Progress in all forms loomed large. New buildings, city parks and avenues, railroads, streetlights, refrigerated ships, and industries were all visible signs of the modernization that had been dreamed of for much of the century. Railroads and armies drew the formerly lawless frontiers more closely into national orbits.

Science and technology, and the people who could best manipulate them, ushered in the new millennium. Some individuals adapted better than others to the challenges and to the feeling that their world was crumbling and a new one fighting to emerge. The Irish immigrant William Grace triumphed because he understood the Peruvian milieu in which he worked (Chapter 13). Brazilian entrepreneur Francisco de Paula Mayrink had such wealth and business acumen that he almost survived the change from monarchy to republic in the 1890s (Chapter 17). José Leocadio Camacho of Colombia, an urban artisan, exercised political influence and improved workers' lives by making only moderate demands on the elite (Chapter 18). The couple Emilio and Gabriela Coni of Argentina offered simultaneously the benefits of medical science and the increasing control that the liberal elites assumed when they began to pass public health legislation for the rest of the population (Chapter 16). All of these winners lived in major cities, in islands of modernity and centers of national power and wealth.

Many other Latin Americans lagged behind, either ignored or patronized in the new age. A new poverty sometimes accompanied the new

187

progress. Former frontiers had become safe for settlement, but what would become of the gauchos and Indians already living in these regions? Some changes rendered helpless the people and institutions that in the past had served as buffers between the national elites and the rural poor and indigenous groups. Police and armies had become more efficient national institutions, which threatened the local patronage of regional caudillos. The church hierarchy had grudgingly accepted a more limited national role as part of its newly structured alliance with Liberal politicians.

Some individuals or groups who challenged the new age met defeat, as did the followers of the mystic Teresa Urrea of Chihuahua, Mexico (Chapter 15). The Mexican sage Nicolás Zúñiga played the clown, and few of his compatriots realized that the dictator Porfirio Díaz was the real joke (Chapter 14). An Indian leader such as Mandeponay used the church to protect his people in Bolivia, but his successors would have to seek other solutions and allies to fit their own times (Chapter 19). Cuba and Brazil outlawed slavery in the 1880s but relegated former slaves to the margins of national life. However much creole leaders might despise the colored masses as inferior to European peasants, they had to acknowledge that Indians, mestizos, *pardos,* mulattoes, and blacks formed the citizenry of their modern nations. Beneath the glittering facade of liberal progress lay the decadence of unresolved social and economic inequality.

The last quarter of the century also saw a resurgence of major conflicts, which were again cast in political terms. The dismantling of old empires and institutions had left behind a feeling of insecurity about what would replace them. The costly independence struggle of Cuba demonstrated the sad impotence of Spain. The shining empire of Dom Pedro II fell in 1889 with hardly a whimper. Colombia had its War of 1,000 Days (1899–1902), and Uruguay its final conflict between Liberals and Conservatives in 1903. The War of the Pacific (1879–1884) destroyed Bolivian and Peruvian optimism and assured Chile's ascendancy, albeit a Chile chastened by the bloody struggle between president and parliament in 1891. In Venezuela the Andean hordes of Cipriano Castro took over the nation in 1899. Political parties to represent new, dynamic economic interests emerged in Argentina and Chile. These struggles and, in some cases, "new men" highlighted the sense of the decay of the old age and the birth of the new.

Do these individuals constitute a single generation? Surely not, for José Leocadio Camacho and Mandeponay were born in the 1830s, and Teresa Urrea in the 1870s. They had neither a common background nor common attitudes toward issues of their day. They shared only in the anxieties and contradictions that marked the end of the nineteenth century in Latin America. Sometimes in their individual lives, and certainly collectively, they exemplify the tensions between progress and decadence.

13

William Russell Grace: Merchant Adventurer

Lawrence A. Clayton

Many Latin Americans were convinced that they had to attract foreign immigrants in order to spur economic development. By the early twentieth century the most successful in attracting the desirable Europeans were the Atlantic coast nations of Argentina, Uruguay, and Brazil. Still, a few hardy souls had arrived earlier, pushed by economic distress in Europe and pulled by rumors of quick wealth in Latin America. Such wealth was to be had especially where there were minerals, where there were natural resources (such as guano in Peru), or where crops that could be exported flourished. Immigrants usually found that their best occupational and investment prospects lay in commerce, mining, sometimes transportation, or the service sector.

Few immigrants had the astounding success of William Grace, who drew upon capital, contacts, and other resources in Europe and the United States. Born in Ireland in 1832, Grace came to America in 1846, driven by the Irish famine and attracted by the prospect of wealth. He arrived in Peru in 1851 and began a modest career in trade. Ultimately dividing his attention between New York and Peru, he laid the foundation for one of the outstanding American commercial empires.

Even with contacts the path was not easy. Most immigrants, if they stayed in Latin America, eventually joined the ranks of the urban middle class. A few became entrepreneurs of such stature that they truly affected the destinies of their adopted homelands. The best of the immigrant entrepreneurs learned the language, cultivated necessary friendships with political leaders, and shrewdly gauged where and when to venture their capital. Misjudging the vagaries of the world market and their effect on the vulnerable export economies of Latin America or alienating politicians could mean bankruptcy. Understandably, most of these immigrants thought not of developing their host societies but of enriching themselves. In response, Latin Americans who espoused traditional communal values sometimes criticized the individualism that accompanied the economic development.

How can we evaluate these immigrants and entrepreneurs? They made major contributions to the modernization of and quickening economic pace in late nineteenth-century Latin America. Their skills and ties, however, also helped to turn the eyes of Latin Americans even more toward Europe and European models of progress. Why bother to deal with, to train, to absorb rural Indians when they could be replaced by European workers? Did successful immigration and modernization distract attention from national social problems?

Lawrence Clayton is professor of history and director of the Latin American Studies Program at the University of Alabama. He has had a special interest in the economic and maritime history of the Andean countries, as revealed by his books *Caulkers and Carpenters in a New World* (1980), *The Bolivarian Nations* (1984), and *Grace: W. R. Grace & Co.: The Formative Years, 1850–1930* (1985).

In the sixteenth century, during the Elizabethan age, English sailors and merchants combed the newly discovered oceans and lands of the world in search of trade, adventure, and empire. They were called merchant adventurers, and they were the pioneers of an empire that would come to span the world. In the nineteenth century a similarly minded youth from Ireland cut loose from his homeland in the 1840s and set out for the New World to make his fortune, to seek adventure, to push to the horizon and beyond. Marquis James, an earlier biographer of William Russell Grace, called him a merchant adventurer because his restless spirit and enterprising ambition reminded James of those same sea dogs and adventurers of Queen Elizabeth's day. This is the story of that latter-day merchant adventurer from Ireland who landed on the faraway Pacific coast of Peru. Grace, and the enterprises that he founded, left a remarkable imprint on nineteenth-century Latin America as he sought his fortune.

William Russell Grace was pulled to Latin America by certain forces just as surely as he was pushed from Ireland by others. Born in 1832, he was only a teenager when Ireland was plunged into hunger and despair. A series of agricultural failures, especially a blight of the potato crop, occurred between 1846 and 1848, and in its wake came famine, dislocation, death, and a massive emigration from the want and horror of the island's misery. Although his family was surviving well enough, young William decided to leave in the spring of 1846 for personal as much as for economic reasons. His father had enrolled him in a Jesuit school in Dublin, and William chafed under the discipline of both the Jesuits and his parents.

Almost naturally he embarked on a vessel bound for America. It landed in New York, and he worked there for a while as a cobbler's assistant and then as a printer's devil. In 1847 he signed as a crew member on a ship that took him to Cuba to load sugar for Liverpool. Perhaps he heard Spanish for the first time in Cuba. Perhaps it was there that the color and beat of Latin America with its warm, tropical, and sensual rhythms touched the boy's Irish imagination. In any event, he returned to Ireland for a few short months and then was off again to Liverpool, the emporium of English trade, the second greatest city in England. Like so many Europeans of the period, Grace was driven by a restless, entrepreneurial spirit; he was determined to make his way in the world.

In Liverpool, at the age of eighteen, he established his own company to broker passages for emigrants bound for America. This was a speculative business; as a broker William accepted a down payment from the emigrants and guaranteed them passage at a set fare, the balance to be paid upon embarkation. Since the shipping company could vary the rates, the broker took his chances. It was the essence of trading, and young William acquired a taste for this type of enterprise that sustained him for the rest of his life and brought him a substantial fortune.

In 1851 his father offered him a new opportunity. A fellow Irishman, James Gallagher, needed people to work on his sugar plantation located near Lima, Peru, and William was invited to go along. Already a seasoned traveler and adventurous by nature, William said yes. The job offered him a chance to round tempestuous, legendary Cape Horn and to taste life in the far Pacific. He once again set out for America, only this time for South America.

Peru at midcentury was in the grip of its first major economic boom since independence. Freed from Spain in the 1820s, Peru had remained moribund for the next three decades, torn apart by an unstable and wild political scene. Constitutions and caudillos rotated as though in a revolving door in the capital city of Lima while the war's devastation, especially in the silver mines of the mountainous interior, cast a blight over the new republic, once the richest of Spain's possessions in its New World empire. When William arrived, however, a revitalizing energy was flowing through the country, fueled by bird droppings. Correct, bird droppings, called guano in the trade.

For thousands of years seabirds such as the cormorant, booby, and pelican had returned to roost on the Chincha Islands off the Peruvian coast after a leisurely day of feeding on the abundant sea life, especially anchovies and herring, populating the cold

Humboldt Current sweeping north along the coast. Their droppings, guano, accumulated to depths of hundreds of feet, and the fertilizing properties of guano, which was especially rich in nitrogen, long had been realized and carefully exploited by the ancient peoples of Peru. Then, in the 1840s, North American and European farmers discovered the splendid properties of guano, and the boom was on.

The first commercial shipment of guano to England, aboard the aptly named ship *Bonanza,* was off-loaded in 1841. By 1850, the year before William arrived at Lima's port city of Callao, almost one hundred thousand tons were shipped to England alone, while the depleted tobacco fields of Virginia too were being rejuvenated by the rich guano fertilizer.

The widespread use of fertilizers only was commencing in the industrializing nations of the Northern Hemisphere. As populations grew and urban areas expanded in response to the industrial revolution, a greater and greater premium was being placed on food production. Increasingly, European and North American entrepreneurs, merchants, and miners looked to Latin America as a supplier of raw materials, from ore to guano, for the ever-expanding markets to the north. When William came ashore at Callao, he quickly took in the situation. Although opportunities were abundant, they certainly were not to be found in working on James Gallagher's sugar plantation. William disengaged himself from that endeavor and got a job in a ship chandler's shop in Callao owned by John and Francis Bryce.

The Bryces were purveyors of naval stores: spars for masts; oakum, pitch and tars for leaky seams; and cordage and sails to drive the tall ships through the world's oceans—the myriad items needed to replenish and refurbish the vast fleet working the new guano trade. While most ships were loading for the ports of North America and Europe, others were bound for the goldfields of California, refitting and revictualing after long voyages from New York around the Horn. Hundreds of New England whalers called in at the Peruvian ports of Callao, Paita, or Tumbes in the course of four- and five-year voyages in the Pacific. Herman Melville sailed on one such voyage, and his memories were transformed by his genius into some of the most memorable classics in American literature, including *Moby Dick.* Of different nationalities, different speeds, and different types, indeed, each unique in its construction and adaptation, these tall ships possessed one important common denominator: they needed naval stores.

Not only did William commend himself to the Bryces by his good business sense and diligent work habits, but the young Irishman also rapidly began to learn Spanish and to enlarge his circle of friends among Peruvians of Callao and Lima. Grace early on was disposed to look for friendship and for business with little prejudice as to an individual's national background or ethnic origin, although he particularly liked Yankee captains and crews. He got even closer to the Bryces when he expanded their business with a brilliant suggestion: Let us take the goods to the buyers rather than wait for the buyers to come to the market.

William convinced the Bryces to anchor a storeship in the roadstead at the Chincha Islands in 1856 and keep it well provisioned with a line of goods similar to that sold in the Callao store. This would reduce the time that captains had to spend in sailing to Callao to refit and revictual before embarking on the long voyage home. It was the perfect idea for the booming times. Not only did William sell traditional products to the guano fleet anchored at the Chinchas, but he also branched out into fresh meats, vegetables, and fruits delivered from the port of Pisco on the nearby Peruvian mainland. He lived a rather spartan life on the storeship for five years, dedicating himself with a passion to the trade. But it was not all work for the young Irishman, just as life among the guano fleet was not all sobriety and industry.

The ships anchored in the roadsteads of the Chincha Islands often were there for two or three months as they loaded guano, and the captains, mates, masters, and sailors entertained themselves with dances, visits, and ship work during this long layover. Wives and children frequently traveled with Yankee ship captains, and their presence fostered a civility and gentleness that might not otherwise have prevailed at the parties and teas celebrated to pass the time.

By contrast, Peruvian convicts and Chinese coolies imported as indentured workers from far across the Pacific labored on the stinking guano piles, mining and loading the guano in hellish conditions. It was not unusual for the Chinese to overdose themselves with opium and hope for a quiet death and relief from their fate. While differences in conditions for new arrivals from Europe and North America, such as William Grace, and Latin Americans were not always so dramatic, there nonetheless gradually developed a double standard in the nineteenth century. Enterprising foreigners most often linked their destinies to the small elite upper classes and the rising commercial middle class, thereby segregating and distinguishing themselves from the great mass of Latin American peasants and workers. The association between foreigners and the Latin American elites was not unnatural. Foreigners were courted by Latin Americans for their skills, their capital, and their knowledge of international markets and trends—from the price that guano was fetching on the London market to the latest fashions from Paris—and foreigners came to associate themselves with progressive elements of the elites who were promoting the modernization of Latin America. That this economic modernization was often accomplished at the expense of the masses set the stage for various revolutions of the twentieth century.

In the late 1850s, William Grace had on his mind both business, which was booming for him, and a seventeen-year-old girl named Lillius Gilchrest. Lillius was the daughter of Mary Jane Gilchrest and George Gilchrest, captain of the ship *Rochambeau* out of Maine. William had met Captain Gilchrest in Callao where the latter had gone to speak to the American consul. Knowing no Spanish, Gilchrest was having difficulty finding the U.S. consul when Grace asked if he could help. He spoke Spanish. What was the captain needing? Gilchrest returned the favor and invited the helpful young Irishman to visit the *Rochambeau*.

A few days later William boarded the *Rochambeau* for tea. There he met Lillius. She had been sailing aboard her father's vessels since she was six and shared in the world the Irishman spoke about—clippers and downeasters, the beautiful, dangerous sea, the exotic settings of the world. Lillius had sailed through the Indian Ocean and the Black Sea and numerous times across the Atlantic. She had weathered a monstrous waterspout in the Indian Ocean, which nearly capsized her ship, and had watched cannonballs tear through the rigging of nearby vessels while they reprovisioned the British during the Crimean War. She knew the rudiments of navigation from watching her father shoot the stars and study his charts in the twilight moments of dawn and dusk when navigators broke out their sextants and charted their courses across the vast oceans.

William was smitten by this lovely, soft, and feminine girl who possessed such a remarkable background and directness. The *Rochambeau* spent three months loading guano, and, in this truly exotic setting, they courted. When the *Rochambeau* lifted anchor and headed for home, Lillius and William were betrothed. They did not meet again for three years, but when they did it was in a chapel in Tenants Harbor, Maine, where they wed in 1859. William brought his bride back to the Chinchas where Lillius set up housekeeping on the old Bryce storeship.

William had extended considerably both his friendships and the business, so much so that by 1860 Bryce & Company (Grace had become a partner in 1854) was the principal purveyor of American goods and merchandise, not just naval stores, in Peru. To keep expanding the business, William sought out his kinfolk as partners and juniors in the tradition of English firms, which integrated brothers, nephews, cousins, uncles, and sons into commercial networks that spanned the seas. The most important of these kin was William's younger brother Michael, who arrived in Peru in 1859 and joined William on the storeship.

Michael first traveled to Peru at the age of nine with his father and the other Irish immigrants who had come over to work in Dr. Gallagher's plantation. When that experiment failed after three years, Michael returned with his father to Ireland, but his warm feelings toward Peru were formed at an early, impressionable age, and these would survive for a lifetime. Another brother, John, followed William and Michael to the Western Hemisphere in the 1870s, and innumerable nephews, especially the sons of William's oldest sister, Alice, and her husband John Eyre, swelled the ranks of the growing Grace business in Peru. The most important of these, Edward Eyre, arrived in Callao in 1867, sixteen years old and eager to please his Uncles William and Michael and get ahead in the world.

The pattern set by the Graces was not untypical of immigration from Europe to Latin America in the second half of the nineteenth century. Once a beachhead was established by a particularly adventurous and enterprising member of a family—such as William Grace—others followed. And they were encouraged to follow by the policies of Latin American governments, which sought European immigrants with great zeal. The goal was to "whiten" Latin American society, to leaven it with enterprising, progressive Europeans who were expected to contribute to the modernization of the economy. That William and Michael and Edward Eyre and many others (millions of Europeans would in fact come to Latin America in the nineteenth century, most of them ending up in the southern cone nations of Argentina, Uruguay, Chile, and Brazil) found a friendly atmosphere very conducive to the activities of competitive, ambitious Europeans was a great advantage to them. The Graces made the most of it.

One day in 1862, however, William heard what sounded to him like a death sentence. Already suffering from a debilitating bout with dysentery, he was told by his doctor that he had Bright's disease (a kidney ailment marked by albumin in the urine) and had not very long to live. The prescription was to leave Peru and get plenty of rest. With Lillius and two babies, William sailed for Ireland to see his family and attend to personal business in the light of the doctor's lugubrious prognosis. The doctor was off by about forty years in predicting William's death (he lived four years into the twentieth century), and the Irish clan was overjoyed at seeing the prosperous son return.

After resting and recuperating in Ireland, William and Lillius took ship in 1863 to return to Peru, stopping at New York City for an extended visit at the home of Lillius's father, Captain Gilchrest, who had purchased a house in Brooklyn. William's real interest lay across the river in the city then charged with emotion and energy from the Civil War raging between the Union and the Confederacy. A boomtown prosperity prevailed, and for a man of William's nature, the hustle and bustle were intoxicating. He was off to Peru in late 1863; however, he returned in 1866 to expand his business. New York would be his home for the rest of his life, but his business always would be based on trade and commerce with Latin America. William Grace was in fact laying the foundations of the first multinational corporation in Latin America, W. R. Grace & Company.

Why go to New York? After the Civil War, the reunited Union emerged into a dramatic cycle of business expansion and prosperity, and New York drew William like a magnet. Furthermore, he had married an American and had developed close personal and business ties with Americans while in Peru. After settling his family into a house in then-fashionable Brooklyn Heights, William rented a small office at 110 Wall Street in Manhattan, located squarely in the center of the shipping district. It suited William well, for he liked to be close to the action.

From 1866 to 1880, when William was elected mayor of New York, he, his brothers, his nephews, and other associates expanded their trade across the Americas, moving quickly to take advantage of new business opportunities as they arose. Nothing captivated the imagination of entrepreneurs such as William more than the brilliant promise of the railroads, those agents of progress and modernization whose iron-and-steel ribbons were threading their way across the Americas.

In Peru, the government decided to turn the revenue from the booming guano industry into railroads. This desire to modernize the country with the iron horse amounted almost to a national obsession in the 1860s and 1870s, and the great champion of the railroads was Manuel Pardo, who became president in 1872. The agent of this transformation in Peru was a flamboyant North American entrepreneur from Connecticut named Henry Meiggs. In this trio—Pardo, Meiggs, and Grace—we see many of the fundamental forces combining to transform the country in the last half of the nineteenth century.

Pardo's goal was to translate the guano revenues (a nonrenewable resource that would sooner or later be depleted) into permanent railroads, which would in turn trigger economic development. His aspirations were high, for not only would the railroads catalyze increases in production and commerce, but they also would be endowed with a higher mission in Peru: "To create where nothing today exists, to spawn and stimulate the elements of wealth which today are found only in a latent and embryonic state." Pardo thus equated the railroad, as did many of his contemporaries, not only with economic progress but also with the ability to transform his country socially.

"Who denies," Pardo writes, "that the railroads are today the missionaries of civilization? Who denies that Peru urgently needs those same missionaries? Without railroads today there cannot be real material progress; and without material progress there can be no moral progress among the masses because material progress increases the people's well-being and this reduces their brutishness and their misery; without the railroads civilization can proceed only very slowly." Pardo's faith in the ability of the railroads to do all this may have been too generous and optimistic, but men such as Pardo welcomed men such as Meiggs and Grace as the means to these ends.

Henry Meiggs had started his career rather modestly in Brooklyn in the 1840s before being drawn by gold fever to California in 1849. There he parlayed a load of lumber shipped around the Horn to the East Coast into a minor bonanza. A fast mover and speculator, he left California for Chile bankrupt and one step ahead of the law. In Chile he converted his winning charm and innate organizational ability into government contracts to build railroads, and he did this with élan and success. From Chile he passed to Peru, signing a series of contracts beginning in 1869 to build major railroads from the coast into the ore-rich mountains to the east. Throughout the 1870s, Meiggs built and built, and Peru went deeper and deeper into debt until bankruptcy and a catastrophic war with Chile at the end of the decade ended the expansion. But as the boom began in the early 1870s, the Grace brothers were ready to expand their business and link their fortunes to those of the remarkable Henry Meiggs

Michael Grace, then running the business in Peru, was struck by railroad fever and pushed William in New York to make connections as soon as possible with Meiggs's purchasing agent, Joseph S. Spinney. Through Spinney, whose family became good friends of William's, the Graces obtained their first contracts to provide the expanding railroad works in Peru with lumber and ties. William himself traveled north to Canada and south to the Carolinas and Georgia to purchase and arrange for shipment of the materials to the growing Meiggs enterprise in Peru.

There, Michael mingled with Meiggs and solicited more business as the railroad crews drove into the Andes. William traveled down to Peru in the spring of 1871 to meet the king railroad builder and size him up for himself. The extravagant Meiggs set off a warning signal in William's mind. William dragged his feet in late 1871 and 1872, wary of a financial collapse. Michael importuned his brother not to be so cautious.

"Make hay while the sun shines," Michael wrote. "So long as the government is good we fear nothing." That was what William precisely feared, but Michael did not relent. "You still seem to think that Meiggs is not safe. . . . He holds good railroad contracts and although he has thrown money away by the shovelfuls, unless Peru comes to the ground we cannot see that Meiggs is going to fall."

Still, William refused to enter into new contracts with Meiggs. Michael steamed. Then, in 1872, a new bond issue by the Peruvian government to raise money for the railroads fell flat, and by 1873 the Meiggs enterprises were on their way to bankruptcy, spurred by a worldwide depression. William had been proven right. In the heat of the battle he upbraided his brother in no uncertain terms, suggesting that if Michael in the future were to demonstrate no more sense than he had recently, in spite of William's advice, "then as a friend and brother I ask you to finally let me out of the concern [the original Callao-based Bryce-Grace partnership] as I can't see any safety in the present mode of carrying the business on."

When his anger cooled, William apologized to his brother for the outburst but not for the advice. "It would make no difference in my feelings toward you as a brother," William wrote Michael, even if Bryce-Grace failed. "But, no matter what your past record has been, just make a heavy loss by Meiggs and others, use up the capital in your hands, and you will learn the bitter lesson of what it is to fail as a businessman."

William not only did not fail but he also prospered, restructuring and expanding his businesses in the 1870s. His strength was in seeing where to disengage and where to engage and expand. This remarkable business prescience came from constant honing of an entrepreneurial spirit. In the 1870s, for example, while William was disentangling the Grace partnerships from Meiggs and the failing railroads, he also closed the old storeship serving the diminishing guano fleet working the Chincha Islands. In the same decade, he moved more actively into the business of chartering and operating vessels between New York and the west coast of South America, twice relocating his offices to larger and more convenient quarters in the downtown shipping district of Manhattan. He brought new, dynamic partners into the business, such as Charles Ranlett Flint, a young, ambitious New Englander who eventually became a partner of W. R. Grace & Company and figured prominently in the expansion and diversification of the Grace businesses over the next two decades. Charley Flint hit the road running when first sent to South America in 1875, traveling all over Peru, Ecuador, and Chile like an itinerant peddler, sizing up the markets, and looking for orders and more business.

By the end of the decade, the Graces had sold or were selling everything from sewing needles to locomotives, and their geographic field was opening to include other parts of Latin America. In that same decade they entered into contracts to supply new railroads being built in Costa Rica by a flamboyant nephew of Meiggs, Henry Meiggs Keith; they invested in the sugar and nitrate industries in Peru; and they restructured the partnerships to make them more efficient; and, all the while, the enterprises felt the strength and wisdom of William's hand at the tiller.

William imparted to his siblings, nephews, and other young associates such as Flint a warm feeling for Peru and its people. "I like the Peruvians," he wrote to his brother John, who had come over from Ireland in 1872 to join his brothers in the

Americas. "I always enjoyed their society and I never looked upon them as more deceitful than [other] people. . . . The English in foreign lands, I never liked; they are, in my experience, presumptuous and self-opinionated. . . . I know [mercantile] houses in Peru that were in my time hated as haters of Peru."

It was almost inevitable that, being a dynamic individual, William Grace would find additional outlets for his energy. In 1880 he moved dramatically into the mainstream of American politics. He was elected mayor of New York, becoming the first foreign-born mayor of that great city. Grace was elected in 1880 for a two-year term, and again in 1884, both times as a reformer pitted against the boss system of Tammany Hall. His career as mayor carried his attention away from Latin America for much of the 1880s. As Mayor Grace, William's fame and reputation expanded in the United States, just as Peru—the center of the Grace enterprises in Latin America—suffered a disastrous setback in its national destiny.

In 1879, Peru and Bolivia went to war against Chile. The War of the Pacific, as it was called, was not settled until 1883. It established Chile as a major power on the South American continent and humiliated both Bolivia and Peru. The Grace businesses, so closely identified with Peru, inevitably were drawn into the vortex of this war, and it was only natural that the company favored the Peruvians. Even before the war, Michael had alerted Charles Flint in New York to be ready to fill orders for munitions and arms. By the outbreak, Flint already had thousands of rifles and cartridges and ten dirigible torpedoes on the high seas bound for the battlefields.

During the course of the war, William Grace and Flint operated on many fronts on behalf of Peru. They not only sent standard weapons and arms to the combatants, but they also contracted for testing and sending the newest inventions to the Peruvians. They held, for example, great expectations for a new-style torpedo (the one most of us are familiar with: a long, cylindrical tube, self-powered, with a charge at its nose to be exploded upon contact). It was hoped that these torpedoes could turn the tide of the war against the Chileans, who enjoyed naval superiority. But the torpedoes proved unreliable, and the technology did not restore Peruvian parity with the Chileans at sea.

Toward the end of the war—especially after January 1881, when the Chileans took Lima and Peru's military fortunes were at their nadir—Michael Grace argued with increasing vehemence for greater U.S. intervention to preserve the territorial integrity of Peru. But internal political squabbles, and the assassination of President James Garfield in 1881, frustrated a clear U.S. policy of support. When the Peace of Ancón was finally signed in 1883, Peru and Bolivia were stripped of some of their richest provinces along the Pacific coast, and Peru was left saddled with an immense debt, over $160 million, inherited not only from the war but also from the Meiggs railroad-building era of the 1870s.

From New York, William ran his company rather loosely during this period, dedicated, as he was, to the public obligations of being the city's mayor. When he relinquished office in early 1887, his company entered a second major wave of growth and diversification, responding to the strength of his presence once again at the helm.

From sail the Graces turned to steam, and they pioneered the first major steamship line from New York to the west coast of South America in 1894. They became involved heavily in the rubber boom along the Amazon in the late 1880s and early 1890s, reaping healthy profits before being pushed out of the business by none other than Charles Flint, William's former associate. After Flint broke with his old boss, he turned against the Graces. His finely honed business shrewdness and immense ambition eventually led to his founding the United States Rubber Company, one of the first of the great monopolies in the United States.

In 1898, William became involved in one of the greatest enterprises to occupy the attention of Americans at the turn of the century: the building of a transisthmian canal across either Nicaragua or Panama. William assumed the leadership of a powerful faction desiring to build the canal as a private venture across Nicaragua. They were fiercely opposed by the Panama lobby, and the issue came to dominate public affairs in the United States until 1902, when the U.S. Senate finally voted in favor of the Panama route. Although William lost this battle, his company eventually came to profit mightily from the canal fever that gripped Americans in the nineteenth century. When the Panama Canal was completed in 1914, it was no accident that one of the first steamships to navigate it was a Grace Line ship, and it was no accident that Grace Line dominated the inter-American trade for the next half century.

William died in 1904. Like many of the great capitalists of the era he had turned to philanthropic endeavors at the end of his life. Although not a titan on the scale of Andrew Carnegie, who accumulated hundreds of millions of dollars in his lifetime (William left a fortune of approximately $10 million), William gave generously to the Roman Catholic church, and he endowed Grace Institute in New York for the ever-greater numbers of young women then entering the industrial work force.

How does one judge William Grace? In retrospect, his was a life dedicated to trade, commerce, and industry, very much reflecting those ideals that dominated the nineteenth century. He helped weave new and stronger ties between the United States and Latin America, and he laid the foundation for a company that would emerge in the twentieth century as the first great multinational operating in Latin America. One ultimate implication of his activities—the greater dependence of Latin Americans upon the United States for their economic and political destinies—has been the source of much controversy and criticism in the twentieth century.

William's contemporaries, however, remembered a remarkable man. The newspapers of the United States and throughout the world ran long obituaries that invariably praised him as an outstanding businessman and public servant. The *New York Evening Telegram* headlined "Twice Mayor of New York, Mr. Grace Won City's Praise." The *Brooklyn Eagle* said, "End of a Lifetime Filled with Business Enterprise and Public Usefulness. . . . A Man of Strong Ideas, Whose Business, Politics and Charity Were All on a Big Scale." The *New York Times* wrote:

> Even in this country of self-made men, of great business houses, and of great fortunes, the career of ex-Mayor William R. Grace was a conspicuous one. He developed markets, he established transportation lines, he embarked in mercantile ventures, and directed them with such skill that while he was building up a personal fortune he was also contributing to the expansion of this country and of other countries. Whenever he took an active part in politics it was as a man of sound principles working in behalf of honesty and efficiency in public administration.

And the *New York Daily News*, always with a penchant for the colorful, produced this epitaph: "Romantic life story of an Irish lad who ran away from home to be a Robinson Crusoe, who twice became Mayor of New York and died a multimillionaire." That was the embodiment of the American dream at the turn of the century, and the one for which his contemporaries remembered him best.

SOURCES

The Grace Papers in the Rare Book and Manuscript Collection of the Columbia University Library constitute the single most important source for the study of William R. Grace and the company that he founded. This collection, donated by W. R. Grace & Company to Columbia in the spring of 1980, is the finest and most complete collection of papers relating to a U.S. company's operations in Latin America. Over one hundred fifty letter books contain the correspondence of Grace and of his siblings, relatives, and colleagues with each other and with the great and small entrepreneurs and politicians of their times, from Andrew Carnegie to Theodore Roosevelt.

The next most important source on William Grace is a fast-paced, beautifully written biography produced in the 1940s by two-time Pulitzer Prize-winning popular historian and journalist Marquis James. The book, "Merchant Adventurer: The Story of William R. Grace," was never published (a story in itself). The manuscript, which is bound and in galley-proof form, is copyrighted and owned by W. R. Grace & Company, New York.

The third source is Lawrence A. Clayton, *Grace: W. R. Grace & Co.: The Formative Years, 1850–1930* (Ottawa, IL, 1985), which is a history of the company, including its activities as the first major multinational in Latin America, its role in inter-American economic and diplomatic relations, and its contribution to the modernization of Peru. Detailed studies based on careful use of the Grace Papers are only now beginning to appear. One of these is C. Alexander G. de Secada's "Arms, Guano, and Shipping: The W. R. Grace Interests in Peru, 1865–1885," *Business History Review* 59, no. 4 (Winter 1985): 597–621.

14

Mexican Sartre on the Zócalo: Nicolás Zúñiga y Miranda

William H. Beezley

The rule of dictator Porfirio Díaz in Mexico has become synonymous with the modern, positivistic dictatorships of the late nineteenth century. Díaz first seized power in 1876 with the battle cry of "effective suffrage and no reelection." He surrendered power between 1880 and 1884, but he retained the top office after that until 1911. Nonetheless, elections were held at four-year intervals (six-year intervals after 1904). The stability that Díaz's long regime provided allowed Mexico at last to enjoy a burst of economic development. Agriculture for commercial export expanded, thousands of miles of railroads linked Mexico to U.S. markets, and a modest industrial complex appeared.

The political and intellectual elite and the Catholic church hastened to sing Díaz's praises as the necessary gendarme of Mexico. Most prominent in the chorus were his technocratic advisers, known collectively as *científicos* (scientific men), who followed the positivist philosophy of the Frenchman Auguste Comte. Few people dared publicly to criticize either the government or positivism. Many in the growing middle class depended on the expanding government bureaucracy for employment. Entrepreneurs needed the goodwill of government officials to secure their concessions and investments.

Still, some Mexicans questioned the benefits of the new progress. Farm and industrial labor saw their standard of living fall while food costs rose drastically. Employers called in the army or the *rurales* (national police force) at any sign of workers' restiveness. The *científicos* praised education, but they did little to invest in rural public schools. On the whole, they preferred foreign immigrants to native mestizos and Indians.

Nicolas Zúñiga y Miranda was born around 1856. He became a kind of "wise fool" in Mexico City, where he was known for his scientific inventions and earthquake predictions. He confirmed his role as a fool when, in 1896 and in 1900, he ran for president against Díaz, but in running he also drew attention to the farcical elections in a way that made Díaz uneasy. If all must feign compliance with a dictatorship in order to avoid reprisal, then what outlets are there for frustration? As the story of Zúñiga y Miranda illustrates, poking fun at government values, even indirectly, both can provide a release for frustration and begin to undercut the solid front of the regime.

William H. Beezley, professor of history at Texas Christian University and coeditor of this volume, has become well known both as an interpreter of Latin American popular culture and as an expert on the Porfiriato. His extensive publications include articles on teaching, on sports history, and on Mexican historiography. His most recent books are *Judas at the Jockey Club and Other Episodes of Porfirian Mexico* (1987) and, as coeditor, *The Human Tradition in Latin America: The Twentieth Century* (1987), a collection of Latin American biographies that parallels this one.

Modernization, with its attendant crumbling of traditional society, causes some human wreckage. Marginal persons, fools, vagrants, town drunks, all in some way qualify as the human damage of so-called progress. These derelicts lurch through the community, engendering laughter that on inspection reveals a great deal about society's paradoxes and anxieties and what Jean-Paul Sartre called "bad faith" in the midst of change. These individuals, these characters, appeared in multitudes in the past. In the midst of the disheveled society that followed the gold rush in California, for example, there appeared Norton I, self-proclaimed emperor of the United States and protector of Mexico. Norton I, like other socially acceptable fools, personified Cervantes's judgment of Don Quixote that he was "mad in patches, full of lucid intervals." During the flurry of modernization in Mexico promoted by Porfirio Díaz there appeared a "fool" who expressed social apprehensions and represented popular humor.

Nicolás Zúñiga y Miranda belongs to a long and vigorous tradition of mirth and fun, which in Mexico stretches back into the early nineteenth century and includes an emphasis on billingsgate. Ribald commentators were no respecters of rank. They were as ready to poke fun at the misadventures of former President Antonio López de Santa Anna and his wooden leg as they were at the confusion of a country bumpkin in the city. Don Nicolás represents one facet of political raillery during the dictatorship of Porfirio Díaz that survives today. It includes as well numskull jokes about the people of Lagos, Jalisco. These stories lampooned all of the town's residents, but in particular satirized the city fathers. No doubt also Mexicans told political jokes and anecdotes about the dictator and his regime. Much of this humor has not survived, but accounts do exist of the mock challenger to the dictator, Zúñiga y Miranda.

Nicolás Zúñiga y Miranda was born in the city of Zacatecas sometime before 1856. The precocious child of a provincial elite family, he had tutors from his third birthday on. One teacher, a priest, steered him toward the priesthood; Nicolás wanted to study engineering. His father sent him at sixteen to Mexico City to study law. Immediately upon his arrival in the capital city, his misadventures began. He mistakenly took a room in a hotel that normally rented by the hour to lovers. When the young student, who had been reared as a gentleman, heard an argument develop between an insistent lover and his companion, who seemed to have changed her mind, he determined to rescue the woman's honor. Dressed in his bedclothes and a serape, Nicolás burst into the room and discovered that he had interrupted a playful couple who were engaged in a mock lovers' quarrel. Moreover, he had to face a local policeman summoned by the angry couple.

His troubles continued at the law school, where his tall, broom-stick-thin appearance, drooping moustache, and mode of dress led to many jokes. He ignored the catcalls and dedicated himself to his studies, which included mathematics and geology. In his spare moments he practiced his hobby of astronomy, which he had begun under the direction of one of his tutors. His fellow students viewed him as a humorous eccentric.

This apparently harmless eccentric unsuccessfully predicted comets, floods, and other cataclysms. He had no greater success with his seismographic invention, which, he claimed, could indicate in advance the time of earthquakes. When he announced his campaign for the presidency in 1896, he immediately became the choice of the lawyers with whom he had attended law school and of the university students who demonstrated in rallies throughout the city. Thus he became the classic jester, deflecting genuine criticism of the regime through laughter.

Don Nicolás's comic characteristics can be analyzed. Humor, according to one theory, can be defined as the playful impulse deriving pleasure from an instance of life's ambiguity. This explanation stresses the element of play that leaps from words, phrases, actions, and situations in which the expected is replaced by something else, revealing an unsuspected equivoke. A certainty suddenly can be perceived in different ways; ambiguity allows incongruity as one possible perception of the situation. An individual's inability to catch the equivocal character of a word, phrase, action, or situation means that he or she does not get the joke.

Humor performs several social functions. There are jokes that help in the acculturation process, that help in adjustments to new social situations, that serve as cautions against unacceptable or dangerous social behavior, and that act as safety valves for protest and frustrations of all kinds. Joking becomes subversive to political, economic, and social structures insofar as it suggests that principles are not immutable but equivocal. Yet joking cannot itself serve as an agent of social change or revolution because the successful toppling of an institution removes the ambiguity and therefore the humor. The humor substitutes for action that may be risky or impossible. On the other hand, jokes substituted for positive action may hurt society by allowing correctable situations to continue unchanged because no one will protest or act to set matters right.

Social sublimation through the safety valve of joking, sociologist Anton C. Zijderveld has suggested, may be encouraged, even manipulated, by the powerful as a technique to manage conflict and protest. As tempting as it may be to blame the governing elite for bad jokes, atrocious puns, and numskull riddles, it hardly seems likely that any government would manufacture and broadcast jokes deliberately. However, as a technique for managing conflict, for the elite to encourage or at least to ignore antigovernment jokes seems well advised.

This brings us back to Zúñiga y Miranda. The description of don Nicolás provides us with a graphic example of his ambiguity and, therefore, of his humorous character. His effect, through humor, was to confront the Porfirians with a display of Sartre's "bad faith," that is, with the pretense that something is necessary that is actually voluntary. Zúñiga y Miranda reminded Mexicans of all ranks that presidential elections did not have to go uncontested, that Porfirio Díaz did not have to be unchallenged, that technology did not have to come from abroad, and that inventions did not all perform as advertised. Above all, he revealed the people's bad faith because they had adopted the attitude that Díaz was indispensable and that technology was the equivalent of progress. Their notions had produced a collective contented sigh while society awaited modernization. This, don Nicolás performed in a social comedy creating doubts about the Díaz regime. His inadvertent humor offered more than a simple safety valve; it was a form in which to demonstrate graphically the incongruities in everyday Mexican life.

Always dressed in a sombrero with a tall, glittering crown, an elegant frock coat, clean spats, and black, highly polished shoes, Zúñiga y Miranda epitomized the old Mexican elite. Traditional Mexican males invested as much as they could afford in their sombreros. Social standing was expressed from the high, ornate, heavy felt hats of the upper ranks to the small, straw, nearly flat sombreros of the poorest peon. Don Nicolás represented traditional Mexico at a moment of change.

The Díaz government, in its quest for modernity, launched a series of fashion regulations. State governments and the governor of the Federal District decreed pants laws, requiring all adult males to wear European-style trousers while in town. Naturally, a brisk pants-rental business appeared at the city limits of major towns. The government of the Federal District continued with its plan to westernize the appearance of Mexicans. This resulted in a series of required uniforms for different occupations. Porters, hack drivers, and streetcar conductors all had distinct uniforms, including caps to replace the sombrero. Corner newspaper boys dressed in black-and-white vertically striped pants and shirts until Porfirian officials learned that North American tourists avoided these boys because they assumed them to be some kind of prison labor.

The Díaz elite abandoned Mexican clothes for those of European cut, donning tailored coats and trousers, ties, collars, and homburgs. Zúñiga y Miranda thus was an ambiguous figure, representing the Mexican elite to the lower ranks and symbolizing traditional society to the Porfirian plutocrats. This image was accentuated by don Nicolás's drooping moustache, the traditional facial hair. Porfirian government officials and the social *científicos* (Mexican followers of the positivist philosophy of Auguste Comte) replaced their moustaches with trimmed beards, sideburns, goatees, and other European styles.

Because Zúñiga y Miranda roamed the capital's streets and gave his interviews, speeches, and prognostications on street corners, he appealed to the folk tradition of melodrama. For decades there had been street festivals on religious and civil holidays. Carnival, Holy Week, Independence Day, and the Cinco de Mayo each had official rituals, but these were overwhelmed by popular celebrations in the streets. These popular festivals included itinerant puppet theaters, Judas burnings, clowns, and social reversals by the crowds, who acted simultaneously as spectators and participants. Don Nicolás represented a heritage that reached back through the colonial society to medieval Europe and perhaps even earlier. He performed as the classic clown, exaggerating his actions to reveal that which caused either unspoken or unconscious conflict in the society. Thus he overstated the purpose of his mechanical inventions and made hyperbolic claims for the utility of science.

Don Nicolás burst into public consciousness in May 1887. His observations of the heavens led him to predict that at the end of the month there would be an earthquake that would send shocks throughout central Mexico from its epicenter in Oaxaca. He went to the editor of *El Siglo XIX* and explained his conclusions. The paper published don Nicolás's startling prediction along with a sarcastic sketch of this self-made man of science.

On May 24, the day he had predicted for the earthquake, churches filled with Mexicans praying for help. Even the students who had jeered him at the mining and law schools decided to take no chances. Every hour seemed an eternity until at eleven o'clock at night in Mexico City the gas and oil street lamps began to sway, and the capital endured a mild tremor. The following day, don Nicolás was acclaimed for his scientific ability. His father purchased one thousand copies of the issue of *El Siglo XIX* that carried the sketch of his son and the story of his astronomical skills.

His second earthquake prediction did not turn out so well for his reputation. He made a series of astronomical studies that persuaded him of an approaching earthquake that threatened all of the buildings in the republic; during the quake four volcanoes would erupt, new mountains would appear, and the entire Mexican population would perish, to be replaced by a new race. His scientific efforts took him away from his classes for days of intensive investigation, and he determined that August 10, 1887, would be the day of this holocaust. Again he went to *El Siglo XIX,* and the editor eagerly published his story.

Priests sang the Mass; the faithful and the unfaithful made confessions; many made pilgrimages to the Virgin of Guadalupe. On the evening of August 9, the eve of the apocalypse, reports circulated that smoke columns could be seen rising from the volcano Popocatepetl. Near panic gripped Mexico City through the next day and night until the dawn of August 11. Then people relaxed—and many blamed don Nicolás for misleading them. Other individuals believed that his warning had saved them because he had given the faithful enough time to offer sufficient prayers to prevent the catastrophe. His fellow students believed him to be a fool. He was swung up in the air like a Holy Week Judas effigy in the open patio of the National School of Jurisprudence (today, the open-air theater of the Ministry of Public Education). For half an hour he was tormented with taunts and sticks. When he was lowered, his sombrero looked like an accordion and his frock coat was in tatters. He himself dismissed the entire episode by blaming his sources, not his science. Society at large laughed at him.

Don Nicolás created mirth by taking seriously what he was not supposed to and by becoming a character of public derision. Posing as a man of science, he represented a Hispanic tradition of comic figures that served as a parody and a signal of social ambiguity. For example, Spaniards who had gone to the colonies to make their fortunes and then returned home with their riches were called *indianos* and became the butt of humor in their home country because they seemed more colonial than Spanish. The *indiano* became synonymous with new wealth and appeared as a stock satirical figure in contemporary Spanish literature. Nineteenth-century novelists continued this tradition in the literature of the frontier by using laughter to defuse stressful situations, and, on other occasions, by using it to create tension. Humor was also used as a device to undermine authority by challenging it with laughter.

What great fun for the lower ranks to watch don Nicolás try to master modern science and technology. Like the foreigners with their locomotives, factory engines, pumps, presses, and steel plows, don Nicolás produced machines that did very little for most everyday Mexicans, since a majority of them lacked either the money to ride the trains or the skills necessary to work in the factories. His seismograph promised to predict earthquakes; railroad promoters promised to bring prosperity, the plow salesman an end to drudgery. None of it came to pass, but it sounded good and looked modern. Like the Zuni clowns who covered themselves with excrement and mud when they danced, don Nicolás carried his inventions through the streets, displaying things that much of society regarded as abhorrent, or at least as improper and astonishing.

What pleasure for the Porfirian elite to observe Zúñiga y Miranda attempt to master science and technology! He, like those people whom the elite viewed as the downtrodden, retrograde, and primitive lower classes, mixed superstitious predictions and sham science. His wild efforts at invention fit perfectly the elite's perception of indigenous naïveté and stolid ignorance.

For both segments of Mexican society in the 1890s he provoked laughter by exaggerating the stereotype that each group held of the other. At the same time, underneath the humor of his caricature was the growing confidence many Mexicans had in technology as a remedy for their concerns. His inventions might not work, but they did indicate the areas of life that everyday Mexicans believed needed to be explained and, if possible, controlled. Zúñiga y Miranda's performances provided a key to popular attitudes toward modern technology and aspirations for its application.

Equally relevant to his contemporaries were his one-man melodramas of Mexican politics, that is, his campaigns in presidential elections. Don Nicolás ran for the presidency in 1896 and 1900. He conducted his campaigns on street corners, especially those in transitional neighborhoods where the rich were pushing the poor out toward the city limits.

President Díaz found nothing amusing or quaint in Zúñiga y Miranda's initial efforts. The dictator recognized that this comical character, a betwixt-and-between figure, represented a social danger. Don Nicolás acted as though the regime's democratic pretenses were real. In so doing, he disrupted the orderly social system that had been erected so carefully by Díaz and his advisers. The laughter of the people at the challenge to Díaz was anxious as well as amused because the everyday order was being disturbed. By the 1890s the authoritarian administration of Díaz had become a consensual arrangement, and Zúñiga y Miranda threatened to undo the balance.

Liberal journalists attacked don Nicolás's candidacy, declaring that he made Liberal ideals appear ridiculous and that he outraged society with his mockery of sacred political rights. One undercurrent in such newspaper opposition was the journalists' belief in the priority of lucid, rational political argument in written form over the street-corner theatrics of a populist politician, even of one whom the editors regarded as a buffoon populist. The arrogance of the literate Liberals limited their appeal, and they resented don Nicolás's ability to capture public attention by seeming to mock their programs.

In his lucid intervals, don Nicolás, like such fools as California's Emperor Norton, revealed a sensitivity to social problems and popular concerns. The emperor issued decrees in San Francisco commuting John Brown's death sentence on the grounds of insanity, directing that a bridge be built from Oakland to San Francisco, and supporting aerial experiments. The challenger to Porfirio Díaz offered voters a sincere plan for Mexican progress. His political platform called for land reform to increase food production, elimination of pulque production to end drunkenness, and endorsement of European clothing and shoes. His agrarian proposal aimed at making Mexico more productive than Argentina by dividing the land into small plots to be sold on credit with ten years to pay, by offering loans for the purchase of farming equipment and seed, and by demanding no repayment of loans until after the first harvest. He planned to eliminate the problems associated with pulque by giving prison terms without parole to producers. His fashion regulations echoed those of Díaz; he wanted to prevent men from entering the national capital in white peasant pants that he believed were indecent and displayed the backwardness of the people. His declared that if any man could not afford the obligatory trousers and shoes, the articles would be provided by the government, and the individual could pay for them by working on the crews paving the capital's streets.

Mexican police halted don Nicolás's 1896 political campaign. They arrested him on a charge of drunk and disorderly conduct. A night in jail and a four-peso fine stunted don Nicolás's enthusiasm, and he retired from the political arena until 1900. Díaz had had the candidate arrested because he represented a challenge, apparently a mild one but symbolically fundamental, to the orderly system. His campaign blurred the hierarchy and thus created feelings of unease by revealing society's bad faith. In this respect, don Nicolás was a marginal man and a dangerous one for his political challenges to the Porfirian myth of consensus.

During the interval between the 1896 and 1900 elections, Díaz decided that Zúñiga y Miranda actually deflected criticism by his antics. Consequently, the dictator welcomed don Nicolás's participation in the new election. Once the "fool" joined the campaign, he served the views of both the traditional masses and the *científico* elite. For the dispossessed population, Zúñiga y Miranda provided his theater of the absurd, mocking all the highfalutin talk of Mexican democracy. For the elite, he provided a living tableau of the ridiculous results from attempts by semieducated Mexicans to win a role in government. Don Nicolás thus provided an object of humor for all the witnesses. This humorous spectacle gave those individuals who did not benefit from Porfirian progress the strength to stand straight beneath the repressive yoke, not the rage to throw it aside. Laughter renewed the courage to live with reality rather than instilled the bravery to dream new worlds.

Don Nicolás retired as a political candidate after 1900. His last political effort came in 1909, when he offered his assistance to

General Bernardo Reyes, who briefly considered an election campaign against the dictator. Reyes rejected his help and soon discarded his own presidential ambitions. But another challenger appeared in the 1910 campaign, who took don Nicolás's place. Díaz mistook this new aspirant, Francisco Madero, for a fool; he misinterpreted the Anti-reelectionist challenge as another street-corner melodrama. Too late the dictator learned that the short, squeaky-voiced vegetarian from Coahuila took Porfirio at his word. Madero dressed and acted the part of the elite and, above all, sanctioned or not, was nobody's fool.

Don Nicolás, the sanctioned fool, this Sartre on the Zócalo, ultimately had misled the dictator. After abandoning politics, he directed his attention to more general problems, which he wanted to solve with the help of the great men of history. He became a Spiritualist and believed that he received direct counsel from Aristotle. He claimed, for example, that the Greek philosopher had instructed him to negotiate a peace settlement during World War I. A lifelong bachelor, don Nicolás became a favorite with neighborhood children, who loved his stories and his phantoms. His conversion to spiritualism only added to the popular derision about his prognostications, which continued now and again until his death in 1927.

SOURCES

Works on don Nicolás are limited but see the brief biography, Guillermo Mellado, *Don Nicolás de Mexico (el eterno candidato): Vida, aventuras y episodios del caballero andante, Don Nicolás de Zúñiga y Miranda* (Mexico City, 1931) and both *Diccionario porrua* 2:2354 and Carleton Beals, *Porfirio Díaz: Dictator of Mexico* (Philadelphia, 1932), p. 318. A full-fledged study of a similar character is William Drury, *Norton I: Emperor of the United States: A Biography of One of America's Most Colorful Eccentrics* (New York, 1986).

Theories of humor and its social functions are discussed in William H. Beezley, "Recent Mexican Political Humor," *Journal of Latin American Lore* 1, no. 2 (1985): 195–223; Rose Coser, "Some Social Functions of Laughter: Humor in a Hospital Setting," *Human Relations* 12, no. 2 (1959): 171–82; Charles Winick, "Space Jokes as Indicators of Attitudes toward Space," *Journal of*

Social Issues 17, no. 2 (1961): 43–49; and Anton C. Zijderveld, "Jokes and Their Relation to Social Reality," *Social Research* 35, no. 2 (Summer 1968): 306.

Sanctioned clowns receive consideration in two articles: Arlene K. Daniels and Richard R. Daniels, "The Social Function of the Career Fool," *Psychiatry* 27, no. 3 (1964): 219–29, in which is discussed the fool in rigid or oppressive social situations; and Lucile Hoerr Charles, "The Clown's Function," *Journal of American Folklore* 58, no. 227 (January 1945): 33. Charles used the Cross-Cultural Survey of the Institute of Human Relations, Yale University, as well as drawing on her own understanding of Jungian psychology and her years of practical experience in the amateur and professional theater.

The interaction of humor and politics is explored in Alan Dundes, "Laughter behind the Iron Curtain: A Sample of Rumanian Political Jokes," *The Ukrainian Quarterly* 27 (1971): 50–59, esp. 50–51; Stanley H. Brandes, "Peaceful Protest: Spanish Political Humor in a Time of Crisis," *Western Folklore* 36, no. 4 (October 1977): 334–35; and Jan Harold Brunvand, "'Don't Shoot, Comrades': A Survey of the Submerged Folklore of Eastern Europe," *North Carolina Folklore Journal* 11 (1973): 181–88.

Peter Berger discussed Sartre's construct in *Invitation to Sociology*, reprinted as "Society as Drama," in *Drama in Life: The Uses of Communication in Society*, edited by James E. Combs and Michael W. Mansfield (New York, 1976), pp. 41–43. Also see Hugh Duncan, *Symbols in Society*, reprinted as "Axiomatic Propositions" in the same collection, p. 37.

The outstanding work on the Porfirian period for those who read Spanish is Daniel Cosío Villegas's nine-volume study. See especially *El Porfiriato: Vida política interior*, vol. 2, in the *Historia moderna de Mexico* (Mexico, 1972). William H. Beezley discusses society in these years in *Judas at the Jockey Club* (Lincoln, 1987).

15

Santa Teresa:
Mexico's Joan of Arc

Paul J. Vanderwood

In its later years the dictatorship of Porfirio Díaz faced a number of real and imagined challenges. No fool, Díaz chose to respond in a variety of ways. He ordered some rebels annihilated; he bought off others; he warned some, including Teresa Urrea, into exile; and he ignored still others. The crafty old dictator probably recognized that the greatest threat to his government would be from a mass rebellion of the poor and disadvantaged, and from an individual such as Teresa Urrea who could inspire such a revolt. He also may have realized that his killing or imprisoning Teresa would make her even more dangerous as a martyr.

In 1888 at the age of fifteen, Teresa fell into a trance and said that she had met the Virgin Mary. In northern Mexico a cult developed around the young mestiza and her miracle, and the town of Tomochic claimed that she had inspired their rebellion against the Díaz government in 1892. Díaz forced Teresa into exile in the United States, but Mexican rebels continued to invoke her name and spirit even after her death from tuberculosis in 1906.

Given the strength of popular religion among country folk, any person who could link an inchoate political appeal with religious fervor would be doubly dangerous. In some ways analogous to the activities of advocates of liberation theology in the 1980s, in the time of Teresa Urrea the most successful politico-religious leaders placed the Catholic church squarely on the side of the poor rather than of the rich. They tempted the poor with the thought that they themselves could bring about the millenarian ideal of well-being and love, quite a different ideal from the earthly passivity that the more formal church advocated.

Mystics often are seen credibly by their followers and skeptically by historians and nonbelievers. Whatever Teresa herself might have believed about her experience, there must have been other visions that occurred in the barren lands of northern Mexico among the credulous population. Why did Teresa's miracle uniquely become the focus for rebellion?

Returning to the theme of fin de siècle decadence, Teresa's followers can be compared with contemporary Cuban patriots. In both Mexico and Cuba in the 1890s, corrupt and unresponsive regimes may have seemed vulnerable to a popular uprising. The Spanish empire gave way in 1898, after thirty years of struggle, but Díaz's regime lasted until the onslaught of a mass popular uprising in 1911.

Paul Vanderwood, professor of history at San Diego State University, is an authority on the social history of the Porfiriato. He is the author of *Disorder and Progress: Bandits, Police, and Mexican Development* (1981), has published numerous articles on film in Latin America, and most recently has published, with Frank Samponaro, *Border Fury: A Picture-Postcard Account of the Mexican Revolution and U.S. War Preparedness, 1910–1917* (1988).

Newspapers proclaimed her Mexico's Joan of Arc, this comely mestiza, this teenaged maiden named Teresita, who rallied her followers so brazenly to attack the government. Their battle cry, "Viva la Santa de Cabora," echoed across much of northwestern Mexico and even over the border well into the United States. Armed with a hodgepodge of weapons ranging from crude bows and arrows to modern Winchester repeater rifles and, even more important, with amulets, tokens, photos, and potions granted by their "Santa" to guarantee their lives, but if not, at least their salvation, they swarmed to her blandishments and adhered to her admonitions. Her followers were Mayo and Yaqui Indians from their traditional lands in southern Sonora; mestiza laborers from towns such as the Sonoran seaport of Guaymas; and farmers from villages such as Tomochic, located to the east, on the Chihuahuan side of the Sierra Madre Occidental, and even from the llanos below Tomochic, down in the broad, well-populated valley of Papigochic. Adherents even drifted in from Arizona and New Mexico. And as her fame spread, so did her following.

By 1890 thousands of Mexicans were making pilgrimages to Teresa's modest chapel at Cabora, a *rancho* on the hot, arid lands below the more mountainous silver-mining town of Alamos in southeastern Sonora. Daily healings took place at Cabora: a lame person walked, the deaf heard, deformities were overcome, psychologically disturbed individuals regained their senses, and tumors disappeared. She ministered to perhaps two hundred people each day; on some days five thousand people came to Cabora. Some pilgrims came quite long distances, from deep in Mexico and even from the lower tier of the United States. Most seem to have been Yaqui and Mayo Indians from the region, but mestizos also arrived to witness the "miracles" at Cabora, to participate in them, and to adore their "Santa."

The scene at the ranch was something of a carnival. Peddlers with their ropes, huaraches, belts, straw hats, pottery, rosaries, rebozos, tacos, mescal, and fruit juices set up shop around the ranch house and corrals of Cabora. The pilgrims vied to touch her, to see her, at least to hear their venerated saint. And just what did Teresa preach? What was she telling the populace? Certainly she preached love and brotherhood, but as she did so she fiercely labeled clerics, doctors, and money as the world's greatest evils, and she was especially derisive, even vitriolic, about the Catholic church as an institution, as a bulwark of officialdom. The church needed to be reformed drastically, or eliminated, and that admonition she extended to the pope himself. No more corrupt pope. She, Teresa, had received the word of God; there need be no intermediary between individuals and the Lord. People, if they cared to, could marry, baptize, and confirm themselves. In fact, they need not adhere to any authority: "None but the justice of God." This was not only teaching; it also was a battle cry.

How did this extraordinary teenage girl come to all this? Teresa was born into most humble circumstances, the daughter of a fifteen-year-old Tehueco Indian in Mexico's northwestern state of Sinaloa, not in the towering mountains, the Sierra Madre, to the east, but more in the bleak, river valley district that drains into the Pacific. The date of Teresa's birth was October 15, 1873. Her mother, Cayetana Chávez, was herself the daughter of a vaquero, a weathered cowboy who rode herd for prosperous ranchers. Teresa's father, Tomás Urrea, scion of the wealthy and prominent Urrea clan, was one such rancher. The Urreas had accumulated much of their wealth in the silver-mining district around Alamos. Tomás showed little initial promise as an entrepreneur, but he rode his family's coattails to an elevated social position and shared its considerable prosperity. He married a cousin in a match arranged by his uncle, the family patriarch, to assure that Urrea wealth stayed in the family. Cayetana and her father worked for Tomás, and Teresa was the illegitimate child of their patron.

Losers in the contentious politics of Sinaloa, the Urreas left the state precipitously and resettled among the family's interests in and around Alamos, there to await more fortuitous political times. Once in Sonora, Tomás worked the family's ranching business to the west of Alamos. As a wedding present his uncle had given him the ranch called Cabora, and Tomás dedicated himself to making his property the centerpiece of the Urrea ranching enterprise. At the same time, he disencumbered himself of his wife, with whom he shared little affection, although he continued to father their children. Señora Urrea remained in the elegant family homestead in Alamos, and, down on the plains, Tomás's mestiza mistress, Gabriela, with whom he lived for the rest of his life, bore him additional children.

Teresa and her family had been part of the retinue that Tomás Urrea carried north to refurbish the ranch holdings in Sonora. Apparently, because of some family squabble in 1888, when she was a fifteen-year-old, Teresa moved from an outlying ranch to Cabora and to the protection of her father, who adored her. In the following year, Teresa suffered a seizure. For two weeks she lay comatose; funeral arrangements were prepared. Then a kind of consciousness returned to her, and Teresa serenely related to her concerned family and friends accounts of her ethereal meeting with the Blessed Virgin Mary, who had told her of the many things that she must do for God and humanity—help people, cure them, comfort and console her fellow humans. For the next three months or so, Teresa wandered around the environs of Cabora in a kind of stupor; she seemed to be in a mysterious trance. Her father discounted reports of any encounter with the Virgin Mary. He considered himself a rational man, a modern Mexican who had read a good deal on his own about the church and superstition.

Rumors about Teresa's mystical experience and demeanor began to spread, first within Cabora, then to neighboring ranches, arching outward to encompass Yaqui and Mayo Indians, penetrating the Sierra, and on to relatively large towns, such as Guaymas. It was rumored that Teresa had been resurrected from the dead—a miracle. In her serious, enigmatic way she began to predict happenings to her closest friends: Juan Miramontes, she said, was on his way with news of an accident on an outlying ranch; a tornado would soon hurtle into an upland village; a long-missing person was returning to Cabora. All of these predictions came true. And Teresa began healings; at times she would simply speak to the afflicted, perhaps lay hands on them. On other occasions she blended her spittle with dirt into an ointment that she then applied to a sick or injured solicitant. The ill became cured, and soon pilgrims began to arrive to be healed and to receive the blessings of "Santa Teresa, la Niña de Cabora."

Confronted by the realities surrounding him, Tomás Urrea finally professed belief in his daughter's special healing qualities.

At first he fed the solicitants and allowed their horses to graze on his land. But he soon began to feel the financial impact of his largess, or perhaps he recognized an opportunity to profit financially from the extraordinary circumstances. He began to sell forage and food to the pilgrims. Those who sympathized with Teresita judged her father's pecuniary solicitations to be entirely reasonable. Others, more suspicious of or even hostile to the happenings at Cabora, sharply criticized Tomás as an opportunist and a gouger. Newspaper reporters investigated all of this excitement, which is why we know something of what went on at the site.

Among the visitors came a professional land surveyor, Lauro Aguirre, a troubled man in his midthirties with a political consciousness, who seems to have enjoyed considerable rapport with Teresa. Tomás had engaged Aguirre, a former military engineer, to help plan an irrigation system for his ranch. It was a fateful move, for Aguirre was well read, a dreamer, vigorous, and resilient. Although his ideas were not well formulated, he nurtured notions of a better world, one in which there would be more justice and fairness than he had seen and experienced in his native Mexico, one in which the terrible poverty that he had witnessed during his military service along the Guatemalan border would be eliminated. Aguirre spoke of the need for love among all peoples, but at the same time he meant to overturn the present political system. He was something of an anarchist, and his ideas were all jumbled up, but that did not make them any less dangerous to constituted authority.

Much of Mexico's officialdom was invested in the Roman Catholic church, as those at Cabora viewed it, through priests, the subject of Teresa's most strident attack. She caught her target at an especially vulnerable time, for the Catholic church was in turmoil, steeped in debate concerning its attitude toward and role among the common people, especially proletarians, or working men and women. Eventually, in 1893, the pope proclaimed his famous *Rerum Novarum*, declaring the church's social responsibility toward these individuals. But even before the official edict, Teresa had told her following about developments forthcoming from Rome. The church, she said, was about to undergo dramatic reform from the top down. In fact, she insisted, at that very moment emissaries were on their way from Rome to converse with her about the reconstructed church. It is not surprising that nothing has been found in the record to substantiate that last claim, but how did Teresa know about the deliberations in Rome? Certainly, someone could have informed her about them, perhaps Aguirre or her father, who was an avid reader. There had been a good deal about the church's deliberations in the national Catholic press, although how much of this reached Cabora is problematical.

Teresa herself seems to have had some education in a formal sense. She apparently could read and write. At least she was credited with carrying on an avid correspondence with adherents craving her advice. How much that correspondence represented her, was in her own words, or even if she wrote the letters herself, is not known. No examples have been found. Aguirre, too, soon proved himself to be a prolific writer. In fact, he became the publisher of a polemical newspaper for which he provided most of the research and writing.

A decade after her ministries at Cabora, Teresa disclaimed any political persuasion or advocacy of either resistance or challenge to the state. Just the opposite, she said. She claimed that when urged by others to rally the masses surrounding her to rebellion, she had declined, eschewing a call to violence for a message of respect and love. But when one pieces together the tidbits of evidence embedded in her teachings, they leave little doubt that she in fact did intend to turn the world upside down.

Around the year 1890, Teresa's preachings began to mold a cult of perhaps one hundred followers in the small mountain village of Tomochic, on the Chihuahuan side of the Sierra, where the state tilts downward toward rolling plains and eventually the desert. The village's name soon became synonymous with Teresita. It was a tragic relationship in the classic sense, one that was steeped in inevitability and doom but at the same time illuminated the human spirit and, many would say, human greatness.

Tomochic was at the time a village of some three hundred inhabitants, most of them mestizos but with a sprinkling of Tarahumara Indians, remnants of the Jesuit and then Franciscan mission that had marked the place. About midnineteenth century, miners, adventurers, and wanderers had entered the scenic and fertile Tomochic Valley and begun the process of edging the natives from their lands and other holdings. Tomochic was certainly no closed corporate community in any anthropological sense, yet the people there had their own ways of doing things, of dividing up land and influence, a situation that frequently bred more tension than harmony. Formal political authority over the village lay east, down in the Papigochic Valley, a true population center, where the fertile llanos meet the mountains. Authorities there placed little official pressure on Tomochic, which is not to say that the administrators in each place were not in contact with one another.

Precisely why elements in the village became attracted to and started to communicate with la Niña de Cabora is not at all clear. But a group, maybe eighteen to twenty, of the villagers sought her solace and counsel. They had lost faith in any form of government as they knew it, and so they turned to God for justice. At first they solicited succor from a rather bedraggled traveler from central Mexico who called himself "Saint Joseph," professed to perform miracles, and claimed direct contact with the Almighty. Santa Teresa was by no means the only so-called holy person in the region. Several were already in evidence, and more soon would appear. We know little of Saint Joseph, only that some thought him crazed and that the government feared his power to assemble crowds. He might have been preaching sedition, for the authorities arrested him but not before he had brought further mention of Santa Teresa to his listeners from Tomochic.

When the customary itinerant Catholic priest came to Tomochic late in 1891, he berated the parishioners for their growing devotion to Teresa. In response, they literally booted him out of the village church, threatened his life, and warned him never to return. The harried priest then alerted authorities in the Papigochic: the mountaineers at Tomochic were in outright rebellion against the government. He advised sending a public security force to subdue the villagers, and officials in the valley did not hesitate. Such a direct challenge to authority could not be tolerated. A squad of soldiers and militia began a two-day march over hostile mountain roads to Tomochic. The villagers knew they were coming; they had sympathizers in the militia. And as the military guard camped above the village prior to its assault, the soldiers heard the singing, chants, and other incantations to the Santa de Cabora being celebrated in the village church below. The rebels blessed their rifles (up-to-date Winchesters) and waited until the military approached the church.

"Viva Santa Teresa," shouted the rebels, as they burst from the church and hurled themselves at their adversaries. The brief firefight left several soldiers and villagers dead or wounded. The

Tomochitecos dispersed and headed for a planned rendezvous in the mountains west of the town. There some thirty men met with their stern, determined leader, Cruz Chávez, a small land-owner and occasional miner in his midthirties, possessed of an especially strong religious streak and an obstinate morality. Chávez had conducted church services when the itinerant priest was absent, and he seemed more sensitive than most to the changes in politics and economics that had beset the region in recent years. New regulations ordered from the Papigochic and beyond had begun to intrude on village life, and the economic pulse of the place had increased as mining in the region experienced a resurgence. Along with new opportunity came new competition, which had created rifts among the populace of Tomochic. And the adoration of Santa Teresa by the Chávez faction had finally split the village wide apart.

When they fled west to escape the military probe, the Chávez-directed insurgents knew where they were headed: to Cabora, to seek the solace and advice of la Niña. Authorities also recognized the rebels' destination and determined to head them off. Tele-graph lines loosely linked the mining communities in the Sierra with the major cities of Sonora and its capital at Hermosillo. All points were alerted; many raised security forces to engage the rebels. At the same time, the soldiers and militia in Tomochic joined those villagers who had ridiculed and otherwise opposed the Teresita element to root out the remaining rebels, to search their homes for weapons and evidence of their heretical faith, and to identify positively those who had chosen to adhere to no power but God.

Through the deeply cut arroyos and dense pine forests, the rebels carefully picked their way toward Cabora. By the new year, 1892, they were approaching the ranch. So were members of the Sonoran National Guard. When the cultists finally arrived, Teresa had disappeared. She had not, it seems, meant to involve herself directly in armed struggle. Still, Cruz Chávez and his followers remained steadfast to her. They assembled for a full day or more in the chapel at the *rancho,* and in a beguiling ritual they offered prayers and praise to their Santa, pleading for her intercession with God who in His justice would welcome them into a world rid of affliction and replete with peace. Tears streaked their faces as they gave voice to agonized pleas. Eyewitnesses later called the sight both pitiful and magnificent.

The Tomochic rebels could not tarry in Cabora. Chávez left behind his teenage brother, who had been wounded in the initial battle, and headed with his band back toward Tomochic, where, he said, they intended to die with their families. Did he mean that they intended to induce deliberately the apocalypse that would herald the Second Coming? Probably so. They knew that they would be pounded eventually by the army, but they were well prepared, both in morale and materiel, to do battle with the forces of the Antichrist, even to their deaths.

En route to Tomochic the rebels spotted the forces of the Sonora state guard in pursuit. They ambushed the militia, killing a number, including the commander. The humiliating defeat for the military set the tone for what was to come. The rebels reclimbed the Sierra, evaded further skirmishes, and returned to their homes and families. The soldiers had left the village; the clique that had opposed them remained, but not for long. Chávez meant to establish an egalitarian community in which these pragmatists would have no part, although he did not expel them. Nonetheless, feeling threatened, the faithless departed for the safety of the valley of Papigochic.

From February 1892 until September, when the federal army mounted its first campaign against the recalcitrant villagers, little is known about the activities of Chávez and his constituents. The state government attempted to negotiate a surrender and offered the rebels amnesty if they would agree to recognize constituted authority. Although in the talks the authorities employed a *político* from the Papigochic, an official previously trusted by the Tomochitecos, a negotiated settlement was not to be; the rebels adhered to Santa Teresa and to God—no one else. Visitors traveled to Tomochic to learn what was going on, but none of them overtly supported the movement just as no one, including the authorities, actively opposed it. Chávez established his utopian community; all members were proclaimed equal. In the military arm of the group, soldiers were to receive equal pay, four pesos per day, which were extremely high wages for the region and the times. The rebels do not seem to have had much money, perhaps just enough for arms and ammunition, which they could purchase from nearby mining centers, and Chávez probably did not pay his soldiers any such amount. But he was making a point. The villagers valued themselves highly, as the equal and more of almost everyone else in the area. In assuming this stance,

Chávez certainly had not considered money per se the evil that Teresa had assigned it. Moreover, he respected private property. When persistent drought curtailed food production even in fertile river valleys like that of Tomochic, the rebels broke into the storage houses of their rivals who had left. In keeping with their moral stance, they sent these adversaries a receipt for the grains and animals that they took. But the national government headed by the dictator Porfirio Díaz was losing patience with the rebels.

Why Díaz took so long, eight months or more, to pluck out the thorn of Tomochic is not certain. Chihuahuan state politics were in transition, and he may have preferred to iron them out before attending to unfinished business in the Sierra. Besides, he had other disorders to contend with—a genuine military uprising in the state of Guerrero and nettlesome incursions by self-proclaimed revolutionaries along the Texas border. Moreover, Díaz did not always prefer force to negotiation; perhaps in the case of Tomochic he favored conciliation. No matter, the point is moot, for Santa Teresa de Cabora forced his hand. Díaz ultimately was compelled to recognize the power of Teresa Urrea to mobilize common Mexicans against himself and his government.

Crowds of pilgrims who revered Teresita and sought her healings and ministry had continued to grow and now regularly numbered in the thousands at Cabora. Sonora's bishop, who routinely blessed small sketches and paintings of his parishioners' patron saints, complained that more and more people tried to sneak images of Teresa into the stack of images to be consecrated.

At last came outright revolution. A band of Mayo Indians attacked the little town of Navajoa, southwest of but not very distant from Cabora, shouting "Viva la Santa de Cabora." They carried a variety of talismans from their saint to ensure their protection. The Mayos killed several of the town's officials, including the municipal president, and sacked some buildings before being driven off and pursued by a military contingent.

The incident caused a national sensation, and Porfirio Díaz had to respond. When military investigation disclosed that folk saints predicting the apocalypse were appearing all over the Mayo territory, the prognosticators had to be either quieted or removed. More importantly, it was time to end the spectacle at Cabora, an undertaking that risked inciting widespread riot, even rebellion. Díaz reached an agreement with the Urreas: the security of the family properties would be guaranteed if Teresa and her father,

Tomás, slipped quietly into exile in the United States—not right on the border but inland at least as far as the city of Tucson, Arizona. No one debated the wishes of Díaz in such matters, and, in late June 1892, Teresa and her father quietly crossed the border under military guard into Nogales, Arizona. So far as is known, they never returned to Mexico, although rumors persisted that Teresita crossed the border to agitate against the regime. If she did not stir up the campesinos and urban poor, plenty of others did so in her name.

Once safely beyond the border, the Urreas, father and daughter, reneged on their promise to the Mexican government. Recognizing Teresa's commercial potential, the businesspeople of Nogales offered the Urreas a home from which Teresa could continue her healings and preachings. The scheme derived immediate profits for all those involved. Meanwhile, Lauro Aguirre, more politically radical and polemical than ever, joined the Urreas in exile and brought news of the events at Tomochic.

In September, Díaz ordered his military buddy from the days of the resistance to the French intervention, General José María Rangel, to subdue the rebels at Tomochic once and for all. Rangel marched on the village with banners flying over a military column of some four hundred soldiers supported by local militia. He disdained and underestimated his enemy; he meant to subdue his adversary by show of force alone. And where the main dirt wagon road to the village wandered past the cemetery on its outskirts, the battle was joined. In a sharp exchange, Rangel's units were tossed into a panicked dispersal. He and his staff narrowly escaped capture; they hid in cornfields at the edge of town and sneaked away under the cover of night. But a dozen of his men and officers were captured, and another group lay slain.

The rebels credited their spectacular victory to the Santa de Cabora and sang hosannas in her name. Correspondence later recovered by the military proved that Teresa and the rebels had been in direct contact during this period. One packet that was found even included some printed broadsides, apparently advocating the overthrow of the government. One cannot be sure whether these messages emanated from the United States or Mexico, before or after the expulsion of the Urreas. But someone who sent them had a printing press, probably Aguirre.

The military mapped its new campaign against Tomochic for late October 1892. General Rangel, in disgrace, was granted a reprieve; this time there was to be no foul-up. He would march with some seven hundred fifty men, reinforced with a Hotchkiss cannon, upon the village from the Chihuahua side. Meanwhile, Sonoran troops under Colonel Lorenzo Torres would converge on the defenders from the west. Rangel and Torres would unite and coordinate their forces on the rim of the mountains surrounding their quarry before the actual assault began. Of course, the Tomochitecos knew that the soldiers were coming and calmly confronted the odds. Perhaps eighty-five men, including teenagers, would defend their adobe homes and their village church, strewn like so many pillboxes in a field, against some twelve hundred federal soldiers and state militia. Their families stayed with them, and a small group of men under Pedro Chaparro joined them from a nearby mountain village. Chaparro and his comrades, considered bandits by many in the area, were the only ones to proffer assistance to the rebels. However, when the situation got toughest, Chaparro's gang fled.

The resistance as a whole, viewed from any standpoint, was heroic; no doubt in the defenders' view it was divinely inspired. Santa Teresa had promised them deliverance from their enemies, or at least salvation. Although they fought like demons, they lost. They gained respect and glorification, however, like the Greeks had at Thermopylae or the Jews at Masada. To this day the events of October 1892 at Tomochic are celebrated in novels, in those peculiarly passionate, popular Mexican songs called *corridos*, and certainly in every Mexican schoolchild's national history textbook.

The rebels fought to the last man. For nearly one week the village was enveloped in firepower from above. And federal soldiers crept down the hillsides and into the ravines intersecting the valley to get a more direct shot at the insurgents in their homes. As each adobe house was cleared of its defenders, federal forces moved in. Meanwhile, the rebels herded their wives and children into the church. As the resistance waned, soldiers crept forward (a good many died in the attempt) to pile fagots against the wooden doors of the church and set them afire. The roof of the church collapsed in smoke and flame, killing many in the conflagration. By the seventh day all of the surviving defenders were wounded, some grievously, Cruz Chávez among them. Food was scarce, ammunition all but gone. General Rangel offered to provide military escort for the surviving women and children, something under one hundred of them, to the safety of the city of Guerrero, municipal seat of the Papigochic. For the men there would be no such mercy. Imagine the good-byes made under those circumstances!

The last six defenders, including Chávez, exhausted their energy and ammunition but certainly not their willpower. General Rangel forcibly removed them from their adobe bastion. Once outside, he offered them cigarettes before proceeding with their executions. What a waste of life! But President Díaz had ordered exemplary punishment for Tomochic's defenders. The echo of his intransigence would sound in his ears. In the months that followed, a good many villagers returned to remember and to rebuild on the ashes of their community. Díaz would hear the battle cry of "Remember Tomochic" in the revolution that brought him down within two decades. Meanwhile, Teresa wept for the martyrs to her cause.

Muleteers who transported supplies to and from the mining districts near Tomochic still caught the stench of death five days after the final battle. Little was left alive, only packs of wild dogs that gnawed at the putrefying cadavers. A military squad arrived to burn and bury the dead, nearly one hundred counted on the floor of the valley alone. No one knew how many more bodies lay in the environs of the place, on the mountainsides, in the surrounding forests, and in the rugged arroyos. A civil official canvassed personal property found at the site; there would be an attempt to return such goods to survivors—the women and children who had been moved to the Papigochic.

The results of this affair satisfied no one. True, the army filed a series of efficient reports with superiors in Mexico City in an attempt to tidy up what had been a very messy campaign. But much of the citizenry of Chihuahua seemed to be in shock or at the very least deeply saddened. To the populace at large, it had all been so unnecessary, but then most of these people never did understand the millenarian hopes that Teresa had engendered.

The governor launched a charity drive to aid the survivors, and contributions arrived from throughout the state. Several families in the state capital, Chihuahua City, offered to adopt and to educate youngsters who had been orphaned by the fighting. And the governor pleaded for public peace to allow the wounds to heal. But there was to be no peace in the Papigochic, in the Sierra, and elsewhere in the state. "Viva la Santa de Cabora" echoed across the countryside amidst reports that the Tomochitecos fought on.

No, the bloodletting at Tomochic had ended; there were no survivors among the rebels, no escapees. But rebellion in Chihuahua certainly had not ceased, especially in and around the Papigochic. U.S. newspapers reported that all northern Mexico was about to erupt in revolution. Among the journalists, some feared for Díaz's hegemony; others thought he had it coming. Catarino Garza's raids along the lower Rio Grande had been stilled, but in the spring of 1893 serious upheaval occurred around the towns of Temosachic and Santo Tomás, north of Ciudad Guerrero along the Papigochic River. Unlike Tomochic, this revolt was not in essence millenarian; it did not seek to create an entirely new world of harmony and justice, even though some of its warriors dashed into battle screaming "Viva la Niña de Cabora." Rather, its goals concerned the here and now; rebels meant to overturn politics as practiced in the Papigochic and to bring down the national dictatorship. The leader of the rebellion was Simón Amaya, a former ranking official in the district whose political adversaries had gained local control and forced him into exile to the United States. News of events at Tomochic probably stimulated him to try a comeback; he even averred that he had been heading for Tomochic when strong federal army units intercepted him at Santo Tomás. He should have known, and probably did, that the resistance had ended at Tomochic five months earlier.

Díaz meant to take no chances with the Amaya uprising; it was overtly political. He ordered one of his best military commanders, General Rosendo Márquez, to Chihuahua to quell the affair. Amaya had attracted some two hundred followers as he marched through hamlets such as Yepomera and Matachic, on his way through Temosachic, and then into Santo Tomás. There the federals finally surrounded him, drew a cordon around the village, and determined either to beat him into submission or starve him out. House-to-house fighting ensued; Amaya was killed along with some thirty-five of his followers and perhaps sixty-odd federal soldiers. After two days of heavy assaults, the remaining rebels surrendered. But a number escaped; somehow they broke through the cordon and fled to the countryside.

These events led to terrible repression throughout the region; many innocent persons lost their lives as the military scoured the area seeking revenge for its own shortcomings. Soon the army had other troubles on its hands as well. Officials accused of election fraud were tortured and killed in Ascensión in the northern part of the state. Militia units restored an uneasy peace. Then radical leftists who had sought refuge along the border in the United States raided down toward Namiquipa, also in the Papigochic. These anarchists, people like Lauro Aquirre, Teresa's friend and confidant, no doubt intended to rally ordinary Mexicans and others into a mass movement against the dictatorship. They demanded Díaz's ouster. Federal soldiers caught up with them at a *rancho* called the Canyon de Manzano, killed several, and dispersed the rest. But these radicals would be heard from again, and U.S. immigration records show that they were in touch with Teresa, her father, and Aguirre.

It is difficult to establish precisely Teresa's role in these continuing forays against the Mexican government. Although her name was frequently invoked by the rebels, she denied any complicity. It is fair to assume that she endorsed their activities. In August 1896, for instance, a band of Yaqui Indians attacked the customshouse at Nogales (on the Mexican side) and plundered the place, killing several public officials in the process. Then they headed south toward their homeland, shouting "Viva la Santa de Cabora." Investigators found incriminating evidence on the bodies of several raiders who had been slain in the streets: amulets, scapulars, and religious trinkets, also letters, all of which proved that Santa Teresa had sanctioned the raid, even helped to plan it, and had provided powders and ointments that would shield the attackers from the bullets of their adversaries. Response on both sides of the border was immediate. Prominent citizens and others from the U.S. side of Nogales strapped on their pistols and toted their rifles across the line to hunt down the perpetrators and to prevent any repetitions. Mexicans also responded to the emergency. And the U.S. Army, still mired in its Indian war mentality, sent reinforcements to the scene; some even crossed to the other side without being asked to do so.

Despite the evidence, and perhaps it was not totally conclusive in the minds of the authorities, the Urreas suffered no real consequences. U.S. authorities refused to honor extradition appeals by the Mexican government. Instead, they urged the Urreas to move farther inland, and Teresa and her father did so, settling in the copper-mining town of Clifton, Arizona, but on the New Mexican border, where they were in daily touch with Mexican migrant laborers. Such a move certainly would not impede their political work should they choose to continue it. Aguirre urged them on. In 1896 he published a book about the happenings at Tomochic and about the millennial dreams spawned by Santa Teresa. He equated the repression at Tomochic with the injustice that infested all of Mexico, and he endorsed the call for justice issued by Teresita. The book is a hodgepodge of spiritism and of a vague anarchism that urged workers to address their plight with force. The border raids continued to occur in the name of "la Niña de Cabora."

These forays were easily contained and then defeated for they raised little support in Mexico. Meanwhile, the U.S. government had infiltrated the ranks of the raiders with treasury agents who confirmed that the Urreas and Aguirre had participated in planning the incursions. Mexico urged extradition, but the United States declined to comply; it argued that there was insufficient proof that the trio had participated directly in any attempt to overthrow a government that was friendly toward the United States. Other individuals had been and soon would be extradited or jailed on much less evidence.

Throughout this period Teresa's healings masked, at least to some degree, her political intentions and activities. Perhaps the healings also protected her from prosecution; she simply was too popular to be extradited into the hands of authorities spoiling to convict and sentence her for sedition. Or perhaps she deliberately tried to distance herself from revolutionary politics. Aguirre broke with her on this assumption. Teresa increasingly concentrated on her healings, and Aguirre turned to publishing a bombastically anti-Díaz newspaper in Spanish out of El Paso, Texas.

Teresa even claimed that she had fallen in love. She was twenty-seven years old in 1900 when a miner in Clifton began to court her. Over her father's objections she married, but on the wedding night the young man acted strangely; the next day he went out of his mind. They separated after just one day of matrimony. At the behest of a friend, Teresa traveled to San Jose, California, to treat a three-year-old girl who had failed to respond to the ministrations of five doctors. When Teresa cured the child, the major newspapers in the region recorded the event. Teresa's fame spread and entrepreneurs caught the scent. A so-called medical company, in reality more a traveling carnival, offered Teresa the substantial sum of two thousand dollars per year to circle the country, even the world, performing her good works.

She agreed, and the next year "the fanatical Mexican 'Miracle Worker'" appeared in New York City.

As Teresa spoke only Spanish, family friends back in Clifton furnished an interpreter, their son, a teenage ne'er-do-well with whom she took up residence. In 1902, the year that her father died of typhoid fever, Teresa had a baby girl, Laura. The "show" then moved back west to Los Angeles. After eighteen months of ministering to the Mexican and Mexican-American population in that growing city (it is reported that even in California, Teresa preached revolution against the Díaz regime), she apparently became tired of her hectic schedule.

In June 1904, Teresa, again pregnant and now reasonably well-to-do, returned to a more tranquil life in Clifton. Her retirement, however, was cut short by tuberculosis; there was no cure for her diseased lungs. Teresa died on January 11, 1906, at age thirty-three. Musicians played "Las Golondrinas" at her wake, and hundreds mourned as she was buried beside her father in Clifton's Catholic cemetery. Only five years later, rebels were fighting the Mexican Revolution in her name: "Viva Teresita. Viva la Santa de Cabora." More recently, feminists have acclaimed her as one of Mexico's most illustrious liberated women, and people who know of her through the oral tradition—Yaqui and Mayo Indians, and others around Clifton and Alamos—still speak of her miraculous healings, of the manner in which she preached the love of both God and man, and of her vision of a world devoid of war, poverty, and injustice, indeed the plea for all humanity then and now.

SOURCES

There are few secondary sources that deal with Teresa Urrea, "the Santa de Cabora." The only book in English worth mentioning was written by William Curry Holden and is called simply *Teresita* (Owings Mills, MD, 1978). Holden, history professor emeritus at Texas Tech University, first heard of Teresita while he was doing fieldwork in Mexico in 1951. The following year he began his research on her in Yaqui Indian villages. For more than two decades he dug into the "Santa's" background and activities through interviews, newspapers, and whatever evidence he could find. The result is an interesting book, well written, with much reliable detail as well as a good deal of fanciful description. The interviews, mainly with individuals who claimed to have known Teresa or heard relatives speak of her or both, caused the author to romanticize his subject far beyond the bounds of sound historical interpretation.

The only other secondary works are in Spanish and treat the tragedy of Tomochic and therefore necessarily mention "la Niña de Cabora." The more genuine, and certainly more fascinating, story of Santa Teresa lies in primary materials found in regional and national archives in both the United States and Mexico. For example, much of this essay is based on material found in the Papigochic holdings in Ciudad Guerrero (a magnificent set of historical records), the Sonoran State Archives, the Porfirio Díaz holdings at Iberoamerican University in Mexico City, the Archivo General de la Nación in Mexico City, and the National Archives in Washington, DC.

Equally important for our knowledge of the "Santa" are newspapers of the epoch. Admittedly, searching for the mention of Teresita in newspapers is frustrating, but an occasional glowing nugget does appear. And it is surprising how the nuggets begin to add up. U.S. newspapers from New York, San Francisco, St. Louis, Las Cruces, and El Paso among other cities at one time or another carried lengthy and informative stories on Teresa. So, too, did Mexican papers in Sonora and in Mexico City. Even so, there are never enough sufficiently detailed reports to satisfy the historian. Why did not the journalists of times past think to ask the "right" questions of their subjects, meaning, of course, "our" questions? Nevertheless, the evidence eventually does surrender its rewards, and the drama unfolds.

16

Emilio and Gabriela Coni: Reformers, Public Health, and Working Women

Donna J. Guy

By the end of the nineteenth century, Argentina bristled with confidence and optimism. After the conflicts that had resulted in Juan Manuel de Rosas's overthrow in 1852 and the subsequent dispute over whether Buenos Aires should become the national capital (resolved by 1880), the nation settled down to enjoy peace and prosperity. With its fine public educational system, its broad avenues and public buildings, and its prosperous middle class, Buenos Aires became the Paris of Latin America. Thousands of European immigrants streamed into Argentina, residing primarily in the capital and drawing attention to critical urban problems.

Gabriela Laperrière, a French schoolteacher and journalist, was one of these immigrants. After her marriage to Emilio Coni, a Buenos Aires doctor and city council member, she continued to write, became a factory inspector, and, like her husband, joined the Socialist party. Both worked for implementation of measures that would improve the lot of the working class in the capital city.

A belief grew in Argentina that the traditional political parties were exhausted and incapable of leading the nation into the twentieth century. The immigrants, the growing working class, and the concomitant penetration of European ideologies encouraged the rise of new parties. The Radical Civic Union and the Socialist party proposed an end to the laissez-faire philosophy of the old Liberals. They advocated a more activist government, one that would assume some responsibility for the well-being of its citizens. Buenos Aires and other cities became the major beneficiaries of the new social reforms, heightening the disparity between the quality of life in rural and urban areas of the country.

The careers of Emilio and Gabriela Coni illustrate some unresolved dilemmas that accompanied the new politics of social welfare. Civil liberties had not been a strong part of the Hispanic tradition, so few Argentines criticized Emilio Coni's efforts to control people's behavior for their own and for the public good. With the best of intentions, Coni saw illness as a metaphor and implicitly blamed the poor for their tuberculosis or syphilis. In the hands of liberal reformers science and technology could become additional tools with which to manipulate and control the less educated and the powerless. What were the implications of having the *científicos* (scientific men) replace the traditional caudillos and political bosses as the intermediaries between governments and their citizens?

Donna Guy, associate professor of history at the University of Arizona, is the author of *Argentine Sugar Politics: Tucumán and the Generation of Eighty* (1980) and numerous articles on social history and women in nineteenth-century Argentina. She is currently at work on two monographs, one a study of cotton cultivation and Argentine industrialization between 1860 and 1940 and the other on white slavery and prostitution in Argentina between 1875 and 1937.

Dr. Emilio R. Coni and his wife Gabriela exemplified the commitment and dedication of health workers and social reformers in the Argentine capital city, Buenos Aires, during the late nineteenth and early twentieth centuries. Confronted by rapid population growth, outbreaks of epidemic and pandemic diseases, and inadequate housing, the Conis helped shape public policy and private efforts aimed at reducing the alarming rates of infant mortality and communicable diseases. To accomplish their goals they identified women who worked and the work that women performed in the home, the factory, and the bordello as subjects for reformist activities.

Emilio was a *higienista* (public health physician) and, intermittently between 1880 and 1909, a member of the Buenos Aires health board. Gabriela Laperrière de Coni had her own multifaceted career as a journalist, novelist, factory inspector, and feminist Socialist activist. Although we know little about their private lives, their influence on public health strategies and protective labor legislation for women and children are important contributions to the history of Buenos Aires.

Both Conis wanted to improve women's health, but they disagreed about the best way to accomplish this. Emilio exemplified the nineteenth-century male liberal reformer. A doctor and city council member, he wanted first to control and then to change the behavior of women in order to make sure that they raised healthier children. In contrast, Gabriela had little experience wielding power and authority. She, too, wanted to keep the children of Buenos Aires healthy, but Gabriela believed that this goal could be met without coercion. A feminist Socialist, she believed that women would be better mothers if they were given more control over their lives. Therefore, she worked to relieve women of household tasks, of unhealthy working conditions, and of ignorance.

Physicians and social reformers in Argentina had to contend with a number of factors. From the 1860s until World War I, the country experienced unprecedented growth and modernization. During this time the young nation encouraged European immigrants to come and provide the labor and technical expertise needed by Argentine agriculture and industry. Argentina's search for a foreign-born work force coincided with the exodus of millions of Europeans who traveled to the New World in search of economic advancement and a new life. Between 1857 and 1890 the country's population tripled.

Argentine cities, particularly the capital and port of Buenos Aires, were completely unprepared for rapid urban growth. In 1854, Buenos Aires had a population of 90,000. In fifteen years it had almost doubled to 177,000, only to increase to 670,000 by 1895 and to 1,575,000 in 1914. Most of the population growth was due to the arrival of Europeans or the migration of native-born workers from the Argentine interior. As the city grew, unsanitary living conditions and exposure to epidemic diseases threatened to decimate the newly arrived working class.

In 1858, Buenos Aires experienced its first yellow fever outbreak, and in 1871 more than thirteen thousand residents died from the disease. Epidemics of cholera, measles, and smallpox also periodically ravaged the city until the 1890s, while tuberculosis and syphilis were persistent causes of both infant and adult mortality. The city's first response to these problems was the creation of a municipal public health board in the 1850s and the subsequent passage of ordinances to control the purity of water and food and the disposal of garbage. Throughout the latter part of the nineteenth century teams of physicians and neighborhood officials periodically entered tenement houses and businesses in search of unsanitary conditions or people infected by disease.

By 1873 the University of Buenos Aires began to teach principles of hygiene, or public health, at its medical school. Graduates of these courses formed the next generation of public health physicians, and many of them were called upon to serve in municipal hospitals and to formulate city ordinances. With the advice of the *higienistas*, Buenos Aires officials began to target specific groups of potentially infectious individuals, such as prostitutes, beggars, wet nurses, and domestic servants, and monitor them from a medical as well as, in some cases, a police perspective. At the same time health officials began campaigns of public education to inform city inhabitants, both rich and poor, of the need to practice good health habits within the home. Strained by limited budgets and having few medicines with which to treat the many diseases that threatened Buenos Aires, physicians and public officials came to rely on a combination of modern water and sewer systems, vaccinations, increased hospital and clinic facilities, and preventive medicine based upon principles of hygiene in order to protect the city's health.

EMILIO R. CONI (1854–1928)

Emilio Coni was among the first class of doctors at the University of Buenos Aires to graduate with a specialization in public health. Considered a brilliant student, he soon embarked on an equally impressive career of public service. Even before he graduated he had collected and analyzed health statistics. Subsequently, he continued his statistical work, proposed and implemented public health programs in Buenos Aires, and published more than thirty books and pamphlets. Many of his ideas came from his reading in the field and from his observation of European public health organizations during trips abroad.

The young *higienista*, an idealistic liberal reformer, was convinced that Buenos Aires could be a healthier city provided that it had laws to enforce good medical practices. All he had to do was convince the ruling urban elite of the need to implement an extensive public health program to control, as well as to cure, sick inhabitants.

The formation of a municipal organization controlled by *higienistas* was one of Emilio's main goals. The proposed Asistencia Pública (Public Assistance) would centralize the administration and improve the efficiency of hospitals, laboratories, cemeteries, garbage collection, slaughterhouses, and social services. Without the vigilance of disinterested physicians, health conditions in the city would be at the mercy of doctors and politicians who might be unscrupulous or poorly informed. From the late 1870s until the early 1890s, Emilio worked unceasingly, often without compensation, to implement Asistencia Pública.

His years of public service spanned the critical decades from the 1870s until the 1920s. Emilio had started his career fighting epidemics, and many of his authoritarian tendencies were reinforced by the need to take swift, often arbitrary action in order to contain the spread of diseases such as cholera or smallpox.

Teams of health workers literally had to invade tenement houses, identify the sick, isolate them, and disinfect or destroy their possessions. Because of his early experiences fighting the disease, Emilio favored mandatory smallpox vaccinations. He was willing to advocate often unpopular policies because he believed that the public's interest in health matters should take precedence over individual rights.

Emilio's determination to control individuals for the sake of the group's health can be seen clearly in his campaign against syphilis. In January 1875 the Buenos Aires municipal council had legalized female prostitution in licensed bordellos, provided that the women be examined twice each week and, if necessary, treated by a private physician. Emilio believed that medical examination of the prostitutes should be more rigorous and conducted by city physicians and that infected women should be more securely isolated in municipal hospitals. He began to campaign for these reforms in 1877 when he published an article that blamed infected prostitutes for all of the deaths from syphilis of infants in the city orphanage.

Doctors at the time had no simple cure for syphilis and few effective treatments for gonorrhea. They did know, however, that syphilis could be inherited by the children of infected mothers. Many European and Argentine physicians in the late nineteenth century also believed that women infected men but that men rarely infected women. Since prostitutes had many sexual partners, they were considered to be medically dangerous as well as immoral. Consequently, European authorities sought to control syphilis by monitoring female prostitution. The Buenos Aires ordinance of 1875 was a pale reflection of European laws, and, therefore, the young *higienista* believed that the alarming incidence of venereal disease in Buenos Aires would not be lowered without a more comprehensive system of medical control.

For similar reasons he began to advocate municipal medical inspection of wet nurses who could transmit syphilis through their milk. The hiring of a woman who had given birth recently to provide milk for another's infant was a common practice among middle- and upper-income families in different parts of the world. Medical discoveries during the nineteenth century had revealed that the mortality of infants nursed by these women depended upon the level of care provided the babies and the wet nurses' health and milk quality. Furthermore, poor women supposedly often ignored their own children's needs in order to have breast milk for sale. Emilio urged mothers to either breast-feed their own infants or seek medical examinations of any wet nurses they hired. He recommended that the authorities create a system to inspect potential wet nurses and to regulate their business.

In 1880, Emilio was asked to join the Buenos Aires municipal council as a member of the Public Health Board. During his short time on the board he supported many neighborhood petitions to have women evicted from their lodgings because they were suspected prostitutes. He was unsuccessful, however, in his efforts to modify undesirable aspects of the bordello ordinance. Frustrated by the lack of action on his proposed health ordinances, such as new laws covering bordellos and prostitution, Emilio resigned from the board in 1881 and worked for other provincial and municipal authorities as a specialist in medical and census statistics.

Emilio envisioned a public health system that, in addition to protecting urban inhabitants, particularly children, from contagious individuals, complemented the work of charities and ultimately replaced charitable institutions. He wanted health care for indigents and the protection of poor and unwanted children. He was one of the first defenders of vagrants and successfully launched a municipally sponsored program to provide transient men with lodging and breakfast. He started hygiene programs in the schools and had milk distributed to schoolchildren. He translated pamphlets on sex education for children and adults as part of a campaign to inform the public of the dangers of venereal disease.

At the same time as he strove to bring about social and medical reform, Emilio was quite willing to sponsor municipal or national laws to take civil liberties away from alcoholics and to confine female prostitutes in medically supervised bordellos until they either married or died. He also advocated a ban on alcohol and tobacco consumption as a way to lower the incidence of tuberculosis. His advocacy of coercive and charitable laws, fines, and public education demonstrate that he often had conflicting ideas on how to improve sanitary conditions in the city. While he hoped that people would learn about hygiene and voluntarily change their habits, he also was willing to force them to live healthier lives.

In 1887, Emilio established the first comprehensive service in Buenos Aires to register and monitor wet nurses. Subsequently, he worked on a number of national, provincial, and municipal committees related to public health issues. Then in 1890 the *intendente* (mayor) of Buenos Aires invited Emilio to study the causes of infant mortality. Two years later Emilio's committee published its report, and the Patronato y Asistencia de la Infancia (Children's Welfare Board) was established. The committee recommended ways to provide better services to poor and defenseless children and thereby reduce infant mortality. Their suggestions included encouraging parents to put children up for adoption rather than abandon them; instituting more rigorous and scientific vigilance over wet nurses; preventing children from working more than six hours per day; and teaching mothers about nutritious liquids and foods to feed young children.

By this time Emilio was at the peak of his energy and highly respected by city officials in Buenos Aires. Again the mayor called upon him, this time to reorganize completely municipal health facilities. With his typical zeal, Emilio set out to change the world, or at least the city. He divided public health facilities into two categories, Asistencia Pública and Administración Sanitaria (Sanitary Services). Within these institutions he organized an ambulance system, introduced evening medical clinics, centralized many hospital facilities, and defined standards for burials, autopsies, and disinfection of localities contaminated by infectious diseases.

He was willing to do almost anything to implement his program and often ended up in acrid verbal and written battles with the mayor, the city council, and the principal charity of Buenos Aires, the Sociedad de Beneficencia, an organization run by prominent society ladies that controlled most hospital services for women. A dispute with the new mayor in 1893 led Emilio to resign once again from municipal service. He left for Europe where he spent several years representing Argentina in a number of public health matters. When he returned, he stayed away from Buenos Aires until the turn of the century when he was invited back to the city to serve on the Public Health Board.

At the same time as he returned to the health board, Emilio began his great campaign against tuberculosis. He was president of the international commission on the prevention of tuberculosis in Latin America, and, in May 1901, he founded the Argentine Anti-Tuberculosis League, serving as director of the league's clinics until 1909. Earlier public health campaigns had led to a decline in mortality from yellow fever, cholera, smallpox, and other epidemic diseases. In their place, tuberculosis had become a major cause of illness and death among children and adults. Emilio set out to conquer tuberculosis, but once again he encountered resistance from public officials who were reluctant to commit scarce municipal funds to a campaign that would need vast amounts of money. Moreover, Emilio was bitterly disappointed by the scarce numbers of private citizens who were willing to pay dues to and support the league. By 1917, at the end of Emilio's career, he had concluded that only the national government had the resources necessary to finance the expansion of hospitals, centralize hospital administration, and, eventually, lower the incidence of diseases such as tuberculosis in Argentina. He drafted a law to carry out his program, but it was not acted upon. He died in 1928, embittered and frustrated by government officials who did not heed his expert advice.

In contrast to his boundless energy in pursuing the ideal of healthy children, his interest in mothers, particularly if they were working women, was more limited. Emilio saw all women as potential mothers. Since he assumed that women bore primary responsibility for *puericultura* (child care), he believed that they needed to learn how to take care of their children and how to keep the home hygienic. For good mothers and mothers with good intentions, he had unbounded time, energy, and ideas. All he needed was the financing, either public or private, for his programs.

On the other hand, while Emilio's writings demonstrated an awareness of the latest developments in public health technology, he rarely contemplated the impact of industrialization and modernization on women workers. Not until after the death of his wife did he go into factories nor did he concern himself with industrial health conditions unless they threatened children. After all, in his estimation working women were merely ignoring their primary roles as mothers.

Emilio's concern for women and children was part of his great campaign to make Buenos Aires a healthier place in which to live. At times he worried about the need for coercive measures to prevent the spread of illness, but he justified their use to protect all of the city's inhabitants. A biographer once wrote that Coni was "not the physician of the individual but rather of the collectivity; he was the physician not just of the ill, but also of the towns and cities." Without such dedicated doctors, cities like Buenos Aires would have been unable to control many of the health problems brought on by rapid population growth.

GABRIELA L. DE CONI (1866–1907)

Gabriela's early biography sheds little light on her preparation for a political career. In fact, we know little about her at all. Born in France and trained as a schoolteacher, Gabriela worked for several French newspapers before migrating to Argentina as a young woman. As Emilio's wife (there are some indications that she may have been married prior to meeting him), she continued her interest in writing, and only after 1900 did she turn most of her energy toward politics. Her brief political career was truncated by her death in 1907 at the age of forty. Despite the disparate lengths of their activist years, Emilio and Gabriela both deserve to be remembered for their efforts to improve the health of the working class, particularly of mothers and children, and to find appropriate ways to maintain safe and hygienic conditions in the home and workplace.

Emilio's and Gabriela's approaches to these problems were as different as the span of their careers. Emilio formulated public health policy to protect the city as a whole and ill children and indigents as groups. He concentrated on teaching urban mothers how to keep children healthy and on providing medical services for the poorest city residents. Gabriela focused on a somewhat different group. Deeply influenced by her husband's efforts to reduce infant mortality and prevent tuberculosis, she also was committed, as a Socialist and feminist, to the defense of working-class women and children. Hence, Gabriela targeted the unhealthy factory and the working-class home as the objects of her scrutiny, and she championed the political, economic, and hygienic rights of women and children who worked and lived in those environments. Unlike the unemployed and the desperately poor, working-class people in Buenos Aires often earned too much to qualify for the municipal programs established by her husband, yet they were too poor to escape the need to work in insalubrious factories and businesses.

When, then, did Gabriela develop her political ideas? Her novel, published in Paris in 1900, indicated that she was committed to social reform even before she began to be active politically. Her principal female character, Anita Kerven, was a young teacher who became a doctor and worked at the Children's Hospital. Anita was guided in her career by a kindly physician, Dr. Mendel. From him she learned many secrets of science and medicine and the difference between good physicians and those who were incompetent or inhumane. Anita also married a physician, Eduardo Larsan, who was both well trained and caring. These fictional characters had much in common with Emilio and Gabriela, although Gabriela herself never became a doctor. Nevertheless, it is clear that she learned much from her husband about the plight of sick children, and she used her knowledge to buttress her own political speeches about unhealthy working conditions.

Gabriela began her political career in 1900 as the press secretary for the Argentine National Council of Women, but she resigned that same year because of the council's conservative policies. After that, she became Buenos Aires's first factory inspector. As a member of the city's board of health, Emilio probably suggested that the mayor appoint Gabriela to the position. One of the goals of the league to combat tuberculosis that Emilio headed was to encourage factory owners to ensure the health of their employees. In August 1901, three months after the Argentine Anti-Tuberculosis League began to operate, Mayor Adolfo Bullrich named Gabriela L. de Coni to be an inspector of city factories employing women and children. Her job was to visit the factories, analyze their hygiene and health conditions, and prepare a report that would be sent to the national congress.

Gabriela took her assignment seriously and prepared an in-depth four-part study. Her first report, delivered in November 1901, was designed to tell the mayor of her personal fears and anxieties about the unhealthy working conditions that she encountered. She was disturbed that children less than ten years old were working and that the air was filled with all kinds of impurities that could damage workers' lungs. Her recommendations culminated in her April 1902 proposal that protective legislation for women and children be enacted.

The law suggested by Gabriela consisted of eighteen articles and copious explanations in footnotes. Children were to be banned from factories and workshops until they were fourteen and could prove that they had been vaccinated for smallpox. They could work for only six hours per day. Women and children over eighteen could work eight hours but not before 6 A.M. or after 6 P.M. They would also be forbidden from working in factories considered dangerous or immoral. Finally, all women and children would be guaranteed Sundays off, and lactating mothers would have a room within the factory where they could breast-feed their children.

Although Gabriela did not live to see all aspects of her legislation enacted, parts of it were incorporated into another piece of protective legislation presented to the congress by Joaquín V. González in 1904. Although González's bill was rejected by the Socialist party as well as by the congress, the cause of protective legislation was, nevertheless, a key issue for Argentina's Socialist party. Indeed, it was Socialist Deputy Alfredo L. Palacios who drafted the legislation that was finally passed by the congress in 1907.

As Gabriela explored the factories of Buenos Aires, she realized that her position as inspector could help the campaign against tuberculosis. Accordingly, less than a month after her appointment, she wrote Dr. Samuel Gache, president of the league established by her husband, and offered to give talks about hygiene in the home, nutrition, and other topics related to the antituberculosis cause. As she put it, "Surely there are many female apostles, more competent and appropriate than myself, who could talk to upper-class women, but I want to serve the working women because they are more threatened and less prepared to combat disease, and thus their needs are more critical." Gache was delighted to have Gabriela's help and accepted her offer. By October 23, 1901, after less than one month, Gabriela already had given ten conferences.

Her 1902 speech to the Unione Operari Italiani (Italian Workers' Union) was published by the Argentine Anti-Tuberculosis League, and it enables us to recapture the intelligence and social commitment of an unusual woman. Gabriela, after citing a number of recent publications on the subject, identified the causes of tuberculosis to be "alcoholism, unhealthy habitations, poor nourishment, excessive physical, mental, or moral labor, and poor hygiene." She informed her audience that these perils endangered men and women alike, although men tended to suffer more frequently from alcoholism while women and children experienced more poor health from working too strenuously. This was especially true for women, who were expected to perform domestic chores in addition to salaried labor, and Gabriela described the daily schedule of a typical working woman:

The typical working-class woman has to be in the factory at 6 A.M.; if she is a mother and married, she arises at 4 or 4:30 to prepare breakfast, dress her children, and sweep and straighten out her lodging. Of course I am presuming all of this can be accomplished in an hour and a half, and the woman lives close to her place of work. At 11 A.M. she returns home, makes a fire, and prepares lunch for her family, all within an hour and a half. Some factories—very few—grant them two hours, others one. . . . At 6 P.M., having finished her work at the factory, she must begin the preparation of dinner, washing the dishes, and the children, if they need it. She must also mend, sew, iron, etc. . . . How many hours do these beasts of burden, these women who are perhaps pregnant, have to rest? Add them up yourselves: by 9 P.M., they have worked without rest for seventeen hours and not for themselves, but rather *for others,* for this family they have given birth to.

Throughout 1902 the league's magazine continued to publish speeches and reports by Gabriela. In September the league responded favorably to her suggestion that soup kitchens be set up near factories so that inexpensive but nourishing meals would be available for workers. Such establishments would eliminate the need for women to cook for their families at lunchtime. Given the insufficient financial base of the league, no soup kitchens were established immediately. Nevertheless, by 1917 subsidized restaurants were operating throughout the industrial parts of the city under the auspices of the Salvation Army, the Sisters of the Sacred Heart, the Sisters of Mary the Provident, the St. Vincent de Paul Society, the Charity Dames, the Conservation of the Faith Society, the YWCA, the League for the Protection of Young Women, the Irish Sisters of Mercy, and the Dowry Society for Working Women. Most of these establishments served working-class people full-course meals at very low prices.

Other activities undertaken by Gabriela after 1902 had a more immediate impact. Working more directly through the Argentine Socialist party, which had been organized in the 1890s, Gabriela was the first woman to support Socialist politicians at public political meetings. The only female member of the party's Executive Council in its early years, she was also one of the founders of the Centro Socialista Femenino (Socialist Women's Center) in 1902. The center endeavored to organize dressmakers, espadrille makers, telephone operators, and cigarette workers. Gabriela's support for the Centro Socialista Femenino was evident when she tried to use her influence as an inspector to mediate labor disputes between factory owners and striking women. In November 1904 she represented the women on strike against La Argentina Espadrille Factory after management had refused to accept an eight-hour work day. Gabriela bravely addressed more than eight hundred angry women workers, exhorting them to stay away from their jobs until their demands were met. Eventually, Gabriela's formal efforts to mediate the strike were rejected by the factory owners because she was not an employee.

Until national legislation mandated an eight-hour day for men and women, striking workers could rarely force employers to limit the number of work hours, although they could obtain higher wages. Gradually, Gabriela came to the conclusion that women should not offer their services to factories unless it was a matter of economic necessity. Instead, they should accept financial privation in order to make sure that their children were cared for and fed. Of course, for many workers in Buenos Aires unemployment was unacceptable. Given the prevailing high rents and low salaries in the city, it was usually imperative that women and young children contribute to the family income if they could.

News of Gabriela's activities after 1904 is impossible to find. Her tumultuous and active career as a defender of the rights of women and children ended as suddenly as it had commenced. According to the memoirs of Enrique Dickmann, a prominent Socialist physician, Gabriela was forced out of the party after she left Emilio for another man. More likely, she already was stricken with the illness that caused her death on January 7, 1907. Her brief, but intensive, efforts to defend working women and children and document their abuse had to be taken up by others.

Alfredo Palacios and Emilio Coni continued Gabriela's campaign to enact municipal and national legislation to protect the working class and provide government-sponsored inexpensive medical care. In 1913 the Argentine feminist Socialist Carolina Muzzilli wrote a prize-winning study of the conditions faced by working women. Gabriela's work for the Argentine Anti-Tuberculosis League was continued, partly by municipal public health education programs, partly by the hygiene classes offered by the Socialist popular university program, the Sociedad Luz (Society of Light), and partly by charitable organizations.

Emilio's work was also carried on by others. When he died in 1928 his plan to provide a centralized and well-financed program of hospital care and preventive medicine in Buenos Aires and other Argentine cities had not been fully implemented and funded. Twenty years later, during the presidential administration of Juan Perón (1946–1955), Dr. Ramón Carrillo, a *higienista* as dedicated as Emilio, started an ambitious program that incorporated many of Coni's 1917 suggestions. Under Carrillo's guidance, a new national program rapidly expanded the number of hospital beds, doctors, and nurses ready to serve public health needs. Because of the availability of penicillin and other modern medicines, communicable diseases that had endangered women and children finally were scientifically controlled.

CONCLUSION

The careers of Emilio and Gabriela Coni set the course for future public health programs and strategies to help mothers and working women. Efforts to ameliorate the health problems and working conditions of women and children appeared to have common goals but in fact were quite different. Generally speaking, these goals could be divided into two categories: plans to help women and children by regulating their behavior and health; and programs to give women more control over their jobs as mothers and as workers through education and improved working conditions at home and in the factory. One strategy sought to control women, the other to empower them.

Municipal programs to improve the nourishment and health of poor children were vital to the well-being of the inhabitants of rapidly growing cities. Planned by members of the governing class, the programs rarely contemplated the problems of the working-class mother who had to combine child care with salaried labor. Similarly, programs to monitor medically suspect women such as prostitutes and wet nurses rarely considered the fact that these women could contract diseases as easily as they could infect others. While these programs may have had laudable goals, often they were resisted by those whom they were supposed to benefit because they were too coercive.

Socialist feminist plans to help working-class women offered a different approach to the problems of public health. Reformers geared to helping working women and children ignored the need to provide public health information to the middle and upper classes. They also presumed that insalubrious conditions in the home or factory would affect women and children more than men, and they believed in the ability of the working class to demand health reforms in the workplace. When strikes and labor demands were not successful, people like Gabriela de Coni suggested that women and children withdraw from the labor force, an often unrealistic strategy.

Countries like Argentina and cities like Buenos Aires needed a combination of programs, some multiclass as they were in Emilio Coni's dream, others class-specific and sensitive to gender issues as in the feminist-Socialist vision of Gabriela. The aspirations of both Conis relied upon the commitment of personnel and funds by private and public agencies. Over the years, many of their plans reached fruition. In 1918, Emilio published a book documenting the various agencies providing social, medical, economic, and charitable services to the working class in Buenos Aires. In his book he took credit for initiating many public facilities. He also acknowledged Gabriela's role in suggesting many programs aimed at working women. Together they left a legacy of concern about public health, child care, and working conditions that would continue to spur public and private efforts to tackle the social and medical consequences of modernization.

SOURCES

Among the books and articles written by or about Emilio Coni, see Dr. Emilio R. Coni, *Higiene pública: El servicio sanitario de la ciudad de Buenos Aires* (Buenos Aires, 1880); idem, *Memorias de un médico higienista* (Buenos Aires, 1918); idem, *Higiene social: Asistencia y previsión social. Buenos Aires caritativa y previsor* (Buenos Aires, 1918); Ernest A. Crider, "Modernization and Human Welfare: The Asistencia Pública and Buenos Aires, 1883–1910" (Ph.D. diss., Ohio State University, 1976); Osvaldo Loudet, *Figuras próximas y lejanas al margen de la historia* (Buenos Aires, 1970); idem, *Médicos argentinos* (Buenos Aires, 1966); Drs. Horacio Madero and José Penna, *La administración sanitaria y asistencia pública en la ciudad de Buenos Aires*, 2 vols. (Buenos Aires, 1910); Estela Pagani and María Victoria Alcaraz, *Las nodrizas de Buenos Aires: Un estudio histórico, 1880–1930* (Buenos Aires, forthcoming); and Hugo Vezzetti, *La locura en la Argentina* (Buenos Aires, 1983).

For materials about Gabriela L. de Coni, feminism, or the Argentine Socialist party, see Maryfran Carlson, *Feminismo! The Women's Movement in Argentina from Its Beginnings to Eva Perón* (Chicago, 1988); Nicolás Cuello, *Acción feminina* (Buenos Aires, 1939); Gabriela L. de Coni, *Proyecto de ley de protección del trabajo de la mujer y del niño en las fábricas presentado á la Intendencia Municipal* (Buenos Aires, 1902); María Carmen del Feijóo, "Las luchas feministas," *Todo es Historia* 128 (January 1978): 6–23;

Enrique Dickmann, *Recuerdos de un militante socialista* (Buenos Aires, 1949); Asunción Lavrin, "The Ideology of Feminism in the Southern Cone, 1900–1940," Wilson Center Working Paper, no. 169 (Washington, DC, 1986); Maryssa Navarro, "Hidden, Silent, and Anonymous: Women Workers in the Argentine Trade Union Movement," *The World of Women in Trade Unions,* edited by Norbert Soldon (Westport, CT, 1985); María Silvia Ospital, "Un antecedente del proyecto de ley nacional del trabajo: La labor de la Sra. Gabriela de L. de Coni (1901–1904)," *Investigaciones* 1 (1976): 68–95; and Richard Walter, *The Socialist Party of Argentina, 1890–1930* (Austin, 1977).

17

Francisco de Paula Mayrink of Brazil: A Bourgeois Aristocrat

Steven C. Topik[1]

Brazil enjoyed an easy political transition from colony to independent nation under Pedro I in 1822. Emperor Dom Pedro II (1831–1889) presided over the economic development and modernization that eluded the more politically troubled Spanish-American countries. By midcentury a new coffee-growing area was flourishing from Rio de Janeiro south through São Paulo. The liberal monarch abolished the slave trade in 1850 and encouraged capital investment in railroads, streetcars, small industries, banks, and commercial agriculture. English capital also flowed into the country.

Economic modernization, however, prompted the growth of a stronger liberal republicanism, especially after the expensive War of the Triple Alliance (1865–1870) briefly halted economic expansion. Although Dom Pedro II was liberal and popular, the feeling grew in Brazil that the monarchy, like slavery, was an outmoded, decadent institution. Brazil's ability to attract European immigrants and to experience further economic growth depended upon the creation of modern institutions. Slavery was abolished in 1888, and the monarchy fell in 1889.

Francisco de Paula Mayrink, born in 1839, had built one of the largest fortunes in Brazil by the 1880s. His many business endeavors—banking, railroads, coastal shipping, urban services, and real estate—grew from his close association with the emperor and with foreign capitalists and from his own keen business sense. At first it seemed that he would weather the change of government, but suspicions of his monarchist sympathies caused the republican government to persecute and ruin him in the 1890s.

Much has been written about the Latin American elites' reluctance to invest in their own nations. Mayrink's example points out both the opportunities and the dangers. Were the risks any greater for him than for a foreign investor? What investment fields seem to have been the safest, or the riskiest?

Mayrink's fall also may provide a clue to the link between political stability and economic development. In nineteenth-century Latin America, political victors usually seized the property and jobs of the vanquished or denied to the losers the political favors that were essential to economic

249

success. Some shrewd or lucky individuals kept their skills, capital, and contacts intact and were indispensable to all regimes. Other citizens like Mayrink met a combination of unfortunate economic reverses and political suspicions that ruined them.

Steven Topik is associate professor of history at the University of California at Irvine. His specialty is the economic history of Brazil, from the end of the monarchy to the end of the Old Republic in 1930, with an emphasis on the role of the state. After earning a doctorate from the University of Texas (Austin), he published *The Political Economy of the Brazilian State, 1889–1930* (1987).

Brazil's *Conselheiro* Francisco de Paula Mayrink (1839–1906) largely has been forgotten. Only a neglected monument in an obscure plaza and a small road in Rio de Janeiro together with the name of a small, decadent town in the province's interior commemorate him. Yet, in the last years of the empire and the first of the republic, Mayrink was the richest and among the most politically influential men in Brazil. Today, Brazilian historiography and the popular imagination champion the viscount of Mauá as the mightiest, most progressive entrepreneur of the nineteenth century; in fact, Francisco de Paula Mayrink's activities far outstripped those of Mauá in size, vision, and, for a time, economic success. Mayrink was a tropical J. P. Morgan.

Clearly, Mayrink was not a typical Brazilian and his life story was extraordinary. But because the *conselheiro* was so intimately involved in the economic, social, and political aspects of the country, discussion of his life illuminates much about the imperial and early republican elites. His role in shaping nineteenth-century Brazil underlines the importance of the financial bourgeoisie; the bourgeois nature of the imperial aristocracy; the close links between the state and civil society, and between economics and politics; the central economic importance of Rio de Janeiro; and the nature of the Republican Revolution of 1889.

FAMILY BACKGROUND

Francisco was born into an influential family close to the imperial court. His ancestors first had come to Brazil in the early eighteenth century from Madeira and apparently became landlords in the state of Minas Gerais. The family remained there as *fazendeiros* (planters) through the eighteenth century, although little is known of their activities. Francisco's grandfather, Lieutenant Colonel Francisco de Paula Mayrink, broke with this agrarian vocation to join the military. In that capacity he helped quell a revolt against the future emperor of Brazil, Dom Pedro I, in the capital of Minas Gerais in 1821 for which he received the title of "Benémerito da Patria" (Benefactor of the Fatherland). The lieutenant colonel's brother, José Carlos Mayrink de Silva Ferrão, was even more successful in winning royal favor. Having moved to Pernambuco, he was named president of the province in 1824 and was later chosen senator (a lifetime post) by the emperor.

Francisco's father, also named José Carlos, became intimately linked to the royal house and to the economy of Rio de Janeiro city, known simply under the empire as "a Corte" (the court). Born in Minas Gerais, he also began his career in the military but soon moved to Rio to participate in commerce and finance. Within a couple of decades he rose to such prominence that he was named a director of the largest bank in the country, the semiofficial Banco do Brasil. José Carlos served for a time as president of the Banco Brasileiro-Português, which later became the English Bank of Rio de Janeiro, and founded one of the largest banks in the country, the Banco Comercial do Rio de Janeiro, in 1861. He presided over the latter as president until his retirement in 1876.

It appears that José Carlos's success was based on both his close relationship to the emperor and his connections overseas, especially in Portugal. José Carlos's friendship with Emperor Dom Pedro II and his wife was demonstrated in the banker's appointment to the noble Order of the Rose. He also served in honorific positions as keeper of the emperor's wardrobe for five years and then as the empress's huntsman. When the emperor's only daughter Princess Isabel married, José Carlos was one of the few nonroyal Brazilians invited to the banquet. He had the honor of being seated next to the emperor. To maintain his close relationship to the Crown and demonstrate his financial success, Francisco's father built a palace next to the imperial summer palace in Petropolis. José Carlos's political position was confirmed by his election to the Chamber of Deputies.

José Carlos's European connections were demonstrated in his presidency of Portuguese- and British-owned banks and in his trips to the continent at a time when international travel was quite rare. One of his sons, João Carlos, lived almost his entire life in Portugal, probably assisting his father in business arrangements.

EARLY YEARS

It was to this strangely bourgeois and aristocratic world that Francisco was born in 1839. The son of a capitalist courtier, young Mayrink had an upbringing more similar to that of an English merchant than a Brazilian aristocrat. His father apprenticed him at the age of fourteen to a friend's drygoods store. After Francisco had repeated squabbles with other employees, his father used his influence to gain the young Mayrink admission into the military academy in the southern city of Porto Alegre in order to teach the boy discipline. There Francisco underwent army training and was promoted to lieutenant of artillery before his mother prevailed and had him returned to Rio where he apparently abandoned his military career.[2] Again José Carlos exercised his influence; Francisco entered the imperial Escola Central, the country's most prestigious high school, where he studied engineering for two years. He left the school without graduating to enter his father's bank as a scribe. Over the next twenty-one years he worked his way up the bank's hierarchy. He became a director after his father retired.[3]

Francisco's education diverged from the usual pattern for the offspring of the urban elite. Although higher education was restricted to a tiny portion of the Brazilian population, most of the scions of the urban elite earned law, medical, or engineering degrees or had graduated from military academies. Mayrink, instead, concentrated on acquiring practical experience in the workplace. This background would serve him well in future years.

Francisco enjoyed the fruits of his father's influence not only in gaining him admission to elite educational institutions and a career in banking but also in winning recognition for him at court. When the young banker turned twenty-one, the emperor bestowed the title of *moço fidalgo* (young noble) upon him. (Aristocratic titles in this New World monarchy were honorific; they carried no privileges of substance and were not inheritable.) Eleven years later, Francisco was made a *comendador* (commander). In 1879, Dom Pedro awarded Francisco the title of *conselheiro* (councillor).[4] Three years after that the emperor offered the banker the title of "baron." Mayrink had been very helpful in convincing a group of North American bankers that Brazil deserved a loan to rebuild its armed forces. The head of the group, who was particularly taken with Mayrink, was a Philadelphia banker. To reward Francisco for his services to the country, the emperor wanted to make him baron of Philadelphia. The banker rejected the title, however, because it would erase the name "Mayrink." That, in turn, would reduce his ability to trade on his father's reputation, which was an important asset in the personalistic world of finance and commerce. (He could not be made Baron Mayrink because his brother already had received the title Viscount Mayrink in Portugal.)

SOCIAL STANDING

Mayrink inherited wealth, business contacts, and an esteemed place at court. But he knew that to consolidate his position and expand his financial empire, he had to cultivate the Brazilian elite. Although Brazil was 90 percent rural, with its sparse population dispersed over vast distances and its economy dominated by coffee exports, the elite was concentrated largely in the court, Rio. The political capital was also the country's financial, commercial, social, intellectual, and cultural capital. "Tout-Brésil" lived in the city's districts such as Engenho Velho, São Cristoval, Catete, Larangeiras, and Botafogo. In this world, family, style, and contacts counted almost as much as wealth.

Mayrink enjoyed his regal life-style. In 1874, at the age of thirty-five and with his career secure, he married Maria José Paranhos, the widow of his cousin, who was the son of the wealthy marchioness of Itamaraty. To establish his place in high society, Mayrink purchased, in Engenho Velho close to the imperial palace, a mansion where his three daughters would be raised. Eight years later, after becoming a director of the Banco Comercial and a magnate in his own right, he had the mansion completely renovated and a fourth story built onto the already imposing edifice. Few other buildings in Brazil at the time had more than two stories. The Mayrink palace held dozens of bedrooms, several large ballrooms, a billiard room, a chapel, and one of the city's larger libraries. Outside spread large, well-manicured gardens and woods graced by a covered swimming pool, stables, tennis courts, grottos, and ponds and populated by exotic birds, Shetland ponies, and even zebras. And, as befit an aristocrat in a slave society, neat rows of slave quarters stood off to the side. The house and gardens bustled with activity as the elegant carriages and litters of aristocratic neighbors such as the Princess Leopoldina or prominent visitors such as Prime Minister Cotegipe came to call. In his sumptuous ballrooms the portly, bearded Mayrink hosted some of the city's most lavish festivities. Sometimes the guests were entertained by Italian opera singers the councillor had brought to Brazil. To be invited to the Mayrink residence was to be a member of high society.

Although Mayrink's Engenho Velho palace surpassed his father's Petropolis mansion, the younger banker was not satisfied. In the last year of the empire, 1889, he purchased for 1,800 contos (almost $1 million) a three-story mansion in the Catete district of Rio that had belonged to Brazil's richest coffee planter, the baron of Novo Friburgo. European architects and artists had joined with Brazilian slave artisans to fashion one of the country's most imposing residences. When the plan to use the Catete mansion as a hotel failed, Mayrink kept it as a weekend and summer house, which he occasionally lent to friends and family. He also commissioned an enormous yacht built in England and tied it up to the docks on Flamengo Bay.[5]

The next year the family purchased for a weekend home the mansion and grounds of the marquess of Bonfim in the beautiful forested hills above Rio known as the Alta de Boa Vista. The banker did not stop there. If he wished to go to the country for a cure, he traveled to the nearby Caxambu springs, which was the favorite watering spot for the imperial family and the elite. Mayrink directed the spa for the first fifteen years of the republic. If the councillor tired of this retreat or the Catete or Engenho Velho palaces he retired to his *fazenda* in Minas Gerais.

Philanthropy as well as a luxurious life-style won Mayrink standing and influence. In Brazil, in which Catholicism was the established religion and the emperor defender of the faith, it was prudent to donate to Catholic charities. Mayrink donated substantial sums to orphanages in the surrounding provinces of Minas Gerais, São Paulo, and Rio de Janeiro as well as at court. He also contributed to a sanitarium, poorhouse, and hospital in the capital. He was named to the Order of Christ for his services.

The *conselheiro* ingratiated himself with important members of civil society as well through his donations. Despite his not finishing high school, Mayrink's donation to the Engineers' Club won him election to the board of directors of this prestigious civic organization and the post of vice president in 1888. A large loan to Rio's Commercial Association (the most important economic pressure group in the country) helped Mayrink secure that organization's presidency in 1890, although he was unable to take office because of other responsibilities. He was also a member of the country's most distinguished intellectual (and social) organizations: the Real Gabinete Português de Leitura, the Instituto Histórico e Geográfico Brasileiro, and the Sociedade Brasileiro de Geografia.

ECONOMIC ACTIVITIES

While Mayrink's life-style and gifts won him considerable prestige, it was the income from his business holdings that made his generosity and ostentation possible. He made his fortune principally as a banker, although his undertakings were so diversified that Rio's commercial directory, *Almanack Laemmert*, listed him in 1889 simply as a "capitalist." He attempted early on to transform the country's conservative financial institutions into more aggressive entrepreneurial actors. At the time, institutions concentrated on short-term commercial loans, note discounts, and exchange operations. Mortgages and developmental loans were virtually nonexistent. Banks also rarely helped launch new companies or invested in their stocks.

Mayrink campaigned for the imperial government to implement an 1875 law that would create a large national mortgage bank that could tap European capital markets by issuing mortgage bonds. Finally in 1883, over the objections of many competitors, the government authorized Mayrink to create the Banco de Crédito Real do Brasil, which could issue up to 200,000 contos in mortgage bonds once it realized its 20,000-contos capital. He resigned from the directory of the Banco Comercial and assumed the presidency of this new institution. This was a tremendous political coup for a man who had never been president of any bank. It demonstrated the considerable influence he and his father exercised at court and in European capital markets. This concession gave Mayrink a national monopoly on the issuance of mortgage bonds and permitted him to create what would have been the second largest bank in the country. Unfortunately, the bank never succeeded in attracting either much capital or many buyers for its bonds. Mortgages were a risky business because of the uncertainty of land titles.

The Banco de Crédito Real's failure to reshape Brazilian banking did not daunt Mayrink's spirits. He founded several other banks in the empire's last years. He combined influence, vision, and luck. Mayrink's star began to rise in the 1880s at just the time that the Brazilian economy was enjoying rapid growth. The imminent abolition of slavery (which finally came in 1888) freed capital that had previously gone into human chattel. At the same time, the size of some cities was reaching critical mass, factories began to appear, and the pace of commerce quickened as the transportation system burgeoned. Both the court and the western part of the province of São Paulo prospered. That they would experience simultaneous good times was not coincidental. Rio investors sank some of their profits into the expanding Paulista frontier.

Mayrink was one of the leaders in founding new undertakings and launching the Carioca (residents of the city of Rio de Janeiro) assault on São Paulo. His main weapon was mortgage banks: the Banco de Crédito Real do Brasil, the Banco Predial, and the Banco Constructor. The financier employed his newly won prominence in capital markets to launch many companies in other sectors. He operated, as J. P. Morgan would later, as an intermediary between investors and entrepreneurs. Mayrink usually did not serve as either a director of or a large stockholder in the companies that he helped found; rather, he placed trusted lieutenants on the boards.

The *conselheiro* joined in the rapid extension of Brazil's railroad network. As a representative of the Banco Comercial and a shareholder in his own right, Mayrink was elected in 1880 president of the financially troubled Sorocabana Railroad, a relatively small line in western São Paulo. He oversaw its expansion from under one hundred miles when he took over to more than five hundred miles by 1893. He also bought a majority of the shares of the sizable Ituana Railroad, a neighbor of the Sorocabana. In 1883 the banker founded the E. F. Bahia and Minas, which sought to connect the dry region of Minas Gerais with the coast of Bahia. It was the only purely developmental railway of the empire in that it hoped to stimulate an area not yet developed rather than tap existing production as other lines did. In addition, Mayrink controlled a number of smaller lines around the nation's capital: the Petropolis, the São Fidelis, the Tereza Cristina, and the

Muzambinho. Together these lines constituted about one fifth of Brazil's rail network at the end of the empire.

Mayrink controlled an even greater share of the nation's coastal shipping fleet. In 1876 he helped found the Companhia Brasileira de Navigação. During the next decade he added the Companhia Nacional de Navigação and the Espírito Santo e Caravelas. By the end of the empire these three shipping lines represented more than two thirds of all maritime capital on the Rio stock exchange. He also participated in creating the modern docks at Santos that allowed the São Paulo port to surpass Rio as the principal coffee entrepôt.

The fourth major area in which the *conselheiro* invested was urban services and real estate. He owned the most important tramway companies in São Paulo, Santos, and the court as well as water and drainage companies in São Paulo, Campinas, Barbacena, Ouro Preto, and Pelotas. In addition, he had valuable real estate holdings in the desirable Carioca districts of Tijuca, São Cristoval, Botafogo, Vila Isabel, Engenho Velho, Rio Comprido, and Copacabana.

As is evident, the great majority of the banker's investments were in urban or technologically innovative areas. He combined foreign and national capital with foreign technologies and engineers to "modernize" Brazil. A relatively small portion of his capital was invested directly in the countryside even though the Brazilian economy depended on coffee exports. He owned several sugar and wheat mills in the province of Rio de Janeiro and Pernambuco. He also founded the Agricultural Colonization Company in São Paulo to attract European immigrants and settle them in agricultural colonies to provide rural labor. Indeed, he believed that agriculture, not industry, was the key to Brazil's future greatness: "because the truth is . . . that for many years to come the foundation of our wealth and our finances will be almost exclusively agricultural production." But the financier does not appear to have invested much in either coffee plantations or slaves. While coffee *fazendas* were profitable, they were risky and slow to show returns.

Mayrink preferred to limit his risk. While he appears to have placed his own and his banks' assets boldly in farsighted progressive enterprises rather than routinely sink money into the soil or into human property, his motives were often less heroic. Mayrink traded on his close relationship with the emperor and the imperial elite to garner government guarantees of profits.

His rail, maritime, and tram companies received monopoly routes and government subsidies. The banks received government loans and privileges such as the issue of mortgage bonds. He purchased the sugar and wheat mills only after Parliament promised a 5 percent return on capital to encourage investment in modern machinery. And the colonization company received grants of government land for its colonies. The link between economics and politics was extremely close. Because of his influence in Parliament, Mayrink received the right to create joint-stock companies, and his companies received special privileges. Other foreign and national investors, knowing of Mayrink's *pistolão* (pull) in official circles, invested in his companies. Conversely, the financier was able to wield such influence in the court and the Chamber of Deputies because many aristocrat-politicians were brought into his companies and profited handsomely from them. The *conselheiro* was a major financial contributor to the Liberal party.

Mayrink's political ties became particularly strong during the cabinet, the empire's last, headed by the viscount of Ouro Preto (June–November 1889). Intimate with Ouro Preto and many other influential members of the Minas Gerais Liberal party, the councillor himself was elected a federal deputy for Minas in the empire's last election, although the monarchy fell before he could take office. It is a commentary on the empire's political system that the Carioca banker who had lived his entire life in the court was to represent the neighboring province. Mayrink won the seat without himself campaigning in the province by relying on the local elite and their representatives in Rio. He had ingratiated himself with Liberal leaders through campaign contributions to them, by participating in a number of economic ventures with them, and by building the Bahia and Minas railroad. Friends sent members of the cavalry from Rio into the district to cast votes for the banker and used fraud in totaling the votes to ensure his victory.

Francisco de Paula Mayrink, then, belies the conventional image of imperial Brazil as a neofeudal monarchy dominated by routine-minded slavocrats. Much of the political, economic, and cultural life was dominated by urban aristocrats, often not closely tied to the soil. The financial bourgeoisie was of central importance. At the same time, the imperial state shaped the urban economy. While Brazil's aristocrats were members of the bourgeoisie, the bourgeoisie under the empire was integrated into the aristocracy.

So closely was the *conselheiro* linked to the monarchy and to the Liberal party in the popular imagination, that when the military-led Republican Revolution overthrew Emperor Dom Pedro II on November 15, 1889, one of the first acts of then marshal and future president Floriano Peixoto was to order the arrest of Mayrink. After all, the financier had been a major figure of court life, a bankroller of the Liberal party, and an aristocrat and a slaveowner himself. Moreover, he had incited the ire of the army when he arranged European financing and training for an expanded National Guard in the empire's last year. Army officers feared that the emperor was creating a praetorian guard to defend himself against the resentful armed forces. Added to these "crimes" was the fact that when Dom Pedro and his family were forced to sail to Europe into exile, they sailed on one of Mayrink's personal ships.

The most militant republicans wanted to create a new, more democratic, modern Brazil. They abolished aristocratic titles and sought to loosen the state's grip on the economy. One would assume that a monarchist aristocrat such as Mayrink, who based so much of his success on his influence at court, would be one of the republic's first victims. In fact, Mayrink was able to seize the moment, and for a few years he had a large hand in directing the new republic.

THE PROVISIONAL REPUBLICAN GOVERNMENT AND THE ENCILHAMENTO

Mayrink not only avoided arrest under the Provisional Government, but he also found himself named lieutenant colonel in the National Guard, elected deputy from the Federal District (the official designation of the city of Rio de Janeiro under the republic) and later from Minas Gerais,[6] elected to the presidency of the Commercial Association of Rio, and made the single most powerful banker in Brazil. How was this self-professed monarchist, who converted to republicanism only on the day the empire fell, able to survive the change in regime and to prosper as well?

The *conselheiro* had made important contacts with key members of the new republican regime. Of particular importance was his close relationship with one of the leaders of the Provisional Government, the republican leader and minister of justice Quintino Bocayuva. The two were close friends; moreover, the banker lent the minister money and placed him on the directorship of a number of companies. It was the minister of justice who intervened to prevent Mayrink's arrest. The minister of finance, Rui Barbosa, sat on the board of directors of two Mayrink companies, and Barbosa's brother was closely involved with Mayrink in stock dealings. João de Matta Machado, first secretary of the Constituent Congress and then president of the Chamber of Deputies, was a partner with Mayrink in many ventures and a director of many of the banker's most important firms. Other prominent republicans received positions or gratuities from the *conselheiro* as well. Although Mayrink had direct access to government since he served as deputy, he rarely participated in Chamber debates, preferring to operate behind the scenes through intermediaries.

The banker was able to win favor with some members of the new military regime because of his own military training and that of his father and grandfather. Also, Mayrink had ceded a large building to the imperial government to be used for the Colegio Militar just one month before the founding of the republic. Moreover, a number of prominent officers, such as the first minister of war, Benjamin Constant, and the nephew of the first republican president, Hermes da Fonseca, asked favors of the financier. The military had been poorly paid under the empire; many officers consequently were willing to peddle influence under "their" republic.

The most important ingredient in Mayrink's initial success under the republic had been his wealth. Because of his longstanding business undertakings with Portuguese, English, French, and German financiers and considerable prestige abroad, Mayrink's support was important for the republic's foreign credit.[7] Domestically, he was one of the three or four most important bankers in the country. Having cofounded in Rio only two months before the collapse of the monarchy the Banking Clearing House, which facilitated the exchange of drafts between banks, the *conselheiro* had his hand on the financial and commercial pulse of Brazil. And as president of the recently created Banco Constructor he presided over potentially the third largest bank in the country.[8]

Perhaps most importantly, a rapid expansion of the money supply and bank credit combined with the abolition of slavery and substantial foreign investment in the empire's last year to create the stock market frenzy known as the Encilhamento.[9] Mayrink was in the center of the boom, creating many opportunities for influential members of the imperial elite and for important republicans.

In June 1889 the Ouro Preto ministry sought to ease the impact of the abolition of slavery one year earlier by offering to lend to private banks, interest free, the unprecedented sum of 86,000 contos (about \$43 million); the banks in turn were to match the sum and lend it to agriculture. Mayrink's banks received one quarter of the loans.

To facilitate credit further, Prime Minister Ouro Preto authorized thirteen banks to issue currency that would have doubled the money supply. Mayrink's banks received the right to issue about 10 percent of the total. This made him the second largest beneficiary of the government's reforms. The most favored recipient of state privilege was the count of Figueiredo, a close ally of Ouro Preto. His Banco Nacional was authorized to issue over 80 percent of the new currency. Figueiredo and Mayrink would have momentous clashes in the republic's first years.

This tremendous amount of new credit and new currency, combined with buoyant foreign capital markets, led to the Encilhamento. More capital was invested in the Rio stock market in the last six months of the monarchy than had been placed there in the previous sixty years. As the *Jornal do Commercio* exclaimed in December 1889, "The taking up of stocks was done not only with excitement, but with madness, with delirium, with swooning and punch-drunkenness." Far more people began to participate in the stock market than had ever before. As the viscount of Taunay observed in his famous and critical 1893 novel *O Encilhamento*: "Everyone gambled [in the stock market,] the businessman, the doctor, the attorney, the government bureaucrat, the broker and the bum." Mayrink, a key character in Taunay's novel under the name "Meyermayer," was an important player in the imperial boom. But it was only with the rise of the republic that, for a few short years, he reached the pinnacle of financial power because only then had the stock excitement reached a fever pitch. As the famous Brazilian novelist Machado de Assis has a character reminisce in *Esau and Jacob*: "Surely you have not forgotten the word 'boom,' the great season of enterprises and companies of every sort. He who did not see it, has not seen anything. Cascades of ideas, of inventions, of concessions, rolled out every day . . . to make thousands of milreis, thousands of millions, millions of millions of milreis."

The republican Provisional Government allied itself with Mayrink. Rui Barbosa met with him in January 1890 to draft new banking legislation after military leaders had been impressed by Mayrink's plan. The law created three large banks of issue and stripped Figueiredo's Banco Nacional of its special relationship with the government. In its place was put a new bank that was not created until six days after the legislation, Mayrink's Banco dos Estados Unidos do Brasil (BEUB). Ironically, Mayrink received such favored treatment because Figueiredo had been even more closely tied to the imperial Ouro Preto regime than had the *conselheiro* and there were no prominent republican bankers.

Mayrink's bank was given the most far-reaching privileges in the history of Brazil. It could single-handedly more than double the money supply; found railroads, industries, and colonization companies; receive tax exemptions; and serve as the government's official agent for foreign exchange and debt. The BEUB had a capital of 100,000 contos, three times that of the Banco Comercial, Mayrink's previous flagship. The BEUB organized the São Paulo bank of issue and bought large interests in five other banks.

The BEUB was the leading institution in the Encilhamento. Minister of Finance Barbosa said at the end of 1890, "Rare are the companies floated this year here or in São Paulo that have not been effectively and powerfully aided by the BEUB and its auxiliaries." At the end of the year, Mayrink's position in the market was strengthened still more when the government forced the BEUB and the Banco Nacional to merge to create the Banco da República. This new entity was by far the largest bank that Brazil had ever known. In fact, it would be more than fifty years before another bank was authorized to capitalize at the Banco da República's level. Mayrink presided over the bank as president while his competitor, the count of Figueiredo, was forced out. Figueiredo vowed revenge and spent the next few years undermining Mayrink's empire.

The BEUB and later the Banco da República attempted to create enterprises on a scale unprecedented for Brazil. As the *Mail and Express* commented, "There seems to be a thirst for . . . monopolies at the head of which is Mr. Mayrinch [*sic*] an able schemer and financier." In addition to creating the Banco da República, the *conselheiro* launched the Lloyd Brasileiro shipping line, which consolidated most of the national coastal fleet; established the Companhia Geral de Estradas de Ferro do Brasil, which brought many smaller railroad companies together to create the Leopoldina line; merged the Sorocabana and the Ituana railroads; and joined the tram companies of São Paulo city into the Companhia Viação Paulista.

Mayrink and his banks promoted and invested in companies throughout Brazil and in virtually every sector of business activity. He was now the prime beneficiary of government privileges, including the right to issue currency and to receive treasury loans, as well as concessions for railroads, tram companies, and shipping lines, land awards for colonization projects, and tax exemptions for the import of machinery. From a rich and important person under the empire he rose to be the wealthiest and mightiest person under the republic. But all was not well in the financier's world. Mayrink's daring and access to government concessions and foreign capital allowed him to lead the charge during the boom's upward swing. Once the Encilhamento began to wane, however, in early 1891, and the financier lost favor with government officials, his empire began to cave in.

Mayrink's success was based in part on large loans taken from the federal government and from Europe that he used both for his personal account and as reserve funds for the Banco da República. He bought stock on a small margin and then used it as collateral for further borrowing. He piled debt upon debt. As long as the economy was expanding and stock appreciating this was a profitable strategy. But once investors lost confidence in the stock market Mayrink found himself with devalued stocks and a great debt.

The banker's political fortunes declined at the same time as his economic prospects. Many militant republicans were suspicious of the imperial aristocrat who had become the republic's principal financier. They believed that he was subverting the new regime intentionally with speculative endeavors intended to depress the value of currency, provoke inflation, and, ultimately, undermine capital markets. As Afonso Pena, a future president of Brazil, complained: "The axis of all financial fraud is the Banco da República, which tries to impose itself as the incarnation of the new regime, making the stability of the latter dependent on its fate." Another critic protested hotly that because of this speculative boom, which bankrupted many honest investors, the Encilhamento became "synonomous with armed robbery." This suspicion was reinforced because many of the empire's establishment—the rich aristocrats, merchants, and planters who dominated under Dom Pedro II—were the major actors in the stock splurge. The Banco da República counted among its stockholders twenty-one barons, three counts, and eighteen viscounts and viscountesses. Indeed, the first republican administration was overthrown in November 1891 in large part because President Deodoro and the baron of Lucena (minister of finance) shut down the congress when the deputies refused to expand vastly the Banco da República's right to issue currency.

Mayrink ran afoul of President Floriano Peixoto (who took office after the 1891 military coup) when a naval revolt broke out in Rio in 1893. Mayrink was quite friendly with the admiral who led the revolt. Moreover, Mayrink had retired to his *fazenda* in Minas Gerais shortly before and ordered many of his shares in the Banco da República sold. When the revolt erupted, the rebels seized some of Mayrink's personal ships. Floriano suspected that the banker had initiated and financed the rebellion, which the marshal characterized incorrectly as an attempt to restore the monarchy. While it is true that one of Rio's most important financiers, the count of Leopoldina, probably did participate in the rebellion, Mayrink was not in fact guilty. But his name was cleared only later. For ten months he had to remain essentially under house arrest in Minas, far from the Banco da República and his Rio investments. Although Floriano allowed Mayrink to remain free, the marshal speeded the decline of the magnate's business career.

At the end of 1893 the now-ailing Banco da República was merged with the second largest bank in Brazil, the Banco do Brasil. This time, however, Mayrink was removed from the bank's presidency and lost control over its resources. Instead, the federal government appointed the bank's president. Floriano chose a banker allied with the count of Figueiredo and hostile to Mayrink's interests. Mayrink spent the last thirteen years of his life battling to stave off disaster as the legacy of the Encilhamento continued to haunt him.

Floriano's attack on Mayrink's interests was not isolated and not motivated by personal animus. The collapse of the Encilhamento in 1891 coupled with the overthrow of the first republican president, Deodoro da Fonseca, crushed the imperial establishment that had so profited in the 1889–1891 period. Removed from office after 1891 (many aristocrats had weathered the fall of the empire and the republic's first two years), and verging on bankruptcy because of the devaluation of their stocks, the Carioca haute bourgeoisie were no longer a major political force. They were replaced initially by politicized military officers and militant members of the urban middle class known as the Jacobins, who provided the main support for Floriano's regime.

After November 1894 the Republican party of São Paulo in union with republicans from the provinces of Minas Gerais and Rio Grande do Sul took the reins of power. They primarily represented coffee planters. Mayrink was not trusted either by Floriano's confirmed republican followers, who saw the *conselheiro* as an aristocratic monarchist, or by the Paulista planters who saw the financier as an architect of the Rio effort to subordinate and control São Paulo.

When the Paulista republican president Prudente de Morais took office at the end of 1894, the assault on Mayrink's fortune did not abate. The government faced large foreign debt demands and budget deficits as the economy slumped. Consequently, the Treasury demanded that the Banco da República repay loans extended in the republic's first years. The bank itself tottered on the brink of failure. Its aggressive participation in the stock market during the Encilhamento left it with many worthless investments and bad debts and with depreciated collateral, so it in turn called in Mayrink's debt to the bank. Mayrink believed that this move was politically motivated; it was an attempt by republicans and his enemy the count of Figueiredo to end the relationship between the *conselheiro* and the bank.

This action raised the concern of other creditors, who feared that Mayrink might not be able to repay them. An American coffee-importing firm and a German banking house demanded immediate liquidation of outstanding debts. The Brazilian government also became worried and opened proceedings to recover loans granted to Mayrink.

As a result of these pressures the *conselheiro* had to cede the stocks and in large measure control of his most valuable holdings. Ironically, or perhaps justly, Mayrink's most important enterprises, which he had created or enlarged because of government favor and foreign capital, eventually either became state property or fell under foreign control. The Leopoldina railroad was taken over by its British creditors, and the São Paulo, Rio, and Santos tram companies were obtained by a Canadian firm. The Banco da República was reorganized as a public bank and renamed the Banco do Brasil in 1905. The federal government eventually also took over the Lloyd Brasileiro shipping line, the country's largest, and sold the Sorocabana Railroad to the government of São Paulo.

The banker had to surrender many of his urban properties as well. Twenty of his buildings were torn down to create the Rio equivalent of the Champs Elysées, the Avenida Central (now known as Avenida Rio Branco). The banker's personal estates also fell into the public domain. The Alta de Boa Vista mansion and chapel became a public park. The Caxambu springs were taken over. So was the elegant Catete Palace, which mirrored (and anticipated) the development of Brazil's economy as it passed first from the hand of a coffee baron to the financier Mayrink to finally, in 1897, the federal government. Mayrink ceded the palace supposedly because it was smaller than his own residence in Engenho Velho. Catete was, however, one of Brazil's most elegant mansions. Prudente de Morais decided to make it the presidential residence, moving from the Itamaraty Palace, which had housed the republic's president since 1889 and which before that had belonged to Mayrink's aunt.[10] It remained the presidential residence for the next sixty-three years. The move into the sumptuous residence and the nationalization of Mayrink's elegant custom-built yacht moored to the palace's dock must have pleased the Paulista president; they symbolized São Paulo's hegemony in the new empire, which had been built on the wealth and splendor of the Rio financial bourgeoisie that the Paulista planters now eclipsed.

Mayrink spent his last years comfortably but out of the national limelight he for so long had occupied. Like Brazil's other great nineteenth-century entrepreneur, the viscount of Mauá, the councillor expanded his empire faster than the nation's economy would permit; he ended his life with little left of his once vast fortune.

When Mayrink died in 1906 newspapers ran glowing eulogies. His memory, however, faded quickly. Politicians continued to praise Floriano, President Campos Sales, or Minister of Finance Rui Barbosa as national heroes. The viscount of Mauá remained the symbol of national initiative and drive, the representative of progress and modernity. But history was less kind to Francisco de Paula Mayrink, a man who straddled two eras and two political regimes and was uncomfortable in both. Playing by the empire's rules in his first decades, he was able to prosper but not to break out of its narrow constraints. He threw himself headlong into the euphoric first years of the nascent republic to lead Brazil vigorously into the twentieth century, but he fell victim to his own grand vision. This bourgeois aristocrat, this tropical J. P. Morgan, for a time defied the limitations of nineteenth-century

Brazil; ultimately, he surrendered to them. He had little wealth left in the end to pass on. One neighbor remembers his daughter and grandson decades later living in genteel poverty, with no pretensions and few visitors. After Francisco de Paula Mayrink died, his regal mansion and stately gardens were bulldozed to make room for an English flour factory. The tall brick building and the noisy machinery that now stood on the Engenho Velho site signaled the victory of the twentieth century.

NOTES

1. I would like to thank the Committee on Research and Travel of the Academic Senate of the University of California, Irvine, for a 1988 grant to research this essay. I also would like to thank Marilia Velloso of the Museu da República, Rio de Janeiro, for her assistance.

2. The extent of Mayrink's military training is unclear. Data on his early life are sparse. All of his biographers claim it was quite short while he stated in a speech in the Chamber of Deputies in 1891 that he had been in military service between the ages of fifteen and twenty-two. No one contradicted him.

3. The date is 1876 according to the *Jornal do Commercio* (December 8, 1939). The contemporary *Almanack Laemmert* first lists him as a director in 1881.

4. The title was honorific since Mayrink was not made a member of the Council of State, a body that advised the emperor and ministers on key issues of state.

5. Today the Catete Palace is some distance from the bay because of landfill done in the 1950s.

6. The congressional delegation from the Federal District displayed the conflicts within the capital. Along with Mayrink were elected not only the rich banker the count of Figueiredo but also the radical republican Lopes Trovao and the labor leader Augusto Vinhaes.

7. Surprisingly, despite his close relations with European capitalists and his imitation of European fashion, Mayrink himself never traveled to Europe. This was probably a result of his personalistic business style and the still rather cumbersome transportation and communications technology of the era; he feared to leave his empire for long.

8. The success of Mayrink's banking enterprises is something of a mystery. The public never subscribed the capital that the government generously authorized. Mayrink's three banks in 1889 had an authorized capital of 104,000 contos, more than that of the largest bank in the country, which had an authorized 100,000 contos, but only 7,340 contos actually were subscribed. In other words, his banks had 21 percent of all authorized bank capital but only 5 percent of realized capital.

9. Horse-racing slang for the last moments that the betting windows are open before the race begins. It is a comment on the speculative nature of stock investments and the sense of excitement that accompanied them.

10. Technically, the first presidential resident of Catete was Manoel Vitorino, Prudente's vice president, who served as chief executive while the president recovered from an illness.

SOURCES

This essay was based on a number of sources. The archives of the Casa Rui Barbosa and the Instituto Histórico e Geográfico Brasileiro in Rio de Janeiro, the Rothschilds and British Foreign Office archives in London, and U.S. consular reports in the National Archives in Washington, DC, were all quite useful. So, too, were publications of the day, particularly the *Jornal do Commercio, Rio News,* and the *Almanack Laemmert.* Mayrink himself published three short books: *Refutação das objeccoes feitas a organização do Grande Banco de Crédito* (Rio de Janeiro, 1881); *O Cambio, a produção, o governo* (Rio de Janeiro, 1881); and *Questão financeira* (Rio de Janeiro, 1898). There is a wide secondary literature. Some of the most important works are Francisco de Paula Mayrink Lessa, *Vida e obra do Conselheiro Mayrink* (Rio de Janeiro, 1975); João Gualberto de Oliveira, *Conselheiro Francisco de Paula Mairink* (São Paulo, 1958); Lucio Floro, *Silhuetas parlamentares* (Ouro Preto, 1898); R. Frank Colson, "The Destruction of a Revolution: Polity, Economy, and Society in Brazil, 1750–1895" (Ph.D. diss., Princeton University, 1979); and Gustavo Henrique Barroso Franco, *Reforma monetaria e instabilidade durante a transição repúblicana* (Rio de Janeiro, 1983).

18

José Leocadio Camacho: Artisan, Editor, and Political Activist

David L. Sowell

The North Atlantic economy in which Francisco de Paula Mayrink and William Grace participated had some less visible members: urban workers and farm laborers. Neither group of workers found an effective way to join the political debate in the nineteenth century. José Leocadio Camacho's political achievements probably represent the height of success for an artisan, because of his long life and his skill at accommodation with the political elite. Born in 1833, Camacho worked as a carpenter in Bogotá, Colombia. He edited newspapers, founded workers' organizations, and served in a number of political organizations. He remained active as an advocate for workers until his death in 1914.

Camacho's story is a counterweight to the lives of the grand entrepreneurs. The investors and entrepreneurs who depended upon commerce usually opposed tariffs. In contrast, local artisans, who might have been either nascent industrialists themselves or just skilled workers in an industrial society, advocated protection of local industries in order to keep the domestic market from being flooded with foreign goods. Nevertheless, Bogotá's artisans were, like artisans elsewhere in Latin America, a relatively well-off sector of skilled, urban labor. After all, Camacho not only had had an education that prepared him to write for newspapers, but he also was able to secure the economic backing to publish the papers and possessed the political shrewdness necessary to placate the authorities.

The truly forgotten members of society were the unskilled and semi-skilled workers and farmers. Other city workers may have benefited from Camacho's programs indirectly, but neither Camacho nor they shared much in the way of a community of interest or held common goals. Some artisans vaguely may have hoped that gradualist tactics would benefit the more worthy first and that subsequent reforms would help the less fortunate. Others among Camacho's colleagues may have feared that any improvement in the lot of those poorer than themselves would compromise their own tenuous hold on economic security.

It is worth stressing that artisans belonged to both the Liberal and Conservative parties and that their partisan interests often outweighed their individual or economic class concerns. What does that say about

269

the ideological basis of Colombian political parties? Partisanship high-lights another difficulty for workers, that of organization. Strong mass or political movements in Latin America often rested on folk religion, on regional or ethnic identity, or on family and personal ties. Modern forms of mass organization, that is, numbers of unrelated individuals joined nationwide by their economic interests or by a formal political ideology, were less characteristic of the Hispanic tradition.

David Sowell, an assistant professor of history at Juniata College, has specialized in and published on the history of labor and artisans in nineteenth-century Colombia. He received his Ph.D. from the University of Florida in 1986. He has held Tinker, Fulbright, Doherty, and Organi-zation of American States fellowships.

> The history of workers, considering all of the ramifications of human labor, would be the most extensive, the most general of all histories; it would be the same as the history of civilization.
> —José Leocadio Camacho, 1886

The day-to-day lives of the inhabitants of nineteenth-century Colombia were profoundly affected by the country's integration into the world market. Few groups were touched more directly than the skilled, independent craftsmen living in Bogotá, the nation's capital. Artisans had enjoyed considerable economic pro-tection for their trades during the colonial period, formally through tariffs imposed by the Spanish government and infor-mally because of the obstacles to trade presented by the country's tortuous terrain. Such protective barriers slowly were removed during the nineteenth century because of changes in national economic policy and improved transportation, leaving artisans little choice but to adapt their industries to new economic con-ditions. Craftsmen did not passively watch their economic well-being erode but struggled at every turn to maintain the economic independence and social status they thought rightly theirs.

José Leocadio Camacho began his adult life as a carpenter making coffins and furniture. His own economic fortunes appear not to have suffered great losses that might have provoked him to undertake political activity. He nevertheless emerged as an ardent defender of Bogotá's artisan sector in the latter half of the nineteenth century and the leading spokesman for artisans' interests. In the years after 1864, Camacho edited at least five newspapers dedicated to issues of concern to workers, helped found several workers' organizations, and served in various positions in local, state, and national government. In all of these activities, Camacho represented the aspirations and needs of Bogotá's artisans in a political system that avidly sought the votes of workers but did little to advance programs that would improve their economic or social lives.

Born into a relatively well-to-do family, Camacho (1833–1914) enjoyed the luxury of a good education, one that prepared him well for the challenges he faced during his lifetime. At an early age he was apprenticed as a carpenter, and by the 1860s he had established his own shop. It was an exciting time to come of age in Colombia, a period of intense political activity in the nation's capital but a perilous era for artisans seeking to maintain their economic independence.

The law of June 14, 1847, one of the central planks of the Liberal Reform era that had begun in the mid-1840s, had lowered tariffs on imported goods by more than 30 percent in the hope of spurring the expansion of international trade. The measure posed a dire threat to native producers who barely had held their own against foreign competition before that date. Craftsmen formed the Society of Artisans in 1847 to attempt to raise tariffs, but they had no success. The Society of Artisans promptly became embroiled in the intense struggle between the Conservative and Liberal parties for control of the nation's government. Political struggles between members of the two parties plunged the nation into civil war in 1859, a conflict that persisted for three years. The dual impact of that war and the accelerated flow of foreign goods into Bogotá's market resulted in economic crisis for the city's artisans, a crisis that spurred Camacho to his first efforts to defend his fellow craftsmen.

In late 1864, Camacho began publishing *El Obrero* (The worker), a modest paper dedicated to the interests of the capital's working classes. His political philosophy was clear from the start. While he favored Conservative politicians, Camacho declared that the paper would "work independently and seek guarantees and protection from those elected to represent our interests." The carpenter noted that it was his hope that the government would begin to look after the welfare of workers. The government should educate and inspire them to improve their professions because, Camacho reasoned, workers produced most of the goods consumed in the country and were its social foundation. The objective of the paper was to remind the government of its responsibilities to all citizens and to serve as a forum for debate on topics of interest to workers.

Camacho further sought to unite craftsmen in the capital to work together politically. This task was especially arduous as artisans recruited during the previous decade by Conservative and Liberal politicians into electoral societies had become bitter enemies. Many artisan leaders had attempted to reduce these partisan differences but with disappointing results. In the wake of the civil war of 1859–1862, the time was ripe for another effort. As Camacho explained: "We have a cause of solidarity: that of defending our mutual material interests. Enough of the hatred and quarrels that bring us nothing except disgrace. . . . Do not forget that we constitute a majority [of the population] and are called to raise the country from the prostration in which it lies."

Not everyone agreed with Camacho's approach. Numerous artisans wrote to the paper, expressing the opinion that his Conservative political orientation was too apparent. There was some truth to the charges, as his political endorsements went primarily to candidates of that party. Nevertheless, Camacho and other *El Obrero* editors also gave space to Liberal politicians sympathetic to workers, a policy that soon earned Camacho the respect of several key Liberal artisan leaders. After this early effort, many of these individuals joined his more nonpartisan endeavors.

The Union Society of Artisans was founded in 1865 to unite the artisan class of the capital. The Union Society published the paper *La Alianza* (The alliance), which Camacho helped to edit. For two trying years the Union Society fought for the interests of Bogotá's artisans, presented candidates for public office, petitioned the national congress for tariff protection, and attempted to mend the partisan rift within the craft sector. During much of the Union Society's existence, Camacho served as its president and one of its leading spokesmen.

In the pages of *La Alianza*, Camacho honed his editorial skills and further developed his concept of proper government. A nation, according to Camacho, consisted of numerous social groups, the most important being the producers and the consumers. Manual laborers were not the only producers. So, too, were merchants, lawyers, and farmers, all of whom helped to circulate goods. In an ideal society these elements were positively balanced in a symbiotic relationship, which for Camacho defined the "social function of property." Workers (the poor) produced by way of their labor and their skills; their social partners (the wealthy) consumed the products of labor and thereby put capital into circulation. It was the government's obligation to facilitate such relationships. In a nation in which the social function of property was fulfilled, neither the rich nor the poor abused their role, and a balance existed between producers and consumers, lamentably not the case in Colombia, according to Camacho.

Tariff protection was the single most important initiative that the government could undertake on behalf of artisans and, by implication, for the nation. As the Union Society prepared a massive petition to the national congress, Camacho complained in the group's paper that craftsmen suffered from high city taxes, cut-throat merchants who sold them poor materials, and prejudicial tariff rates: "Can the worker who knows that the consumer will pay ten pesos for what is worth 40 use materials whose cost is more than the promised payment and make a piece whose merits are not appreciated or, if they are appreciated, will not pay for the time employed in making it?" Artisans, Camacho claimed, lived better in the colonial period, when the government recognized its social responsibilities by protecting industry. Independence and liberty, he reasoned, had brought only misery for the worker, but misery that could be alleviated by protection of industry, immigration of foreign masters to teach new arts, and vigorous prosecution of the merchants who sold contraband at very low prices. "Freedom of industry without protection," he concluded, "is not only useless but prejudicial." The congress, however, dismissed the society's petition without debate.

Formal political efforts were not the only arena in which artisans sought to protect their collective interests. Bogotá's newspapers were often the forum for polemics regarding aspects of the city's highly politicized intellectual life. Camacho joined one such debate, in late 1867, with one of the nation's leading Liberal intellectuals and most ardent defenders of free trade, Miguel Samper. The debate centered on the causes of the economic crisis within the capital and on possible remedies. Samper offered his interpretation of the origins of Bogotá's miserable social and economic conditions in a series of open letters to the press. His letters forcefully suggest that much of the misery in the region stemmed from Colombia's failure to accept wholeheartedly principles of economic liberalism. Bogotá's artisan class in particular, Samper claimed, had blocked progress by fighting so tenaciously for protectionist tariffs. Camacho did not let this attack on artisans pass unanswered, writing four open letters in response to Samper.

The thirty-four-year-old carpenter began his analysis by humbly noting Samper's widely known reputation as an honorable man of science and letters. Nevertheless, according to Camacho, in his accusations Samper had maligned artisans unjustly and had misstated the nature of the crisis facing the city and country as a whole. Artisans, Camacho maintained, rightly deserved the central role that Samper assigned them; they were the first victims of the crisis afflicting the capital, a crisis of much deeper proportions, however, than Samper had indicated. Many workers lived for months on end without meat and subsisted on only one meal per day, and their trades, Camacho alleged, were so ravaged that the practitioners barely could survive.

The origins of their plight lay not with the workers themselves, however, according to Camacho, but with an elite-dominated government that refused to legislate with the welfare of the general populace in mind. The Colombian upper class suffered from the "spirit of foreignism," a "disease" that caused them to worship foreign goods while belittling national products. Because of this condition they refused to protect native industries. At the same time, the elite lacked an appreciation of the manual arts, causing the economically and socially advantaged sectors of society to seek employment at public expense instead of in performing honest labor. Camacho observed that many children of the elite who went abroad to get an education "learned two languages, although they forgot their own, learned some accounting and the beautiful practice of buying for two and selling for six, for which one does not need talent or training."

In 1867 the Union Society collapsed in the aftermath of an attempted coup by the country's president, Tomás Cipriano de Mosquera. Partisan political divisions slowly sapped the organization's unity. Even Camacho, despite his nonpartisan rhetoric, began to work with members of the Conservative party, and that same year was elected to the state legislature as a representative of both the Conservative party and the Union Society. He earned a reputation as an able member of the congress. In the early 1870s the Conservative party used Camacho's political experience and reputation among artisans to appoint the carpenter a member of the party's local organizing committee. Several times Camacho was nominated again by his party to serve in the state legislature but as Liberals controlled the reins of government, he failed to win election.

Furthering the interests of the capital's workers continued to occupy much of Camacho's abundant energy. Having failed to maintain a large organization to look after the general welfare of artisans and other workers, Camacho helped to found in 1872 the Mutual Aid Society for the benefit of the more well-to-do craftsmen, the first organization of its kind in Colombia. The Mutual Aid Society endeavored to cooperate to the mutual advantage of its original eighty-three members, principally to provide them assistance in times of sickness or death. Members paid regular dues and extra amounts in cases of special need. Not only artisans joined the Mutual Aid Society; merchants, lawyers, and others could join, although the majority of its members appear to have been craftsmen. After some initial difficulty in getting members to pay their dues on schedule, the society functioned smoothly, operating at least through the 1920s. Through most of his life, Camacho held some office in the organization, usually the orator, who spoke at funerals or at the group's meetings.

Camacho praised the contributions of workers to society through these speeches and argued for the protection of workers by the government. "Work," he remarked in 1886, "is an honorable function of social life that should not imply degradation and disappointment for those who do it." Work was the foundation of social well-being, the wellspring of production that deserved all possible "public honor." Moreover, as he commented on another occasion, "to establish sources of work is to redeem the vagabond and the woman with 'lost honor.' " "To put capital into the hands of those who employ idle arms is to raise a barrier and deny poverty entry into people's houses." "Praise to the Governments that . . . raise on high the moral force of work." In a country whose Spanish heritage included a disdain for manual labor, Camacho's voice represented an effort to acknowledge the dignity of those who toiled with their hands for a living. The Mutual Aid Society did not seek to help directly the average artisan, only the more privileged members of the trade, but its concerns were shared by most workers. It urged that the government provide industrial training for the city's craftsmen, petitioned for tariff protection, and protested against the threat of war.

In 1876 a split in the Liberal party inspired Conservatives to revolt. The Mutual Aid Society urged its members to help calm passions wherever possible and pleaded with the government to avoid armed conflict, but to no avail. For over one year a war raged, disrupting lives, reducing economic gains, and shattering political tranquility. From this war emerged a new political party, made up of disillusioned members of the major parties, united behind Rafael Núñez, who wanted to recast the nation's economic, social, and political fortunes. Called at first the Independents, in time they assumed the name of the National party. Camacho turned his loyalties to this movement in 1879, helping in the campaign to win Núñez's election to the presidency in that year.

Camacho himself was elected to Bogotá's city council, the first time since the late 1860s that he had held public office. Camacho and other craftsmen had very sound reasons for supporting Núñez, who had signaled his support for higher tariffs, for stimulating national industry, and for an end to partisan conflict. Artisans publicly campaigned for the tariff package, which passed over the objections of old Liberals such as Miguel Samper. A second initiative of the new president, to establish "model shops" where craftsmen could learn new methods of production, won equal praise from the artisan community. Camacho and four others were appointed to a committee to select five young men who would travel to Europe and learn new techniques so that they could introduce them to the workers of the capital. By the early 1890s the model shops had become a reality, although their contributions to the local economy were somewhat limited.

Yet another civil war, in 1885, provided the opportunity for Núñez and his followers to sponsor a constitutional convention wherein the programs he had begun in 1880 would shape a new law of the land. The new regime, the Regeneration, centralized authority in the hands of the executive, restored the Catholic church to an important role in education and other social services, and helped sustain a program of industrial development and export expansion. Camacho ardently supported this turn of events from the pages of his new paper, *El Taller* (The shop), founded in 1884. Camacho praised the government's moves to aid workers, measures that included the establishment of an "Artisan Institute" to provide education for craftsmen and their children. His defense of the Núñez government won him the nomination for the state legislature in 1888, a contest that he handily won. In his legislative position, Camacho campaigned unsuccessfully for establishment of state-sponsored housing for workers, a plan that met stiff opposition in the congress.

At least one of the programs of the Núñez government caused considerable hardship in Bogotá and throughout the nation. The newly founded National Bank released large amounts of paper money into circulation, hoping thereby to stimulate economic development. While it may have succeeded in that goal, the paper money set off a devastating inflationary cycle that lasted until the end of the century. Workers and other residents of the city suffered from the rising prices and increasingly inadequate wages. Camacho urged local authorities to impose price controls on goods in the local marketplace, but to no avail. High prices and low wages continued to cause considerable tensions in the city.

These tensions served as a backdrop to a riot in 1893 in which Camacho, then sixty years old, played a major role. High food prices and low wages were not alone in inciting the urban upheaval. Bogotá's officials had begun to "modernize" their police force in the early 1890s, bringing to the city a French police official to undertake the reform of that agency. By late 1892 armed, uniformed police began a crackdown on crime, especially on prostitution in the downtown area. Police agents were recruited from outside the city, helping to drive a wedge between the local populace and the police force.

In early January 1893, Camacho pushed the Mutual Aid Society to condemn the author of a series of articles in a local paper that had criticized the moral habits of the capital's working classes. José Ignacio Gutíerrez Isaza had singled out artisans as particularly notorious abusers of alcohol, a vice he alleged to be responsible for deteriorating families and mendicancy. Camacho insisted that the author retract his allegations and that the government censure him for violation of the nation's press law that prohibited inciting one class against another. (Camacho was well aware of press censorship, having served on a review board in the late 1880s.) Neither demand was met. Several days later the city's populace erupted into a major riot that released the various pressures that had built up during the early 1890s. The rioters, described as mostly artisans and workers, first attacked Gutíerrez's house before taking aim at the city's police force. All but one police station in Bogotá were sacked before order was restored by regular army troops. Some forty to fifty people were killed and an unknown number injured.

Some analysts identified Camacho as a central protagonist in the riot. They claimed that his call of protest to the Mutual Aid Society had galvanized workers against Gutíerrez and fueled their anger. For his part, Camacho, who again had a seat on the city council, blamed the riot on the taxes that had left the populace in poverty. Other members of the council vehemently disagreed and censured him for his allegations. In the months following the riot, Camacho personally engineered the removal of the government's ban on meetings of the Mutual Aid Society, an edict imposed in the wake of the riot.

Curiously, Camacho's standing in local politics was not permanently damaged by his role in the riot. In the presidential election of 1897, he played an active role recruiting artisan support for the National party candidate and reminding craftsmen through *El Grito del Pueblo* (The cry of the people) of all of the government's positions on tariff policy and craft training. The War of 1,000 Days (1899–1902), during which Colombia lost possession of Panama, closed the vicious circle of nineteenth-century partisan conflict. Now approaching his seventieth birthday, Camacho had seen the Colombian capital experience numerous changes. Its population had doubled during his lifetime while its craft tradition had been undermined by foreign competition, and now native manufacturing had developed, giving rise to a generation of wage laborers.

Camacho's last decade was spent in continued pursuit of the goals he had followed during his long life. In 1904 some moderate Liberals founded the Union of Industrialists and Workers to unite the growing numbers of industrial workers and artisans in a nonpartisan effort to gain the government's economic protection. Once again a massive petition was prepared by the organization, which helped result in the implementation of higher tariffs the following year. At its formal session of organization on June 8, 1904, the union selected Camacho as its president. In his speech of acceptance, he informed the members that their task was to build unity among all workers in Bogotá for their mutual improvement. As had been the case since the 1860s, workers' unity was his central message. Camacho happily reported that workers' unity was more feasible now than ever before because workers possessed a stronger awareness of their shared social reality. Once again, Camacho served as editor of the organization's newspaper, *Paz y Trabajo* (Peace and work). The union proved to be short-lived; nevertheless, it clearly indicated the arrival of a new thrust for the Colombian labor movement, one that addressed the needs of wage laborers over those of independent craftsmen.

Camacho remained active in the Mutual Aid Society and in the Family Insurance Society, which he had helped to found in 1890. Multiple honors were bestowed upon him by these groups. Upon his death in early 1914, the press in Bogotá temporarily abandoned its partisan accusations to pay tribute to Camacho's lifelong efforts on behalf of workers. One editorialist noted of Camacho that "one noble thought perennially occupied the mind of this most proven and modest citizen with singular persistence: the education of the people." Surely the "human tradition," the ongoing struggle for a dignified and just life not only for one's self but for others as well, is captured in this sentiment.

SOURCES

Most of the information on Camacho's life is found in Bogotá's newspapers in the latter half of the nineteenth century. *El Obrero, La Alianza, El Taller, El Grito del Pueblo,* and *Paz y Trabajo* reveal his thoughts most directly. His speeches, published by the Mutual Aid Society, are valuable insights into his social ideology. Unfortunately, most of the day-to-day record of his family, his work experience, and other aspects of his life are lost.

An overview of urban artisans in the colonial period is Lyman Johnson, "Artisans," in *Cities and Society in Colonial Latin America* (Albuquerque, 1986), edited by Louisa Schell Hoberman and Susan Migden Socolow, 227–50. An introduction to the world of nineteenth-century artisans can be gleaned from Paul Gootenberg, "The Social Origins of Protectionism and Free Trade in Nineteenth-Century Lima," *Journal of Latin American Studies* 14, no. 2 (November 1982): 329–58; Alan Middleton, "Division and Cohesion in the Working Class: Artisans and Wage Labourers in Ecuador," *Journal of Latin American Studies* 14, no. 1 (February 1982): 171–94; and Frederick Shaw, "The Artisan in Mexico City (1824–1854)," in *El trabajo y los trabajadores en la historia de México* (Mexico City, 1979), edited by Elsa Frost, Michael C. Meyer, and Josefina Z. Vásquez, 399–418. For an account of the Society of Artisans, see David Sowell, " 'La teoria i la realidad': The Democratic Society of Artisans of Bogotá, 1847–1854," *Hispanic American Historical Review* 67, no. 4 (November 1987): 611–30.

19

Mandeponay: Chiriguano Indian Chief in the Franciscan Missions

Erick D. Langer

Bolivia enjoyed a rather splendid isolation during the quarter of a century following independence in 1825. The Catholic church, the state, and elites generally ignored the country's indigenous population as long as the Indians paid tribute, which was the principal source of government revenue in the first years of the republic. By midcentury, an economic renaissance had begun. Foreign and local capital revived silver mining and made possible some agricultural expansion. Greater profitability of commercial farming naturally inflated the value of land and threatened the isolated harmony of many Indian communities. By what tactics could the Indians guarantee their economic and cultural survival?

Passive accommodation would mean the rapid loss of land and of cultural autonomy, and the transformation of independent farmers into a pool of reserve day workers for plantations owned by others. Rebellion would mean even quicker destruction. Ethnic and regional differences among those whom others termed *Indians* also limited the possibility of real unity among Bolivia's indigenous people. The state, even if it had wanted to protect the indigenous population, increasingly embraced a laissez-faire ideology that tacitly favored the wealthy and powerful. Individuals such as Manuel Isidro Belzú in Bolivia and Juan Bustamante in Peru, who tried to enact reforms, met with derision from their recalcitrant colleagues and even death.

Mandeponay, chief of the Chiriguano Indians from 1868 until 1904, combined the skills of a caudillo and of a traditional chieftain. The Chiriguano chief found a solution that worked—for a while. He invited one powerful institution, the church, to place a check on the encroachments of the government and the elite. Still, the Franciscan fathers pacified as they protected, and their exhortations to the Indians to be good Christians and good citizens ultimately undermined the cultural autonomy of Mandeponay's people. So, too, did Mandeponay's policy of encouraging Indian migration to Argentina to seek jobs. In the short run, it gave the Indians independence, but in the long run, it threatened communal unity.

We cannot but admire the wily stratagems of a proud chief who secured the best deal he could for his people and himself in a changing world.

Yet as historians we might ask what Mandeponay's story tells us about the "development of underdevelopment." How and why did the modernization of Bolivia contribute to increasing misery in the countryside?

Erick Langer, assistant professor of history at Carnegie-Mellon University, received his doctorate from Stanford University. He has done research on the rural society and economy of southern Bolivia in the critical period between 1880 and 1930. His published articles treat hacienda labor, debt peonage, Andean banditry, community peasant organization, and the commercialization of barley. Langer is the author of *Economic Change and Rural Resistance in Southern Bolivia, 1880–1930* (1989).

Mandeponay became chief of the Macharetí Chiriguano Indians when his chieftain father, Taruncunti, was murdered in 1868. A group of Chiriguanos from Cuevo cut open Taruncunti's mouth from ear to ear because he had betrayed the Indians' cause and spoken to the Franciscan missionaries. Taruncunti's brother and a niece also were killed and a number of his relatives kidnapped and taken to Cuevo. Mandeponay, the oldest son of Taruncunti and the next in line for the Macharetí chieftainship, was not present and so escaped the massacre. Filled with rage, he immediately asked that a mission be established in Macharetí as revenge for his father's death. Within one year the missionaries had built a fort at the Indian village. Despite a concerted attack by dissident Chiriguanos while the fort was still unfinished, the mission at Macharetí had become a reality. As we will see, there was more than just revenge as a motive for Mandeponay's request.

Together the murder of Taruncunti and Mandeponay's request for the establishment of a mission were one episode in the conquest of the Chiriguanía, a vast region of rugged jungle-covered Andean foothills in southeastern Bolivia, ranging from one hundred miles south of Santa Cruz to almost the northern outskirts of the city of Tarija on the edge of the desolate Chaco region. The Chiriguanos had held out against Spanish forces since colonial times. Viceroy Toledo mounted a large expedition against this ethnic group in the 1560s, but he suffered defeat at the hands of the Chiriguanos, who effectively used guerrilla tactics to combat the better-armed Spanish soldiers. Only in the late colonial period did Indian resistance weaken. After the failure of the Jesuits to convert the Chiriguanos in the first half of the eighteenth century, the Franciscans finally achieved some success. In the late eighteenth century the friars, based in Tarija, established a string of prosperous missions in the Chiriguanía.

However, patriot guerrillas and their Chiriguano allies during the wars for independence destroyed the missions and sent the Spanish friars packing.

The Chiriguanos were known as fierce warriors since the sixteenth century, when they migrated from what is now Brazil into southeastern Bolivia. They were able to survive the onslaught of the Spaniards and early republican society because of their military organization, their political decentralization whereby a number of regional chiefs lorded over chiefs of allied villages, and the training in the art of ambush and weapons that every Chiriguano boy underwent at a relatively early age. The Chiriguanos were superb practitioners of guerrilla warfare and frequently raided white settlements throughout the early republican period. The village-based military society, the warriors' unconditional obedience to their chiefs, and the perpetual state of warfare between Chiriguano village alliances as well as against the whites kept the Indians well trained in all manner of death and destruction.

The Chiriguanos were largely left alone until the 1840s, when the Bolivian economy began to quicken again. The government set up a series of military forts along the Chaco frontier on the southern borders of the Chiriguanía. Also, settlers from Tarija entered Indian territory and joined the small garrisons in periodic raids deep into the frontier, destroying Chiriguano villages and kidnapping women and children. However, the cattle that the settlers brought proved even more destructive. Buoyed by increased demand for cattle in the highland silver mines, the colonists drove their herds into the Indians' cornfields. As a result, entire villages lost their means of subsistence and either had to migrate farther north, into the core of the Chiriguanía, or submit to the settlers and work for them under extremely poor conditions as hacienda peons. Many villages resisted violently the encroachment of the white settlers, but in the long term this proved futile.

The only other alternative was for the Chiriguanos to accept a Franciscan mission on their territory as a way of preserving their homeland. By the 1840s the Bolivian government had retreated from its earlier anticlerical stance and, in fact, encouraged the Franciscans from the Tarija convent to resume their missionary activities as a way of neutralizing the still formidable Chiriguano military threat along the frontier. By 1854, under increasing pressure as settlers and cattle ranches encroached on their land, Chiriguano chiefs in Itau (1845), Aguairenda (1851), and Tarairí (1854) had accepted the establishment of missions as the lesser evil.

Macharetí, farther to the north, became the next goal for the settlers. This location was particularly strategic, for it was the main meeting place between the Tobas, adept Indian horsemen who controlled much of the Chaco, and the Chiriguanos. Taruncunti led the resistance to the establishment of the mission in Tarairí and, in alliance with the Guacaya Chiriguanos, attacked the mission in 1855. The assault failed. In revenge for this attack the mission Indians of Tarairí joined with the soldiers in the military colonies farther south and launched a punitive expedition on Macharetí. This expedition was completely successful, and as a result of the sacking of Macharetí and the capture of numerous women, the place was abandoned by Taruncunti's people. Only a small faction of Macharateños, under the leadership of Guariyu, returned to Macharetí six years later after making peace with the missionaries. Taruncunti, outraged by this betrayal, attacked with his people and allied Tobas, wiping out the new settlement. His erstwhile subordinate Guariyu barely escaped naked to the safety of the hillside. Flush with success, Taruncunti marched on Tarairí but again failed to take the mission.

Mandeponay was a young boy during these assaults and counterassaults and probably did not participate in these wars. His father certainly inculcated in him a fierce sense of independence and of Chiriguano ethnic identity. However, Taruncunti could see that his position was tenuous at best on the frontlines in the war against the white settlers. In his later years, in exile in an allied Chiriguano village, he became convinced that he would have to live with the whites and that friendship with the missionaries held the key to the reestablishment of Macharetí as the most important Chiriguano settlement. In 1866 he decided to visit Tarairí mission and make peace with the Franciscans. Settlers were already moving their cattle herds into the Macharetí area, and Taruncunti saw that returning his people to the area was the only way of maintaining his claim there. Almost certainly Mandeponay, as the oldest son and heir apparent of his father, helped Taruncunti negotiate with the friars on the conditions for the Chiriguanos' return to Macharetí.

Despite his wishes, Taruncunti could not move his people back to the old settlement. The Chiriguano bands farther north, in Guacaya and Cuevo, who knew that if Taruncunti buckled under white pressure they would be next, refused to let him return to his ancestral grounds. Deeply suspicious of Taruncunti's motives and his steadily improving relations with the missionaries, they launched a sneak attack on Ñaunti, where Taruncunti was hiding, and killed the old chief. It is in this way that Mandeponay became chief of the Macharetí Chiriguanos and invited the friars to establish a mission at his birthplace.

For the Tarija Franciscans, gaining Macharetí was the greatest triumph of their careers as missionaries in republican Bolivia. Mandeponay controlled more than three thousand individuals, including the dissident band under Guariyu, almost certainly the largest concentration of Chiriguanos in the whole region. Moreover, establishing a mission at Macharetí helped alleviate the constant threat of Toba and Chiriguano alliances against the whites, since it was the chief of Macharetí who traditionally controlled Chiriguano-Toba relations. This move isolated the Tobas and made possible the colonization of the vast Chaco regions on the border with Paraguay. The Tobas, who were well known to the white colonists from Argentina to Bolivia as cattle and horse thieves, relied on the Chiriguanos in Macharetí to provide them with corn, a crop that the nomadic hunting and gathering Toba groups found impossible to cultivate in the difficult climate and soil of the Chaco desert. Traditionally, Tobas came after the rainy season to help the Machareteños harvest their corn crops and, in return for their labor, received part of the crop. The Franciscans hoped that the Tobas might even be persuaded to accept the missionaries among themselves if they got to know the fathers when they came to work and trade with the Macharetí mission Indians.

Mandeponay knew that he had a strong bargaining position, and he was able to get concessions that none of the other Chiriguano chiefs ever got once they agreed to have missions. For one, Macharetí had only a single central plaza. Unlike earlier colonial missions, the Franciscans could not force the Indians to convert if they did not want to, for there were no soldiers to back up forced conversions and the subsequent modifications in behavior required of the converts. However, the missionaries in the Chiriguanía usually segregated *neófitos* (converts) from the heathens as a way of better indoctrinating their charges and preventing the heathens' "savage" ways of life from infecting the Christianized natives. To do this, they had the converts build their houses around a separate plaza, which would assert in spatial terms the separation of heathens and *neófitos*. The *neófitos* gradually received different authorities as well and lived accord-ing to the dictates of the missionaries, not the traditional chiefs. This Mandeponay did not permit when setting up the Machareti mission. Instead, converts and heathens all lived around the one central plaza, although each group lived along different streets. The settlement's layout, however, allowed Mandeponay to main-tain his authority over the whole mission population.

Mandeponay made sure that he kept his authority even over his father's old nemesis, Guariyu. Despite serious misgivings, the missionaries and Guariyu had to accede to Mandeponay's demands; Guariyu kept his group separate from the larger group, but he was placed under the chief's overall jurisdiction. Man-deponay himself never converted to Christianity and kept up traditional customs, much to the chagrin of the Franciscans. For example, he had six wives, clearly a violation of Christian injunc-tions. There was little the friars could do. It was Mandeponay who ran the mission and kept everyone in line. When problems arose, the missionaries had to rely on this traditional chief to correct them, and thus they needed his full cooperation. In Chiriguano society, the chief played an extremely important role in regulating the community and had tremendous power over his followers. Mandeponay kept up the custom of giving large feasts, to which he invited the whole mission population. Showing his largess in this fashion, the chief was able to bind the mission Indians in a web of reciprocity. The feasts thus not only served to demonstrate his wealth and power, a desirable attribute in any Chiriguano leader, but also created ties of mutual obligation upon which Mandeponay could call when necessary.

Mandeponay's example was very important, and, as a result, the friars had little success in converting their charges to Chris-tianity. In 1882, at the apogee of the mission's population and fully thirteen years after the foundation of the mission, only nine families out of a total of over six hundred had converted. In the past five years, only three families had been baptized. Obviously, Mandeponay maintained a significant hold over his people, as evidenced by the tiny number of conversions. The chief clearly wanted to have his cake and eat it too: enjoy the protection of the missionaries and maintain the cultural integrity of his people and their land without giving up anything essential in return.

At this Mandeponay was remarkably successful. In 1890 the missionaries decided to try and modify his behavior. In 1888 a new Franciscan had arrived from Italy. Terencio Marucci was appalled by the licentious behavior of Mandeponay and the liberties he enjoyed with his many wives. Not only did Mandeponay maintain a harem but his son, Napoleón Yaguaracu (also called Tacu), also kept three wives. Many of the chief's "soldiers" practiced polygamy as well. At first, the Franciscans called upon local authorities to punish Mandeponay for his unlawful behavior, but the officials refused to antagonize the powerful Chiriguano ally. The authorities had very good reasons not to punish the chief of Macharetí. In the late 1880s the national government began to explore the uncharted reaches of the Chaco beyond the foothills of the Chiriguanía and support colonization of that region. To accomplish this settlement they needed Mandeponay's support, for in his capacity as the head of the Macharetí Chiriguanos he possessed extensive links to the Tobas and other Chaco tribes. The Daniel Campos expedition in 1886, for example, employed a number of Macharetí Indians to act as porters and attempted to use Mandeponay's influence to keep hostile Indian bands at bay. Other, later expeditions into the Chaco also usually made an obligatory stop at Macharetí to get Mandeponay's assistance and gather intelligence from the Indian chief.

After their appeal to the authorities brought no results, the missionaries resorted to ostracism, isolating Mandeponay from the rest of the mission as much as possible. At first, they reported some success, asserting that now Mandeponay found himself "scorned by many of his soldiers and is fearful of some punishment." This optimism, however, did not last long. With Mandeponay cut out of the authority structure, the unconverted Chiriguanos, the vast majority, refused to obey the missionaries. Afraid that they would lose much of their liberty in this crackdown, many Chiriguanos either left the mission for the Guacaya region, where the whites only recently had penetrated, or simply went out into the countryside adjacent to the mission, away from the influence of the friars. In one year the mission lost over 700 individuals, or about 20 percent of the total population of 3,577. The missionaries were forced to back down. They asked Mandeponay to resume his duties in 1891, which immediately helped get things under control at the mission. Mandeponay exiled a troublemaker, helped return a number of families who had fled into the hills, and prohibited polygamy among the *catecúmenos*, those who had made a commitment to converting to Christianity and were learning the requisite rules.

The reincorporation of Mandeponay into mission life occurred just in time. In 1892 the last revolt of the Chiriguanos broke out

under the leadership of a messianic leader, Apiaguaiqui, from
Ivo. Apiaguaiqui called himself a *tumpa* (messiah) who would rid
the Chiriguanía of its white interlopers and return all lands lost
to their rightful owners. By this time, colonists had insinuated
themselves in virtually every corner of Chiriguano territory and
were forcing the Indians to work as poorly paid peons on their
ancestral lands. Guacaya had fallen to the settlers in a war in
1874; the Franciscans from Potosí took the opportunity to establish a new mission in the area. Even Cuevo, at the heart of
nineteenth-century Chiriguano resistance, in 1887 had accepted
the establishment of a mission after the Cueveños' attempt at
building a huge fence to keep out colonists' cattle had failed.
Only Ivo and a scattered number of smaller settlements remained
outside the control of the settlers.

The 1892 war was doomed to failure from the start because
no mission Indian chiefs joined their brethren from Ivo. A number of Chiriguano chiefs visited Apiaguaiqui to determine
whether to follow the rebel leader or not. This group included
Mandeponay, who by this time was among the two or three most
powerful Chiriguano chiefs in the whole region. He refused to
join in the growing movement but, on the other hand, also never
denied Apiaguaiqui's claims. Although the missionaries and local
authorities liked to believe that Mandeponay was their ally, in
fact he was only against bloodshed and remained essentially
neutral during the conflict. The assembly of Apiaguaiqui's followers declared war on the whites in January 1892, and Mandeponay, when he got the message, is reputed to have said: "War
is bad. There is no advantage in it. It means no homes, no *chicha*
[corn beer, used as a staple in the Chiriguano diet]." It was
rumored, however, that his son Tacu left to join the movement.

The Indians under Apiaguaiqui had planned to revolt during
Carnival, when the whites would be celebrating and most men
would be drunk, but the rape and murder of a Chiriguano woman
by a colonist during New Year's brought about a premature
uprising. The Chiriguano army gained control over an extensive
territory between the River Parapetí and Camatindi, a few miles
north of Macharetí. At this point, the Indian warrior bands
suddenly retreated to the vicinity of Ivo to celebrate their victory
over the white colonists. Almost certainly the failure of the movement to spread among the missions just outside this area precipitated this retreat. Thus, the refusal of Mandeponay in
Macharetí and of the Cueveños in the new mission limited Apiaguaiqui's success and doomed the movement. Reaction by a

hastily mobilized militia and some troops from the regular army was swift. The Ivo Indians and their allies fought bravely from a hillside near Ivo with their bows and arrows, spears, knives, and occasional firearms. They hastily dug trenches and erected walls of fallen trees, but even this tactic was of little use against the much better armed whites. A bloody pitched battle at Curuyuqui, where the fighting soon degenerated into hand-to-hand combat, decided the fate of the rebels. As a result of this battle and the subsequent repression, six thousand Indians were killed or taken prisoner. Those Indians who survived were given to white families in the region, and some children were sold to work as servants in households in Sucre, Monteagudo, and other towns.

Mandeponay, it seems, had been right. Violent resistance was futile. Rather, it was necessary to adapt to changing circumstances. The mission was the most viable alternative to becoming exploited hacienda peons or fleeing into the Chaco to join the Tobas. On the mission, the Chiriguanos enjoyed their own authority structure and, to a large extent, despite pressure from the missionaries to change their ways, were able to maintain many traditions. For example, while the friars forbade consumption of the beloved *chicha,* such an injunction had little effect in a mission such as Macharetí, where the heathen population remained so large. In the aftermath of the 1892 uprising, Mandeponay gained even more power. In 1894 his archrival Guariyu, who had to a certain extent been a counterweight to Mandeponay's influence, was sent with his followers to a new mission, San Antonio de Padua, to help control the Tobas who were congregated there.

Mandeponay's project, of preserving Chiriguano ethnic identity and projecting political power from the missions, could not work in the long term. Although adults had a choice of converting or not (something which they rarely did, leading a missionary to exclaim in frustration that "to baptize an Indian adult who is in perfect health is the same as asking for pears from an elm tree"), all children above age seven were required to attend mission school. This practice, of course, led to the progressive conversion of the mission population, a process that Mandeponay could do little to halt. Not only were the children taught the catechism, but they were also required to wear European-style clothes and speak Spanish instead of their native Guaraní. They also learned how to play brass instruments for the mission band and some type of craft such as carpentry or shoemaking, and the brightest boys learned some elementary reading, writing, and arithmetic. The girls received instruction in sewing, cooking, and other "womanly skills." The friars also often hired the children out to neighboring haciendas, where they were further imbued with Western ideas and habits. Thus, although the conversion process was lengthy, at least in theory by the second generation the mission population would be completely converted.

The process was more lengthy than the missionaries or national authorities had counted on. It is quite possible that Mandeponay helped delay the inevitable, for there were persistent reports that many families hid their children in the surrounding dense scrub forest to prevent them from being indoctrinated. Mandeponay certainly knew about this circumvention but elected to do nothing to help the friars retrieve the children. Moreover, Tacu refused to hand over his own children, setting a dangerous example for the rest of the mission Indians. Another circumstance that made the conversion problem more intractable was the constant turnover of Indians in the mission. Some families found temporary refuge on the mission during the various uprisings or when the corn harvest was poor in other regions, a recurrent phenomenon in the arid climate of the southeastern Andean foothills. Once families moved on again, the missionaries had to return the children to their parents, making many conversion efforts futile.

Nevertheless, the *neófito* population continued to grow. By the 1890s they constituted approximately one third of the total population living at Macharetí, which during this period fluctuated between twenty-five hundred and three thousand individuals. Although mission residence patterns gave Mandeponay a larger say over even those who had converted, in the long term his authority was threatened by the ever-larger Christian population on the mission. The converts tended to heed the friars more and thus obviated the necessity for an intermediary such as Mandeponay. The number of mestizos who lived either on mission grounds or in the near vicinity also increased significantly during the 1890s, from about two hundred fifty at the beginning of the decade to double that number at the end. It was clear to Mandeponay that Chiriguano ethnic identity was threatened even in the relatively benign conditions of the missions.

Another threat to traditional ways of life was the increasing integration of the mission Indians into the market economy. The mission's natural pastures and scrub forest provided abundant fodder for the cattle that the Indians were beginning to raise.

By the 1890s mission residents raised over seven hundred head
of cattle themselves, in addition to the large herd of almost two
thousand head belonging to the mission. In the 1890s a new trail
connecting Argentina with Santa Cruz to the north was developed
that passed through Macharetí. The Indians began to grow fruits,
cotton, and other goods for their own consumption and for sale
to the merchants who passed with ever-greater frequency through
the mission. However, the land around Macharetí was not as
fertile as that at other missions because of the sandy soil and its
proximity to the arid Chaco, making agriculture a difficult enterprise. Nevertheless, as more Indians entered the monetary economy, the emphasis on reciprocity through large feasts that showed
the generosity of the chiefs, and the art of traditional crafts such
as hand-weaving cotton cloth and making beautifully ornamented
pottery, slowly began to wane. Instead, many mission Indians
refused to participate in the mutual shows of largess; others
purchased ready-made clothes and iron pots rather than engage
in time-consuming artisanal activities.

Mandeponay tried to adapt himself and his people to these
changes and used his great influence to provide his followers
with the best alternatives. The most important role the Chiriguanos played in the regional economy was not as producers or
consumers, but as laborers. All white settlers who received land
grants from the government in the Chiriguanía attempted to
include as many Indian villages as possible so as to provide an
adequate source of hacienda peons for the new estates. Unfortunately, labor conditions were miserable on the haciendas, where
the Chiriguanos were treated as virtual slaves, lost their indigenous culture, and were perpetually mired in debt. Mandeponay
was very much aware of this situation, and certainly his awareness
of labor conditions in the region's estates had led him to ask for
a mission rather than subordinate himself and his people to the
white colonists. At times, of course, Mandeponay had permitted
some of his people to work on surrounding estates. At least the
Franciscans, who had considerable clout with the region's landowners as well as local and national authorities, were able to
protect the mission Indians from the worst abuses. However,
even there, pay was low and conditions far from ideal. How was
Mandeponay going to give his people the best possible deal as
the valuable labor resource that they were?

The solution presented itself in the 1880s, when a few labor
contractors from the sugar mills in Jujuy, Argentina, came to

the mission. Jujuy had a relatively large rural population, but most lived in the highlands and, because of their subsistence mentality, rarely came·down to the valleys to help harvest the sugarcane. As a result, labor contractors began to look for other sources of workers, particularly among the indigenous peoples of the Chaco. These contractors, knowing full well who had control over the majority of the mission population, offered Mandeponay a fee for each Indian that he could deliver to Jujuy for the sugar harvest. The deal seemed too good to be true. On the one hand, his people could make more than double the wages that they received in Bolivia. On the other hand, the work was only temporary and did not require permanent migration away from the mission. Mandeponay used the fees that he collected to strengthen his ties with his soldiers and so increase his authority over the mission's inhabitants.

Thus, in the 1880s, with Mandeponay's help, Macharetí Chiriguanos began to trickle over the border into Jujuy, particularly to the Ledezma Valley, to work in the sugarcane harvest. The missionaries were against this temporary migration for a number of reasons. They complained that when the mission Indians returned, the men had been corrupted by their experience in Argentina. The missionaries saw their tutelage over their charges and their efforts at conversion threatened by this absence. Many Indians brought back with them to the mission what the friars considered to be terrible habits. Most returning migrants had learned to fight with knives over even trivial matters, as was the custom among the gauchos of the Jujuy lowlands, creating serious problems of insubordination at the mission. Also, since many of the men had left their wives behind during the harvest, the friars became very concerned about the breakup of family lives. The women and children often had insufficient resources to fend for themselves for the whole period that their men were gone. After they returned, many Chiriguano men, the Franciscans complained, became abusive to their mates, leading to frequent instances of wife beating. The friars also worried about problems of infidelity that the prolonged absence of the men caused. However, Mandeponay's power remained such that despite these misgivings the Franciscans were unable to halt the migration.

In fact, in 1896, Mandeponay, by now an old man, went with his people to Jujuy to supervise the work there. On the sugar plantation he resided in a hut made of sugarcane stalks and leaves, just like the other temporary Indian workers. The owners of the mill gave him a monthly stipend and twelve pesos for every able-bodied man that he had work for at least one month. Even a few Chiriguano women joined the caravan; they did not work in the fields but remained home to cook and watch over the meager possessions that they and their spouses had brought along. At the end of the three-month stay, Mandeponay received, as was customary for Indian chiefs to keep them well disposed toward the mill owners, a few mules or mares as going-away presents.

The friars complained in 1896 that not enough able-bodied men remained to carry out even the basic tasks of maintaining the mission. The missionaries could do nothing to stop Mandeponay, but by this time it had become difficult to sustain the large population on the mission anyway. The years from 1897 to 1903 were exceptionally hard. At first, a plague of locusts descended upon the region, wiping out virtually all the mission's crops. For the rest of the century, a prolonged drought dried out the corn plants before they bore fruit, creating even worse problems for those who lived on the mission. Also, as the region's inhabitants lacked food, they resorted to cattle rustling, especially from the mission's herds, leading to an even greater breakdown in the mission economy. Hunger drove many of the Chiriguanos, including a number of the boys in the school, to go to Argentina rather than starve at home. Some friars condoned this migration, for they saw little alternative for their charges, despite the cries of outrage from local hacendados who relied on mission labor for their farms.

In the meantime, Mandeponay as well as his sons became wealthier with their trade in mission workers. As a good Chiriguano chief, Mandeponay distributed this wealth to his followers in the form of more expensive feasts, which he supplied with copious amounts of rum. The missionaries, who were already concerned with discipline problems brought about by the migrants' new habits learned in Argentina, were appalled at this drunkenness but again could do nothing about it. They continued to need Mandeponay, especially as the drought got worse, to prevent the mission from losing all its population. In fact, Mandeponay's ability to hold these feasts attracted for the first time large numbers of Tobas and Tapietés (another Chaco tribe), who were affected by the prolonged drought themselves and sought food and refuge on the mission. Thus, Mandeponay maintained his position as the indispensable intermediary between the missionaries and the indigenous population of the region.

This situation could not continue, however. The drought persisted into the twentieth century. Even Mandeponay's ability to purchase large quantities of alcohol could not prevent the Indians from noticing that they had no food for their children and themselves. As a way of keeping the Indians on the mission, Mandeponay became more and more autocratic and, according to the friars, abusive. The feasts, in the context of the increasing commercialization of the mission and the subsequent breakdown of traditional ties among the Indians, were simply no longer adequate for keeping his followers in line. Instead, Mandeponay relied to a greater extent than before on force to maintain his authority. This tactic backfired, especially as the drought worsened. First to depart were the Tobas and Tapietés, who left for regions that had been spared the disastrous crop failures.

The remaining heathens at the mission, Mandeponay's power base, left in increasing numbers as well. Once he had alienated his followers, there was little reason for them to remain. Many instead elected to go to Argentina with their families and to stay there permanently. As the twentieth century arrived, the exodus turned from a trickle to a flood. The missionaries in 1901 had to turn over seventy of their pupils to families leaving the mission, a fact that they blamed on the drought and on Mandeponay's despotism. In 1903, ninety heathen families and forty *neófito* families left for greener pastures. The Franciscans threatened to depose him, and Mandeponay agreed to reform his ways. It was too late. By 1904, three hundred left, more than halving the mission population from its high point in early 1901 of over three thousand. Of the fourteen hundred people remaining, most were *neófitos,* since they had a greater stake in staying on the mission. As a result, for the first time in 1904 the mission contained more Christian Indians than heathens (in fact, twice as many), making Mandeponay's position as intermediary superfluous. The friars could finally act against the old chief, and they deposed him as the supreme Indian authority of the mission. Although Mandeponay continued to send Indians to Argentina, his power was broken, and he died soon thereafter.

What does Mandeponay's life tell us about the human condition in nineteenth-century Latin America? Mandeponay was representative of the leaders of indigenous groups who, during the course of the nineteenth century, were forced to accommodate themselves to the expansion of the frontier into their territories. In a sense, Mandeponay's experience was relatively fortunate; neither he nor his band suffered total extinction as happened to many other, smaller native groups in, for example, the Amazon basin. Mandeponay wielded significant power during most of his long adulthood because he was able to act as an intermediary between his people, as well as to a certain extent other frontier tribes, and national society. Even in these frontier conditions, where the strong subjugated the weak, Mandeponay was able to carve out a breathing space for his people and help them adapt to changing conditions.

Mandeponay's experience shows that even relatively powerless indigenous groups, when led by creative leaders with political savvy and a firm understanding of their indispensability as intermediaries in the ever-changing circumstances along the frontier, were able to maintain a semblance of ethnic cohesion and pride. Tragically, this could be only temporary. The acceptance of a Franciscan mission spelled, through the indoctrination of the indigenous children, the eventual end of traditional cohesion and culture. Also, by bringing the Indians into the regional economy, the missions guaranteed that the Chiriguanos would move away from their customary ways of life. Even so, Mandeponay seized the initiative and gave his people the opportunity to work for much larger monetary rewards than were available in the immediate vicinity of the mission. This Macharetí chief tried to maintain his traditional control over his people by sponsoring more festivals and distributing large quantities of drink. However, this effort failed. The immediate cause for this failure was the prolonged agricultural crisis that afflicted the area at the turn of the century, making it difficult for Mandeponay to keep his people in the region. In the long term, his political project was doomed anyhow; the drought probably accelerated his eventual downfall. By encouraging the mission Indians to migrate to Argentina, he helped expose his people to the full force of the market and to ideas that entered the mission only in a filtered form. This circumstance alone would have converted the Chiriguanos into the agricultural proletariat that by the first decades of the twentieth century the vast majority of these Indians had become.

SOURCES

Sources on Mandeponay, considering his importance in southeastern Bolivia for a generation, are relatively scarce and scattered. The founding of Macharetí and Mandeponay's role in it is related in Antonio Comajuncosa and Alejandro M. Corrado, *El colegio franciscano de Tarija y sus misiones* (Quaracchi, 1884). Numerous reports highlight the conditions in Macharetí and the other Chiriguano missions. Among them Manuel Jofre O., hijo, *Colonias y misiones: Informe de la visita practicada por el Delegado del Supremo Gobierno, Dr. Manuel Jofre O., hijo en 1893* (Tarija, 1895); A. Thouar, *Explorations dans l'Amérique du Sud* (Paris, 1891); and Doroteo Giannecchini, *Diario de la expedición exploradora boliviana al Alto Paraguay de 1886–1887* are most revealing. In this study, I have relied extensively on the annual reports of the Tarija mission prefects for Macharetí, which are in the archive of the Franciscan convent in Tarija, and on the annual reports of the minister of colonization, available in the Archivo Nacional in Sucre, Bolivia.

For the 1892 revolt the basic secondary source is Hernando Sanabria Fernández's excellent *Apiaguaiqui-Tumpa* (La Paz, 1972). For conditions in the Chiriguanía in the late nineteenth and early twentieth centuries, see Erick D. Langer, "Franciscan Missions and Chiriguano Workers: Colonization, Acculturation, and Indian Labor in Southeastern Bolivia," *The Americas* 62, no. 1 (January 1987): 305–22; Langer and Robert H. Jackson, "Colonial and Republican Missions Compared: The Cases of Alta California and Southeastern Bolivia," *Comparative Studies in Society and History* 30, no. 2 (April 1988); and Langer, *Rural Society and the Mining Economy in Southern Bolivia: Agrarian Resistance in Chuquisaca, 1880–1930* (Stanford, 1988), chapter 6. By far the best analysis of the colonial Chiriguanos is Thierry Saignes, "Une 'frontière fossile': La Cordillère Chiriguano au XIXe siècle" (Ph.D. diss., Ecole des Hautes Etudes, Paris, 1974).

General studies on the Chiriguanos include Bernardino de Nino, *Etnografía chiriguana* (La Paz, 1912); Alfred Métraux, "Chiriguano and Chané," in *Handbook of South American Indians,* vol. 3, edited by Julian H. Steward, 465–85 (Washington, DC, 1948); Bratislava Susnik, *Chiriguanos* (Asunción, 1968); and Lorenzo Calzavarini, *Nación chiriguana: Grandeza y ocaso* (La Paz, 1980).

Index

297